CHURCH LEADERS HANDBOOK

To my Hereford friends

With Christian love & every good wish,

Harold Rowdon

August 2002

Church Leaders Handbook

General Editor
Harold Rowdon

Foreword by
Ian Coffey

Published for

by

paternoster
publishing

British Library Cataloguing in Publication Data
A catalogue record for this book is available from the British Library.

ISBN 0-900128-23-2

Cover design by Paulo Baigent.
Typeset by Profile, Culmdale, Rewe, Exeter,
Produced by Jeremy Mudditt Publishing Services, Carlisle,
and published for Partnership by Paternoster Publishing,
PO Box 300, Carlisle, Cumbria CA3 9AD.
Printed and bound in Great Britain
by Bell & Bain Ltd, Glasgow.

Contents

PART THREE: CHURCH MANAGEMENT

PART FOUR: PASTORAL MATTERS

PART FIVE: LEGAL, FINANCIAL AND PRACTICAL

FOREWORD

I have lived and worked in Plymouth for the past nine years. During visits to churches across the United Kingdom and other parts of the world I am frequently asked the same question: 'What is happening with the Plymouth Brethren?' The answer to that question is, in part at least, contained within the pages of this comprehensive handbook.

Historians suggest that the name of the city of Plymouth became attached to the Plymouth Brethren by virtue of the fact that the largest 'assembly' in the early days of the movement was located here. But since the early 19th century the influence of this Christian group has extended far beyond Devon, to the four comers of the world.

At a personal level, it is impossible for me to escape the movement and its influence. My maternal grandfather was converted in the early 1900s in Consett, County Durham, and was grounded in his new-found faith through the local Brethren assembly. My mother was the first child born after her father's conversion and she – together with her brothers and sisters – grew up in a family deeply affected by the local assembly and its teaching.

My wife, Ruth, grew up in a Brethren assembly in the South-East of England – both her parents having been converted at the same church in their teenage years. She received her grounding in the faith under the influence of the Christian Brethren – and gratefully acknowledges the valued foundations laid in her life in those early days.

Although I grew up within the traditions of the British Baptists, I trace my own spiritual journey through two landmark events. Both of these took place at Christian camps organised by Christians from Brethren assemblies which I attended as an interloper and at both of which God touched my life.

In my ministry I have been blessed through the encouragement and support of those within the Brethren movement. I have also been intrigued to discover many leaders in various denominations and streams who trace their spiritual roots to a Brethren assembly, youth ministry or camp. I am not alone in saying 'Thank God for the Brethren!' – for the debt owed by the wider church to this small but influential group is enormous.

In assessing the extent of this contribution I would highlight five areas in particular.The Brethren have always had a strong commitment to biblical teaching and preaching and this has been reflected in their work with children and young people. Coupled with this is an emphasis on prayer as a priority for an individual Christian and a local church. Third I would cite the sharp focus on personal discipleship with practical training to the fore. Many men who have gone on to become outstanding preachers and Bible teachers first cut their teeth in Brethren assemblies. (I have often wondered how a branch of the church can produce so many gifted people yet somehow fail to retain them all. Or perhaps that is an unfair way of looking at the phenomenon – part of God's purpose may be that the movement should be an enabling group to serve the wider needs of the Body of Christ.)

A fourth contribution of the Brethren can be seen in the sphere of mission and evangelism. From what I can judge there has always been a seriousness of intent among assemblies concerning the Great Commission of Christ. At home and overseas, prayer support, financial backing and human resources have never been lacking from the Brethren movement. A final strand of the Brethren contribution to the global church would be their emphasis on the place of the local congregation of believers. It has always been spelt out by them that the Christian life is to be lived in the context of other local believers meeting, breaking bread, praying and learning together.

All of this may suggest that I am describing a group without faults but, in my experience, many of those at the heart of the renewal that has been happening in parts of the Brethren movement would be the first to point out its failures. As study of any Christian group or denomination reveals, strengths can become weaknesses, rediscovered truths can easily become altars on which we sacrifice life and liberty for the sake of the letter of law.

That is what makes this handbook so interesting. In my travels I have been privileged to catch a glimpse of the renewal taking place among a significant group of Brethren churches. I have studied it with interest. It seems to me that many of those caught up with this are on a journey back to their roots and are rediscovering some of the radicalism that captured the founder members of the movement. In the words of Isaiah, I would encourage them to 'look to the rock from which you were cut and to the quarry from which you were hewn' (Isaiah 51:1). This is a healthy exercise if it uncovers some of the principles that gave the early assemblies such sharp cutting edge.

In the chapters that follow you will find fifty-one subjects addressed by forty-four contributors. Each of the five areas I have highlighted are included in this handbook – and more besides. This is a readable, practical and biblical introduction concerning what it means to be a local church. Though it comes from a Brethren stable, its usefulness will extend far beyond. It is intensely practical, offering wise insights into how to 'do' church in biblical, thoughtful and relevant ways. A wide range of subjects are addressed. Church leadership, organising a spiritually enriching programme of activities, management, pastoral care, legal and financial matters are dealt with by people living at the coal face of local church life. The result is a collection of material that makes sense and provides ideas.

Some maintain that we live in a post-denominational age – or at least in an era where people are encouraged to move beyond the orbit of one particular type of church. One of the undoubted benefits of this approach is the cross-fertilisation that results. Ideas and methods that have been tried and tested in one corner of the church are transferred and adapted for use elsewhere. I believe there are insights and lessons contained in this handbook that will benefit others as well.

What I find most exciting is not only what this book says – but what it represents. God is at work within the Brethren movement in the United Kingdom. That is good news for the Brethren and good news for the wider church too. And – if they remain true to those radical roots – it will be good news for society in Britain as a whole.

Ian Coffey,
Senior Minister,
Mutley Baptist Church,
Plymouth, Devon.
Summer 2001

INTRODUCTION

From Fair Havens in Crete to the island of Malta is some 1000km on a bearing 275 from True North. In Paul's day, sailors would not normally sail that distance to such a small island since they would have to stay on that course to a fraction of a degree throughout the voyage or they would miss the island altogether. When the ship on which Paul was sailing tried to do it, all hope was lost in the midst of a storm (Acts 27:20) but God had the ship under control throughout the voyage and, in the end, his planned destination was reached.

As leaders appointed to serve the church, we do well to remember that it is his church. In all our decisions, we can afford to allow him to be captain. Acts 27 contains detailed descriptions of excellent practical seamanship. It seems that the crew were experienced and well trained. They worked well together as a team and carried out their duties in the face of great difficulty. They considered, planned and took action as best they could for the comfort and safety of all on board. God may well achieve his purposes despite us, but we surely have a duty to carry out our responsibilities in diligent partnership with him. How many church leaders feel adequately trained or experienced for their task?

The vision for this book grew out of my own experiences as an elder in a large Brethren church in Aberdeen. I was first asked to be an elder in 1976, and served for ten years. As a consultant in the oil industry, I had a very busy life, travelling all over the world, looking after a family of three children with my wife, Alison, and trying to run the youth group, the Sunday school and summer camps, as well as taking preaching engagements. I was not a very good elder. I barged ahead in some things and procrastinated in others. If it were up to me, I would have commended anyone who asked for full-time service, or even foreign mission, if they were keen. I almost split the church with my seminar on the 'Toronto Blessing' and I would have spent the entire church budget in a month had it not been for wiser influences on the leadership team.

This ideally qualifies me to compile such a book as this. I moved away from Aberdeen to Kent in 1996 and this gave me time to reflect on my achievements. I recognised that leadership teams need training and advice. I spoke to David Clarkson in Motherwell about the possibility of compiling a series of articles by experienced church leaders. David put me in touch with Harold Rowdon and in time the network widened till Harold, David and I found forty-four appropriately qualified contributors for fifty-one subjects. Naturally, these subjects do not exhaust the issues facing church leaders today, let alone tomorrow.

The task has not been easy but Harold has dedicated himself to the project and has edited this very exciting and readable handbook for church leaders. All the contributors to this book have done so freely out of a shared willingness to help their fellow workers. Peter Cousins has advised on content, and Margaret Helps has done sterling work polishing the manuscripts. Anthea Cousins has kindly compiled the index. I would like to express my thanks to those who have selflessly given their time and energy to this project and it is my prayer that God will bless you and your church as a result of their efforts.

Angus Jamieson

Contributors

Barbara Baigent is currently a church leader at West Side Church, Wandsworth Common in SW London. Now mother and grandmother, she has worshipped at West Side for 45 years. During this time she has been Girl Covenanter leader, women's evening club leader, house group leader and the mission deacon for 15 years, during which time she was able to visit about 20 countries. In retirement from pharmacy she still hopes to give more time to her recreational interests – reading, gardening, walking and travelling abroad. *(Stimulating involvement in world mission)*

John Baigent has been a church elder in SW London for over 20 years, with a career in Religious Education, first as school teacher, then as training college lecturer. For the last 15 years he has been engaged in a full-time pastoral and Bible teaching ministry in the UK and abroad. He is a member of the council of Partnership, and chairman of its Partnership Link Up Service committee. *(Leadership: roles, tasks, qualifications and styles. Baptism)*

Keith Barnard taught modern languages for nine years, then studied at London Bible College and began work with a local church in Huntingdon in 1982. He moved to Cambridge in 1990 to become a full-time elder at Queen Edith Chapel, and also taught New Testament Greek and Communications as a visiting lecturer at Romsey House, a Cambridge theological college. He is married, with four children. *(The Lord's Supper)*

Fran Beckett is chief executive of The Shaftesbury Society, a national Christian social action charity. She is chair of Rebuilding Community, vice-chair of the council of Evangelical Alliance and member of a number of committees and councils of reference. As a Christian leader, speaker and author, she is wholeheartedly committed to seeing the church as 'good news' to those in great need. *(Serving the community)*

Donald Black is depute rector of a Scottish secondary comprehensive school and one of the leadership team of Holm Evangelical Church in Inverness. At various times he has served as Crusader leader, SU school group leader, Bible class leader and Sunday school superintendent. Married to Fiona with a family of three, they have two grandchildren. *(Pastoral care of young people)*

Russell Blacker is a psychiatrist who has written an MD thesis and over 40 articles and chapters on the subject of depression. He obtained the Laughlin Prize for his MRCPsych examination and was made a fellow of the Royal College of Psychiatrists in 1994. He does a considerable amount of teaching, including twice-annual UK and international lecture tours, and runs the membership training course for psychiatrists in the south-west. He was co-founder and for many years secretary of the Association of Christian Psychiatrists. He now works with the Priory Hospital Group in Bristol which allows him to do more clinical work – always his first love. *(Depression)*

Donald Bridge was brought up in Hebron Church, Stockton-on-Tees, served as an evangelist with the Open Air Mission in the 1950s, pastored an independent church in Newcastle-on-Tyne and Baptist churches in Sunderland and Frinton during the '60s, '70s and '80s. He has led the planting or renewing of several churches; served as chaplain of the Garden Tomb, Jerusalem, 1984-5; and subsequently acts as consultant to Partnership and The Evangelisation Society. The author of numerous books and articles, he is now enjoying a busy retirement in Cleveland. *(Discovering and using spiritual gifts. Church discipline)*

David Clarkson was headteacher of a large secondary school in Dumfries for 15 years. He retired early and became involved in the work of Gospel Literature Outreach as a lecturer in Tilsley College. His particular remit focuses on the development of leadership materials and seminars for local churches. David also works with a large church in Glasgow where he is involved in Bible teaching and pastoral work. *(Identifying and training new leaders)*

Peter Cousins has successively been a schoolteacher, head of the Religious Studies department at Gipsy Hill College, editorial director of Paternoster Press and editor of *Third Way* magazine. He lives in Exeter. *(Providing balanced teaching. Encouraging godly living)*

Beth Dickson is a teacher of English at St Aloysius' College, Glasgow and a council member of the Evangelical Alliance. She is married, with two daughters. *(Interchurch activities)*

Max Donald is pastor of Holme Evangelical Church, Inverness, has ministered in Glasgow, London and Sussex, and made several preaching and music ministry trips to the USA, France, Germany, Austria and the Indian sub-continent. His doctoral dissertation explored the relationship between gifts of inspired utterance and the revelation which came to be inscripturated in our NT canon.

Max and his wife, Ruth, have five children. Over the years they have been actively involved in music ministry, both in the context of worship and in the presentation of Christian truth. They both play keyboards and sing. They have composed a number of songs together, and have produced three music cassette albums. *(The place of music)*

Madge Ford is an accredited counsellor with the Association of Christian Counsellors. Currently staff counsellor with World Relief, she worked with Merton Bereavement Service for 14 years, three of them as a group supervisor. She has also worked as a part-time counsellor in general practice, as well as being active in her church fellowship. Originally trained as a nurse and midwife, she served for 20 years in Peru before training as a counsellor. *(Bereavement counselling)*

Billy Gilmour is pastor emeritus of Riverside Evangelical Church, Ayr, having served there as an elder for many years, 14 of them in a full-time capacity. Prior to taking up his full-time role, he was headmaster of a Scottish primary school. *(Pastoral care of older people)*

Peter Godfrey has been involved in church life in Eastbourne, Ramsgate, Ipswich, Sevenoaks, Houston, Texas, and now in Hucclecote, Gloucester. In Sevenoaks he served as an elder for over 20 years during which time the church experienced very significant change. He is currently a member of the leadership team of a new congregation planted by Hillview Evangelical Church, Hucclecote. Peter is happily married to Pat and has six grandchildren. Before retiring he was a director of a consulting company working in the chemical industry and travelled widely in Europe, Africa and the Middle East. *(Handling differences and managing change)*

Tony Hobbs, with his wife Anne, runs Mission to Marriage and Christian Marriage Ministries. They focus on biblical marriage enrichment weekends and helping churches to develop their own effective marriage ministry. He is a church elder. *(Marriage enrichment)*

Stanley Jamieson was for more than 50 years an active member in a traditional Open Brethren assembly and subsequently in an evangelical church of Brethren origin. Pastoral care and youth work were his particular interests, but he was regularly invited to preach the gospel in a wide variety of churches. He was a teacher of geography in schools and establishments of higher education. *(Knowing when to close)*

Peter Kimber was born in India, educated in Kent and Oxford, and has worked and travelled in Antartica, the Americas and Iceland. After training as a teacher in Scotland he had various teaching posts and spent the last 21 years with the Scottish Examination Board. Peter has been involved in Scripture Union, Scotland and International, and joined Scripture Union, England and Wales, in 1996 as chief executive. He is married to Hilda, and they have two adult sons. *(Pastoral care of children)*

Jonathan Lamb is associate general secretary and head of Bible Ministries for the International Fellowship of Evangelical Students. For several years he worked in a pastoral-teaching role in a large British church, and he has also served as chairman of the Keswick Convention. He is the author of several titles, including *Making Progress in Church Life* (Partnership), the *Crossway Bible Guide* on 2 *Corinthians* and *Tough Minds, Tender Hearts* (IVP). He lives in Oxford with his wife and three daughters. *(The authority of leaders)*

Peter Maiden lives with his wife, Win, in Carlisle. They have three grown-up children. Peter is an elder at Hebron Evangelical Church and the associate international director of Operation Mobilisation. He is also chairman of the board of the International Christian College in Glasgow and of the Keswick Convention. His preaching takes him throughout the country and to many other countries. He is a voracious reader who, when not reading, can be found long-distance running, often in the fells of the English Lake District. *(Commendation for service)*

Brian Mills is founder and director of Interprayer, which is committed to encouraging prayer for the nations and has developed ministries in USA, Brazil, Uganda and Switzerland, as well as UK. He visits more than a dozen countries a year, helping to develop prayer movements in relation to church-planting and evangelism, and has written numerous books. For 10 years he served the Evangelical Alliance, first as evangelism secretary and then as prayer/revival secretary. During the three years he was seconded as assistant national director of Mission England he launched the first prayer triplets, now replicated in many countries. Prior to that he was general secretary of Counties for 14 years. Married to Ruth, a singer/song writer, he has three grown-up sons. *(Stimulating corporate prayer)*

Archie Naismith was born in India of missionary parents. Educated in India and Britain, he qualified as a chartered accountant in Glasgow in 1951 and worked in professional offices, the Department of Health for Scotland, and the Scottish Office, mostly based in Edinburgh. His main outside interest is preaching and teaching the word of God. *(Providing balanced teaching)*

Alastair Noble is a head of educational services for South Ayrshire Council in Scotland with responsibility for curriculum development and special educational needs. Formerly a chemistry teacher, he has worked as an adviser, an education officer for the BBC, and a schools inspector. A lay preacher for over 30 years, he has been involved in several major evangelistic and Bible teaching projects. In 1991, he was national co-ordinator for Mission Scotland with Billy Graham. His wife, Ruth, is a primary school teacher. His son, Douglas, and daughter, Rosalyn, are both at university and have significant involvement in overseas missions. He lives in the village of Eaglesham and is an elder of Cartsbridge Evangelical Church, Busby, near Glasgow. *(The place of preaching)*

Don Palmer is married to Kirstin and they have three boys. He worked with York Community Church for just over eight years prior to January 2001, seeing it grow considerably during that time. He is now senior pastor with Forest Brook Church in Ajax, near Toronto, Canada. He has published one book, *The Kingdom of God* (Evangelical Press, 1986) and regular articles in Partnership publications. *(Church-based evangelism)*

Graham Poland has been one of the leaders of Grosvenor Church, Barnstaple, for about 12 years. He has served in church leadership in Weston-super-Mare, Southend and Boswell, Scotland. He and his wife, Maureen, spent 11 years with Gospel Literature Outreach. *(Small groups. Handling growth)*

Edward Pratt came to faith in Christ whilst in the Royal Navy and at university, became an Anglican minister and worked in parishes for 31 years, including 19 in Portsmouth. Owing to severe and increasing hearing loss he retired to Dorset early in 1997. He has been chairman of Marriage Resource since its inception in 1993. He has been married to Jo for 35 years, and they have three children and two grandchildren. He is an amateur botanist. *(Marriage enrichment)*

Gwen Purdie (née McDowell) became a Christian at the age of 13. After qualifying, and working as a social worker for 19 years, she was sent out by Bruntisfield Church, Edinburgh, to launch a Christian counselling service. Dove Christian Counselling was set up in Edinburgh, where Gwen trained other counsellors, and now operates in Edinburgh, Glasgow, Linlithgow and Costa Rica. In June 1996 she married Sandy and they work together as Christian counsellors in the Scottish Borders. Gwen is about to publish her first book, *There is LIFE after Abuse*. *(General principles of pastoral care. Addiction)*

Alistair Purss hails from Ayrshire, SW Scotland. A graduate of the Bible Training Institute (now The International Christian College) in Glasgow, he has been in the ministry since 1991 and is presently pastor of Sawyers Church in Brentwood, Essex. Alistair has been involved in Partnership since 1996, serving as council member, minister-at-large, and member of various sub-groups including future vision/purpose, training and leadership development, and conference planning. He is married to Sharon and they have three young boys. Alistair enjoys reading, classical music, golf and red wine. *(Church membership)*

John Redfern was, until two years ago, the chair of the elders of West Street Chapel where there was a full-time pastor. For many years he was and still is heavily involved with Crusaders at local, national and international levels. He is currently chair of Anorexia Bulimia Care, a Christian charity concerned with eating disorders. He also serves as a governor of a well-established Christian school. For many years he was the managing director of a scientific instrument company. He is now a director of F.I.R.E (Fire Instrumentation and Research Equipment Ltd). *(Pastoral care of leaders and their wives)*

Harold Rowdon taught church history at London Bible College for 37 years and has been deeply involved in the work of Counties. Now living in retirement at Lymington, his major involvements are with Partnership, as its general editor and international secretary. *(Leadership structures)*

Robert Rowe was thrust into church leadership when the assembly he attended with his wife split in 1986. With the other six remaining members, Roger grew a large new church in the same building. Whilst broadening his theological knowledge from 1995-98 at Oxford University, Roger pastored another small church in north Hertfordshire. Having moved back to his home county, East Devon, in April 2000, he is impatient to discover the Lord's plans for his future ministry. *(Reversing decline)*

Paul Sands comes from a Brethren/Presbyterian background in Northern Ireland. For the last 20 years he has been involved in Woodcroft Hall/Evangelical Church, now International Gospel Church, a multi-cultural cell church with a charismatic flavour, where he is team leader. He has been involved in several church plants. He has been married to Ruth for 24 years, and they have three children. *(Planting a new church)*

David Short is a retired hospital doctor and lecturer in Aberdeen, with over 25 years' experience of church eldership. *(Home visiting. Divorce and remarriage. Homosexuality)*

Joan Short is a retired part-time general practitioner and mother of five children, active in church prayer fellowship and visitation. *(Pastoral care of women. Home visiting)*

Alistair Simmons has been pastor of Riverside Evangelical Church, Ayr, since 1994. Riverside is a church of 300+ members, including many young people. Prior to this he was a secondary school teacher for 25 years, latterly as principal teacher of Religious Education at Hamilton Grammar School. He is married to Jean and has a son, Ross. He plays golf badly and skis too infrequently. Two of the greatest joys of living in Ayr are the views of the island of Arran (still there in spite of David Icke's prediction) and the superb, and cheap, golf courses. *(Evangelism in a postmodern world)*

Max Sinclair lives near Sevenoaks, Kent. He has been married to Sue for 32 years and they have three grown up children and two grandchildren. Max was an accountant in the City and then became a youth worker. A car accident left him paralysed from the neck downwards. He made an unexpected and remarkable recovery which changed the course of his life, as related in his book, *Halfway to Heaven*. Sue is a full-time homemaker who has many years' experience in working with children and families. They are now much in demand, speaking individually or together on practical Christian living and on marriage and family issues. Their book *Heaven on Your Doorstep* tells the story of their own marriage and family. *(Pastoral care of men)*

Corinna Summerton worked with homeless young people for the Shaftesbury Society for almost six years, managing their Homeless Service. She has been involved in church leadership, youth leadership and the leading of Bible study groups. Corinna lives in Devon with her husband, Matt, and their son-Joel. *(Pastoral care of young people)*

Neil Summerton has been involved in local church leadership virtually all his adult life, first at Cholmeley Evangelical Church, Highgate, and since 1991 in planting a church in Crouch End, London. He has been a council member of Partnership and its predecessor since 1980, and executive chairman since 1997. He is a council member of the Evangelical Alliance and has been a council member of a number of other national parachurch bodies. He was a civil servant for many years and now directs two research institutes at Oxford on environmental and water matters. He was appointed Companion of the Bath in 1997 for his services to the Department of the Environment. *(Worship)*

Pauline Summerton, a practising counsellor, has been Free Church chaplain at a large acute general hospital in north London since 1992, and was acting head of its Spiritual and Pastoral Care department in 1999. For three summers (1994-6) she was locum chaplain at a large general hospital in Charleston, South Carolina, and was a businesswoman before retiring at age 46 in response to the Lord's call to full-time service. She trained at the Westminster Pastoral Foundation and Oak Hill College, London. Brought up in a church leader's household, she has been active in church work all her life. *(Pastoral care of the ill and dying)*

Mark Thomas is married to Julie and has two adult sons, Luke and Andrew; his family roots are in Bridgend, South Wales. He runs a company specialising in leadership development and people management. Mark has been involved in leadership with local churches in Manchester and Basingstoke and, as the Partnership council member responsible for developing training, he has set up a leadership development course. In addition, he is committed to leadership development within international mission and currently works in India, the Middle East and the UK. He also supports his wife in running a charity (The CHILD's trust) that helps provide for the spiritual, physical and educational needs of underprivileged children throughout the world. *(Vision building and goal setting)*

Keith Tondeur is director of Credit Action, a Christian money education charity. After training in accountancy he spent 22 years in stockbroking. Keith became a Christian in 1981 and, three years later, trained in debt counselling after a family in his church got into financial difficulty. He joined Credit Action in 1990, is a regular speaker at conferences and churches, and has written several books. He is increasingly in demand by the secular media as a commentator on personal money matters. *(Wealth, poverty and debt)*

Bob Tripney trained at Edinburgh University and worked as a medical doctor in general practice for 36 years, and also in cardiology at Northampton General Hospital. A long-term member of Duke Street Evangelical Church, he has served as an elder for some 20 years. He is married to Molly, and they have three children and six grandchildren. Now retired, Bob's main interests are preaching, teaching, pastoral work, and arranging seminars and conferences, His hobbies are mountain biking, climbing Munros and travel. *(The funeral service. Marriage preparation)*

Helen Walker has been a social worker for more than 20 years, mainly in child care and child protection work with the local authority. Currently she is a lecturer in social care at Dumfries and Galloway College. An active church member, she is involved with Samaritans and Christian Care for the Homeless. *(Social care legislation)*

Gerald and Eileen West Eileen has for many years been an authorised person at Cholmeley Evangelical Church which is within the Harringey Registration District. She is also a JP and sits on an Inner London bench. She and Gerald have been married since 1958 and have three children and four grandchildren. Gerald has been an elder since the mid-70s. He is a member of the council of Stewardship Services (UKET) and has particular responsibilities in connection with the properties of which they are owner or trustee. Until a few years ago he was chairman of Partnership. He has recently retired as chairman of the elders at Cholmeley Evangelical Church in Highgate, London where he and Eileen are still active members. *(The marriage service. Trusts and trusteeship. Church accounts. Premises)*

PART ONE:

Church Leadership

CHAPTER ONE

Leadership Structures

HAROLD ROWDON

Christian churches have rarely been in any doubt of the necessity of some kind of leadership structure, but they have not been able to agree on the form it should take. The major alternatives are as follows.

Major options

Episcopalians (from the Greek word *episcopos*, meaning bishop) argue for a three-fold ministry comprising bishop, presbyters and deacons. They appeal to the examples of James in Jerusalem, and Timothy and Titus in Ephesus and Crete respectively, for the concept of a single bishop as well as presbyters and deacons. Traditionally, they have claimed that apostles, or apostolic delegates like Timothy and Titus, conveyed their unique powers of oversight to chosen individuals who, in turn, passed on their powers to individual successors. The researches of J B Lightfoot, more than a century ago, provided a more likely explanation of the rise of episcopacy with the suggestion that, from within the ranks of the presbyters, one emerged who received precedence and the distinctive title of bishop (*episcopos*) which had hitherto been used interchangeably with the title presbyter, or elder (*presbuteros*).

Presbyterians (from the Greek word *presbuteros*, meaning presbyter or elder) focus on the NT presbyters, denying any essential difference between 'bishops' and 'presbyters' and maintaining that a group of elders should form the governing body in every congregation. They also include deacons. However, they distinguish a single 'preaching elder', known as 'the minister', from the rest of the 'ruling elders', appealing for support to the evidence of 1 Timothy 5:17. The local congregation has its role, notably in choosing office-bearers and exercising church discipline. There are also provincial, national and even international synods, comparable with the so-called council of Jerusalem (Acts 15:6-29).

Independent churches almost always have a single 'minister' who in theory and, nowadays, often in practice is one of the elders (*primus inter pares*: first among equals) sometimes described as the presiding or teaching elder, together with a group of deacons. In theory, final authority rests with the congregational meeting of the church, but generally it is held that when there are office-bearers, much of that authority is delegated to them

Brethren views vary considerably. J N Darby's view, that because of the so-called 'ruin of the church' (dating from late apostolic times) NT practice has become irrelevant, has influenced some Open Brethren who may have no recognised leadership other than that exercised by a 'brothers' meeting'. More generally, a few of the brothers known as 'brethren in oversight' or 'the oversight' have provided slightly more focused leadership. Occasionally throughout 'Brethren' history, and increasingly since World War II, the term elder has been used of such leaders, and in some churches they have been relieved of much administrative work by the appointment of deacons. Quite recently, there has been a tendency to appoint leadership teams, usually with elders retained.

New Testament evidence

One thing that is clear is that in NT times leadership structures varied from church to church. At Jerusalem, apostles (Peter in particular) and subsequently James, the brother of the Lord, stood out as undisputed leaders, with deacons (the term itself is not used) being given responsibility for specific tasks (Acts 6:1-6), and elders mentioned in passing as sharing in leadership with the apostles (Acts 15:6).

At Antioch, however, the leaders are described as 'prophets and teachers' (Acts 13:1). During Paul's first missionary journey, elders (but not deacons) were appointed to care for the newly established churches (Acts 14:23), but not during his second. Stephanas in whose home the Corinthian church evidently met exercised some kind of leadership role (1 Cor 16:15, 16). It is quite likely that the earliest churches, which met in homes, would have recognised the head of the household in which they met as being in some sense their leader. One wonders whether this would have been true in the case of Lydia (Acts 16:15, 40) and Nympha (Col 4:15). Paul's letter to the Philippian church mentions elders and deacons (Phil 1:1), though it has been suggested that this means nothing more formalised than the older men and those who served the church.

It is interesting that no other Pauline letter to a church mentions leaders (apart from 1 Thess 5:12 which refers to 'those who work hard among you, who are over you in the Lord and who admonish you'). It is the church as a whole that is addressed by Paul, even when delicate moral and doctrinal issues are under discussion. The letter to the Hebrews, which may have been addressed to the church in Rome, mentions 'leaders' (Heb 13:17, 18) but gives them no formal title. Paul instructs Timothy and Titus to appoint elders and deacons in Ephesus and Crete, and it is commonly assumed that this is binding on all churches and means that the variety of styles of church leadership hitherto prevailing was to end – for all time.

This may not be so. If it was the intention, certain problems arise. For example, no job description is given for deacons. (Even Acts 6:1-6 which does seem to provide one does not actually use the term '*diaconos*'.) And why do we not follow equally literally the instructions regarding widows who appear to be given a recognised role in the church – and a job description! (1 Tim 5:3-16)? The argument that because the Pastoral Epistles were written later they override earlier practice is, interestingly, similar to the argument that the examples of Timothy and Titus establish once and for all the principle of episcopacy!

Far more important than these minor issues, which are nevertheless not without significance, is the undoubted fact that, contrary to what has often been taught, the NT was not intended to provide a blueprint for church leadership in all parts of the world and for all time. There is no NT equivalent of the 'pattern shown thee in the mount'. Those who maintain that there is have to contend, as we have seen, with the paucity and conflicting nature of the evidence. But the decisive argument is that if there had been, it would have been in conflict with the nature of the new dispensation, which is of the Spirit, not the letter; and it would have bound the Christian church everywhere and for all time to the cultural forms of the first-century Near East, with the result that Christianity would never have become the universal religion that it is – and was meant to be.

Church leadership and culture

The NT provides plenty of evidence that the church did – and always may – adopt contemporary cultural models, where these do not conflict with clear biblical teaching.

The NT world almost universally looked to older men to provide leadership. And for good reasons. They were the major channels through which the accumulated wisdom of the past was conveyed to the next generation. They represented stability and possessed maturity as the fruit of long experience. Of course there were some older men who were anything but role models but, generally speaking, leadership in the ancient world was synonymous with age (hence the need for Paul's reassurance to young Timothy in 1 Tim 4:12 – though Timothy was no teenager!).

It has been plausibly argued by R Alastair Campbell (*The Elders*, T & T Clark, Edinburgh, 1994) that the term elder in the NT refers purely and simply to the older men in the church and that it is only the term *episcopos* which carries with it the notion of formal office. Whether or not this is totally accurate, the fact is that Jewish regard for older men as natural leaders has a long history – as any student of the OT will know – and also has parallels in non-Jewish society.

The meticulous research of scholars like E Hatch in his book, *The Organisation of the Early Christian Churches* (London, 1909) shows that the Christian church, from its earliest days, was prepared to utilise existing models of leadership, Gentile as well as Jewish.

The church in NT times was clearly prepared to draw on the practices of non-Christian society, where these were deemed appropriate.

An alternative to elders and deacons

For a number of decades, many Brethren churches have been well served by the recognition of elders and deacons as church leaders. There was biblical precedent for them. They often provided more effective leadership than was available previously.

But there have been problems. One of those who had been a foremost advocate of the recognition of elders, the late K G Hyland, came to see that, just as missionaries who were slow to recognise 'national' leaders damaged the future of the church, so elders who yielded to the temptation to cling on to their position, to fail to promote younger leaders, and, sometimes, to be dictatorial, were damaging the future prospects of the church.

Over and above this, is the cultural shift. No longer is age regarded as a prerequisite for leaders. Today, younger people (women as well as men) may possess greater knowledge and even greater wisdom than those who are more advanced in age but may be deficient in both qualities. There is also a marked trend towards sharing the tasks of leadership more widely than hitherto – terms like 'middle management' and 'team leadership' evidence this.

In a Christian context, the vital component of spirituality may be at least as marked in younger people as in older. And careful study of the NT shows that women shared with men in just about everything in the church (except apostleship and eldership, which, despite the NT's record of going against convention on all manner of matters, would have been culturally unacceptable).

An increasing number of churches (not only those with Brethren roots) are looking for leadership not to those archaically described as elders and deacons but to a leadership team comprising men and women with proven spiritual and natural gifts of leadership. Sometimes, as noted above, the traditional elders remain in place, but with a modified overseeing role. Other members of the leadership team are given portfolios – for pastoral care, teaching, evangelism, youth work, women's work, children's work, finance, administration, etc. Each in turn shares responsibility with a number of others, where this is appropriate, thus widening the leadership still further.

One disadvantage of this leadership style is that meetings of a largish leadership team require good chairmanship and, perhaps, longer discussion before arriving at conclusions. But most matters can surely be remitted to the portfolio holder and sub-team concerned and the leadership team need not be involved in detailed discussion – particularly if it has confidence in its members!

One advantage – for those who believe that there is a place for women in church leadership – is that it makes it much easier for women to be afforded that place. It preserves shared leadership – an essential, if NT precedents and principles are to be followed – and it escapes the overtones of the term elder which we have undoubtedly overstated in the past.

A vexed question which merits inclusion in this brief discussion is the way in which leaders should be chosen. It has usually been the practice in Brethren churches for leaders to be co-opted by the existing leadership group though, in the case of deacons, the precedent of Acts 6 is often followed. Some churches have applied the same principle, in a limited way, to the appointment of elders. Existing elders have their own nominees, but also invite suggestions from the congregation. After due consideration, the existing elders inform the congregation of their final conclusion and invite personal reactions before inviting those concerned to join them as elders. While it is undoubtedly appropriate that existing church leaders should take the initiative in the choice of new leaders, they would be well advised to involve the church as a whole in the process.

The objection is sometimes made that, using a pastoral metaphor, sheep do not participate in the choice of their shepherds! This, of course, is to ignore the fact that spiritual sheep and shepherds share the same form of life and, for good measure, are indwelt by the same Holy Spirit. There is plenty of evidence, some of it already adduced, that in NT times congregations were more active in leadership issues than is sometimes imagined. (See also Acts 15:12 where the whole church was present when the leaders discussed a crucial doctrinal issue, v.12, and the church was involved in the choice of delegates sent out with the conclusion, v. 22.)

It is of crucial importance that church leaders should possess in some measure (for none of us has reached perfection) the qualities to be discussed in chapter 2 in this handbook by John Baigent on 'Leadership: roles, tasks, qualifications and styles.' That granted, I doubt very much whether the terms we use to describe our leaders are of much importance.

Full-time leadership

In Brethren history, full-time leadership has been confined largely, though not exclusively, to cross-cultural missionaries, itinerant evangelists and Bible teachers. Modern conditions in the West have given rise to a renewed concern for full-time leaders at local church level. It was possible to dispense with them – for the most part – when there were available spiritually gifted men with private means, businessmen and others who could forego promotion or take very early retirement in order to make time available, and when family and other pressures seem to have been less than they are today. The writer, however, once belonged to a church whose leaders came to realise that no-one was available for any kind of pastoral ministry until late in the evening, apart from an elderly man in indifferent health, and the leaders had too little time to plan and carry out new initiatives. They were led by God to a man who has been able to help remedy this situation by working full-time in the church, supported by it in accordance with 1 Timothy 5:17.

An increasing number of churches are finding it impossible to cope with the growing demands placed upon them, or meet the increasing number of opportunities that present themselves, without the help of one or more persons who are able to devote themselves to Christian leadership full-time.

The introduction of such a person into the leadership of a church which has hitherto been led by a group of men whose church leadership has been of necessity a part-time occupation is no easy matter. Clear thinking, as well as earnest prayer, is called for in making the necessary arrangements, and much grace is required in putting them into operation.

By the very nature of the case, the role of the existing leadership will be modified with the introduction into it of someone who may be particularly gifted, may have received specialised training, and will be much more available than they to care for the needs of church members and others. Unless functioning as a community or youth worker, the full-time leader should be regarded as one of the elders (if the church uses this term). Some may have been deterred from this by the perception that the full-time leader is in effect being employed by the leadership, but this represents a failure to appreciate that any church leader is in fact the servant of the church.

In the present writer's view, the consequence that the full-time person comes to be regarded as having a position different in kind from that of the other church leaders should be resisted. It would be a strange irony if churches which have been known for upholding the principle of plurality of leaders should compromise it at the very time when other churches which have not practised it are moving towards it! Plurality of leadership is well worth preserving, though this need not mean (and has not meant in the past) that there is no place – or value – in the principle of one of the church leaders being *primus inter pares*.

It is vital to the success of any appointment to full-time ministry in a church that matters such as the following should be attended to with utmost care:

• Terms and conditions of service should be spelled out in some detail and in writing – and be subject to review.
• They should include provision of accommodation, remuneration ('the labourer is worthy of his hire'), holidays (weekly as well as annual!).
• Legal aspects demand careful attention – e.g. whether the worker is employed or self-employed.
• Liaison between the full-time and part-time leaders is essential.
• Provision should be made for appropriate pastoral care for the full-time worker. Ideally, he or she needs pastoral support from a trusted friend outside the church. (See chapter 34 on 'Pastoral care of leaders and their wives'.)
• The length of time envisaged for the appointment should be agreed.

Church leaders contemplating the appointment of someone full-time would be well advised to consult a book published by Partnership, *Don't muzzle the Ox*, which gives careful consideration to the whole issue. It is included in the list of further reading below. Partnership also provides a matching service, PLUS, which assists churches to find workers.

Introducing change

As is the case when any kind of major change is introduced, leaders contemplating changes in leadership structures would be well advised to take the church into their confidence at an early stage, explaining the proposed changes, showing why they are needed, providing biblical and practical justification, answering objections, and easing fears and anxieties. While seeking unanimous agreement as the ideal, they should not allow a small minority, however vocal, to exercise the right of veto over the proposed changes, if they command general approval. (See chapter 22 on 'Handling differences and managing change'.)

Further reading

A Batchelor, *Don't muzzle the Ox* (Paternoster Periodicals, for Partnership, 1997)
S B Ferguson, D F Wright (eds.), *New Dictionary of Theology* (IVP, 1988), articles on 'Church Government' and 'Ministry'.
N Summerton, *A Noble Task* (rev. ed., Paternoster, 1994)

CHAPTER TWO

Leadership: Roles, Tasks, Qualification and Styles

JOHN BAIGENT

This chapter makes two assumptions. First, that leadership refers to the work of the overall leaders of a local church, those whom the NT calls elders or overseers, and not to the work of those referred to in the NT as deacons. (Deacons may be regarded in some sense as leaders and their qualifications as listed in 1 Tim 3 are almost identical with those for overseers, but they have a different role.) The second assumption is that there will normally be a plurality of leaders in a local church, although in NT times the plurality probably applied to the city-wide church rather than to the constituent house churches who might have just one overseer. (See chapter 1 on 'Leadership structures'.)

Roles

The NT uses two main pictures to summarise the overall role of a church leader. The primary one is that of a shepherd, the other is that of a father.

Shepherd

The church leader is to act as a shepherd of God's people ('flock'), representing and accountable to Jesus Christ the 'Chief Shepherd'. The task of a shepherd is the total care of his sheep: leading, feeding, watering, protecting, healing, retrieving strays, etc.

This picture is used in the OT in passages such as 1 Kings 22:17, Psalm 23 and Ezekiel 34, and in the NT in passages such as John 10:1-18; 21:15-17; Acts 20:28; Ephesians 4:11; and 1 Peter 5:1-4. The word pastor is simply the Latin word for shepherd; in English, however, it may convey the idea of someone who is distinct from the other leaders (elders), whereas in the NT all elders are pastors. Moreover, the use of the word 'pastoral' to refer only to activities like visiting, caring and one-to-one counselling is a narrowing down of the biblical concept. As we shall see, it also includes teaching and managing.

The picture must not, of course, be pushed too far. The spiritual shepherd is not tending his sheep in order ultimately to fleece them, nor fattening them up for market! Literal shepherds do not provide an example to their flock; no one expects sheep to walk on two legs and carry a crook! Above all, the church leader is not a different kind of animal from those in his care: all Christians are sheep, members of God's flock. This picture does not justify a clergy/laity distinction.

Father

On occasion Paul refers to himself as a 'father' (and even 'mother') to his converts (1 Cor 4:15; 1 Thess 2:7, 11), but in 1 Timothy 3:4, 5 he compares the role of a church leader (overseer) with that of the father of a household (an extended family with slaves as well as children). The father's role is to manage his household in such a way that everyone is cared for (fed, clothed, accommodated, educated, etc.) and functions productively and appropriately. The church is God's household or family (1 Tim 3:15) and the church leader represents and is accountable to him as supreme Father.

Tasks

To be more specific, the task of a local church leader may be seen as five-fold: teaching, caring, managing, modelling and praying.

Teaching

The NT seems to see this as the main task of a church leader (Eph 4:11; 1 Tim 3:2; Tit 1:9), although some may specialise in it (Acts 13:1; 1 Cor 12:28; 1 Tim 5:17). Church leaders may on occasions delegate this work to others in the fellowship who have teaching gift and even invite suitable speakers from outside, but it remains their responsibility to make sure that teaching is provided and that it is suitable to the people under their care. (See chapter 5 on 'Providing balanced teaching.) If the teaching given is not just theoretical but applies biblical truth to the particular needs of those addressed, it will make emergency pastoral action (the 'ambulance syndrome') less necessary. People will be warned of dangerous ideas and destructive behaviour (2 Tim 4:2-4) and equipped to live confident godly lives. (See chapter 5 on 'Providing balanced teaching'.)

It should, perhaps, be pointed out that such authoritative teaching by leaders is not the only form of verbal communication during meetings of the church envisaged in the NT. Leaders should ensure that other members of the congregation have the opportunity to share any message that they believe the Lord has given them (see e.g. 1 Cor 14:26; Col 3:16).

Caring
Church leaders have a responsibility for the spiritual well-being of each member of their congregation (Acts 20:28; Heb 13:17). This implies that they know which people the Lord holds them accountable for (i.e. that there is some kind of notion or mechanism of membership: (See chapter 19 on 'Church membership'). Whilst part of this pastoral caring is achieved through teaching and other forms of communication to the congregation as a whole, much more is required. It will be essential for leaders to spend time with individuals on their own (in their homes or elsewhere) monitoring their spiritual progress and offering specific help when needed. This kind of pastoral care should be proactive and not simply reactive (when a problem or crisis arises).

Although the leader's prime responsibility is the spiritual health of the members, physical, emotional and social needs should not be ignored. People must be treated as whole persons and each of these areas impinges on the spiritual aspects (see e.g. Acts 4:32-35; Jas 5:14-16). This does not mean, however, that church leaders must become social workers, psychologists or professional counsellors. They must be concerned about the whole range of people's needs, but they must be prepared to delegate some of the more practical aspects (to deacons?: see Acts 6:1-7) and also know when to refer them to qualified practitioners. (See the chapters in part 4 on 'Pastoral matters'.)

Managing
In the NT one of the descriptions of the church leader is overseer or supervisor (*episkopos*). I take it that this implies not only the task of monitoring the spiritual progress of individuals but also the managing or ordering of the life and activities of the local church as a whole (1 Tim 3:5; 5:17). This does not mean that church leaders have to make all the decisions or spend their time on organisational matters such as planning services, booking speakers or making rotas, nor should they have to discuss practical details of buildings, finance, furnishings, etc. Their responsibility is to make sure that such necessary functions are carried out satisfactorily. They should establish policy in each area and then delegate the execution of it to trusted and suitably gifted people (deacons?) who will be accountable to the leaders but also supported by them. Above all, they must make sure that the organisation of the life and activities of the local church serves the overall spiritual purposes and is

consonant with the leadership vision. (See chapter 21 on 'Vision and goal setting'.)

The managing function may also be seen as including the overseeing of initiation (by baptism), admission to church fellowship/membership, discipline and (when necessary) exclusion from fellowship; but perhaps some of these activities would be better regarded as part of the caring role. (See chapters 19 on 'Church membership' and 20 on 'Church discipline'.)

Modelling

The church leader is called to be a role-model, an example, modelling the life of faith (Heb 13:7; 1 Pet 5:3). That is why Paul told the elders of Ephesus to 'keep watch' over themselves as well as over the flock (Acts 20:28). He was constantly drawing attention to his own behaviour as a model of how other leaders should live and act (Acts 20:18-21; 2 Tim 3:10, 11). This implies that church members will have contact with and be able to observe their leaders in a variety of contexts (e.g. the home) and not just in church activities.

Praying

This could be included under Caring but it is so important that it warrants a separate entry. There is no NT verse that specifically tells leaders to pray for their people (except perhaps Jas 5:14-16), but praying is clearly a vital part of 'watching over' the flock (Acts 20:28; Heb 13:17). Moreover, Paul has set all leaders a formidable example in the way in which he constantly remembered his converts (and others) in prayer. Leaders would do well to study carefully the kind of things that he prayed for (see e.g. Rom 15:5-6; Eph 1:15-19; 3:14-21; Phil 1:9-11; Col 1:9-14; 1 Thess 3:12, 13; 2 Thess 2:16-17).

Qualifications

Character

The main passages in the NT which relate to the appointment of church leaders (1 Tim 3:1-7; Tit 1:6-9) focus almost exclusively on their personal qualities. However gifted and willing people may be they should not even be considered if they do not have the basic moral and spiritual requirements. Briefly (as described by Neil Summerton in *A Noble Task*, pp.24, 25), these are deep spirituality (a close relationship with God which issues in goodness, holiness and humility); spiritual maturity (having a good grasp of Christian doctrine and a life-style that matches it); emotional stability (sensible and even-tempered); personal discipline (being able to control body and time); sexual probity (beyond reproach in relationships with members of the opposite sex). I do not think that Paul is limiting church leadership to married men when he says, 'husband of one wife'); competence managerially and in personal relations (demonstrated particularly in the home, but also at work); practical generosity (in use of home, money and property); and social approval (having a good reputation both within the church and in the wider society). The implication of 1 Timothy 5:24, 25 is that no one will be appointed as a church leader without a period of careful scrutiny of his life.

Gifting

These personal qualities are essential but not sufficient: a church leader also needs a range of natural and spiritual gifts. The only one mentioned in Paul's instructions in 1 Timothy and Titus is 'apt to teach'. This confirms our emphasis on teaching as a primary function of the church leader (at least in NT times). Ephesians 4:11 refers to 'pastor-teachers' (probably one role) as one of Christ's gifts to the church. This must imply a number of specific gifts that are required for such a role: not just the ability to teach and communicate, but gifts such as prophecy, encouragement, discernment, wisdom, leadership, administration (or the ability to guide) and faith (see Rom 12:3-8; 1 Cor 12: 8-10, 28; cf. James 5:14, 15). Not all church leaders will possess all these gifts but they should be found somewhere among the leaders. If there is a team of leaders there is also likely to be a variety of temperaments and personalities present which will complement and enhance one another.

Suitability

Even with the requisite character and gifting qualifications a person cannot function properly as a church leader without first being willing (1 Pet 5:2) and then having sufficient time to fulfil responsibilities at home, at work (if employed) and in the church. In addition, the person needs to be generally healthy (physically and mentally). Church leadership is an onerous role and those who accept this responsibility must be prepared to work hard (see 1 Thess 5:12). These considerations have implications not only for the appointment of leaders but also for their retirement. Experience shows that it is wise for a church to agree on a maximum age (say 70) at which a church leader will normally retire. It may be necessary to ask someone to continue a little longer, but that situation should not be allowed to run on without periodic review. Retired leaders could well be regarded as consultants who do not attend regular leadership meetings but are available for wise counsel.

What about women?

At this point I must face the question, Is being male also a qualification for church leadership? This is obviously a controversial question, but in today's world it has to be tackled. There are three main responses among evangelical Christians.

The traditional view

Men and women are spiritually equal before God (Gal 3:28), but the man is the 'head' of the woman both in the home and in the church (1 Cor 11:3; cf. Gen 2:18). 'Headship' is understood as meaning that the man has a leadership, decision-making (as well as caring) role in the home in which he is responsible to God for his wife, and that the male church leaders have a similar role in the church. Women should be submissive to this divine order both in the home and in the church (Eph 5:22; 1 Tim 2:11-15). Proponents of this view would claim that it is exemplified in the practice of both the Lord Jesus and Paul. Despite valuing women more highly than his contemporaries, Jesus still chose only men to be his accredited representatives ('apostles'). Paul was very willing to have the help of women in his evangelistic work and to recognise their contribution to church life (Rom 16:1-7; Phil 4:3; 1 Tim 3:11), but as far as we can see he expected church leaders (elders or overseers) to be male. If this view is maintained it is important to ensure that women are encouraged to play a full part in the life of the church and use the gifts that God has clearly given them (Tit 2:3-4).

The equality view

This is based primarily on Galatians 3:28 and Genesis 1:26, and on a particular interpretation of Genesis 2:18 which stresses the equality of the man and the woman. The claim is that the only significant differences between men and women are biological not spiritual; that Paul's teaching (and Jesus' practice) are culture-bound (i.e. that Paul provides theological reasons for conforming to the accepted social conduct of his day); that women receive the same range of spiritual gifts as men; and therefore there is no reason why a woman should not be a church leader (if she satisfies the biblical qualifications outlined earlier) and engage in teaching the church. (We should notice that some writers believe that the NT teaches male 'headship' in the home but not in the church.)

The complementary view

This view takes seriously what it sees as the implications of both Genesis 1:26 and 2:18 – that men and women were created equal as far as their relationship to God is concerned but different in their relationship to one another (a difference signalled by physical and emotional characteristics). Headship is thus a permanent theological principle which should be expressed in differences of role both in the home and in the church, but it puts on the man the responsibility to set a lead and care for the woman rather than simply the right to dictate to her (Eph 5:25, 28). This view may not sound much different from the traditional one, but in practice it means that women are treated as partners and can play a much fuller role in church life and leadership than they have in the past. In some churches there will still be elders who are all male, but they will associate with them a leadership team which includes women. (See chapter 1 on 'Leadership structures'.) In other churches the leadership team will consist of men and women who are considered of equal status, but the team will be led by an overall male leader (often a full-time worker or pastor). Different stances will be taken on the extent to which such women leaders are permitted to engage in teaching in the church, but if they do this (as the men also should) in clear submission to the Bible and in partnership with their male colleagues, there need be no threat to permanent biblical principles.

Styles

Style is the way leaders carry out their functions and how they are perceived by those they attempt to lead. Leadership styles can be classified in a variety of ways. The simplest is to distinguish three main categories (as listed by David Spriggs, *Christian Leadership*, ch.4).

Authoritarian

This is where leaders impose their will on the group (in this case the local church) on the basis of position, personality (gifts) or power. They may simply announce their decisions (tell), or also explain them (sell), or first ask for suggestions (consult).

Democratic

This is where leaders encourage participation in decision-making and enable the group to reach a consensus and to work together to implement it. They may give the group a strong lead with firm recommendations, or they may delegate these functions to others, or they may simply allow open and a free vote.

Permissive

This is where the leaders leave the group to get on with its own affairs, giving few or no structures or suggestions. People are free to take their own initiatives with a minimum of supervision or interference from the leaders. In its extreme form it hardly seems to constitute leadership at all!

In practice most leaders use (and should use) a mixed style according to the circumstances and needs of the church at a particular time. What is important is that leaders are aware of their own preferred style and of its advantages and disadvantages. (See Spriggs, ch.4.)

Much more important is the basic attitude of a leader. I began this chapter by drawing attention to two pictures used in the NT to describe the role of church leaders, shepherd and father. There are two more, but these apply to all Christians, whether they are leaders or not. They are steward and servant. The latter really encompasses the former, but it may be helpful to consider them separately.

Steward

A steward's job is to be in charge of someone else's property and to administer it in accordance with the wishes of its owner. The description of Moses as 'faithful as a servant in all God's house' (Heb 3:5) means that he acted as a 'steward' (cf. Joseph in Gen 39:4ff.). We see the role and requirements of stewards in the parables of Jesus (e.g. Luke 12:42-48; 19:11-17). Paul describes himself as a 'steward' of the gospel, and of 'the secret things of God', and therefore ultimately accountable only to God (1 Cor 4:1-5). Peter says that all Christians should 'use whatever gift they have received to serve others, faithfully administering God's grace in its various forms' (1 Pet 4:10). Similarly church leaders must see themselves as stewards: first of all of God's church, his prized possession (Acts 20:28, 1 Pet 2:9); then of the gifts that have been given them (2 Tim 1:6); and then of the gospel which has been entrusted to them (cf. 2 Tim 1:13-14). Most of the passages that refer to stewards emphasise that the overriding requirement is faithfulness, that is, obediently and consistently carrying out the will of the master.

Servant

To serve someone is to carry out his wishes, to provide for his needs, or to further his purposes. All Christians should be servants of God and of one another, but this is particularly true of church leaders. The teaching and example of Jesus, given to the apostles, applies especially to them: 'You know that those who are regarded as rulers of the Gentiles lord it over them, and their high officials exercise authority over them. Not so with you. Instead, whoever wants to become great among you must be your servant, and whoever wants to be first must be slave of all. For even the Son of man did not come to be served, but to serve, and to give his life as a ransom for many' (Mark 10:42-45).

Paul also makes it clear that both he and Apollos were to be regarded simply as servants of God and thus fellow-workers: one planting and the other watering in God's field; one laying the foundation and the other building the superstructure in God's temple (1 Cor 3:5-17).

So church leaders are first servants of God, obeying his orders, seeking to fulfil his purposes; second they are servants of their congregation, not in the sense of doing whatever the people want nor of being doormats who allow themselves to be trampled on, but as those who put first the needs and spiritual good of those entrusted to their care.

Church leaders who humbly accept the position of a servant and adopt the attitude of a servant, who faithfully serve as shepherds of God's people, are assured that one day they will hear their master's approval and receive an eternal reward (Matt 25:19-21; 1 Pet 5:2-4).

Further reading

P Beasley-Murray, *Dynamic Leadership* (MARC, 1990)
D Prime, *Women in the Church: a pastoral approach* (Crossway, 1992)
D Pytches, *Leadership for New Life* (Hodder & Stoughton, 1998)
M Scott, *The Role and Ministry of Women* (Word (UK)/ Pioneer, 1992)
D Spriggs, *Christian Leadership* (Bible Society, 1993)
A Strauch, *Biblical Eldership* (Lewis & Roth, 2nd. ed., 1988)
N Summerton, *A Noble Task* (Paternoster, rev. ed., 1994)

CHAPTER THREE

The Authority of Leaders

JONATHAN LAMB

On a recent visit to a university education department I noticed that a special programme was being advertised for hard-pressed teachers entitled 'Assertion Training'. The three-week in-service training programme was designed to equip them to face the daily onslaught in the classroom by projecting a more aggressive image. A similar form of training is undertaken by footballers in their pre-match warm-up as they huddle together and mutter angry words about the opposition, strengthening their communal resolve to annihilate them.

Assertion, dominance, aggression, self-assurance, self-reliance – these are the words which have often been associated with secular leadership styles. As in all areas of the Christian life, it is easy for us to be squeezed into the world's mould when thinking about the challenge of leadership in the church. 'It is difficult to use the conception of leadership without being misled by its non-Christian counterparts', said Lesslie Newbigin. 'The need is not so much for leaders as for saints and servants.'

At the same time, both within our culture and within the Christian community, there has been something of a reaction to the superstar mentality. We have become cynical about authority, uneasy about any form of hierarchy. We reject dominant leadership. There is less and less respect for politicians and the political process. Some observers suggest that the Western world faces a crisis of leadership, with fewer people ready to face the challenge of exercising leadership in the context of suspicion, cynicism and ever-present media intrusion.

In such a context, exercising godly leadership within the Christian community is a demanding challenge. It represents an important opportunity to model Christian values within church and society, for if the old styles of business management represented dominance and aggression, it is significant that the new styles are much more open to a more human – even a more

Christian – style of leadership. The exercise of leadership according to biblical standards of authority will not only be healthy within the Christian community but could also model new ways forward in secular contexts too.

Despite accusations to the contrary, the apostle Paul was not interested in building his own empire or promoting a personality cult. He was committed to serving God and serving God's people, not securing a more powerful platform for advancing his own interests. In several of his letters he replied to those critics who suggested that he was a control freak, bent on manipulating Christian congregations for his purposes of self-aggrandisement. In his first letter to the Thessalonians Paul demonstrated the foundations of Christian leadership, giving us guidelines for the exercise of authority within the Christian community. I have selected four themes.

The authority of God's calling

'We speak as men approved by God to be entrusted with the gospel' (1 Thess 2:4).

In Paul's reply to his critics he stressed that his ministry flowed from his being commissioned by God. The main plank of his defence was that God had approved him and sent him. He felt a deep sense of responsibility because he had been 'entrusted' with the gospel. He was a steward of God-given resources. It was this sense of conviction that transformed Paul, and made him the leader that he was. It was in his bones: God had called him.

It would be wrong to draw the immediate parallel to church leadership today, for we certainly do not inherit that same apostolic calling and authority which Paul evidenced. But these verses remind us of two important principles upon which every leader should reflect.

First, leaders need to feel the sense of stewardship of the gospel which so clearly marked Paul. As we shall see in a moment, we are called to proclaim that gospel and should feel a responsibility to ensure that the church keeps that message at its heart. But second, Paul described his calling in verse 4 as being 'approved' by God. 'Approve' implies testing. Through the demanding circumstances of his life God had been forging Paul's character, making him the person God wanted, preparing him for Christian ministry. Paul's passion for proclaiming the gospel, his commitment to care for the Thessalonian believers, and his ability to rise above criticism arose from his deep sense of being prepared and set apart by God.

For us, the sense of being approved for the task will also result from God's testing in our lives. It is a forging process that goes on within us, producing a maturity and godliness which will make us fit for ministry. We need an inner conviction that God has placed his hand upon us and that he has prepared us for the task of leadership. Without such conviction, accompanied by a reliance upon the Holy Spirit, we will buckle easily when we encounter difficulty or opposition.

Paul also indicates that his fundamental motivation was clear. 'We are not trying to please men, but God, who tests our hearts' (2:4). 'We were not looking for praise from men' (1Thess 2:6). Motivation is a basic issue in Christian leadership. It is easy for us to drift towards personal pride or self-promotion. The result can be a kind of professionalism which separates personal faith from public ministry. We fail to see our personal need, and become arrogant or spiritually dry or exhausted. It is vital that leaders see their need to re-focus on a regular basis, to be renewed inwardly and to return to the fundamental calling to serve the Lord and his people with a wholehearted determination to please God.

The authority of God's word

The Christian leader is a person *under* authority. All aspects of the leader's life come under the authority of God's word. Any authority which he has is therefore a derived authority.

'We thank God continually', Paul wrote, 'because, when you received the word of God, which you heard from us, you accepted it not as the word of men, but as it actually is, the word of God, which is at work in you who believe' (1 Thess 2:13). Here Paul demonstrates both the authority and power of the word. 'You received it as the word of God', with the words 'of God' given special emphasis. It is authoritative precisely because it is God who is speaking. So leaders are able to teach, reprove, correct and train, on the basis of the authority of that word. The leader cannot speak authoritatively other than in those areas where scripture speaks clearly. He or she may offer pastoral advice about personal choices of all kinds, but it would be entirely inappropriate to command or to exercise authority over others where there is no scriptural warrant.

Leaders must therefore be people who themselves are submitted to that powerful word, whose lives are being shaped by its teaching, and whose ministry is enlivened and empowered by its dynamic effects. Leadership teams of all kinds need to ensure that the Bible is at the centre. It should be the controlling principle of church life and the daily sustenance of its leaders. More than ever, our churches today need a renewed understanding and application of its message. Leaders are responsible to ensure that they are actively defending the truth when it is under attack, nurturing the congregation with spiritual food, proclaiming that message with conviction and steering the work of the church by biblical principles and values. Such a teaching and pastoral ministry, based on the authority of God's word, will not control fellow Christians but will liberate them in their own service (Eph 4:11-13).

The authority of moral example

Today's cynical reaction to public figures, whether priests or politicians, arises from the fact that we perceive a credibility gap between words and deeds. We are suspicious of manifesto pledges and political programmes that do not square with reality. We are weary of tabloid stories of politicians who embezzle funds or vicars who run off with the church secretary. Stories like that sell because they are blatant examples of hypocrisy. There is an understandable reaction from the man in the street when he sniffs religious humbug or double standards.

Paul was acutely aware of the dangers facing Christian leaders. 'Keep watch over yourselves and all the flock of which the Holy Spirit has made you overseers', he told the Ephesian elders (Acts 20:28). And to Timothy, 'Don't let anyone look down on you because you are young, but set an example for the believers in speech, in life, in love, in faith and in purity. Watch your life and your doctrine closely' (1 Tim 4:12, 15, 16).

The order is significant: watch your own life first. In Christian leadership, our first responsibility is to sustain and develop our own spiritual and moral life. Paul was fearful of the potential danger of helping others but himself becoming a shipwreck. There is therefore a seriousness about Paul's writing, not least because of the special temptations which leaders face. Calvin once wrote, 'It is an artifice of Satan to seek some misconduct on the part of ministers which may tend to the dishonour of the gospel.'

The NT writers were less concerned about the technical issues of how leaders were appointed, or what kind of leadership structures were to be adopted, or even what duties they were to perform. They were much more concerned about what kind of people they were to be. In today's culture, Christian leaders will have an earned authority if their own lives are a strong moral example to others. It is the result not of authoritative pronouncements from the pulpit but of the quality of life in day-to-day service. Paul demonstrates this in several ways when he says: 'Our gospel came to you not simply with words, but also with power, with the Holy Spirit and with deep conviction. You know how we lived among you for your sake' (1 Thess 1:5).

Paul's expressions here are worth noting. They represent a vital combination. The message was delivered in God's power and with conviction, proclaimed in the Holy Spirit who empowered them and who pressed home the truth to the hearers. But it was not only a combination of word and Spirit. There is a further phrase in verse 5 which in the original text is closely connected to the rest of the verse: 'our gospel came to you . . . with power', so 'you know how we lived among you for your sake'. On several occasions Paul encourages the believers to 'remember how we lived'. The gospel was clearly bearing fruit in his own life, and it was this gospel combination that was so effective: God's word proclaimed in the power of the Spirit, demonstrated and embodied in the messenger himself.

Authentic Christian ministry is when word, Spirit and life combine as they did in Paul. This is the kind of authority that really matters, and which carries the integrity and consistency for which people are searching. It is spelt out further in 1Thessalonians 2:10-12: 'You are witnesses, and so is God, of how holy, righteous and blameless we were among you who believed. . .' Godly example is an enormously influential ingredient in a healthy church. It is often observed that character is caught rather than taught. So Paul could say, 'Follow my example, as I follow the example of Christ' (1 Cor 11:1). It was also why he was concerned to avoid the opposite effect. 'We put no stumbling block in anyone's path, so that our ministry will not be discredited. Rather, as servants of God we commend ourselves in every way' (2 Cor 6:3).

As a child I was involved in a small congregation in north London. When I was ten I encountered failure within the Christian community for the first time. It was discovered that the treasurer had been taking funds from the church over a period of years. In a small church like ours, the impact of this discovery was considerable. A prominent leader had been deceiving people. Someone whom we had seen as beyond failure had acted inconsistently. In many churches, such failure can paralyse the Christian community. In fact, by God's grace, failure in our church was handled in a gracious and firm manner. The man was eventually restored and, with great humility, served the church in a number of quiet ways. I came to respect him enormously. But as a very young believer I learnt some important lessons: that we must pray for leaders, all of whom are vulnerable; that those who name the name of Christ must live his life; and that God can redeem failure.

In 1 Thessalonians 2 Paul is reinforcing the fact that there was nothing in his life which could be made an excuse for others not believing the Christian gospel or walking the pathway of Christian discipleship. His message and ministry were wedded to a godly life that made the gospel believable. And not only that, he states in verses 11 and 12 that this also shaped his pastoral ministry. Like a father he encouraged, comforted and urged those believers to 'live lives worthy of God'. The same is clear from the pastoral epistles, with their deliberate emphasis on the character profile of leaders. The leader must be 'above reproach' (1 Tim 3:2), displaying a rounded spiritual maturity that shapes the whole of life. As the Puritan Richard Sibbes wrote to Christian ministers, 'we must study as hard to live well as to preach well'.

People learn best by being alongside such godly believers. The term 'mentoring' has crossed the Atlantic and become a vogue word for British Christians too. But it represents a vital part of Christian leadership today. It means giving time to the shaping of other Christians through 'parental care'. The best leaders are those who model the Christian walk with integrity, whose vision and decision-making processes are shaped consistently by godly standards, and who display a Christ-like attitude to those for whom they are responsible.

This is the leadership authority that is respected by a congregation, and leads to the appropriate emulation of leaders to which scripture points (Phil 4:9; 1 Thess 1:5-7; Heb 13:7). As the American Puritan, Cotton Mather, expressed it: 'Examples do strangely charm us into imitation. When holiness is pressed upon us we are prone to think that it is a doctrine calculated for angels and spirits whose dwelling is not with flesh. But when we read the lives of them that excelled in holiness, though they were persons of like passions with ourselves, the conviction is wonderful and powerful.'

The authority of identification

Part of that godly example will mean an ability to draw alongside those for whom God has given us responsibility. There is no hint in Paul's writing of a hierarchical leadership style, a professional indifference to the needs of those to whom he was speaking. Quite the reverse. There is probably no better description of pastoral ministry than his words in 1 Thessalonians 2: 6, 7. 'As apostles of Christ we could have been a burden to you, but we were gentle among you, like a mother caring for her little children. We loved you so much that we were delighted to share with you not only the gospel of God but also our lives as well, because you had become so dear to us.'

Paul's leadership is described here in terms of an unreserved commitment to them. His ministry was wholehearted. He not only worked hard to support himself but he constantly gave himself to others. The metaphors he uses convey a deep love for them, a motherly tenderness and gentleness. Teaching and preaching are very demanding ministries, but they are not as demanding as sharing your life with those for whom you have leadership responsibility. Self-sacrifice lies at the heart of servant leadership, and this is simply following in the steps of the Lord Jesus himself (1 Pet 5:1-4).

It is all the more important in our postmodern culture which has become weary and cynical about words. Authenticity and authority in Christian leadership require that our lives embody our message, and that inevitably means a costly identification with those whom we are called to serve. As Colin Morris has written, 'It is not from a pulpit but a cross that power-filled words are spoken. Sermons need to be seen as well as heard to be effectual. Eloquence, homiletical skill, biblical knowledge are not enough. Anguish, pain, engagement, sweat and blood punctuate the stated truths to which men will listen.'

Identification begins with listening. Leaders are often known as good talkers, but the ability to listen is probably one of the most important gifts for a leader to possess. In the church context it is a vital part of understanding pastoral needs and also managing change effectively. I must draw alongside others to feel their pain, hear their concerns and gain their advice.

The NT emphasis on 'one another' provides a much needed counter-balance to the 'them/us' distinction which so often characterises a church with a distant leadership. Leaders need to ensure that they are accessible. They need to be open in their communication. They need to do everything possible to let the congregation know what is being discussed, and have a proper sense of mutual accountability. We should never lose sight of the fact that leaders are no different from other believers within the church: we are fellow members of the body, equally called to serve the Lord of the church, and equally sharing in the privileges of priesthood.

Paul's letter to the Thessalonians demonstrates how authoritative leadership is more spiritual than technical. It is founded on a sense of God's calling, shaped by a commitment to the authority of God's word, supported by the authority of godly example, and welcomed by the congregation because of its compassionate identification. A proper emphasis on the authority of leaders should lead to a greater use of the diverse gifts within the body and to the building up the church towards a Christ-like maturity.

Further reading

C Greene and D Jackman (eds.), *When God's Voice is Heard* (IVP, 1995)
R Longenecker, *Patterns of Discipleship in the New Testament* (Eerdmans, 1996)
D Pytches, *Leadership for New Life* (Hodder, 1998)
D Tidball, *Builders and Fools. Leadership the Bible Way* (IVP, 1999)

CHAPTER FOUR

Identifying and Training New Leaders

DAVID CLARKSON

Christian leaders today feel themselves increasingly under pressure. One reason for this is that the issues facing the local church are significantly more complex. The pace of life is faster, people's lives and circumstances are more complicated, and the demand for instant communication is such that less time is available to think and pray over issues. The nature of leadership itself has also changed. Leaders are held to be more accountable. The increasing influence of the democratic process in society is such that, even in church, leaders are now open to greater scrutiny and challenge.

In addition, the secularisation of society has brought about the subtle change that faith has become more personalised and marginalised. The idea of a community of faith subject to the word of God does not find ready acceptance. The danger is that pragmatism, personal preference or majority view becomes the basis for decision-taking rather than biblical principle.

In the light of factors such as these it is all the more essential to train new leaders so that they can share the burden and also find fulfilment in the exercise of their God-given gift. It is important to keep in mind that the young people we are training now will be in leadership in the early decades of the third millennium. If the issues are complex now, what will they be like in 2020? We need to ask:

- What kind of skills will be required for effective leadership?
- How can these skills be developed and encouraged?

But first we must look at:

Identifying potential leaders

Andrew and Jennifer were obviously excited as they spoke about their new role in their new church. For several years after their marriage they had been peripheral members in another church without much real involvement and little evidence of personal spiritual growth. Two years ago they transferred to their present church and within months became involved in ministry. They are now key members of two different ministries within the church. Andrew has recently been invited to join the eldership. There has obviously been a radical change in their involvement and commitment over these past two years. Why did the first church fail to recognise their potential and what was it about their present church that enabled the potential to come to the surface so quickly and so fully?

Before we jump in too quickly to condemn the first church we should reflect on our own assessment of people over the years. How often have individuals we have rated less highly gone on to be outstanding servants of God, while others regarded as very promising dropped out after a few years. These reflections should make us focus more carefully on how we identify potential leaders. Our track record in this regard has, I suspect, been very mixed.

In one sense identifying leadership is a fairly easy process. Leaders identify themselves. To discover this we need only observe a group of people working together and note whose opinions are valued, whose suggestions are taken up, whose leadership is followed. Using this basic technique it soon becomes obvious that there are plenty of people in the church with ability in leadership. Unfortunately some of them use their gifts negatively and occasionally destructively; others direct their energy and ability to causes outside the church; and yet others simply lack the required spiritual qualities. But there are some who are committed to the service of God. We need to recognise and encourage these.

There is a danger, however, of equating leadership qualities with a strong extrovert personality. Some quieter people possess a depth of conviction and, if encouraged, can grow into effective and reliable leaders. Perhaps the following will be of help in ensuring such are not overlooked.

Some questions
What kind of skills will be required for effective leadership? The NT places much more emphasis on character than on skills and abilities, but there are a number of questions we can ask of an individual in order to ascertain if he or she might be a potential servant leader. Any evaluation of a person's character is difficult, but questions like the following may give us some pointers as to leadership potential:

• Does the person demonstrate a basic underlying spirituality and desire to grow in grace and the knowledge of God?

* Does the person honour Christ in his or her lifestyle and demonstrate integrity in relationships with others?
* Does the person have a teachable spirit and is he or she able to work with other people?

In more practical terms we might also ask:

* Is the person reliable or does he or she frequently fail to deliver on promises made?
* Is the person prepared to accept responsibility or does he or she blame someone else when things go wrong?
* Is the person in the habit of missing deadlines, turning up late or not at all?

With regard to skills, we might ask:

* Is there any evidence that this person can take initiative and motivate others?
* Is there any evidence that this person can introduce change constructively?
* Does the person strive for the best in all that he/she does?

Questions like these enable us to evaluate the potential of a younger person. However, the important point to remember is that consistency and commitment are more important than skill and ability. 'No amount of charisma can make up for deficiency in character.' A well known national athletics coach giving advice to other coaches said: 'If the trainee lacks the qualities of reliability and perseverance, he is not worth coaching, no matter how gifted.'

Training new leaders

Many of us in leadership positions today received no training for the task. We watched others from a distance and tried to apply what we saw to our own particular style and preferences. Often it was a case of 'sink or swim', with only minimal guidance given for the task. This approach, however, is totally unacceptable in our more demanding and sophisticated age. We are selling the next generation short and leaving them at a disadvantage. We must not allow this situation to continue.

But we need to be aware that embarking on a strategy of training a new generation of leaders will bring its own problems. We may, for example, raise expectations which the church might not be able to meet. There is also the extremely difficult task of providing feedback which may be negative on occasions to young leaders. In many of our churches our pursuit of excellence makes it difficult to provide trainees with real ministry opportunities, particularly those of a public nature. If, for example, a young person has the gift of preaching, we may need to take risks in order to provide him with real opportunities to gain the required experience and expertise.

How then can we equip tomorrow's leaders for truly effective leadership?

The model of leadership training

The example of Jesus in the gospels provides us with a biblical mandate and model for training. The gospels describe how Jesus took twelve unlikely people and transformed them into powerful leaders who were to 'turn the world upside down'. In his prayer recorded in John 17, Jesus declares that he has 'finished the work' (v.4). No doubt he was speaking of the task of accomplishing redemption, but he was surely also referring to the 'training of the twelve'. He has revealed the Father to them (v.6) and has given them the words of the Father (v.8). He prays for them (v.9), has kept them safe (v.12), and now sends them into the world (v.18). In this respect his work is done. He has left in place a team of people equipped to continue the task.

What can we learn from the model Jesus left us?

As we look at Jesus' method we discover several things about how to train and equip leaders:

- Jesus selected his team. These men were not ready-made leaders from other organisations but rather men who had the potential to be taught and moulded in the spirit of Jesus himself.
- Jesus modelled leadership. These men knew exactly what Jesus wanted them to be, for they saw it in him.
- Jesus spent a disproportionate amount of time with them. True, he spoke to the crowds and dealt with individuals, but he always came back to explain to the twelve the significance of his actions.
- Jesus taught them. He taught them as they were able to bear it, sometimes by straight teaching and on other occasions by questions and answers. His teaching was not abstract and theoretical, but always had a bearing on real-life situations.
- He gave them responsibility. Having demonstrated how to be involved in ministry he sent them out with clear instructions for the task given to them.
- He provided feedback. Often he encouraged them, but he was also prepared to rebuke and confront.

- He prayed for them. In his prayers and actions Jesus demonstrated that he was totally and unconditionally committed to this group of men.

His concerns were not primarily about skills such as how to preach or how to counsel people. His major emphasis was to bring his disciples into a fuller relationship with himself and into a deeper knowledge of God. The development of character and godliness had much greater significance than the imparting of skills. Also, in focusing on the few, Jesus demonstrated the principle that God can do more with a handful of totally committed people than a multitude of half-hearted individuals. Would our ministries be better served if we learned to concentrate our attention on the spiritual development of a few key people?

The context of leadership training

So, how does all this apply in a local church? It begins with the attitude of the leaders. They must see as their core function the development of people. They must be committed to the concept of lifelong spiritual development, embracing all the people of God, from 'new born babes' to mature believers. Paul describes this process as 'presenting everyone full grown in Christ' (Col 1:28).

This kind of attitude creates a climate in the church where the expectation is that people will grow, that God will raise up individuals for new ministries, that gifts will be utilised, and everyone in ministry will receive appropriate training and support.

A strong commitment to training and development will be demonstrated by the leaders themselves. It will be seen, for example, in a willingness on the part of leaders:

- to attend courses for their own spiritual growth and development;
- to read widely and keep up-to-date with modern trends;
- to share their expertise with others;
- to develop and be involved in a planned programme of training for the church;
- to give time and attention to younger people, in spite of the time required and the inconvenience caused;
- to commit themselves to the principle that involvement in leadership will only be possible after due training has been undertaken;
- to be training or mentoring someone at all times.

In this way leaders give credibility to the claim that they are committed to developing a new generation of leaders. Their example proves that their commitment is more than mere lip service to the idea.

A practical proposal for the local church

In practical terms the outworking of the above principles will require some kind of structure to ensure delivery. One church has developed a model by developing a personal development programme with the following elements:

Foundation courses: Just Looking; Basic Discipleship; Knowing my
    Bible; Finding my Gift; Sharing my Faith; Joining the Church.
Preparing for ministry courses: Working with Children; Working with
    Youth; Pastoral Care; Learning to Preach; Learning to Lead.
Life skills courses: Marriage Matters; Parenting for Today.
Short courses: Giving an Epilogue; Chairing a Meeting; Leading a
    Small Group.

The emphasis is on the personal spiritual development of all, with emerging leaders being encouraged to take more specialised courses. The foundation courses are offered annually, with every member encouraged to take all the options over a period of two or three years. The other courses are offered on a rota basis over a period of several years with members being given the opportunity to opt in as they see their needs.

This kind of provision could not be made available overnight. It would evolve over a number of years and in fact the development of such a programme could provide some very meaningful leadership training experiences. Nor would every church have the necessary resources to provide its own training, but often much more can be done from within the fellowship than is realised. Where particular needs cannot be met from within the church, a training budget could allow an expert to be brought in or individuals to be sent out to national courses, where available.

Thus, the philosophy of the church would become such that everyone involved in Christian ministry would be given training, support and feedback. This would apply at all levels whether the persons concerned are cleaners, welcomers, pastoral team members or elders. In short, everyone would be part of this culture of people development – being developed and in turn developing others.

The content of leadership training

Again it must be emphasised that, while leadership training includes the development of skills, it must also embrace the development of character and knowledge. Generally, leaders need to grow in such areas as:

Knowledge. The leaders should, for example, have a knowledge of the books of the Bible and its main themes; people and society; the history and practices of the church; how to share and defend the faith.

Character. The leader must be a man or woman of integrity whose mind and heart are set on the glory of God. There should be obvious signs of growth in maturity and holiness. He or she should be characterised by humility, reliability and teachability, and be committed to the service of others.

Skills. The leader must be competent in a whole range of areas. For example, he or she must be able to communicate; to organise effectively and to have vision; to solve problems constructively; to motivate other people; to empower others; and to work effectively with others.

If the above accurately reflects what future leaders need, then the existing leadership has the responsibility to ensure that opportunity is given for growth in each of these areas. Obviously, the trainee leader will be committed to his or her own spiritual growth, but there is a level beyond which the individual cannot progress without the help of others. The trainee needs someone to speak on their behalf, introducing them to people who have special knowledge or expertise and who will ensure that they are given new experiences or responsibilities. It must also be recognised that it is the responsibility of existing leaders to ensure that a guide or mentor who can oversee the trainee's development programme is made available.

The personal dynamics of leadership training

The focus of attention thus far has been on organisation of programmes and, while it is essential that proper structures are in place, it is even more important that leaders give priority to the personal relationships involved in developing new leaders. Nothing will take the place of time spent by a leader in developing a younger person. It demonstrates commitment to and recognition of the younger person, and gives the potential leader a sense of personal worth and value.

It is often very helpful to have a formal system of mentoring. The mentor will seek to develop a relationship with the mentee within which praise and encouragement can be given and constructive criticism offered. In this atmosphere of trust, successes can be celebrated and mistakes, seen as part of the learning process, can be turned to advantage. As the mentor shares his experience and acts as facilitator for the younger person, the mentee grows with the knowledge that there is a respected leader who will provide unconditional support.

Sometimes it is helpful to give a structure to the mentoring relationship by seeking to provide an individualised development programme. At the beginning of each year, the mentee in consultation with his or her mentor identifies a series of goals embracing the three areas of knowledge, character and skills. At the end of the year a Personal Development Profile is produced which is essentially a record of what has actually been achieved over the year.

An example of a partially completed profile is shown below.

PERSONAL DEVELOPMENT PROFILE

Name of Mentee...

Name of Mentor...

Year 1

KNOWLEDGE

Acquire an overview of OT history.

Prepared a reading plan based on: 1 & 2 Kings, 1 & 2 Chronicles, Ezra, Nehemiah, Amos, Isaiah and Malachi. John Bright, *History of Israel*, chapters 10 – 17. Discussed progress at the monthly meetings.

CHARACTER

Establish the habit of a daily quiet time.

Oswald Chambers' book, *My Utmost for His Highest*, was used as the basis for daily devotional readings. A chapter a day from the NT was read. There were brief weekly reporting back sessions.

SKILLS

Learn how to lead a small group Bible study.

N F McBride's book, *How to lead small groups* was read and discussed. Observed two elders, each leading a group. Discussed the different approaches. Took a discipleship group for four months.

Year 2

KNOWLEDGE

Acquire deeper understanding of gospel message.
Produced a summary of the arguments of Romans and Galatians. Read John Stott's book, *The Cross of Christ*. Prepared several talks, two of which were delivered – one at a family service and the other at a youth meeting. Positive feedback was obtained from each.

CHARACTER

Learn how to participate effectively in public prayer and worship
Knowing God by J I Packer was read over the year. A journal was kept of preparation and readiness to participate. Discussed contributions at monthly meetings.

SKILLS

Learn how to preach effectively.
Read and discussed: John Stott, *I Believe in Preaching* and M Lloyd-Jones, *Preaching and Preachers*. Attended a GLO course on 'Homiletics'. Discussed sermon construction/delivery. Given opportunity to preach on six occasions with de-briefing in each case and video recording on two occasions.

Year 3

(To be completed)

One problem is that the goals set are too ambitious, but if regular review is built in, these can be adjusted in mid-year and replaced by something more realistic. Even allowing for over-ambition, it is obvious that, over a period of say five years, a fairly wide training experience could be available to the trainees.

It may be thought that this model of leadership training is too mechanistic. The real key to its success, however, is not so much in the structures the church may put in place, but in the mentoring relationship. We have all experienced the positive impact on our lives of an individual whom we respected and admired giving time to us, rooting for us and generally being there for us. It is in this context that spiritual leadership is developed. The structures are there simply to help us achieve that end.

Conclusion

The task of leadership training is difficult. We all feel a sense of inadequacy and hesitate a little at the thought of mentoring another. We know there will be occasions when we will be disappointed and that a huge time commitment will be required. We can list all the difficulties and conclude that it would be easier to press on with the task on our own. But this temptation must be resisted. It is an intrinsic part of the leadership task to ensure that ministries continue after we have gone. We must take the long view, adjust our priorities and give ourselves to the next generation. If we are to discharge our duty we have no other choice in this matter.

As someone has said, 'There is no true success without a successor.'

Further reading

A Baumohl, *Grow your own Leaders* (Scripture Union, 1987)
J C Maxwell, *Developing the Leaders around You* (Word)
V Thomas, *Future Leader* (Paternoster, 1999)
P White, *The Effective Pastor* (Christian Focus, 1998)

PART TWO:

Church Activities

CHAPTER FIVE

Providing Balanced Teaching

ARCHIE NAISMITH AND PETER COUSINS

There can be no doubt about the emphasis laid on teaching in the NT. Our Lord commissioned his disciples to 'make disciples of all nations, teaching them to observe everything I have commanded you' (Matt 28:19, 20). Those who accepted Peter's message at Pentecost 'devoted themselves to the apostles' teaching' (Acts 2:42: note that the teaching is mentioned first). Later when Barnabas was sent to investigate the situation at Antioch where large numbers of Gentiles had responded to the gospel he saw that the new converts needed teaching and arranged that Paul and he should provide intensive teaching for a year (Acts 11:25, 26). The importance of teaching is stressed in Paul's epistles, particularly to Timothy, where ability to teach is laid down as a qualification for eldership (1 Tim 3:2; cf. Tit 1:9).

The word of God is likened to food (1 Pet 2:2) and teaching to feeding believers. The figure of the shepherd, often applied to elders (e.g. Acts 20:28; 1 Pet 5:2-4), surely implies that their work includes leading the sheep into green pastures for feeding. Peter was specifically commanded by the risen Lord to 'feed my lambs' and 'feed my sheep' (John 21:15, 17). Paul speaks of feeding the Corinthians, and the same figure is used by the writer to the Hebrews (1 Cor 3:1, 2; Heb 5:13, 14). The effect of providing food through teaching should be that Christians are spiritually nourished and grow up in their salvation.

Just as a balanced diet is necessary for healthy physical growth, so a balanced diet of spiritual food is the foundation for good spiritual health and helps to protect from heresies and sins. The Pastoral Epistles lay stress on the need for sound/wholesome teaching (1 Tim 1:10; 2 Tim 4:3; Tit 1:9; 2:1; cf. 1 Tim 6:3; 2 Tim 1:13, where 'sound words' means 'healthy' ones).

Sometimes it may be necessary to feed the church on milk rather than solid food, as Paul did to the Corinthians, because it is composed of new converts or Christians who have made little progress in their faith or Christian living. In most congregations, however, different stages of growth will be represented, and so a mixed diet is necessary.

Expository preaching

But how can we ensure that our church gets a balanced diet? My own view is that the systematic teaching of the scriptures is the most effective way of achieving this purpose. Some of the Reformers taught this way. Zwingli preached consecutively through the NT between 1519 and 1525. Calvin expounded in some detail book after book of the Bible, covering every one except Revelation in preaching or writing. I am aware that outstanding preachers like C H Spurgeon and Alexander McLaren could expound isolated texts Sunday after Sunday, usually in no recognisable sequence, and yet maintain a balance in their teaching. This was because they did not confine themselves to certain favourite passages or doctrines in their selection of texts. Spurgeon said: 'I think it well frequently to look over the list of my sermons, and see whether any doctrine has escaped my attention, or any Christian grace has been neglected in my ministrations.'

One advantage of expounding a book is that the teacher, if he is conscientious in his work, is forced to tackle difficult passages and sensitive subjects which he might otherwise have avoided. Harold St John clearly saw the value of systematic teaching. He has told how he asked some young people when they last had a series of lectures on the Epistle to the Romans. They looked surprised and replied that they had never had such a thing. 'And', said St John, 'I shook my head at those elders and wondered what they'd been up to, not feeding the flock properly.' (P St John, *Harold St John*, p.126)

In recent years there has been a welcome shift towards systematic expository preaching. When I came to my present church in 1965 there was no consecutive teaching apart from a sparsely attended Bible reading on a Friday evening, and very occasional series of three or four addresses at the midweek prayer meeting. We now have a regular teaching hour on Sunday evenings in which consecutive teaching is given, usually in the form of expositions through a book in the Bible. Some churches have been following the studies in *Journey*, by Robbie Orr. This consists of notes on each book designed eventually to cover the whole of the NT. It is obtainable from The Bellevue Publishing Trust, 8 Grierson Square, Edinburgh EH5 2AR.

Expository preaching does not, however, of itself guarantee a balanced diet, especially if a different preacher is responsible for each chapter or section of the book being studied. There are some who, having read the passage, in the words of Spurgeon 'touch their hats, as it were, to that part of Scripture, and pass on to fresh woods and pastures new' (*Lectures to my Students*, p.72). Another temptation, to which others yield too readily, is to select a favourite theme or hobby-horse from the passage, without due regard to its message as a whole. Care is therefore required by the elders in the selection of speakers.

Teaching from the Old Testament

For a balance to be maintained there must be teaching from both OT and NT. So much is missed if the OT is ignored. One of its wonders is the unerring accuracy of its predictions of the coming of the Christ. The apostles clearly believed that the OT scriptures preached Christ, for he had said of them: 'These are the scriptures that testify about me' (John 5:39; cf. Luke 24:27). In addition to direct prophecies there are a number of types, teaching on which, if not over-spiritualised, could serve to give a greater appreciation of the glories and work of Christ. The tabernacle ritual prescribed in Leviticus 16, for example, forms the basis of much of the teaching in Hebrews on our Saviour's atoning and high priestly work. The pages of the OT should be read in the light of their fulfilment in our Lord. It has been well said that 'Christianity started on her way with the OT in her hands. But it was a new book; the coming of Christ had brought a great change.' (R Davidson, quoted by F D Coggan in *The Ministry of the Word*, p.80)

Nevertheless, the OT in its own right has much to teach us. Paul's oft-quoted words to Timothy about the role of the 'Holy Scriptures' in teaching us God's truth and ways, and his salvation, refer to what we know as the OT. It reveals to us so much about the nature of God, including his holiness and his grace, and his work in creation, in providence and in redemption. Its stories about men and women of faith exemplify relationship with God. The Psalms are important sources of inspiration for Christian spirituality (witness the use made of them by hymn writers). The Pentateuch and the writings of the prophets teach God's concern for righteousness and justice both in personal relationships and in society. If we neglect the OT, or indeed any large section of the scriptures, we are failing to declare the whole will of God.

That is not to say that in our teaching we should devote time to every book commensurate with its size. I have heard it said that all scriptures are of equal importance. This is manifestly absurd. While they each have their particular place in the canon of scripture it would be ludicrous, for example, to suggest that in our teaching as much attention should be devoted to Esther as to Ephesians. A series of 20 talks on the latter could be highly profitable, whereas the same number devoted to the former, though it is longer in size than Ephesians, would require considerable ingenuity on the part of the teacher and no small modicum of tolerance on the part of the audience, to whom such a detailed exposition would be of doubtful benefit.

Teaching doctrine

There is great need for the basic doctrines of our faith to be expounded. A surprising number of Christians would probably be stumped if asked to give a reason for the hope they have (1 Pet 3:15). This makes it of the utmost importance that they should be taught all that God has done in Christ 'for us men and our salvation'. Such teaching would cover, *inter alia*, the doctrines of the incarnation, the atonement and the resurrection. Occasional series on the attributes of God and the articles of the creed might help to supply the deficiency in our understanding of the doctrines of our faith. Teaching on the Sermon on the Mount and other ethical passages, important though that is, does not of itself provide the impetus for living out the Christian life. We need the great doctrines of the faith as a stimulus to godly living.

Even in evangelistic preaching there is surely a place for the exposition of Christian doctrine – provided that it is presented in a way that is both interesting and relevant to the hearers. Peter's 'gospel message' on the day of Pentecost recorded in Acts 2, for example, while it might be classified as preaching (*kerugma*) rather than teaching (*didache*), contains a wealth of doctrine. He covers the miracles of Jesus (v. 22); God's purpose in his death (v. 23); the necessity of his resurrection (v. 24); his holiness (v. 27); his exaltation and its connection with the promised Holy Spirit (v. 33); and the fulfilment of prophecy in the outpouring of the Spirit (vv. 16-21), in the Lord's resurrection (vv. 25-32) and in his exaltation (vv. 34-36). A similar doctrinal element can be traced in the preaching to other Jewish audiences recorded in Acts. Even in the preaching to Gentiles doctrine is not absent, as is evident from Paul's address to the Council of the Areopagus in Athens where he dwelt on the doctrine of God as creator of the world and of men and as judge (Acts 17:22-31). Taking these as models, our gospel preaching, while mainly targeting unbelievers as that of the NT preachers did, could well include doctrines which take account of their background and beliefs, or lack of them. Believers, who very often comprise 90% or more of the audience in the evangelistic services of many churches, should also profit from a reminder of the doctrines of our faith.

Ethical teaching

While the doctrines we hold should affect our conduct, the connection between what we believe and how we should behave is not always grasped. We cannot therefore concentrate on teaching doctrine to the neglect of the practical application of the great truths of our faith to our day-to-day living. Even in the pursuit of secular qualifications, it is recognised that theoretical knowledge is not sufficient and, in a number of disciplines such as medicine, architecture and language study, an elective year given to practical work away from the classroom is a prescribed part of the course. Paul recognised that Christianity is not just theory. He saw the need for the Christians to whom he wrote to apply what they believed to their behaviour and conduct. The gospel of what Christ has done for our salvation, set out in Romans 1-8, is the basis of Paul's appeal to his readers in chapters 12 to 16 to live lives worthy of such a gospel. Significantly, chapter 12 commences with the word 'Therefore' which provides a link between the doctrinal exposition which precedes and the detailed guidance as to the readers' conduct in their particular circumstances and environment which follows. Other epistles of Paul possess a similar balance between doctrine and ethics, being divided into two sections, usually of nearly equal length (e.g. Ephesians and Colossians). Anders Nygren, in his commentary on Romans (p.412) deplores the unprofitable practice of drawing a sharp line between doctrine and life, saying: 'Such a differentiation is alien to Paul. A doctrine, a gospel, which has no significance for man's life and conduct is no real gospel: and life and conduct which are not based on that which comes to us in the gospel are not Christian life and Christian conduct.' The teaching of the NT is given to us not just in order that we may know its truth but in order that we may obey it, that our character may be shaped by it so that we might live a new and Christlike life. Even when the teaching expounds a wholly doctrinal passage some practical application should be made. Remember that NT Christians would probably have heard the epistle sent by Paul to their particular church at one service, and so would have heard both the doctrinal and the practical sections at one sitting.

Doctrinally balanced teaching

Many have unbalanced views on biblical teaching in consequence of an emphasis on one aspect of the truth to the exclusion of another. Thus hyper-Calvinists, while rightly stressing what scripture says about the sovereignty of God, have ignored or watered down the plain scriptural statements about the responsibility of man. Some Arminians, on the other hand, have so stressed the part of man that they have left little room for the sovereignty of God. It is imperative that we be loyal to all that scripture says on a particular subject. Charles Simeon, who sought to do this, discovered that 'the truth is not in the middle, and not in one extreme, but in both extremes'. Applying this principle to Calvinism and Arminianism he says: 'Sometimes I am a high Calvinist, at other times a low Arminian, so that if extremes will please you, I am your man; only remember, it is not one extreme, but both extremes.' (H C G Moule, *Charles Simeon*, p.77) This means that we accept at their face value and faithfully teach both those scriptures which set forth the truth of unconditional election by God and those which emphasise the response of man as conditional to salvation.

In Paul's day and since, there have been those who have so concentrated on one side of Paul's teaching on grace that they have misrepresented it to mean that since we are saved by God's grace it does not matter how we live; we can continue in sin. Paul himself, in Romans 6, refuted such a misrepresentation of his teaching. While he taught, as Martin Luther proclaimed so loudly in the sixteenth century, that we are justified by faith alone, he made it clear, as Luther also did, that it is not by a faith which remains alone. If Paul stresses that we cannot be saved by good works he is equally emphatic that we cannot be saved without good works, and so is not in conflict with the intensely practical James whose teaching should also form part of the church's diet.

Again, while we should affirm confidently that all true believers are eternally secure, as stated in a number of scriptures, such as John 10:27-30, we should not allow any to be lulled into a false sense of security. We have to balance the affirmations of the security of believers by drawing attention to those scriptures which show the need for perseverance (e.g. John 8:31), those which give warnings about false profession (e.g. Heb 6:4-6) and those which exhort us to examine ourselves to see whether we are in the faith (2 Cor 13:5).

Teaching by group Bible study

The traditional mode of teaching is by sermon. While this has distinct value it suffers from the disadvantage that the audience is passive. While some may listen attentively, the minds of others may wander and there may even be a Eutychus who is overpowered by sleep. Those who do listen may not always grasp what is being taught, but generally they cannot interrupt and they may not have the opportunity afterwards of discussing with the speaker questions they might wish to raise, or may have forgotten.

This is where group Bible study (whether in homes or in the church) comes into its own. Preferably, groups should not be large and all those in each group should be free to contribute such understanding of the scriptures as they have, or to seek help from the others in the solution of doubts and problems that perplex them. Some may need a little prompting to speak and others to refrain from speaking. The business of the group is to discover the meaning of the passage under consideration and to apply its lessons. Ideally those in the group should have done their homework beforehand. By the sharing of the fruits of their study and their experiences they can receive new light on the scriptures and fresh impetus for living as Christians. In my church, every two or three weeks we have at the midweek service a joint prayer session followed by Bible study, for which we split into groups with a maximum of ten in each group. The study is based on the passages expounded on the preceding Sundays, which follow a sequence. Suggested questions for discussion, designed to clarify the meaning or purpose of the passages and to bring home their practical implications, are issued in advance. As we study the scriptures together in this way, differing views are bound to be expressed, but controversy should be avoided. What is of prime importance is that we hear God speaking to us from his word.

Group Bible study, where there is freedom to contribute or to ask questions, is particularly suitable for new converts and for persons who are interested but have not yet come to faith in Christ. For these, a course covering the fundamentals of the Christian faith or basic aspects of Christian living could be prepared, or courses available in book form or video could be adopted, such as the widely publicised Alpha course, produced by Holy Trinity Church, Brompton. (A cautionary note is needed on its sections dealing with the Holy Spirit because of the imbalance some will perceive in the emphasis placed on the gifts of healing and tongues.) A few years ago we followed up a church outreach with a visiting evangelist, in which a number professed faith or were restored, with the 'Fellowship with God' course, the first in a series under the overall title of 'Walking with God' produced by Willow Creek Community Church, Illinois. It covered such topics as our relationship with God, the assurance of salvation, reading and studying the word of God, prayer, the 'Quiet Time' and the importance of the Holy Spirit in Christian living. The course was spread over a 10-week period and was conducted in an informal atmosphere with a 15-minute introductory talk by a selected speaker before discussion in groups of the questions and scriptures suggested. Our experience was that members in each group participated freely, including some who had recently made a commitment, and the consensus was that the studies had been of real benefit. This was confirmed by the evident spiritual progress in a number who took part in them. (See chapter 13 on 'Small groups'.)

Conclusion

The object of Bible teaching, whether by address or group study, should not be allowed to slip out of sight. This is not only to help towards a better understanding of the scriptures but also, through them, to lead to a more intimate knowledge of our Lord and a closer walk with God. (See chapter 6 on 'The place of preaching'.)

Further reading

F D Coggan, *The Ministry of the Word* (1945)
C H Spurgeon, *Lectures to my Students* (Christian Focus, 1998)
J S Stewart, *Heralds of God* (Hodder & Stoughton, 1946)
J Stott, *I Believe in Preaching* (Hodder & Stoughton, 1982)

ARCHIE NAISMITH

TEACHING

When the Plowden Report on 'Education in the Primary School' appeared in 1967, it generated a good deal of surprise, not to say shock-horror, because according to its critics, it did not contain the word 'teach'. The critics were not silenced when it was pointed out that the really important thing in education is not that children should be given 'teaching' but that they should learn. Indeed at the time it was quite normal for teachers to speak of the importance of 'learning strategies'. Of course it is true that one way of describing the role of a teacher is to say that a teacher should *teach*. It is equally true, however, that a teacher's job is to help students *learn*. There is still a widespread assumption that children will 'learn' more or less inevitably if only they are (properly) 'taught'. But, however conscientiously teaching may be given in churches or schools, there is no benefit if the students fail to learn.

Not only is it important to distinguish learning from teaching. Those who teach need to remember that the verb 'teach' has two objects. As a teacher I may teach, for example, maths. But my efforts to teach maths will be largely unsuccessful if I forget that I am also teaching Mary. And Michael too. Also Melvin, who may very likely learn best in a second or third way, different from what is appropriate for the other two. There is no 'one size fits all' method of teaching.

How do people learn? When I learn maths, for example, the teacher explains to me how to do simple subtraction. The teacher works a few examples for me. And yet I have not learned. I learn by doing some examples myself. When I get them right, the method which has been taught me is reinforced. Getting some of them wrong is helpful if it makes me realise that I haven't yet mastered the procedure.

Another example. It is not difficult to learn what is produced on the farm down the road. I am given a list to memorise. I do a test paper. Ten out of ten and I've obviously learned the names of the products. But can I tell which of these fields contains wheat and which barley? How does the milk get into the churns? If I am well taught I shall learn by seeing and even by doing. Also by associating and relating – do all the beetroots in that field really get put in vinegar and eaten in salads? If not, what happens to them?

That's almost enough generalising about learning and teaching. But there's still space to pose one significant final question. What do we mean when we say – as we do – that people 'learn by experience'? How does this happen -in school, in everyday life, in church life?

Method

In too many churches it is still taken for granted that teaching is done by somebody speaking from up front and using a lecture format. This technique may be useful sometimes but it doesn't correspond to the methods commonly used today, whether in schools and higher education or in business and manufacturing. Nor, for that matter, to NT practice, which would have entailed far more interaction between teacher and taught, even (or especially) in a situation such as the one in Ephesus, which we find recorded in Acts 19:9, where Paul based himself in the lecture hall of a philosopher called Tyrannus and there discussed (NIV) and argued

(NRSV).

When Paul revisited Ephesus, he reminded the elders of the church (also described in verse 2 as bishops) of how he had taught the church. They knew, he said, that he '[had] not hesitated to preach anything that would be helpful to [them] but . . . taught [them] publicly and from house to house'. Imagine that you are a member of such a household. Would you expect Paul to walk in, sit down and launch into a discourse? Surely far more of this teaching was done in conversation or as individuals raised questions about Christian belief and conduct.

Similarly, it is not difficult to see that the 'teaching/ training' referred to in Titus 2:3-4 was not delivered in a formal setting. Paul tells Titus to 'teach the older women to be reverent in the way they live, not to be slanderers or addicted to much wine, but to teach what is good. Then they can train the younger women to love their husbands and children.' As Gordon Fee points out in his New International Bible Commentary volume, the word used 'probably implies nothing more than informal teaching by word and example'.

It was not only Cretan women who needed to learn the Christian way of life. In the first century – as still today – an important aspect of Christian teaching concerned conduct. How should a believer behave at home, at work, in the community? Had the Lord said anything which would give guidance? If he had not, then were there any principles to follow when responding, for example, to an invitation to a birthday meal in one of the local temples? 1 Corinthians 10:14-23 is only one example of teaching about conduct which – then, as today – was surely based on a number of informal conversations.

Content

The word *training* (Tit 2:4) is interesting. We still tend to think of teaching as something purely cognitive. 'People should be *taught* the things they need to *know*.' Churches should teach believers biblical content, Christian doctrine, Christian ethics and information about missionary endeavour. But Titus was told to ensure also that young wives are *trained* in what they ought to *do*.

A church which is doing the right thing by its members and thus by the head of the body of which they form part will take care to teach them how to *do* things. It will ensure that training is provided in a number of skills; for example, how to have a 'quiet time', how to witness, how to function as a husband, wife or parent, how to study the Bible, how to lead a Bible study, how to handle a youth group, how to lead a Bible study or a service, how to welcome people to a service, how to preach, how to lead someone to Christ, or help someone who is suffering. Where teams work together to clean the church, it may be necessary to train some people in floor-cleaning skills!

Church and community

One result of the development of parent-toddler groups is that more and more churches are realising the importance of teaching parenting skills. This is an immensely important ministry which is valued not only by parents but frequently also by local councillors, who know only too well the price the community pays for family breakdown and parental failure.

During the eighteenth and nineteenth centuries, the church made an immense contribution to the life of the nation through its teaching ministry but also, to a substantial extent, in the twentieth. I am not thinking so much of the role of church schools but of the way in which local churches have empowered individuals. The role of nonconformity in shaping the tone and influence of the trade union movement is – or should be – well known. How did this happen? Very simply and almost inevitably. Men and women who had been disempowered by economic and social forces were touched by the Holy Spirit and found themselves in communities where they learned to read and think.They learned to work alongside other people with a shared purpose. They discovered that in this way they could affect outcomes. They learned to take responsibility for their own lives and also for their involvement in a common enterprise within which they had voluntarily accepted a significant role. Examples commonly referred to are Methodist churches and the vigorous life of Welsh churches, which supplied so many working-class politicians to the rising Labour Party.

In Latin America, the charismatic movement has likewise empowered many. Even today in the UK a church which down-loads responsibility to that traditional British institution, the committee, is training people to work together with integrity for a shared goal.

As I write, I am thinking of a church which is engaged in an ambitious development project which depends to a significant extent on the labour of members. The end product will have immense potential. But meanwhile, the shared experience of being part of a group of believers working together teaches lessons the importance of which it is impossible to over-estimate. When the former county engineer is working alongside an unemployed truckdriver as brothers in Christ there is a two-way 'learning situation' of incalculable value.

Formal and informal

We have seen how wide the 'teaching ministry' of a church may be; how it is in no way limited to formal sessions, and how important personal interaction may be. It would be interesting for readers to examine their own experience of informal learning. Who were the people who shaped your understanding of what it means to be a Christian and how to serve God? To what extent was what they gave you supplied by means of formal instruction? How much by informal contact? What did you learn and how? The odds are that you will remember unscheduled conversations, books recommended or lent, occasions when you asked for advice. One important common factor in all these is the importance of personal contact for this kind of informal teaching.

It may be helpful to mention some of the various means a church can employ in its formal teaching programmes. Whatever skills or fields of knowledge are being handled, it is important to make use of current teaching techniques as appropriate. One obvious resource is the overhead projector. Although this is increasingly employed there are still churches where a speaker wouldn't dream of using one to display the main points of what he or she is saying. (Incidentally, having to reduce one's discourse to a series of points is a very good discipline as well as helpful to the learners.) Also important are small-group learning, examining in detail how principles already learned may apply to specific situations, and, of course, computer programmes. It is important that learning should include an element of interaction.

Home groups. Besides providing an opportunity to learn more of the scriptures and of what Christians believe and how they should live, home groups can empower people who might otherwise never try to formulate their thoughts or to express themselves aloud in worship or discussion. Home groups should also inculcate good practice in committee work and in helping others. (See chapter 13 on 'Small groups'.)

Alpha and *Just Looking* courses differ from much traditional evangelism because they teach the faith to enquirers – sometimes also to the believers who are helping to run them.

Marriage preparation classes. If a church lacks people able and willing to run its own courses there is a wide variety to choose from. (See chapter 43 on 'Marriage enrichment'.)

Parenting classes are likewise valuable. They can be a great help to single parents who may attend toddler groups and who may come to faith as a result of personal interaction and through seeing how faith, practice and commitment are related.

Working alongside others with greater experience. This method may be used in youth work, catering, visiting homes, sermon preparation . . . The possibilities are endless although their potential is not always recognised.

Visits by Christians from other cultures, whether at home or abroad. These may inform members about what is going on elsewhere, help them to see new ways of applying old truths, or become aware of new possibilities for their own lives.

Visiting and working with Christians from other cultures. This could include sending teams to evangelise or work on development projects. Young people – although not only they – may experience renewal and receive valuable training in this way. (See chapter 17 on 'Stimulating involvement in world mission'.)

Training courses, church-based, local or national. An obvious example is training in leading Bible study and home-groups. But there is also a great variety of part-time and distance learning possibilities.

'Some . . . teachers'

Whatever is being taught and whatever methods are used, it is important to recognise and make use of people who have (whether by nature or training or the special anointing of the Holy Spirit or all three) the gift of teaching. This does not depend on gender nor solely on knowledge/skill. It should go without saying that somebody who is entrusted with a teaching role should be well acquainted, in breadth and depth, with what they are charged to teach. This is important if they are to reduce their subject to 'bite-sized chunks' or even liquidise it for learners with weaker digestions. A teacher needs to know how to think clearly. Also to exercise self-discipline rather than self-indulgently to ride off on hobby-horses. Also – and just as vitally – to have good interpersonal skills.

These skills will include the ability to ask and find answers to three vital questions.

- Where is this student coming from? What relevant knowledge do they already have? Do they find it easy or difficult to think in abstract terms?

- What – if anything – does he or she want to learn? Students have their own agendas. These may need to be modified but it is important to know what goals they may have set themselves.

* How is this student motivated? They may want to be of service to others, to strengthen their CV, to enjoy learning something new, to outdo other members of the group, to gain approval. Knowing what motivates a student will help in teaching them more effectively.

However respected a senior church member, their possession of these skills must not be taken for granted. Nor should their vital importance be overlooked. Under God the long-term strength and vitality of a church is closely related to the quality of its teaching.

Some resources

London Bible College, Green Lane, Northwood, Middx HA6 2UW (01923 45600)

The Open Theological College, PO Box 220, The Park Campus, The Park, Cheltenham, GL50 2QF Website: www.chelt.ac.uk/cwis/otc.htm E-mail: otc@chelt.ac.uk Tel: 01242 532 837 Fax: 01242 532801

Workshop is not a distance learning provider. It offers an extremely valuable and wide-ranging course. which takes the form of a number of non-residential weekend sessions – one a month for eleven months – available at various centres in different parts of the UK. Fran Beckett (Shaftesbury Society), Graham Cray (formerly principal of Ridley Hall), Philip Mohabir, (president of the African and Caribbean Evangelical Alliance), Nigel Wright (Spurgeon's College). Contact Anvil Trust Central Office, 104 Townend Lane, Deepcar, Sheffield, S36 2TS Tel: 114 288 8816 Fax: 114 288 8817 E-mail: office@anvil.org.uk

PETER COUSINS

CHAPTER SIX

The Place of Preaching

ALASTAIR NOBLE

I am honoured, if not best qualified, to write on the place of preaching in the church. My views on preaching and teaching derive from more than 30 years of lay ministry alongside full-time and demanding employment, and mainly within a network of independent evangelical churches. Although I greatly appreciate the work of ordained ministers and professional preachers, I remain committed to the role of lay-preachers in enriching the life of the church and in the wider work of evangelism. Come to think of it, a good number of the disciples and apostles of Jesus, whose preaching transformed the Roman Empire and gave us our Christian heritage, fell into that category.

Biblical and historical perspectives

Preaching is largely an NT phenomenon, as most of the references to it in any concordance will demonstrate. The prophetic and teaching ministries of the OT come close to it and the Christian pattern must have drawn on previous means of instruction (see, for example, Luke 4:18, Acts 9:20). Preaching and teaching are at the heart of the Lord's commission to his disciples, both before and after his resurrection (Matt 10:7; 28:19-20). It was the subject of Paul's solemn charge to Timothy (2 Tim 4:2) and the practice of the other apostles (1 Peter 1:25).

Primarily, preaching was 'the public proclamation of Christianity to the non-Christian world' (C H Dodd) and we should continue to encourage its use in that evangelistic way. However, it is clear that the preaching and teaching of the word became a regular feature of the life of the early church (2 Tim 4:2). Preaching in one form or another has been consistently used in the church both to win and to instruct converts. For many centuries, preaching made the Bible accessible to the illiterate of the world; in some countries the pulpit set the national mood; and in modern societies it has remained a source of challenge and comfort. It is salutary to note that many great movements in church history had at their centre individuals who were called to preach.

After almost 20 centuries of preaching, it would be short-sighted and perverse to imagine that it no longer has a place in the church. However, its role in the contemporary church cannot just be taken for granted and its practice could well become trapped in the norms of the past.

Cultural relevance

The need for cultural relevance is the great quest of the modern evangelical church and rightly so. In fact, most of our church practices are already shaped by the demands of our times, and, if not culturally relevant, are at least culturally determined or, at worst, culturally convenient. A common objection to preaching, therefore, is that it is outmoded in an age of sophisticated means of communication.

In the current debate about cultural relevance, preaching will struggle to hold its place. Everyone is supposed to know that the highly educated people of the third millennium cannot concentrate on the spoken word for more than about five minutes at a time. Curiously, they can listen to radio, television and tapes for hours on end, creating the impression that this generation can cope with what it wants to listen to – and for remarkably long periods of time. The point Paul made about 'itching ears' (2 Tim 4:3) might have some bearing on this!

The declaration of the gospel and the teaching of Christians must surely remain biblical norms for the church in any age. The range of methods by which these duties were discharged in the early church was extensive. Lecture, debate and conversation supplemented the preaching of the gospel in synagogue, market place and hired hall. The methods of teaching Christians were as diverse as homely discussion of the scriptures, and discourses that lasted till midnight. The methods of communication were those that matched the patterns of first-century life.

Churches should use all the modern means of communication at their disposal and in the delivery of Christian education should take full account of current interactive and practical styles of learning. But my view is that, just as there is no real alternative to the political conference speech designed for rousing the faithful and speaking to the nation, so nothing makes quite the impact on mind and heart as a powerfully delivered sermon.

A question of authority

Arguably, a more fundamental question to be considered in determining the place of preaching is that of authority. Our age, with its existential conditioning and postmodern principles, is one in which clarity and certainty are suspect. The act of preaching derives directly from the authority of the Bible, and if the latter is in doubt, the former becomes vacuous.

A commitment to the place of preaching by the modern church is, in effect, part of its commitment to the authority of scripture and the need to declare its timeless truths. If we flirt with the postmodern notion that there are no unequivocal Bible values, we might as well settle for talks, discussions, panels and workshops, so that every shade of opinion can be fully explored in an unending quest for religious enlightenment. But if we believe that there is such a thing as revealed and timeless truth, we should not apologise for making its declaration through preaching a regular means of communication. A church that rejects preaching as a key part of its learning strategy may well be rejecting much more than it thinks.

Preaching is different

My most basic conviction about preaching is that it differs in kind from all other forms of communication. True preaching is neither teaching nor lecturing, both of which have an important role in Christian evangelism and education. The modern description of preaching as 'a talk' does it a huge disservice. Preaching involves a unique combination of truth and passion which appeals to both intellect and emotion. Although preaching has been described as 'truth through personality', it is much more a phenomenon in which the Holy Spirit uses the spoken word to move the hearers to an immediate and lasting response. (See for example Acts 2:37.)

My experience is that preaching is essentially inspirational. The content of the sermon may not be long remembered and, in any case, the interested mind will pursue the detail later. It is the impression conveyed by the sermon which lives on, generating commitment and action. In this sense it is different from systematic teaching which is more considered and often less immediate in its impact.

I also believe that preaching must involve building a bridge of understanding between biblical truth and contemporary reality. Preaching has to connect truth with the daily experience of the listeners. For that reason it should not deal simply with academic or exegetical matters. It is crucially important that the preacher relates ancient precepts to present dilemmas. The preacher therefore needs to understand something of the politics, sociology, values, and crises of the world in which he lives, and set his message in that context.

None of this is meant to imply that preaching alone is the key to progress in the church. A church that is committed to Christian education will create opportunities for formal and informal teaching, for discussion and debate, and for the illustration of themes through audio, video and computerised resources. Most churches have a fair way to go in the development of these modes of learning. But preaching with relevance and clarity will always enrich these activities.

There must be a down side

The fact that preaching has fallen into relative decline in our age does indicate that there are difficulties with this area of ministry.

The commitment of the evangelical tradition to preaching has sometimes given rise to the view that its quality is in direct proportion to its length. However, it is now more fashionable to imagine that the real drawback with preaching is the length of it! I think it is pointless to speculate about how long a sermon should last. It should simply be suited to the occasion. However, in the general round of church activity, preachers should be able to bring a complete message in around half an hour, leaving plenty of time for the other elements of a service. There are occasions where a powerful impact can be made in much less time, and there are more relaxed settings when the preacher can explore a theme at greater length. A competent preacher should always know when his audience has had enough.

And there are some other drawbacks with preaching, such as the following:

- Preaching is particularly prone to the promotion of the cult of personality with consequent damage to the unity of a church.
- By virtue of their high visibility, capable preachers can imagine that they may speak without accountability to the leadership of the church.
- Uninformed preaching can create a phoney sense of authority with the associated dangers of the adoption by churches of dogmatic and inflexible positions.
- A surfeit of preaching can make congregations lazy and unwilling to explore biblical issues for themselves.

- Poor preaching can alienate people who genuinely want to know what the Bible has to say about their life circumstances.

None of the above, though, is an argument for rejecting the ministry of preaching.

Scheduling preaching

If we accept the continuing need for preaching as a distinctive mode of communicating the word of God for today, there is a need to plan for its inclusion into the programme of the church. There can be no single pattern for the preaching ministry in modern evangelical churches and leaders are wise if they select the configuration of teaching and preaching which best suits the needs of their congregations and communities.

My suggestion is that such planning be done within an agreed set of guidelines for preaching which might look like this:

- The church has a duty to have at least one occasion for preaching and teaching each week.
- A balance needs to be struck between messages with an essentially evangelistic thrust and those that are designed to instruct believers.
- While preaching needs to be undertaken within a programme of systematic coverage of Bible truths, there must be scope for the spontaneous and the prophetic.
- Where possible, a preaching team should be created and encouraged to work together in their ministry.
- In recognising the place of preaching, the church will make it part of its wider programme of Christian education.
- Because preaching aims to address a wide range of needs at once, it should be varied in its content and supplemented by other interactive styles of communication.
- Since preaching can either inspire or alienate the hearers, the church must entrust it to those who are obviously gifted in that direction and whose lives are consistent with their teaching.
- The church has a duty to ensure that its training programme is designed to achieve some succession in the ministry of preaching.
- Churches should recognise other gifted preachers whom God has given to the wider church and should encourage their members to participate in events outside the normal church routine where their ministry can be heard.

Evaluating the quality

Leaders who sense the importance of preaching in the life of the church also need to be prepared to evaluate the quality of what is on offer. My suggestion is that there are at least three criteria by which preaching should be judged. These are the quality of the following:

- *Exposition.* All preaching needs to be rooted in scripture because it is the authoritative rule of Christian life. The preacher's exposition of scripture needs to be accurate, authoritative and accessible. Leaders should bear in mind that the average Christian seldom has time to study scripture in depth and will look to the church to explain it.

- *Explanation.* This is the more difficult task of interpreting scripture in the context of modern life and current realities. Scripture needs to be preached into the circumstances created by modern living. The application of scripture to the lives of the hearers needs to be contemporary, clear and convincing.

- *Encouragement.* People who come to church to listen to preachers expect to be uplifted and encouraged. While wrongs needs to be exposed, the objectives of preaching should be the encouragement and inspiration of the hearers to greater commitment and effort in the service of Christ.

'I have been to church today and I am not depressed', Robert Louis Stevenson once observed. The loyalty of the congregations of past ages has largely gone. People will not continue to come to church if the preaching and teaching is not inspirational and relevant.

Conclusion

At a time when the national government is attempting to promote the well-being of individuals, families and communities through education and various social measures, there is a real opportunity for evangelical churches to display the torch of Bible truth more clearly through preaching.

We should never be afraid, in an increasingly confusing and confused age, to declare the Christian faith through preaching. We are short of preachers who can both inform and inspire. We need some preachers who sound like the prophets of ancient times, who can stir congregations, and whose words are heard beyond the confines of the church. I think we do not have enough of them because we do not value them sufficiently.

Paul's charge to a younger church leader was unequivocal:

'Preach the Word; be prepared in season and out of season; correct, rebuke and encourage – with great patience and careful instruction. For the time will come when men will not put up with sound doctrine. Instead, to suit their own desires, they will gather around them a great number of teachers to say what their itching ears want to hear. They will turn their ears away from the truth and turn aside to myths. But you, keep your head in all situations, endure hardship, do the work of an evangelist, discharge all the duties of your ministry' (2 Tim 4:2-5).

Further reading

G Goldsworthy, *Preaching the Whole Bible as Christian Scripture* (IVP, 2000)
W L Liefeld, *New Testament Exposition* (Zondervan, 1984)
D Martyn Lloyd-Jones, *Preaching and Preachers* (Hodder & Stoughton, 1971)
J Stott, *I Believe in Preaching* (Hodder & Stoughton, 1982)
R E O White, *A Guide to Preaching* (Pickering & Inglis, 1973)

CHAPTER SEVEN

Stimulating Corporate Prayer

BRIAN MILLS

Nowadays it is rare to find a praying church. Of course, all churches include prayer in their services; but few provide opportunities for the development of prayer in the life of the members – either personally or corporately. Yet prayer was one of the four principles on which the life of the early church was based (Acts 2:42). As a result, it grew.

A biblical model of a praying church – Jerusalem, 1st century AD

It was born in prayer. After Christ's ascension the disciples met together to pray and continued to pray until the Holy Spirit was poured out (Acts 1:14; 2:1, 11). Even then, their activity was prayer and praise as they declared 'the wonders of God' in tongues. Before that time the disciples seem to have been failures in prayer – they fell asleep when Jesus took them with him to pray (Luke 9:32; Matt 26:40, 45).

It was devoted to prayer. Daily they met in each other's homes to share fellowship, break bread, be taught and pray (Acts 2:42-47). As a consequence, God added daily to the believing community.

Its response to crisis was to pray. Restrictions were placed on the apostles by the authorities; they were told not to preach in the name of Jesus. Their response was to meet together to pray for more boldness and more evidence of God's power. No wonder the house shook (Acts 4:23-31).

Its response to criticism was to maintain the priority of prayer. When the apostles were criticised over the neglect of Grecian widows, they delegated some of the responsibilities to others so that they could give their undivided attention to 'prayer and the word' (Acts 6:1-6). Leaders today need to follow this example by freeing themselves from responsibilities that others can handle in order to maintain the priority of prayer and the word of God.

Its response to unusual blessing was to 'export' prayer. Samaria had accepted the gospel through Philip's preaching. God's power brought healing, deliverance and great joy to that city. So the Jerusalem church sent Peter and John to the new believers. They prayed for them that they might receive the Holy Spirit – that seems to have been the main purpose of their visit.

It sacrificed to pray. When Peter was put in prison a second time, the church called an all-night prayer meeting. Anything that threatened to curtail the spread of the gospel and the growth of the church inspired urgent prayer. Desperate need required desperate measures. God intervened through an angelic deliverance (Acts 12:5-18).

What is a praying church?

A praying church is one that recognises prayer as one of its foundational functions. It is prepared to sacrifice the time and comfort that prayer sometimes requires. It spontaneously and specifically prays in time of need. Its leaders are committed, praying people who set the example for others.

Prayer is not an optional extra for a church. Paul's letters contain many encouragements for churches to pray – particularly for the spread of the gospel and the growth of the church. In many respects the way a church develops its prayer ministry will depend on its size, its locality, its focus and function, and its denominational or theological flavour. Each church has a unique soil (receptivity), climate (spiritual atmosphere) and mix of gifts. A praying local church will desire to see as many people as possible released into good prayer habits. People of all ages, backgrounds and Christian experience, involved in a variety of ways, will make for an exciting array of informed prayer. In many churches, small group prayer has helped to bring this about. People with a wide or a limited vocabulary and experience of prayer feel at ease with it. In developing a prayer strategy for your church there should be something for everyone. Your church can become a praying church.

Encouraging prayer within a church

Is your church prayer meeting working? Is it the place to be, or has it lost its vitality? Do people attend only out of a sense of duty? Or is it the visible powerhouse for what God is doing? Do you have any special occasions for the church to meet in prayer? If it has lost its direction a number of options are open to you:

Discontinue it

This will either cause a furore, or people will breathe a sigh of relief. If people complain, ask them to meet with the leaders to share why they are so concerned and suggest what they think should be the remedy.

Reshape it

Arrange it at another time – instead of 7.30pm, why not 7.30am? Instead of weekly, why not daily for a while? Instead of spending only an hour, why not spend longer – maybe two or three hours? Why not give the group a new name, a new leader, or a new focus? Most church prayer is inward-looking, focusing on personal needs, church activities and services. Turn the prayer meeting inside out. Focus on the community and its needs, or the streets around you and the people that live there.

Revitalize it

There are many exciting ways of varying the style, content, emphasis and subjects of prayer gatherings. Clearing a space in the middle of the room may be a start! Here are some more suggestions:

- Decide on a theme or themes for prayer.
- Find scripture to encourage prayer.
- Create an upward focus by starting with a time of worship to help focus on the divine intercessors (Rom 8:26, 27, 34).
- Develop an inward focus by a time of personal reflection in private prayer, or forming twos in order to pray for something personal to each.
- Strengthen the outward focus by using a variety of small group sizes to concentrate on prayer related to your chosen theme.
- Change the composition of the groups. For example, if you are focusing on education, ensure that those involved in education – as teachers, students, governors, dinner ladies – identify themselves. Then encourage groups to form around them to pray, asking them to share first within their groups.
- Use the same method for different areas of the town, or different countries or regions of the world.
- If you have many topics, you might wish to give a different topic to each of four in a group so that the topics are covered in every group. Or divide the congregation into four sections and groups within that section, and give each section one of the topics to pray over.
- Intersperse prayer songs to express what is being prayed about

and the manner of praying (e.g., sorrow, repentance, empathy, hope, victory). Introduce a time of open prayer, either led from the front or arising spontaneously from the congregation.

- Allow a period when people pray simultaneously (all together at the same time) either spontaneously or liturgically (or both).
- Finish with a time of praise, sharing or scriptural declaration.

Visual aids in the form of newspaper cuttings, maps, pictures on the walls, overhead projector acetates, or video extracts, are essential components of creative prayer. For example, hand a page of the day's newspaper to each group, asking them to pray over one of the news stories.

Replace it with something else

- Create prayer triplets. Most people are concerned to pray for their friends; most find recurring difficulties in praying on their own. Correct both by introducing triplets, focusing on non-believing neighbours, friends, colleagues or relatives. You can do this initially within a structured church time or home cell group, and then encourage the triplets to develop a life of their own.
- Create church activity groups. All churches have activities – ensure that a praying group (including those leading it) meets during each time of activity. Pray before and during the activity, and see how much more effective it becomes.
- Create special interest prayer groups. These are groups whose focus is on issues such as education, children with special needs, families in crisis, increasing crime, overseas mission, or your neighbourhood.
- Create ministry prayer groups. These are concerned for pastoral needs, physical or emotional ailments, or evangelism. Those involved need to pray together regularly about their area of ministry and the people they are ministering to. Some churches have formed healing or prayer counselling groups; others have deliverance groups.
- Review progress in prayer. From time to time you may still wish to meet as a church to pray. What a creative time could be enjoyed if all the interest groups reported what God had been doing! Your prayer meeting could become a praise, instead of a petition meeting. By bringing leaders of various groups together, you may also identify gaps to be filled, or burdens for more in-depth prayer.

Be really radical

Increasingly, nations are opening up to the world of the internet;

increasingly, young people relate to other young people through the global youth culture. Bring the two together by inviting your young people to introduce the rest of the church to prayer on the internet. On the net can be found plenty of information on global issues for prayer, and stories of answered prayer from around the world. Download some of this to encourage belief in our God who delights to answer prayer. Find out about some of the countries in which church-planting is taking place, or others where catastrophic difficulties are being faced. Obtain FridayFax by e-mail. To subscribe, send a message with the subject 'subscribe English' to <fridayfax@dawneurope.net> DAWN has a web-site (www.dawnministries.org) and prayer co-ordinators around the world. Along with the use of modern music and creative visual ideas, there is an an explosion of prayer among both young people and children around the world. Tap into http://www.24-7prayer.com

Release the intercessors in your church

Identify who they are. Intercessors are not specially favoured by God or more spiritual than anyone else. It is just that prayer is their service to the Body of Christ. As people who are involved in a personal ministry grow, so a church prayer ministry will emerge. Or, as a church becomes a praying church, people with such a calling on their lives will stand out.

Although prayer is key to the life of every believer, God seems to gift some with the desire and ability to devote themselves to intercession for others. They will often spend more time and energy in prayer than others. Anna was an example of such a person. 'She never left the temple but worshipped night and day, fasting and praying' (Luke 2:37).

Link them together in appropriate ways. Although there may be only a few in each congregation, across the community there could be many of them. Identify and develop the unique calling that God has put upon their lives, such as praying for the community, praying for the sick, praying for leaders, praying for the nation. Those who are called to pray for the community or nation may have or may develop a strong spiritual warfare component to their praying.

There are many different kinds of calling and anointing in prayer, and it is important to help people to receive training appropriate to their call. Pastorally inclined people will often want to perform personal ministry, spending longer amounts of time ministering to those who are broken physically, spiritually or emotionally. They will need special training for such ministry. Some will wish to be a prayer back-up group for others (we call this a prayer shield). These intercessors can be a vital and powerful force for effective ministry. It is important to allow each person to 'wear their own armour'. David couldn't fight Goliath in Saul's armour; he had to be himself.

Create a prayer chain with either a pyramid or a ring structure to enable prayer to be communicated to the church. Leaders may need specific prayer over a sensitive subject. Every church is involved in battle, so it will need warriors to engage in battle on its behalf. Urgent, concentrated prayer may be needed for a particular person, or a national need, or a special event. The prayer chain is an important means of providing such cover.

Be open to consider fresh developments. Praying churches are never static. They are always growing – in numbers, influence, ministry – and in problems and opposition. So prayer needs to grow and adjustments made both to cope with changes and to enable growth to continue. Praying churches find that they need to organise a number of innovative prayer events – like prayer concerts, prayer walks, days or weeks of praying and fasting, a 24-hour chain for as long as necessary and practical, prayer journeys and expeditions – to name a few. They may arrange prayer walking, or driving groups who will carry out these activities as their ministry. They will link successful praying people with those less successful in order to help improve the effectiveness of their prayer. They may wish to arrange seminars or run a school of prayer in order to learn more about the principles and practices of spiritual warfare. Some churches have opened prayer houses.

In it all, God will lead, by his Spirit. Prayer doesn't happen merely by good planning and structures. It happens when God pours out a spirit of 'seeking after him' – not for blessing, but for relationship. It will be God who will grow a praying church, but we need to be fertile, well-prepared soil in which the seeds of prayer are planted and take root.

My goal is God himself,
Not wealth or fame or growth,
But God himself, my God,
At any cost, dear Lord, by any road.

Further reading

J Holloway, *Community Prayer Cells* (CPAS, 1998)
B Mills, *Developing a Prayer Strategy* (Challenge 2000, 1994)
M and K Morris, *Praying Together* (Kingsway, 1987)
C P Wagner, *Churches that Pray* (Regal Books [Gospel Light], 1993)

CHAPTER EIGHT

Baptism

JOHN BAIGENT

In the New Testament

Its practice

The practice of Christian baptism derives from the clear command of the risen Lord Jesus to his apostles to go to the world's population, preaching the gospel and making disciples by baptising them (Matt 28:19, 20; cf. Mark 16:15, 16). This would readily be understandable to Jews at that time, familiar as they were with OT washings, (probably) proselyte baptism and, especially, the baptising of John the Baptist. Gentiles also might be expected to be familiar with purification rites in Hellenism and particularly in the mystery religions. The book of Acts shows how the apostles and other evangelists obeyed this command: 2:38-42; 8:12, 13; 8:36-38; 9:18 (cf. 22:16); 10:47, 48; 16:15, 33; 18:8; 19:5 (cf. 1 Cor 1:14-17).

The following points emerge from a study of the foregoing references:

- Baptism was an important and integral part of what was involved when a person became a Christian (a 'believer' in, or 'disciple' of Jesus). It appears that whenever the gospel was preached a call was made not only for repentance and/or faith but also for baptism as the outward, public expression of that inward response.

- Whilst the presentation of the gospel may well have included an element of 'teaching', the main educational process for the new convert began *after*, not before, baptism.

- A person's 'reception' of the Holy Spirit normally occurred immediately or soon after baptism (Acts 8:14-17 and 10:44-49 being explicable exceptions) and involved 'the laying on of hands'. Some kind of outward, vocal manifestation (tongues, prophecy, praise, etc.) was apparently common (if not invariable) in those early days.

- The candidate for baptism was almost certainly required to make a public confession of faith in Jesus as 'Lord' or 'Son of God' (cf. the western text in Acts 8:37; Acts 22:16; Rom 10:9, 10; 1 Cor 12 :3).
- At this time baptisms were 'in (or into) the name of Jesus' (cf. Rom 6:3). This probably meant more than 'on the authority of Jesus', suggesting rather a 'coming-into-relationship-with' or 'coming-under-the lordship-of' Jesus (cf. 1 Cor 1:12-15). Whether it was actually used as a formula by the baptiser is uncertain but very likely. There is no evidence that the trinitarian formulation in Matthew 28:20 was so used until later (cf. *The Didache*, c.150 A.D?).
- Where 'households' are described as being baptised, it is unlikely that this included very young children because stress is usually placed upon people 'hearing' the message and 'believing' it. On the other hand, what the NT describes is the baptism of people converted from Judaism or paganism; there is no mention of what should happen when a child has grown up in a Christian family (1 Cor 7:14 is probably not relevant here).
- The mode of baptism was almost certainly normally by immersion. This follows from the natural meaning of the verb used (*baptizo*, an intensive form from *bapto*, 'dip', 'dye', 'immerse', drown'), the need for sufficient water (a river, pool or tank), and the description of both baptiser and baptised going into the water.
- There is no evidence of baptisms taking place in the context of a church 'meeting' (or 'service'). They took place wherever there was a convenient quantity of water, as soon as possible after the person signified a desire to become a Christian, and in the presence of whoever happened to be there at the time, the minimum being one other person (the baptiser).

Its meaning

In the teaching of the NT we find a rich variety of explanations of the symbolism and significance of Christian baptism. Here they can only be summarised.

Symbolism

The use of water in an initiatory act is not arbitrary: it serves as a potent symbol of both cleansing and drowning.

- *A picture of cleansing from sin* (Acts 22:16; cf. John 3:5; 13:6-11; 1 Cor 6:11; Eph 5:26; Tit 3:5; Heb 10:22; 1 Pet 3:21; Ezek 36:25; [2 Kings 5:13, 14]). I am assuming here that NT references to 'washing' from sin, although primarily about *inward* cleansing, would have suggested to the original readers a link with baptism.

* *A picture of dying to sin* (Rom. 6:1-7; cf. Mark 10:38, 39; Luke 12:50; Col 2:11, 12; [Pss 18:4, 5; 69:1, 2; Jon 2:3, 5]). Paul does not actually spell out this symbolism in Romans 6 but the imagery of being plunged under the water ('buried') seems to underlie his explanation of baptism as a dying to sin by being united with Christ in his death. [I am unable to follow those who understand Paul's references to 'baptism' as connoting 'Spirit baptism' unless he actually mentions water.]

* *A picture of salvation from sin* (1 Pet 3:20-22). This is not an easy passage. Peter sees a parallel (NIV 'symbolises' is literally 'an antitype') between the water of the Flood and the water of baptism. Just as Noah and his family in the ark were saved by being brought through the waters of God's judgment, so Christians are saved from the judgment due to their sins by going through the waters of baptism and thus symbolising their appeal to God for a good conscience. Such salvation is possible only because Christ suffered (3:18) and rose again.

Significance

* *Initiation* (Gal 3:26-29). Baptism signifies entry into the family of God through faith in Jesus. The main point being made here is that *all* who are baptised are equally part of God's family: Gentiles as well as Jews come into the good of the promises made to Abraham. The ethical consequences of being 'clothed' with Christ are elaborated elsewhere. Just as people being baptised apparently stripped off their old clothes and put on new clothes afterwards, so they must 'put off' their old life and 'put on' the new life of someone who belongs to Christ (cf. Col 3:9, 12; Eph 4:21-24).

* *Identification* (Rom 6:1-11). Here the ethical consequences of baptism are drawn from its significance as the expression of union with Christ in his redemptive actions. The doctrine of justification by faith cannot mean that Christians are free to sin with impunity. Their baptism means that they have 'died' to sin because Christ's death has become their death, and that they can and should live new, morally upright lives because Christ's resurrection is their resurrection (cf. Gal 2:20; 2 Cor 5:14, 15; Col 2:11, 12).

* *Incorporation* (1 Cor 12:13). Although Paul is referring here primarily to 'Spirit baptism' it is hard to imagine that there was no link in his mind with water baptism. We have seen already

from Acts that reception of the Spirit was normally associated with water baptism. Baptism has a corporate as well as an individual aspect. To be baptised 'into Christ' (Rom 6:3; Gal 3:27) is to be baptised into his body, the church (cf. Eph 4:4-6). Whilst this means in the first instance the universal church (all believers of all time), baptism was surely also seen as entry to the local, visible community of Christians.

This brief survey of NT teaching on baptism confirms what we found in Acts: that baptism in the early church was an integral part of becoming a Christian. Thus Paul does not ask his readers to recall their conversion (when they 'put their trust in Jesus' or 'decided for Christ') but their baptism. It is a person's baptism that marks so clearly their turning to Christ as Saviour and their commitment to obey him as Lord. (We might compare this to a married couple looking back to their wedding day, not to the occasion when they agreed to get married.) What may surprise us even more is that the NT writers refer to baptism as if it were the *means* by which a person becomes a Christian. Does this imply that baptism *effects* what it symbolises? No, the one essential for salvation is inward faith (cf. Mark 16:16; Rom 3:28; Eph 2:8). Baptism without faith is null and void, but baptism as the outward, public expression of faith can be seen as equivalent to it (cf. 1 Pet.3:21).

Note: I have deliberately avoided using the word 'sacrament' because it is ambiguous and, anyhow, is not found in the Bible. For Roman Catholics there are seven sacraments which 'convey the grace they signify'. For Protestants there are only two (baptism and the Lord's Supper) and they are usually seen as 'signs' (and by some 'seals', by others 'means') of grace. Some evangelicals prefer to speak of the two 'ordinances' commanded by Christ.

In today's church

It is the responsibility of the elders or leaders of a local church to discuss and determine policy on various issues relating to baptism. Decisions on such matters should be clearly communicated to the congregation and consistently adhered to. The following notes are offered as a stimulus to provoke thought and encourage biblical and realistic conclusions.

Pastoral and practical issues

Who may be baptised?
As we have seen, the NT presents a consistent picture of 'believers'

baptism' (a better term than 'adult baptism') for those who respond positively to the gospel for the first time. There is no description or teaching in respect of children who belong to Christian families. The close connection between baptism and repentance/faith/conversion that we have already noticed rules out (for this writer at least) the baptism of babies or infants. Bringing them to church for thanksgiving, blessing or dedication would seem to be wholly appropriate (cf. Mark 10:13-16) but must not be seen simply as a (poor?) substitute for infant baptism: it is a valid action in its own right but it does not carry the theological significance of baptism.

The question then is, What is a suitable age for children (either brought up in a Christian home or brought to faith through children's evangelism) to be baptised? That in turn raises questions regarding the minimum requirements of understanding, responsibility and maturity that should be required before someone is baptised. This is relevant not only for children but also for people who have learning disabilities.

Children as young as 5 who clearly have a simple faith in Jesus and some understanding of what that implies for their behaviour could be baptised, if they ask for baptism and if the parents are willing. The problems here are the possibility of repudiation at a later stage (e.g. teenage rebellion) and the likelihood that young children in the church will simply copy one another and all request baptism. Is it even possible that they would forget the event? Certainly they may feel later that they were too young to appreciate the significance of the occasion and even ask to be baptised again.

If Jewish boys of 13 can be regarded as old enough to accept personal responsibility to keep God's Law, perhaps early teenage is a suitable age for a young person to come to a reasonably mature faith (or crystallise an existing implicit faith) and make a public declaration in baptism, providing they have understood the basics of the gospel and the moral consequences of being a disciple of Jesus. The dangers of later rebellion or repudiation may actually be lessened by the memory of being baptised (quite apart from the action of God's protecting grace). Anyhow, these dangers are possibilities with people of any age and we cannot postpone baptism until we are certain that a person will never give up their faith.

A case could be made for making 16 (when young people are free to marry) or 18 (when they have the vote and are regarded in the UK as legally independent of their parents) as minimum ages for baptism.

The important thing is for the leaders of a local church to have an agreed policy on baptism: either a minimum age and/or definite criteria that must be present. They will also need to decide whether children of Christian parents are offered the elements at Communion (see chapter 9 on 'The Lord's Supper') before being baptised. The normal order in the NT is clearly baptism followed by partaking in the Lord's Supper.

Note: I do not intend to discuss the views of paedo-baptists (those who baptise babies or infants) in this chapter, but there are pastoral problems in a local church which has members from a paedo-baptist background who wish to have their babies baptised. There would seem to be three options in this situation. (1) Only believers' baptism to be taught and practised, but due respect shown to the alternative position. Those who still wish to have their babies baptised would have to go elsewhere for this. In this case the leaders of the church would have to decide whether their attending this ceremony would vitiate their position. (2) A local church could teach and practise *both* forms of baptism, according to parents' wishes. (3) Only believers' baptism would be taught and practised in the local church, but the leaders would be prepared to baptise babies in a home setting at the parents' request, making it clear that this was by way of concession to the genuinely held views of the parents.

When should people be baptised?
This is not a question about the candidate's age, but their suitability for baptism. In some churches the practice has been to expect a considerable gap (sometimes of several years) between conversion and baptism. This has usually been in order to wait for evidence that the conversion is genuine, that the person shows signs of real spiritual life. It also allows time for teaching about the significance and implications of baptism and even for a course in church membership or discipleship. Sometimes people have been encouraged or even pressurised to receive baptism; more often there has been the idea of waiting for people to 'see the truth of baptism for themselves.' The result of this separation of baptism from conversion has been to reduce its significance to that of an 'act of witness (testimony)'.

As we have seen, in NT times baptism normally followed immediately after conversion. Some mention (and explanation?) of baptism was apparently always included in the presentation of the gospel, but the bulk of the teaching for the new convert *followed* baptism. It is true that many of the early converts were Jews and therefore they already had a good grounding in theology and morality, and the earliest Gentile converts were either proselytes or

God-fearers who also had a basic understanding of the Jewish faith. But there is no evidence that procedures changed when pagan Gentiles came to faith in Christ. They just needed more instruction after being baptised (cf. Paul's letters). It might be pointed out that in the early days there was often some outward sign that people had received the Spirit, but that was normally *after* their baptism and anyhow we cannot be sure that there were always outward manifestations.

There would seem to be no valid reason for not continuing the NT practice today – or rather, there is every reason for doing so – providing we make sure that people are sufficiently instructed *before* being asked to make a decision to become a Christian. We might remember how Jesus made people count the cost when they wanted to become his disciples (e.g. Luke 14:25-33). Baptism should be part of our evangelistic preaching and introductory courses for inquirers: they should be challenged to 'repent and be baptised' (Acts 2:38). Anyone who expresses a genuine (as far as can be judged) desire to trust Christ should be offered baptism as the means of expressing that faith and making it definitive. The fear of baptising someone who is not sincere should not prevent us from adopting this policy; the final responsibility rests with the person who makes the request (cf. Acts 8:13-23).

If, however, as a result of upbringing, previous teaching, fear or contrariness, a person wants to become a Christian but does not see the need to be baptised, they should be handled very gently and time given for the Spirit of God to bring understanding. Refusal to be baptised should not be an impediment to full acceptance as a Christian (see further below). Someone who says, 'I want to be baptised again, because I didn't really mean it the first time' could be baptised again if the first time is considered to have been invalid. If it is a case of a Christian who has backslidden being restored, then re–baptism is inappropriate, but such a person could be encouraged to make a public declaration of recommitment to Christ. There may also be value in an occasional or even annual reaffirmation of baptismal vows by all Christians (although this may have no biblical precedent) – there's no need to wait until you visit Israel and stand in the Jordan river!

Is baptism essential for church membership?

The NT picture seems clear: baptism – which did not necessarily take place in a church context – was regarded as bringing a person into membership of the church, the Body of Christ in its universal aspect. But that also meant *de facto* membership of the local church, i.e. the community of Christians in a particular city, town or area. It was expected that new disciples would immediately seek fellowship with others in the locality, although we do not know how a person decided which house church to join (if there was more than one). Only in the case of someone like Saul would there be any problem (cf. Acts 9:26)!

Today the picture is much more complicated. The local church (in the NT sense) is divided into a number of different congregations, owing allegiance to different denominations or traditions and having a variety of practices in regard to baptism and church membership. Some churches have baptism (at any age), others have believers' baptism as a requisite for membership. Some churches welcome any professing Christian into membership, others have no formal membership. Practice regarding eligibility for the Lord's Supper also differs. (See chapter 19 on' Church membership'.)

However desirable we may feel it to be for Christians to have been baptised as believers before joining a local church, this is not always a realistic policy today. Since baptism is not essential for salvation, it should not be made essential for fellowship or church membership. Believers who have never been baptised should be encouraged to consider baptism before they are received into membership. Those who have been baptised as infants (and probably also later confirmed) should be accepted as they are, especially if they are transferring membership from another church; they could be asked to make a confession of faith before the church at their reception and encouraged to consider believers' baptism, but not pressurised into undergoing a ceremony which they might consider 'rebaptism'. If the trust deeds of a church do not permit such an open policy on church membership, either change the trust deeds or move to another building!

Some churches would feel that the policy outlined above is acceptable for most church members but that those in leadership should have been baptised as believers since they are expected to model what they teach.

How should people be baptised?

If we are trying to follow NT practice and to incorporate as much symbolism as possible, we will always endeavour to baptise by total immersion. There may, however, be occasions or situations where this is impossible, difficult or inappropriate, e.g. when there is insufficient water, no suitable pool or tank, or in the case of those physically or mentally unable to be immersed. In such cases *affusion* (pouring water over the head) or even *aspersion* (sprinkling) may be more appropriate, perhaps with the person standing in the pool. In more extreme cases a form of baptism could be administered which involves little or no water being used, or perhaps simply a pouring of water from a jug into a basin and some form of washing. The important thing in this writer's view is that a person's initial commitment to follow Jesus should be marked with a definite and memorable ceremony. Others would be content in such cases to agree to a 'baptism of intention' i.e. where the will is accepted for the deed.

The baptismal service

Despite what I wrote above about the *ad hoc* nature of baptisms in NT times, a good case can be made for making the act of baptism part of a 'service'. Ideally this should take place in the open air (using a river, pool or tank) so that the general public can witness it and hear the explanation of such a vivid picture of salvation. In cold climates it is obviously advisable to use a church building or indoor (public) swimming pool. It would also seem best not to have the baptism simply as a *small* part of a regular service (e.g. a family service) but to devote the whole service to the baptism(s). (Just as we do not normally squeeze a wedding ceremony into the middle of an ordinary service!) This will allow sufficient time to incorporate the aspects mentioned below, which this author feels are valuable, and it will make a greater impact on the attendees, especially if they are not yet Christians. It is not an occasion to be rushed.

The following could form part of a baptismal service, according to local needs and sensibilities.

- *Praise* The service should begin with a good period of up-beat praise and thanksgiving to set the tone for what follows.

- *Explanation* A short (c. 10 minutes), clear account should be given of the meaning and significance of baptism, probably by one of the leaders.

- *Testimony* Candidates for baptism should be encouraged to give a short, personalised testimony of how they came to the Lord, what baptism means to them, etc. This could be written out (and read if necessary) and then later printed in the church magazine. If more appropriate, the candidate could be interviewed in order to elicit the testimony. If there is more than one person being baptised they will probably want to hear each other's testimony and watch the baptisms (assuming the building is warm enough!).

- *Baptising* This can be done by one or two people together who need not be leaders (in some churches it is part of the deacons' role). Some churches allow the candidate to choose the person who will baptise them. The mode can be either to lower the person backwards into the water or to get them to kneel in the water and then gently push their head and shoulders below the surface. This latter method is particularly suitable if there is little depth of water or the person is fearful of slipping. (The baptism is not invalid if a part of the person fails to go below the surface and members of the church should be discouraged from trying to check this!)

- *Confession* Before immersion the candidates should be asked to confess their faith. The following kind of interchange may be used:
  'Do you believe in the Lord Jesus Christ as your own Saviour?' 'I do.'
  'Do you commit yourself to follow him as Lord for the rest of your life?' *'I do.'*
  'Do you renounce the devil and all his works?' 'I do.' (This third question may be regarded as optional but is very important for people from a pagan background who may have dabbled in the occult.)
  'On confession of your faith in the Lord Jesus, I/we baptise you in the name of the Father, the Son and the Holy Spirit.'

- *Prayer* If we are following what appears to have been NT practice we will very deliberately pray and lay hands on each candidate, asking God to send his Spirit, assure them of their acceptance as his children and fill them with his power for Christian living and witness. This prayer may be offered by the baptiser while the person is still in the water. (There is no need for an unseemly rush from the pool – unless the water is cold! A towel can be passed to the person for drying the face, etc.). Alternatively, it can take place outside the pool either before or after dressing and can involve a number of leaders. In pre-baptismal explanations candidates should be told that if at this point they feel the urge to praise the Lord or to speak out in some other way they should do so. (When this practice is first introduced the church will also need some prior explanation.)

- *Participation* Immediately after the prayer for the reception of the Spirit, members of the congregation can be invited to pray for the person, give them a verse of scripture or share a message from the Lord (prophecy). Again, if this is a new procedure it will need to be explained at an earlier stage.

- *Message* If it seems appropriate, a short (c. 10 mins.) evangelistic message, followed by a call for response, can be given while those baptised are dressing. Alternatively an encouraging message can be given to the candidates after they return (the time in between being used for further praise, etc.) or a challenge might be issued to believers who are not yet baptised.

- *Certificate* Many churches give each candidate a certificate of baptism (which other churches may require as evidence of baptism) which also contains the verse specially selected for and given to each person before their baptism. If such a certificate is presented it should be made clear to everyone that it is not an entry ticket to heaven!

Suitable literature for baptismal preparation

P Beasley-Murray, *Why Baptism and Church Membership?* (Baptist Basics Series No. 6, The Baptist Union of Great Britain)

R Chilvers, *Believer* (Counties, 30 Haynes Road, Westbury, Wilts BA13 3HD)

V Jack, *Believe and be Baptised* (Counties)

Further reading

G Beasley-Murray, *Baptism in the New Testament* (Paternoster, 1972)

D Bridge, and D Phypers, *The Water that Divides* (Mentor/Christian Focus, 1998)

S Gaukroger, *Being Baptised* (Marshall-Pickering, 1992)

D Pawson, *The Normal Christian Birth* (Hodder & Stoughton, 1989)

CHAPTER NINE

The Lord's Supper

KEITH BARNARD

In churches with a Brethren background, as in most Christian communities, the Lord's Supper is a regular feature. Whereas for Catholic Christians, it is seen as one of seven sacraments, for us as for other post-Reformation churches, it is an ordinance given to the church by Jesus himself, like baptism. For over 150 years, our local churches have held the Lord's Supper weekly, its form developed (with some variations) from the pattern laid down in the early days of the Brethren movement: an unwritten ritual of 'open worship' when only men spoke, consisting of hymns, readings and prayers, culminating in taking bread and wine together in remembrance of Christ. Often it has been solemn in tone. It has usually been referred to as 'The Breaking of Bread' or even 'The Morning Meeting' in preference to the more formal 'Eucharist' or (until recently) 'The Lord's Supper' or 'Communion'. More recently, however, as churches have responded to changing needs and circumstances, some characteristics have changed: in places, women have begun to take part in open worship; the use of charismatic gifts has affected the content; and it has moved to different times of day. Sometimes open worship has even been abandoned, and a more obviously liturgical form has replaced it, led by an elder or worship-leader. The purpose of this short chapter is to seek from scripture some guidance as to how far, if at all, we can adapt our practices for today's world, and still remain faithful to the principles and precepts given to us in the NT.

Background to the New Testament passages

In Jewish customs at the time of Jesus, we can already hear a distant echo of what has become normal for us. Meals have always been very important in Jewish culture, and at formal meals, it was the custom to use the breaking of a loaf of bread, with thanksgiving, to mark the beginning. Similarly, at the end, the host would give thanks for a cup of wine, which would be drunk by all – this was 'the cup of blessing' (1 Cor 10:16; 11:25). The bread and wine were shared by everyone present. The Passover meal, with its pattern of courses, including at least three cups of wine, and incorporation of worship including the singing of the Hallel psalms, was a familiar part of Jewish household life, and one which Jesus consciously adapted, and transformed for his disciples.

Moreover, in the OT, we find bread and wine used together and separately in worship settings (Gen 14:18; Exod 29:32ff; Lev 23:17), and symbolism used to drive home the teaching of priests and prophets (Num 21:9; Isa 20:2ff; Ezek 4:1ff). Circumcision was the sign of the covenant with God (Gen 17:11) but only obedience could make its meaning clear (Deut 30:6). The use of physical things to teach spiritual truths was very much part of the culture of Jesus' day, akin to wedding rings and funeral clothes in our own.

The New Testament passages

In the NT, there are two contexts where we receive teaching about the Lord's Supper: the gospel accounts of the Last Supper, which are not simply a narration, but are clearly intended to teach us about the Eucharist; and the passages in 1 Corinthians 10 and 11, which seek to correct the abuses found at Corinth. As Howard Marshall points out, this tells us why the elements in each context are different (*Last Supper and Lord's Supper*, pp.33-34), and we should not take either as simply prescriptive.

In the gospels we have a reminder of the covenant relationship which was at the heart of Jewish worship, in the Passover meal. Jesus takes this and adds interpretative words, which transform the meal into something quite different – a demonstration of a new covenant, with him at the centre. He gives to his disciples new gifts: the bread of God's provision becomes a symbol of his own body, also given; the cup of blessing becomes a vehicle for the greater blessing of his own blood, poured out for many. Interestingly, it is apparent that Jesus left aside the symbolism of the lamb being eaten at the meal, using only the bread and wine as potent conveyors of his presence and grace for his followers.

In Corinthians the context is of early church life, and specifically of the abuses which Paul felt were destroying what Jesus had given. There was a regular gathering of Christians, which included a meal, but the teaching and the opportunity to bring Christ to mind were being lost because of the thoughtlessness and divisions among them. As Alan Palmer says, they 'were treating the Lord's Supper like any other banquet' (*Declare His Glory*, p.64). In 1 Corinthians

11:23ff, Paul, like the gospel writers, teaches that bread and wine are the vehicles and symbols of the gifts and blessings that Christ brings. In addition, however, some see an attempt here to bring together the bread and wine as symbols of Christ (vv. 26-29) and to remove them from the full meal which had given rise to abuse. He emphasises the proclamation of the death of Christ, but adds 'until he comes', which points to his resurrection, present life and future coming (11.26). This is in itself a proclamation of the covenant relationship, which brings us into fellowship with God and with each other (see also 1 Cor 10:16-17). Anyone not in that covenant relationship, or spurning it by lifestyle, excludes themselves from the body, understood both as the 'body and blood of the Lord' (v. 27) and the body of believers (v.17).

The only other passages in the NT which have direct bearing on the Lord's Supper are passing indications of early church practices. In Acts 2:42-46, for example, we have the use of 'breaking of bread' to indicate either an ordinary meal, a formal meal or the Lord's Supper – and possibly a combination; these meals may have happened daily or weekly, in homes or in a larger gathering. The lack of ritual structure helps us to understand why abuses should arise at Corinth. In Jude verse 12, the mention of 'agape' as the name for a meal helps us understand the purpose of Christian gatherings; and according to Acts 20:7 this happened on the first day of the week, at least at Troas (cf. too 1 Cor 16:2). Given that Eutychus fell out of the window, we may be seeing a glimpse here of a Saturday evening meeting rather than one on Sunday morning!

We ought also to mention the passages in John's gospel which add to our understanding in two ways. In 6:25-59, Jesus teaches his disciples that they should be so closely identified with him that they can be said to be eating and drinking him (6:51, 53). Although we should beware of the literal-minded (6:52), these verses surely add to our appreciation of what Christ has done for believers. He satisfies their hunger and thirst, and preserves them eternally – he gives them life. If then, the taking of bread and wine together is an expression and symbol of feeding upon Christ, it will be a means by which he blesses them – a 'means of grace'. As Colin Brown says: 'John 6 is not about the Lord's Supper (but) the Lord's Supper is about what is described in John 6'. In John 13-17, which is associated with a Passover meal in some way (13:1), Jesus uses the occasion of a meal to give extensive teaching. This should encourage us, too, to be flexible in the practice as we eat with him at the Lord's Supper. We should not lay down rules of procedure which may restrict what he wishes to give to us.

Conclusions from the New Testament evidence

The fact that there are only two basic contexts for teaching about the Lord's Supper, and only a few other references, should warn us against rigidity in our interpretation. What seems certain is that early Christians met together to eat; that in 'breaking bread' they obeyed the injunction of Jesus to remember him; and that they used the sharing of a loaf of bread and a cup of wine to show their allegiance to him and their union with him. The simple ceremonial was for them a means of receiving his blessing, a reminder of his death and his future coming, and an expression of unity with other believers. Beyond that it would be unwise to insist upon the detail. As to frequency, venue, presidency, content and the question of a meal, the NT is tantalisingly reticent or silent. Providing we can keep the central and common elements, making sure that we have a 'meal with meaning', we are able to adopt a flexibility in approach which is quite different from the practice of our forbears.

Practical considerations today for the Lord's Supper

It is important

Alone among nonconformists, we have traditionally emphasised the centrality of the Communion, rather than preaching, in our worship. Perhaps, given the evidence of John 13-17 and 1 Corinthians, we need to avoid polarisation, but the emphasis is still valuable. While other evangelicals, especially in the Church of England, are moving towards 'Parish Communion', some of us have been relegating the Lord's Supper to relative obscurity, making it less frequent, or moving it to the margins of our Sunday worship. The reason given is often that we need the most convenient time for a service which is more inclusive, allowing enquirers and children to feel at home.

Yet today's culture, full of symbolism and action rather than words and passive listening, should encourage us to look afresh at the Lord's Supper as a means of proclaiming Christ. If Paul writes of 'proclaiming his death' (1 Cor 11:26), and of unbelievers being present (14:24), should we not adapt our worship rather than exclude them? The simple and moving sharing of bread and wine may become for some the means by which they understand what Christ has done for them, as it is for us a means of refreshing, of receiving Christ again and of renewing our allegiance. Perhaps, instead of forbidding unbelievers from participating, we should be asking them why they wish to partake, and so move them on to firmer faith.

It is a fellowship meal

Since the Reformation, Western culture has often emphasised the individual as against the community. We therefore treat the Lord's Supper as an occasion when we come as individuals to commune personally with Christ, while in the presence of others. The NT context is that of a meal together, an expression of a committed community. There is value, therefore, in sharing bread and wine to bring Christ to mind wherever we are meeting, and all the more on occasions when we emphasise community – in home groups, for example. If we remember that the early church met daily in temple and homes (Acts 2:46) and that there were few homes where a church could meet as a large group, we may avoid the trap of insisting on a weekly celebration alone, and that in a formal church meeting context. (On the other hand, if for example, we wish to share in bread and wine with Christians who cannot leave their homes, we do well to take with us a group of believers to underline our fellowship, rather than treat 'home communion' as a ritual for the individual.)

Expressions of Christian fellowship and unity should find a home around the Lord's Supper – handshakes and hugs, coffee-breaks and meals, according to the culture of those who meet; intercessions for those who are sick or absent; and offerings for those in need. What we do today often speaks much louder than words, and so does the atmosphere we create for our moments of close fellowship together with Jesus our Saviour.

It must be a clear means of communicating Christ

Jesus himself gave us a clear but simple symbolism in the taking and eating of bread and wine, and Paul (1 Cor 10:16) adds that we have 'the cup' and 'one loaf'. Notwithstanding fears of disease, and inconvenience, they are still the clearest symbols of Christ and of the unity of the body, only to be left aside if we must. An explanation, such as the words of institution, can also be helpful (if not vain repetition) to ensure that we do not stray into empty ritual. Similarly, if we choose to place the Supper in the context of a meal, often a good setting, its essential focus on Christ must not be lost – conviviality and gluttony are not only dangers for first-century Corinth! This simple meal was given by Christ himself to be a means of blessing for his disciples, and we must always honour that purpose.

The culture of those who are likely to be present at the Lord's Supper is important – because what one generation considers reverent is condemned as boring by another! Hymns, songs, instruments, chairs, versions of the Bible, leaders (or none), worship posture or body language – these are all things which change from one group of people to another. If we insist on any one for a long period, we may be hindering Christ in his purpose of blessing us or others, because we are creatures of our own culture. We must therefore distinguish clearly what is essential and what peripheral, and be ready for change in the non-essentials.

It is for all who wish to identify themselves with Christ and his love for them

From the beginning of the Brethren movement, the normal teaching has been that the Lord's Supper is for all who belong to him. As Groves wrote to Darby, it is the life of Christ in a believer which must govern our fellowship, not the light he or she has received. Despite exclusive influence at times, that teaching has always been central, and it has not been part of our tradition to 'hedge the table'. Today, however, denominational loyalty is not so much of an obstacle; it is style of worship which boxes us in. Our tradition of 'open worship' should be the most flexible of all vehicles for worship – yet it is so easily restricted by unwritten rules. If we wish to encourage the postmodern generation, for example, to build us all up by taking part in open worship, then our expectation that they should stand up to pray, or sing a song rather than listen to it, is as much an obstacle as demanding a letter of commendation from them. Instead, we must provide the equipment and the space needed for them to play CDs, or act out a drama; we must accept that an offering of worship which has been prepared still falls within the limits of 1 Corinthians 14:26, where the only restriction is that the contribution should strengthen the church. Moreover, if the exercise of everyone's gifts needs encouragement or structure, then a worship-leader to guide and stimulate participation may be a help, not a hindrance.

Conclusion

For over 150 years, churches of our background, though sometimes petty and restrictive, quoting 'New Testament Principles' as a kind of Corban, have succeeded in holding together the centrality of the Lord's Supper in worship with the priesthood of believers. If we look afresh into our Bibles, we shall find the same principles, but the Lord Jesus will guide us into new expressions of our worship around his table, which will continue to honour him in a new generation.

Further reading

D Bridge and D Phypers, *The Meal that Unites* (Hodder & Stoughton, 1981)

I H Marshall, *Last Supper and Lord's Supper* (Paternoster, 1980)

H Rowdon (ed.), *Declare His Glory* (Paternoster/Partnership, 1998), article by A G Palmer, 'The Breaking of Bread: a meal with meaning'

D Watson, *I Believe in the Church* (Hodder & Stoughton, 1978), chapter 14

CHAPTER TEN

Worship

NEIL SUMMERTON

The purpose of this chapter is give advice and guidance on that aspect of local church life which now tends to be described in evangelical and charismatic circles as 'worship', but which in former generations used to be known variously, depending on denominational culture, as 'services' or 'meetings' or 'the meeting'. This aspect of church life is of critical importance for local church leaders in this generation, because of the shift in priorities which has taken place over the last half century in the minds of the people in the pew. Not so long ago in evangelical life the priority of Christian meetings was, again depending on the particular tradition and occasion, either the sermon or the communion (breaking of bread); the remaining activities were incidental to that. It is hard to overstate the magnitude of the shift that has now taken place: now for many, particularly those who are younger, the priority in the Christian mind is 'worship' – mainly meaning that part of the Christian meeting which comprises (largely) congregational song.

The reasons for the dramatic change will be touched on later. At the outset, however, the local church leader should note that the significance of the change will be neglected, or resisted, at the peril of the health of the congregation and of successful congregational leadership today. For the shift marks an important and deep-seated cultural change which church leaders must come to terms with, manage and minister to. For better or worse, the character of congregational meetings is crucial to the health and growth of congregations and individual Christians today. Variety, life, interest, relaxed informality, humour, and smooth, competent flow, are vitally necessary features, especially in the light of the competition and benchmark established by TV and other forms of entertainment. And these latter, even if they are entertainment, communicate extremely effectively.

The problem with many church meetings is that they fall well short of these criteria. They are caught in a time-warp. By comparison with the competition, they are ineffective, even at the exercise to which many church leaders still (rightly) want to give priority – teaching. In short, congregational meetings today are often culturally inappropriate – hopelessly so – in form and character rather than content. Nor is this simply a generational phenomenon. Many middle-aged, and perhaps even elderly, people are just as bored by 'church' as teenagers, even if they absent themselves a little bit less (only just!). Effective church leaders simply must address this problem, even if – bar the Holy Spirit – the time and resources available to them are considerably less than are available to a TV show producer.

The conduct of 'worship', and of the local church's meetings more generally, is therefore a crucial question facing church leaders today.

What is worship?

So far, this chapter has referred to 'worship' – deliberately so, because of the danger that both leaders and congregations in this generation are regarding a particular part of Christian meetings as the sum and substance, even the climax, of worship. If church leaders and worship leaders encourage this belief, they will be doing those for whom they are responsible a sad and damaging disservice. Activities at Christian meetings, and particularly those this generation calls 'worship', need to be seen, and led, in the light of a number of key points in scripture. This biblical backdrop is crucially relevant to deciding how 'worship' should be done.

First, 'worship' in the Christian meeting simply must be the heartfelt audible and inaudible expression of the total life (both individual and collective) laid down in the service of God. For scripture makes no distinction at all between worship and life. Here, there is generally a deep contrast between the worship of fallen humans and the worship that God requires. Fallen humans usually radically separate worship from life: worship is a special, sacralised act, usually liturgical in character, performed at a particular time in a particular place, distinct and disconnected from the rest of life. This is the sort of worship that the Hebrew prophets castigated so extensively, and which, frankly, sickens God (Isa 1:13, 14). Non-liturgical Protestantism is not free from it, and neither is charismatic worship which focuses on existential experience (see below). By contrast, biblical worship is the worship of the life laid down wholly and completely in adoration (see Romans 12: 1, where the presentation of the body as a living sacrifice is described as the believer's 'spiritual worship'). This reflects Jesus' call that we should deny ourselves and take up our cross daily. Ultimately, the Christian worships God in the complete giving up of self – life, time, ambitions, pleasures, comforts and convenience. Individual and corporate 'worship' is, therefore, to be an expression of the sacrificed life of the individual and congregation, as the case may be. That being 'church' entails a corporate sacrificed life tends to get neglected in today's individualistic, consumerist society. Paul neatly catches the individual and corporate dimensions when he writes, 'I am being poured out like a drink offering on the sacrifice and service coming from your faith' (Phil. 2: 17).

The problem of splitting worship from the rest of life is hypocrisy. 'Worship' becomes merely an outward physical act which has no counterpart in inward experience and therefore in day-to-day behaviour. Jesus was quite clear that worship was not a matter of outward experience or of show, which is why he said that if anyone had anything against us, we were to leave our gift at the altar and first be reconciled to our brother or sister (Matt 5: 23, 24). For Jesus, it did not matter whether worship was in Jerusalem by Jewish ritual, or in Samaria by Samaritan ritual. Worship has to be 'in spirit and in truth' (John 4: 21, 24). Just as there cannot be faith without works nor works without faith, so there cannot be worship without genuine inward experience, nor can there be worship without the life given up in worship – and genuine inward experience of God in an act of worship cannot but transform the life of the believer. Nor is this point irrelevant to the issue of culture and worship: worship must be authentic, that is the genuine expression of the heart – and the outward form of worship can get in the way of that, if the form is alien to the worshipper.

Second, in the light of this, it can scarcely be too heavily stressed that God's concern is less with what practices Christians follow in detail when they meet for an hour in the week, than with the nature of their lives – whether they live lives of worship (Isa 1: 15). That is why gross moral failing must, if not repented of, lead to exclusion from the church gathering and fellowship. (See chapter 20 on 'Church discipline'.) A persistent theme of scripture is that the truest form of worship is the holy life, the life lived according to the will of God and in the presence of God, in a manner which is pleasing to him, which rises in his presence as a sweet – smelling savour, the incense of the sacrificed life. Paul makes this abundantly clear in Romans 15, by the number of liturgical words he uses: first, in calling Christians to unity, to endurance, to mutual encouragement, to pleasing others rather than self (in the footsteps of their Lord), to bearing one another's burdens particularly in persecution, to bearing with each other's failings, and to tolerant acceptance of one another, despite their differences on secondary questions (Rom 15: 1-12); second, in characterising evangelism as a priestly act of worship in which the convert is the evangelist's sacrificial offering to God (Rom 15: 15, 16 and following verses); and third, in characterising deeds of mercy, service, and Christian giving as acts of priestly worship (Rom 15: 25 – 29). (See chapter 28, on 'Encouraging godly living'.)

Third, the true nature of worship is revealed by the meaning of the words used in scripture with respect to acts of worship. They encapsulate two key thoughts:

- Recognising who God is – his being, nature and character, and the position that he deserves by right. Hebrew and Greek both use two groups of words for this purpose: first, to bow down, to do obeisance, to kneel, to prostrate oneself, to pay homage to, to kiss the feet of – all indicating a radical physical expression of what should be the inward spiritual experience in the presence of Almighty God (cf. Moses at the burning bush, Exod 3: 6b, and John on Patmos, Rev 1: 17); and, second, to revere, to fear (in the sense of terror, awe, and reverence), to shrink back from, to fall back from, to respect. These two groups of words graphically recognise the difference of status between the holy Creator and the sinful, dependent creature.
- That worship is service – initially performed in ordinary life by a slave, an official or a public servant, and then, in transferred meaning, the performance of a ritual by a priest, that is, the priest's action on behalf of others. This takes us back to the sacrificial worship of life discussed above.

How did early Christians worship?

While scripture is thus utterly explicit as to the true nature of Christian worship, it is tantalisingly coy about the form, place, circumstances and incidentals of the acts of worship of the early Christians – though, more strictly, we should speak of their gatherings rather than their 'worship', because the scriptural emphasis is on their gathering together on a regular basis (on their 'fellowship') rather than on the form of their acts of worship.

Jesus' word to the woman at the well was certainly prophetically true. In establishing his church, he established a worldwide society which worships neither at Jerusalem nor Sychar, nor after the manner of Jerusalem or Sychar. The NT church had no temple (though the Jerusalem church did make use of the third, Herodian, one), and John's vision of the heavenly Jerusalem included no temple either (Rev 22:1-5). The holy city is a city where everything goes on in the presence of God and will have a character and quality suitable to that presence; it does not have a temple to which one withdraws to do something different. For some 150 or 200 years, Christians had no special buildings for worship: they met where they could – whether in the temple in Jerusalem, on the river bank, or in the Roman catacombs. Even in the third century their worship spaces had a storefront character, carved out of a number of apartments in a tenement block, for example. Clearly, in NT times they met chiefly in homes – probably the sufficiently spacious homes of well-to-do Christians, who, sometimes their wives, doubled as the key leaders of that household church. Meeting in a house must in itself have affected the manner in which they met, what they did when they met, and how they did it. Once they had special buildings, other possibilities became available, no doubt.

It is extraordinarily difficult to know from scripture and other evidence what the early church did when they gathered, or, more specifically, how they did it. Many scholars have been anxious to demonstrate that liturgy goes back to the very earliest days. It is true that we can see traces of formal material that may well be hymns or songs; and that Paul's reference to the Lord's Supper in 1 Corinthians 11 evidently contains elements of liturgy. But modern liturgical scholarship recognises the variety and flexibility which characterised NT Christian gatherings, and how hard it is to trace subsequent liturgies back to them, rather than to the practices of the third and fourth centuries. Only gradually did a process of increasing standardisation occur.

There is little evidence of the overall form of what the NT Christians did when they met. We have the accounts in the early part of Acts (both of joining in public worship and of meeting in homes for meals and prayer); we have the account of the Sunday meeting at Troas in Acts 20 (possibly on Saturday evening-Sunday morning); we have the references to communion in 1 Corinthians 10 and 11; and we have what Paul says, by implication, in 1 Corinthians 14 about the character of the gatherings in Corinth. But little else.

What can be said is that their gatherings do not seem to have been much like either traditional Brethren worship, or modern quasi-charismatic worship, or the liturgical worship followed in Christendom for some 1700 years! The dominant form in scripture seems to have been an ordinary meal among friends (a kind of supper party). This ordinary meal was made special (sanctified) by the presence of the Christians themselves, by the reality of their faith, and therefore by the presence of the Holy Spirit, and by the prayer and praise that they offered, particularly at the beginning and end of the meal.

If we are in the dark as to the form and practice of the meetings of the early Christians, scripture is, however, clearer as to the broad content of these gatherings. They normally included:

- prayer (praise, thanksgiving and intercession);
- singing of psalms, hymns and spiritual songs (what we tend today, erroneously, to define as the sum and substance of 'worship') – Paul in two places very positively instructs Christians to do that for the benefit of one another as well as God (Eph 5:19-20 and Col 3: 15-17);
- teaching and exhortation;
- prophecy and revelation;
- communion in the context of the agape meal (indeed, it might be true to say that the agape meal was the context of the whole gathering);
- fellowship (which went on all the time, of course);
- if necessary, the transaction of disciplinary business.

It is interesting that they generally seemed to do all these things at the same gathering, rather than separating them out into different meetings (as the Brethren did), or tending to do only some of them (as with Reformed churches, or some charismatics).

From this brief survey of biblical material, some conclusions can be drawn for those responsible for churches today. The importance of the wider context of 'worship' is clear enough. So are its true nature and goal, the importance of the link between 'worship' and life, the extent to which the service of Christ through outreach and social action is worship, and the various generic activities that leaders need to ensure are represented in the life of a local church on a regular basis. What is only very dimly visible, if at all, is the actual detailed practice of the NT churches – what exactly happened when they gathered together as the church. On this point, scripture – very wisely, we may think, for reasons which are explored in more detail below – seems to conceal as much as it reveals. Interestingly, Luke and the various writers of the epistles did not feel that it was necessary to tell their readers/hearers – because they, of course, already knew what happened! And the divine wisdom was that it was not necessary for us to know – lest we be misled by it!

These conclusions point to some implications for us today as church leaders.

Balance in the congregational programme

First, the question of the range of generic activities which took place in the NT churches. The evidence of church history is that Christian leaders have not always been good at ensuring a satisfactory balance between the generic activities recommended by the NT as necessary for the task of bringing Christians to maturity in Christ. At the risk of over-simplification, it can be argued, for example, that the Orthodox and Catholic traditions have considered the purpose of Christian meeting (at what became the parish level, at least) to be cultic act, fundamentally dependent on the observance of a liturgy involving sacrifice, owing its origins both to the OT and to the worship of the pagan temples with which the Gentile Christians of the earlier Christian era were familiar. Frequently, this tradition in practice, if not in theory, has neglected the teaching of the word and fellowship as purposes of Christian gathering.

By contrast, and perhaps by way of reaction, between 1500 and 1950, Protestant worship meetings saw the main purpose to be education (in this, the influence of the Renaissance and the Enlightenment, rather than scripture, was probably greater than latter-day proponents of Reformed practice like to admit). The essential thing was for Christians to learn through the preaching of the word. Church buildings were laid out as lecture theatres, with the pulpit lifted very high. It is wrong, of course, to say that people did not worship, but insofar as they did, it was an inner rather than an expressed experience, a response to the word. To a considerable extent, Brethren churches have lain in this tradition, notwithstanding the rediscovery of the communion, which was central to the emphases of the Brethren founding fathers.

In the West, the twentieth century saw a further dramatic shift. Increasingly from 1950 onwards, meetings became existential experiences in which the focus was congregational worship, expressed principally (and perhaps increasingly) through corporate singing (though originally involving charismatic contributions). This singing is intended to induce a sense of the presence of God, and of meeting with God.

If there is a lesson here for church leaders now, it is of the constant temptation, under the influence of the cultural context, to over-emphasise one or another aspect of church life, at the expense of the others, and at the expense of the balanced set of activities which can be perceived in the NT. It does not follow, however, from this principle that all the generic activities have to be represented in every individual Christian gathering. Clearly, we are at liberty to arrange for the different components to take place at different times.

But we should not regard ourselves as at liberty or wise to neglect any of them, either as church leaders in our arrangements, or as individual Christians by attending only some of them.

Worship and culture

From our detached perspective, with the benefit of hindsight, we can see at each stage the influence of contemporary culture on church practice. This raises a question of crucial importance, especially in a society which is not only highly multicultural in the conventional sense but in which contrasting generational cultures are extremely pronounced.

It is in this respect that the wide margin of flexibility left to us by the NT is relevant. For we can, in fact, see different patterns of gathering there, in which cultural influence can be discerned. In Jerusalem, the Christians clearly made some use of the Temple for worship for quite a long time – they were still doing so in the late 50s, and Paul was willing to go along with it (Acts 21: 26). The organisation of the Pauline churches owed something to the synagogue, even if the practice of worship at Corinth entailed some marked innovations (though the principle of extempore intervention was not new, as is illustrated by Jesus' own interventions at Nazareth and elsewhere, Luke 4: 14-27). And it is clear from Paul that Gentile Christians continued to be influenced by their religious background.

The fact that the NT is so non-prescriptive about the form of worship is helpful in this respect. Unlike Islam and even Judaism, Christianity takes many and diverse cultural forms, depending on the background of the believers concerned. Christianity has always been relaxed about adapting its cultural forms to the circumstances – that is one reason why it travels so well. This is an expression of the Pauline principle of trying to please everybody in every way for the good of many so that they may be saved (1 Cor 10:32, 33). Paul asserts that his principle is Christ's (1 Cor 11:1). Church leaders should, therefore, regard themselves as positively authorised and encouraged to adapt the form and style of congregational gathering to what is suited to the particular congregation, and more generally to the culture of time and place.

It can be argued that much of the success of new Christian movements (like the Brethren and New Church movements in their days) lies in their cultural appropriateness; that is one reason why such movements are generally the work of 20- and 30-year olds, not of older people. There can be little doubt, for example, about the cultural appropriateness of the styles of worship at Holy Trinity,

Brompton, All Souls, St Helen's, Bishopsgate, Kensington Temple and KICC to the particular constituencies (in some cases, multiple constituencies) on which they are drawing. If our forms of gathering are not culturally appropriate, we shall be hindering some from being saved and alienating others whom we desperately want to keep, namely our children. Church leaders need, therefore, constantly to ask themselves whether their arrangements for meetings, of whatever kind, are geared culturally to the particular target group or groups. They need also to take careful account of the range of people (Christian and non-Christian) who are their responsibility; this is a particularly sensitive question in these days of diversity of culture (including what has been described as 'designer cultures').

Of course, it is necessary to ensure always that in the process of adapting our arrangements and practice so as to make them culturally apt, we do not go against either the doctrine which is permanent or the principles which are essential.

This point about cultural variety, and our freedom to adapt and appeal to it in our meetings, is important because many of the tensions and disputes which surround issues of worship are in fact conflicts of culture. Though people often say that the matter is one of scriptural principle, in fact the difficulty is that others are doing or advocating something which is culturally strange to them. Moreover, they are often disturbed because the particular form that they have become used to actually gives them emotional security and makes them feel at home in the world. These factors have been especially important in motivating attachment to the Brethren morning meeting over the last generation, and are compounded by the fact that some think that the form of that meeting adheres closely to the NT pattern – when it is in fact very far from it! Recognition of the emotional factors involved should lead us to great Christian charity, and great leadership skill in trying to make changes which are essential if the congregation is to move forward in a new generation.

Worship and the Lord's Supper

The question of the treatment of the Lord's Supper is of particular interest to those of Brethren background, since it is an article of faith that it should be the absolutely central event in the life of a local church and that it should be associated with open worship led by the Spirit in which all (men) have freedom to exercise (a limited number of) the range of spiritual gifts which the Lord has given to the church. (See chapter 11 on 'Discovering and using spiritual gifts'.) But it is also an issue of significance for the Reformed tradition which, partly to guard the principle of the closed table, has tended to confine the Lord's Supper to a comparatively infrequent, somewhat perfunctory addition to the main 'worship' event; and to that part of evangelicalism (e.g. the 'Faith Mission' tradition and sections of the charismatic movement) which for a variety of reasons has minimised the importance of rites such as baptism and the Lord's Supper.

That the taking of bread and wine, after it had been specially identified in prayer as relating to Christ's saving work for us, was a central practice of the NT church cannot be doubted. That it should be a central and essential practice for us, too, cannot be doubted from scripture. Neither as churches nor as individuals are we at liberty to dispense with it, as some in the 'faith missions' tradition of the 1859 revival were inclined to do.

But at that point the relationship between the particular Brethren practice of the Lord's Supper (or of the other main traditions of evangelicalism for that matter) and the NT seems to me largely to end. The early practice of the Lord's Supper bears a close relationship both to the Passover meal (a special annual event of great religious and spiritual significance) and the ordinary Jewish family meal – a fellowship meal in which the Lord and his work had a very special place as the foundation of all, recognised through the prayers of blessing at the beginning and end of the meal. That prayer had an important role in it is certain. Song may have had a part, as it certainly did in the disciples' Passover meal (Matt 26:30, AV). The role of teaching, prophecy and revelation is a good deal less clear, though it was clearly a large part of the proceedings at Troas (Acts 20:7-11).

On this basis, we may draw the conclusion that the Lord's Supper is an essential practice for all believers, not an optional extra. Leaders must enable the believers to keep it. But, second, exactly how it is observed is not key. There is no biblical reason for arguing that it has to be associated with 'open worship', for example. There is good reason to think that it might be practised as a fellowship meal, either as a whole church or in, e.g., home Bible study groups (there are no biblical grounds for asserting with Brethren tradition that the Lord's Supper can be kept only by a whole local church). But in our cultural situation, there are good reasons for not practising it on the latter part of Sunday morning, for that is the one time in the week when non-Christians are likely to be willing to attend a church event; they cannot and must not then be confronted with the alien cultural form of the Brethren morning meeting. It is scarcely surprising that teenagers who become Christians either drop off, or gravitate elsewhere, when confronted with this antiquarian curiosity (in its form, that is) – or, for that matter, with long, boring, theoretical, unapplied and un-illustrated sermons. What is needed is something lively and challenging, in a form which is culturally accessible to believers and unbelievers. (See chapter 9 on 'The Lord's Supper'.)

Worship and physical and human considerations

If worship is to be in spirit and in truth, what is the place of the flesh – of practical circumstances, of visual assistance, of aesthetics? What is the contribution of natural as distinct from spiritual gift?

These are important questions on which human beings seem to have a tendency to veer wildly between extremes. At the risk of caricature, the Calvinistic Protestant says that worship is entirely in the mind. Picking up from one aspect of Judaism and perhaps from the NT, that there must be no representation of God or images or decoration of our places of worship, all must be plain and simple. Moreover, in worship we can do only what scripture explicitly sanctions. The Brethren have been in this tradition. The Catholic tradition, picking up from another part of scripture (the OT), makes copious use of visual demonstration in worship. The modern charismatic tradition, true to its cultural context, is very free about appealing to the emotions, the senses and even sensuality in worship.

We do not need to adjudicate. But we should take into account a fundamental scriptural principle: humans are not just minds or spirits; they are souls, minds, spirits and bodies, and as such are unitary beings, not tripartite or quadripartite beings. As Deuteronomy 6:5 says (giving expression to the heart of worship), 'Love the LORD your God with all your heart and with all your soul and with all your strength' (where heart means 'will' and strength means 'physical capacity').

The application is very practical. Our worship is necessarily affected by individual physical conditions and circumstances, and also by our collective physical circumstances. For example, what is possible and appropriate for 25 people is not possible for 200 or 300. It also affects our musical and instrumental style – how big the band will be, and of what composition. And it affects the degree of participation and structure. The nature of the building affects worship: a religious sanctuary creates its own expectations, compared with, say, a sports hall. Even the nature of the carpets and furnishings can affect worship – if they are too absorbent, resonance is lost and even a crowd will find singing hard work. The layout of the space, and the topographical relationships between worship leader(s), instrumentalists and congregation, can help or hinder. These practical decisions matter, precisely because we are physical beings. Church leaders and worship leaders need to discuss these matters in detail, decide what is feasible, and alter things to facilitate congregational worship and involvement (see below on Participative worship).

The point is also relevant to the issues of aesthetics and even music. A satisfying worship experience can be manufactured wholly by and in the flesh. A pleasing event can be assembled which appeals to our aesthetic sensibilities (whether high-brow or popular) and a certain sort of individual can go away satisfied. Similarly, popular music can be used to generate quasi-spiritual emotion at a pop concert. Now, this is not to say that we may not take into account and use the physical in worship. But it is to say that we should beware of the counterfeit (which can look very convincing). The standard is worship in spirit and in truth, not a mere work of the flesh. Nevertheless, because we are physical creatures, but made in the image of God, there is every reason to think that worship in spirit and truth will be aesthetically and emotionally pleasing to the worshipper – which does not imply that we have to use only the finest classical music and poetry, and hymns from former generations! We should not reject aesthetic harmony as being necessarily unspiritual. To do so would raise questions about whether we have a biblical understanding of the nature of humanness.

Posture in worship can also be significant. Here, it is surprising how important is what we are accustomed to. People from the UK still tend to be surprised to discover that Germanic evangelical congregations stand to pray and sit to sing! In fact, across the biblical period there is evidence of a wide variety of physical posture in worship. The church in the first few centuries, for example, characteristically stood for prayer with raised arms (see 1 Tim 2:8). Prostration in prayer seems to have been common in the OT and we all know that kneeling in public and private prayer was normal, though British nonconformity has not practised that, presumably by way of simple reaction against previous practice. Adopting different postures for different purposes in worship can be a positive benefit to some. Here is an area in which stimulating variety can be introduced into worship meetings, though the risks of challenging conventional practice ('We have always done it this way.') should not be underestimated. The encouragement of freedom in the congregation to stand, sit or kneel if they wish is also to be recommended, though again it is remarkable how disturbing that can be for those who are used to everyone's adopting exactly the same physical posture at the same time.

Extending the repertoire of acceptable activities in 'worship' should also be considered. This may be the encouragement of the use of spiritual gifts like prophecy. But it can also include testimony (usually an excellent stimulus to adoration and thanksgiving in the congregation as a whole), drama and dance (either on its own or as an accompaniment to praise), for example. Variety in these respects touches on the cultural, physical and aesthetic points that have been made. Culturally, variety is desirable because that is the mode that people are used to in the era of electronic communication. Physically, it is desirable because, in confining itself to verbal communication in church meetings (a phenomenon of its times), Protestantism risked confining its appeal and effectiveness to a limited group of the population – in spite of the fact that there is a case for arguing that the great Puritan preachers were excellent actors and verbal illustrators. The use of the visual to reinforce the verbal message is too often neglected in evangelical churches. In the TV age, it is folly to neglect it. Similarly, it is interesting how resistant Christian congregations were to the introduction of musical accompaniment in the eighteenth and nineteenth centuries. And variety is in itself refreshing.

To make Christian meetings more effective and revive 'worship', church leaders need to pay attention to getting the physical details right, and to expanding the variety and character of what is done in 'worship'. But it needs to be done with skill, subtlety and pastoral sensitivity. It is the physical aspects of worship in respect of which change is most likely to be a source of stress. They include the time and form of the meeting, whether songbooks are issued to the congregation, whether a different songbook is issued, whether the congregation is to be expected to rely only on projected words, whether some members of the congregation raise their hands in worship, whether one or two kneel in worship, whether the usual layout of the chairs is altered, whether new instruments are introduced. Such matters are liable to be the focus of cultural and emotional shock in those who are disturbed by congregational change. Handling this effectively and sensitively will require of leaders the use of skills in managing change. (See chapter 22 on 'Handling differences and managing change'.)

Basic choices in 'worship'

How are we, therefore, to gather as Christians in the UK today, 2,000 years after the foundation of Christianity? As has been discussed, there are some important principles that we must give effect to. Beyond that, church leaders and congregations have much flexibility to choose how they will give effect to them.

It may be helpful to look at some of the main options in use today, and comment on them (the descriptions below involve a degree of caricature in the interest of clarifying the argument).

Consumerist worship

Elsewhere I have called this 'entertainment worship'. Essentially the aim of meeting is to ensure that people go away personally satisfied by what they have seen and heard. People should, of course, go away from a Christian gathering both satisfied and dissatisfied – satisfied that they have met with God and his people, and dissatisfied with what remains to be done in their own lives and spiritual experience. The consumerist worshippers, however, go away as they might from a supermarket or a cultural performance, satisfied with what they have got out of it. This leads us to performance, to platform activity which is directed towards the congregation, rather than towards God or to assisting the congregation in praise, thanksgiving and adoration. In my experience, church services in the USA are often of this character, with a degree of teaching or evangelistic preaching thrown in. This is perfectly sensible in the evangelistic seeker-friendly context – British churches need to adopt this pattern to sharpen up their evangelistic performance – but it does not seem appropriate to term the result 'worship', except to the extent that it may induce in the audience a passive response to what they see and hear.

Platform worship

This is becoming very common in events influenced by charismatic or quasi-charismatic concepts of worship. In this case, the platform (i.e. the worship leader(s) and the musicians) worship in a somewhat priestly way on behalf of the congregation. Form and content are wholly determined, whether in advance or extempore, by the platform. There is little or no scope for the congregation as a whole to influence the course of events. However, since there is usually a lot of congregational singing, there is the possibility that the congregation will be caught up for themselves in genuine worship, but apart from direct private transaction between individuals and God and, perhaps, between God and the congregation as a whole, they are largely limited by the worship leader's own capabilities and experience.

Liturgical worship

Here we change categories somewhat. Liturgical worship can be performed by a priestly caste with the congregation as onlookers. But it can also be done in a way which fully involves the congregation and gives them a major role. The essence of liturgical worship is the concepts of pre-formulation and control. Those favouring it would see control as quality control; those not favouring it would see it as a serious handicap, limiting the scope for the Spirit and for the congregation to exercise their gifts. Of course, virtually all worship, certainly including Brethren 'open worship', is liturgical to some degree – we use hymns, which are pre-formulated and restrict us to the spiritual understanding and perceptions of the writer, unless we use them as a basis for going further ourselves in our own reflection; we use (or should use) scripture extensively in worship; we may use the Lord's Prayer and graces. Preparation and pre-formulation can be a great aid to worship, especially where 'open worship' is dead and something is needed to revive it. The great weakness of liturgical worship in today's culture is, however, its fixed character, its lack of variety, and its distance from the informal and participative modes which are characteristic of society today. This is why many congregations which use a liturgy themselves introduce variety and unscripted items into it – and use a completely different form, a blend of entertainment and platform worship, to connect with younger people. Where the intellectual and technical resources are available, as for example, at All Souls and Holy Trinity, Brompton, this can be extremely successful. Practically, however, this is not within the reach of small or medium-sized churches, particularly those outside major urban centres.

Participative worship

At this point, I recognise that I may simply be revealing my own traditionalism! But there is a danger of throwing the baby out with the bathwater. I am anxious that the platform nature into which charismatic worship is evolving is proceeding in an essentially priestly direction – that is, that a group of specially equipped and recognised people 'do' worship for the congregation. I believe, however, that it remains possible to enable individuals in the congregation to participate by exercising their gifts, leading to a variety of types of intervention, under the leadership of the Holy Spirit, to the blessing of all present. No doubt, this is more practicable in congregations of less than a hundred – though I have seen highly effective participative worship in a congregation of 500 in the USA. A high level of congregational participation, with the flexibility and comparative informality that is essential to encouraging it, are culturally highly appropriate to the rising generations to whom we are now ministering. It fits the cultural styles to which they are well used, both in education and entertainment. Moreover, it is congruent with the freedom for the Holy Spirit and new forms that characterise new movements in times of revival and renewal. It is certainly congruent with Brethren traditions of 'open worship', though its form, tone and structure are somewhat different.

Practical guidance on the encouragement of 'participative worship'

There are certain guiding points which can help to re-establish participation by the congregation at large in 'worship' meetings.

Don't have a slot which is 'led worship' and a separate slot which is 'open worship' (in which the latter suffers by comparison with the former because it never gets off the ground). Let the two be blended. Let led worship lead into participative worship. Let the objective of led worship be to arrive at, to facilitate, effective participative worship. Indeed, let the leader and musicians see themselves not as leaders but as facilitators.

The worship leader's clear objective must be to liberate the congregation into participative worship. This means leaving sufficient time and space to the congregation to express itself. Too often, the worship leader says, 'Let people now lead us in worship', yet within 15 seconds he is himself talking again. (I say 'he' because women are sometimes more sensitive in this respect.) Do not be afraid of silence: resist the temptation to fill it by taking over yourself. It means trusting the Holy Spirit that he will indeed speak and lead through members of the congregation. It means verbally and constantly encouraging the congregation to use their spiritual gifts. It means flexibility on the part of the worship leader and musicians, to follow the lead given by the Spirit in the congregation, rather than dragging the congregation back to the thought that is in the leader's own mind, or to the programme (including the programme of songs) worked out in advance.

Let the musicians and platform singers see themselves not as performers to the congregation, but as worshippers, whose task is to facilitate the participation of others, subject to an essential minimum of musical competence. In both rehearsal and on the day, let their emphasis be on worship and spiritual development, rather than on the achievement of musical perfection, however difficult that is for experts in the group and congregation. Let involvement in the band be an opportunity for congregational gift to be used, not the prerogative of a limited group of experts. Let it be a role in which teenagers and older children can be overtly involved in congregational life.

Don't limit the range of what is appropriate by way of congregational intervention, either in terms of content or of form (e.g., prophecy, exposition – brief, of course – testimony, and solo singing, as well as prayer and the proposition of songs).

One particular difficulty is the link between the music group and the congregation, especially when a song is announced that the group are not expecting. Practically, sort out the music so that it can easily be found by the musicians; this usually means having a full collection of photocopied music, arranged in alphabetical order of first lines (ensuring, of course, that the licence fee is paid annually). The same applies in the case of overhead projection slides. If the group does not know the music of a song proposed from the congregation, the congregation probably do and singing unaccompanied will hurt nothing except (perhaps) the musicians' pride! So have someone to take the lead promptly when necessary, if the worship leader cannot. At all costs, avoid an embarrassed pause while the musicians search for the music, muttering apologies which the proposer of the song may take as criticism.

The provision of the words of songs on OHP slides, or by modern transparency projector, further helps congregational participation. It liberates people's hands from being chained to a hymnbook and enables them to lift their heads in song – a point in which a simple physical factor can have an influence on the character of worship. From that it follows that the practical projection arrangements need to be sorted out. How many projectors and screens are needed for the whole congregation? Can the screens be seen? Are they big enough? Are the projectors of good quality? Do they work properly? Are the overhead slides legible and correctly typed? Are they properly arranged and easy to use? Is communication between the worship leader and the slide manager effective? Is the slide manager competent? Church leaders must ensure that this is sorted out (which does not mean doing it themselves – here, a role can be given to someone who does not necessarily have platform or public skills).

To facilitate participative worship, however, a further step needs to be taken: that copies of words of the main collection of songs are available to the congregation, not for the purpose of singing but to facilitate their search for songs that they think might be appropriate. The disappearance of song books from the chair in the past few years has been a mechanism for suppressing participative worship and asserting the iron control of the worship leader.

Leadership plays an important role in helping a congregation to worship, whatever the form or combination of forms that we are using. In this context, both 'participative worship' and 'open worship' need leadership, whether or not from the platform; that is, they need directional input. If it is not coming from the congregation generally, then congregational leaders need to be willing to step in to give the appropriate direction, whether in prayer, exposition or exhortation, prophecy or simply through a song. But not too much!

Finally, given the prominence that many today give to 'worship' as the essential, if not unique, feature that matters in congregational life, it is important that worship leaders should be properly bound into congregational leadership. There needs to be good communication between the two groups, and the worship leaders do need to be under the direction of the congregational leaders. Worship leaders are visibly prominent to the congregation, sometimes more so than the congregational leaders are. The former need to conduct themselves carefully if they are not to undermine the prior role of the congregational leaders. Neither the worship leader(s), nor the congregational leaders, should allow the worship leader(s) deliberately or inadvertently to become a fount of power and influence in the congregation that effectively supplants the legitimate congregational leaders. That can happen if the worship leader teaches or implies, week in, week out, that there is something special about 'worship' compared with the remaining corporate activities of the congregation.

Further reading

P Bradshaw, *Liturgical Presidency in the Early Church* (Grove Liturgical Study No. 36, 1983)

G Kendrick, *Worship* (Kingsway, 1984)

A Kreider, *Worship and Evangelism in Pre-Christendom* (Cambridge, Grove Books, 1995)

E Kreider, *Enter His Gates: Fitting Worship Together* (Marshall Pickering, 1989)

R P Martin, *Worship in the Early Church* (Marshall, Morgan & Scott, 1964)

C F D Moule, *Worship in the New Testament* (Lutterworth, 1961; reprinted by Grove Books as Grove Liturgical Studies Nos. 12 and 13, 1997 & 1998)

D Peterson, *Engaging with God: A Biblical Theology of Worship* (Apollos, IVP, 1992)

H Rowdon (ed.), *Declare His Glory: Congregational Worship Today* (Paternoster Periodicals for Partnership, 1998)

CHAPTER ELEVEN

Discovering and Using Spiritual Gifts

DONALD BRIDGE

For the local church, the subject of spiritual gifts is one full of potential, yet fraught with complications. The need for a balanced response and a sane, scriptural approach is paramount. We need a policy regarding teaching, preparation, training and practice.

The gifts of the Spirit might be defined as 'working abilities distributed to the churches, to equip them for their task'. That task is daunting and many-sided. The plea for helpers in some new project is usually met by an uneasy silence from the many, and a sighing, 'I'll do it again', from the overworked few. Yet in a striking phrase, Peter says that in the many-coloured grace (*charis*) of God there is a colour to match every need and every situation. So, 'each one should use whatever gift (*charisma*) he has received to serve others, faithfully administering God's grace in its various forms' (1 Pet 4:10). The examples he gives are hospitality, speaking and serving – modest gifts needed in even the most undramatic church.

The analogy of limbs within the body lies at the heart of Paul's classic handling of the subject in 1 Corinthians 12. 'About spiritual gifts I do not want you to be ignorant . . . There are different kinds of gifts but the same Spirit' (12:1, 4). He uses other significant descriptive words, describing the gifts as 'services' designed to help others, not to provide personal thrill or status-symbol. They are 'workings'; divinely initiated actions that render our stumbling efforts effective. They are 'manifestations'; demonstrations that God is at work. Here is variety within unity, as the one God (Father, Son and Spirit) acts within the many situations (12:4-7). (See further, D Bridge and D Phypers, *Spiritual Gifts and the Church*, chapters 2-4.)

This matter of motive and purpose (God's and ours) is crucial. Contention about gifts often springs from confusion about their purpose. They should be seen, *not* as a demonstration of the individual's spiritual superiority, nor as a temporary provision to the apostolic church, available and valid only until the NT canon was complete. Rather, they represent a divine handful of gifts, talents, abilities and exercises which constantly unite, separate and reunite in successive combinations, as circumstances require and God directs.

This expression of variety-within-unity, and provision-within-sovereignty lies at the heart of Paul's great picture of active limbs in the body of Christ. 'The body is a unit, though it is made up of many parts; and though all its parts are many, they form one body. So it is with Christ' (v.12). The very argument used to support the traditional Brethren practices of open worship and shared eldership is also the one used to present gifts in all their rich variety and ordered freedom. 'He gives to each one just as he determines' (v.11). Granted, as they are, by God's generosity, and exercised within his sovereignty, gifts are intended for the good of others and the building up of the church. Understood that way, they should not be subjects of dissension, comparison, boasting or envy (see Paul's gentle teasing in verses 14-26).

How many, and which?

Several clusters of gifts are found in the NT. These are best regarded as samples, chosen to illustrate whatever theme is in view, rather than definitive and exhaustive lists. Some are clearly supernatural in origin, but others are difficult to distinguish from natural talents. What defines them as *charismata* is the use to which they are put, rather than their supernatural character.

Paul mentions the following activities (listed here in probable order of writing):

- prophecies (1 Thess 5:19-20);
- voluntary celibacy (1 Cor 7:7, 8);
- words of wisdom, messages of knowledge, faith, gifts of healing, miraculous powers, prophecy, distinguishing between spirits, different tongues and interpretation (1 Cor 12:7-11);
- charitable giving and willingness to suffer martyrdom (1 Cor 13:1-3);
- the ministry of apostles, prophets, teachers, workers of miracles, gifts of healing, helping others, administration, tongues and interpretation (1 Cor 14:27-31);
- prophesying, serving, teaching, encouraging financial aid, leadership and showing mercy (Rom 12:3-8);
- the ministry of apostles, prophets, evangelists, pastors and teachers (Eph 4:9-13).

Peter, as we saw, mentions hospitality, speaking and serving. The narrative in Acts offers examples of most gifts in action. In Acts, though they are not specifically called *charismata*, they often correspond to those so described in the epistles.

Clearly, a gift-of-grace does not have to be colourful, startling or mystifying in order to qualify. Nor is it easy to 'classify' the varied exercises. Some have to do with *mental activity* (e.g. wisdom and discernment of spirits). Some imply the *exercise of power* (e.g. healing and miracles). Others involve *speech* (e.g. teaching, prophecy, tongues). Several suggest *administrative ability* (help, service and administration). The Ephesian list suggests *task* or *office* (e.g. pastor, evangelist, teacher). Some are exercised in *prayer* and *worship* (e.g. prophecy, singing, praying in tongues). Note that the use of music in 'spiritual worship' is assumed in 1 Corinthians 14:15; Ephesians 5:18-20; Colossians 3:16. There is linguistic support for the view that, in the Ephesian passage, 'singing' implies use of the voice and 'making music' implies the use of instruments. Orthodox writers throughout the centuries, as well as modern charismatics, assume 'singing with the spirit' and 'spiritual songs' to be spontaneous songs from individuals or congregations, in which the (human) spirit, or the heart, is engaged. (See chapter 12 on 'The place of music'.) Perhaps such varied gifts as hospitality, mercy and voluntary poverty might be classified as *attitudes*. Cessationists who regard the first of the Corinthian lists and the Ephesian list as 'sign-gifts' appropriate only for the apostolic age nevertheless, in practice, only question the use of tongues, interpretation and prophecy in today's church. They prefer to speak of 'prayer for the sick' rather than 'healing' and 'apostolic ministry' rather than 'apostles'.

Different gifts obviously overlap and interweave. A pastor needs to serve and help, will require wisdom and may well speak prophetically. A speaker may either teach, prophesy or evangelise. A ministry of help may involve healing, generosity or hospitality. Administration of church affairs requires more than mere secular 'man management'; wisdom or discernment of spirits or prophetic insight are needed. (Management skills and spiritual administration sometimes combine happily, but not always. Beware of the automatic assumption that your church treasurer should be the available bank manager, your leading Bible teacher borrowed from the local comprehensive, or your chairman of elders a business executive. Maybe . . . maybe not. I could tell some tales!)

Structuring for gifts – or do we sit and wait?

How do gifts emerge, and how does the 'gifted' individual recognise them? Should I personally seek gifts? What role is played by leadership? Is there a place for teaching and training? What place do gifts have in public worship? How may misuse and excess be checked?

With such questions in mind, John Baigent rightly maintains: 'Opportunities must be provided and structures set up which will allow for the emergence, recognition and exercise of such gifts.' (*Partnership Perspectives*, January 1997, pp. 9-13). That idea should hardly be novel to the kind of church that has historically stood for shared leadership, open patterns of worship, sensitivity to the Spirit, and the priesthood of all believers.

We therefore need to examine: individual discovery and awareness; the role of leadership in care, encouragement, training and discipline; and patterns of corporate activity: i.e. how the gifts are exercised 'in church'.

Finding my gift and role

The NT often urges Christians to discern their gifts and exercise them responsibly (e.g. Rom 3:6-8; 1Tim 4:14-16; 2 Tim 1:6; 1 Pet 4:10). But how do I recognise my gifting? Some simple tests may help. For example, do I feel drawn to a particular gift? Am I increasingly aware of the need for it in my church or personal life? Does it often find a place in my prayers? Have responsible fellow-Christians encouraged me to venture on some exercise? When I move forward with cautious faith, does anything *happen*? Are my natural talents surrendered to God? Have I discerned new, hitherto unsuspected abilities as my spiritual experience deepens?

The Holy Spirit is divinely sovereign and free in his working, 'giving to each one, just as he determines' (1 Cor 12:11). Disconcertingly, his guidance and provision may not slot conveniently into our particular theory, whether that be Pentecostal, charismatic, Reformed or dispensationalist. Nevertheless, we should avoid the attitude that rejects all caution and ignores all advice as 'dead tradition'. Most of all, experiences and perceptions must be submitted to the written word.

Releasing and encouraging gift

One task of eldership is to guide Christians into fruitful living, through formal teaching and informal guidance. That includes the discovery of gift. Elders meeting together will regularly vet both character-growth and service, arranging to offer personal help when its need is evident. This writer recalls how sensitive elders guided him into every forward step during his teens. That involved, in his case, encouragement to pray aloud (midweek first, then at Communion), offers of the Sunday pulpit, opportunity to join in conversational study, and appointment to youth leadership. Elders protected me from negative criticism when I made mistakes, and showed me how to do better next time. This kind of exercise is equally necessary for those developing obviously supernatural gifts, and those developing low-profile abilities that may escape notice.

Leaders should give occasional teaching on the subject of the *charismata*, sometimes as a special series and sometimes in the course of regular biblical preaching. House groups should be offered published or home-grown materials for teaching, discussion and prayer. The small group is the ideal place for early steps in the exercise of gifts. Here, in a non-threatening atmosphere where beginners learn together, mistakes matter less, and can be corrected with little pain. Obviously, leaders holding to a fully Pentecostal two-stage view, will encourage people to seek this (hopefully, without pressure, manipulation, emotionalism or public fuss). However, the Pentecostal route is observedly not the only path to the release of gifts, and the kind of gentle encouragement outlined above can be very fruitful, as well as avoiding the confusion of exaggerated and then disappointed expectations. The NT offers no simple, invariable pattern, as I have pointed out in *Partnership Perspectives* (January 1997, pp. 2-5).

To sum up this section: wise and sensitive leadership will encourage, stimulate, guide and correct, 'to prepare God's people for works of service' (Eph 4:11, 12).

Leadership and structure in worship

'Everything should be done in a fitting and orderly way' says the apostle to a congregation and its leaders (1 Cor 14:40). His context is the exercise of gifts within public worship ('In the church'. . .'When you come together', 1 Cor 14: 1-19, 26-33).

The traditional open worship (familiar to many), offers opportunity for prayer, prophecy, shared discernments, testimony, spiritual songs, etc. But there are limits. Long-cherished customs, habits and traditions (not to mention dominant personalities) can render the meeting open in theory but closed in reality. Moreover, a congregation of over a hundred will encounter practical problems in the exercise of widely-varied gifts within a 75-minute time-slot.

If worship time is largely devoted to Communion, not all gifts are appropriate (not even all the 'verbal' gifts). The apostle urges caution and restraint if unbelievers (literally the 'uninstructed') are present (1 Cor 14:13-17, 23-25). Significantly, large Pentecostal or charismatic churches usually have firm leadership up-front in their Sunday congregations. The widespread exercise of gifts is then channelled into midweek small-group activities, with an occasional joint celebration organised for larger numbers.

Freedom in public worship does not mean licence. Paul's advice to Corinth has several implications (1 Cor 14). Prayers, though addressed to God, should be relevant and meaningful to the congregation (vv.2, 3). Prophecy (assumed to be spontaneous speech) should 'strengthen, encourage and comfort' (v.3). Gifts that build up the whole church should have priority (v.12). Unless interpretation is available, tongues should be restricted to private worship. ('Interpretation' need not mean word-by-word translation, but a perception of the general sense; rather as a piece of literature or music is 'interpreted'.) None of the gifts is regarded as inspired, infallible or canonical. If they were, how could we be urged to judge their appropriateness or otherwise (1 Cor 14:29)? Freedom should be exercised with courtesy and concern for others having something to contribute (vv.26, 27). A 'gift' is not self-authenticating or infallible; the whole congregation exercises discernment and 'weighs carefully' (v.29). Those exercising gifts are in control of themselves, not driven by emotion or ecstacy (vv.32, 33).

The tone of the whole passage implies the duty of leaders to guide, encourage and stimulate godly order. Congregations should be reminded of this from time to time. It may be desirable to appoint trusted people to superintend (or at least open and close) the allocated time of unstructured worship. Some scholars suggest that the 'administration' of 1 Corinthians 12:28 is the ability to 'steer' a flexible and open liturgy. Certainly the judicious mixing of responsive, liturgical, spontaneous and led prayers is an aid to spiritually free worship – not a threat. And, remember, our deservedly beloved hymns are simply set-prayers put to music, and function as a liturgical framework within which free worship can operate.

All of this may seem daunting. It is sad, but hardly surprising, that some Christians prefer to forgo (or even forbid) the free exercise of gifts, fearing the problems of misuse, and wincing at the demands imposed on responsible leadership. But the best reaction to misuse is not disuse, but right use. John Owen, 17th-century theologian, wrote in his *Discourse on Spiritual Gifts*: 'By some . . . gifts have been abused. Some have presumed upon them beyond the line and measure which they have received; some have been puffed up with them; some have used them disorderly in churches and to their hurt; some have boasted of what they have not received . . . all which miscarriages also befell the primitive churches. (But) I had rather have the order, rule, spirit and practices of those churches that were planted by the apostles, with all their troubles and disadvantages, than the carnal peace of others in their open degeneracy from all these things.'

Further reading

D Bridge and D Phypers, *Spiritual Gifts and the Church* (Christian Focus, 1995)

D A Hubbard, *Unwrapping your Spiritual Gifts* (Word, 1985)

J Owen, *Discourse on Spiritual Gifts* (Banner of Truth, 1965)

T Smail, A Walker and N Wright, *Charismatic Renewal. The Search for a Theology* (SPCK, 1993)

CHAPTER TWELVE

The Place of Music

MAX DONALD

The Old Testament

Since the time of Jubal (Gen 4:21) music has had an important place in human life. Music also had a significant place in the religious life of Israel. The appointment of singers and musicians who accompanied the ark into Jerusalem (1 Chron 15:16-28), and the Levitical praise at the time of the completion of Solomon's temple (2 Chron 5:11-14) represent two fascinating examples.

Several psalms include instructions to 'the director of music' about the kind of instruments which are suitable for the particular sung praise or prayer. Especially popular were stringed instruments (Pss 4; 6; 61; 67; 76); flutes are also specified (Psa 5). And one supposes that at least Psalm 150 involved the accompaniment of trumpets, harps, lyres, tambourine, strings, flutes and various cymbals – since they are all mentioned in the psalm. In addition, there are several Hebrew words which we suppose to be musical terms, the exact meaning of which are now lost to us. These include *sheminith, shaggion, gittith, mitkam, alamoth, mahalah* and the popular *maskil*. Some of the psalms have the names of tunes attached to which the psalm was to be sung (Pss 9; 22; 45; 56; 57; 58; 59; 60; 69; 75). The tune 'Do not Destroy' seems to have been a particular favourite. Certain psalms were designed for specific occasions: e.g. the dedication of the temple (Psa 30), a wedding (Psa 45), the sabbath day (Psa 92). Others mark specific experiences and events, notably in the life of David (e.g. Pss 3; 7; 18; 34; 51; 52; 54; 56; 57; 58; 60; 63; 102).

There is clear evidence that the words of the psalms were carefully crafted, as well as being divinely inspired. For example, nine of the psalms are in acrostic form (Pss 9; 10; 25; 34; 37; 111; 112; 119; 145). Psalm 119 is worthy of special note. The psalm is divided into 22 sections of 8 verses each, and each verse in each section begins with the letter in the Hebrew alphabet which heads the section. If the

English alphabet were used in this way, verses 25-32 which all start with the Hebrew letter *Daleth*, might read something like this: (25) Depressed low in the dust am I . . . (26) Declared have I your ways and you answered me . . . (27) Declare to me the teaching of your precepts . . . (28) Dropping is my soul with sorrow . . . (29) Deceitful ways remove from me . . . (30) Determined am I in choosing the way of truth . . . 31) Deliberately I hold fast your statutes . . . (32) Day by day I run in the way of your commandments . . . A gold mine for those who like alliterations, not only in sermons, now also in songs, and presumably a good aide-memoire.

This OT background is not merely of theoretical or academic interest. In the absence of teaching and/or information in the NT to the contrary, it would seem fair to assume that the early church adopted and adapted significant aspects of OT praise and worship.

Several practical lessons emerge from this brief dip into the OT (although this list is offered in recognition that not every church has the luxury of having numerous musicians in its midst).

- There is a place for a variety of different musicians and singers in the leading of congregational praise and worship.
- We might consider the appointment of a music director or praise leader, who is both spiritually sensitive and musically skilful.
- Items of praise and worship should be carefully chosen to suit the occasion.
- Particular instruments are appropriate for different styles of praise items.
- There is a place for liturgical worship (i.e. the communal singing or speaking out of set praises/prayers, e.g. from the Psalms) as well as spontaneous praise.

The New Testament

One of the most important passages in the NT for our present purpose is Ephesians 5:18b-21. Several things may be noted from these verses.

First, our singing should be the expression of Spirit-filled worshippers. 'Go on being filled with the Spirit' is the main verb of the text. It is a present continuous imperative, and it thus highlights what must be the constant source and inspiration of our praise and worship. It is therefore essential that worship leaders give due practical emphasis to the necessity for our praise to flow from Spirit-filled worshippers.

Second, our congregational praise should be an uplifting experience for the congregation. In 'speaking to one another' the wonderful content of praise to God, we minister encouragement to one another as we remind one another of God's grace and goodness to us.

Third, the substance and style of our worship should be varied and diverse, as we use 'psalms, hymns and spiritual songs'. 'Psalms' probably refers to the psalms in our OT and could perhaps be broadened today to refer to scripture set to music. 'Hymns' probably refers to NT praise of Christ (examples include Phil 2:6-11 and 1 Tim 3:16), and today would include some of the great classic hymns which glorify the Lord Jesus. 'Spiritual songs' probably refers to other items of praise inspired by the Spirit, perhaps including songs sung (and even composed) spontaneously in a time of open worship, corresponding to at least the best of new praise and worship songs today. We thus have a rich heritage of material from which to draw, and a healthy approach will express a balance of old and new hymns and songs, some setting scripture to music. It will also resist the urge evidently felt by some to use newer material just because it is new!

Fourth, our praise should be consciously and gratefully directed to the Lord – 'singing and making music in your heart to the Lord'. When we 'worship by the Spirit of God' we will 'glory in Christ Jesus' (Phil 3:3) as our minds are filled and our hearts thrilled with the glorious truths we are singing. 'Making music' in true spiritual worship is 'in the heart . . . to the Lord' and not just with our voices. Most of us will know that it is quite possible to enjoy singing, to sing 'heartily' and yet not be truly praising Jesus in our hearts or genuinely glorying in him.

Fifth, our worship in song should be characterised by thanksgiving – 'always giving thanks to God the Father for everything in the name of our Lord Jesus Christ'. We are exhorted to come into God's presence with thanksgiving and praise (Psa 100:4). The words 'always' and 'for everything' stress the importance of this. When we meet together as a congregation we may not feel like giving thanks. Sometimes we need to remind ourselves, encouraged by the worship leader, of the many blessings and benefits we receive from God's gracious and generous hand (Psa 103). It is important to 'count our many blessings', even when we are most aware of our battles. We may not be able to praise God for every circumstance we encounter, but we can certainly 'give thanks in all circumstances, for this is God's will for you in Christ Jesus' (1 Thess 5:18). And as we offer praise, so we glorify God.

Sixth, our praise and worship should be trinitarian. Paul's mention of 'God the Father', 'our Lord Jesus Christ' and 'the Spirit' in these verses is an important reminder that our worship is of one

God in three persons. Again, our music should reflect the diversity
of the ministry of the triune God, as each person plays his part in
the great and glorious plan of salvation. (See H M Carson,
Hallelujah!, pp.33-44.)

Seventh, we are also exhorted to 'submit to one another out of
reverence for Christ'. This phrase is usually connected with verses
22ff, but it is also the concluding phrase of what flows from 'going
on being filled with the Spirit' (v.18) and in the context of our praise
and worship it is also very appropriate. Paul is here reminding us
that our worship should express a gracious mutual submission.
Many Christians (perhaps especially musicians) have strong views,
opinions and tastes concerning music. It is essential that those
involved in leading God's people in praise and worship and,
equally important, that the worshipping congregation have a
submissive spirit and a servant heart. It is a tragedy and a travesty
when music becomes a battleground on which individuals or
groups within a church insist on their own way.

A smorgasbord of suggestions

Pray – Practise – Praise Pray together for the ongoing experience
of being filled with the Spirit (both at practices and immediately
prior to leading praise). Practise well and hard, so that you produce
the very best you can. And then praise together as you lead God's
worshipping people, so that you model praise and worship for the
congregation.

A flow of praise Our structure of praise would do well to avoid both
the traditional four-hymn sandwich and the more recent endless
repetitive singing of short choruses. The former style engenders a
stop-start attitude to praise. Following the singing of the hymn, the
congregation typically switches off, sits down and waits for the next
(and sometimes quite unrelated) item to be announced. The latter
style can be both exhausting and mind-numbing. A carefully
designed time of praise might incorporate the linked singing of two
or three brief songs, perhaps connected by the reading of an
appropriate scripture while the keyboard continues to play quietly.
The worship leader will also have the sense and sensitivity to invite
the congregation to stand and sit at appropriate moments.

Music and song as ministry versus performance Many of our
churches have abandoned the regular practice of having a guest
soloist because of a general feeling that the cutting edge of ministry
had often given way to the tired performance of an oft-sung solo.
However, there is an undoubted value in being genuinely
ministered to through the medium of music, provided it is done

with freshness and a sense of reality.

Form and freedom Within a structured service, there may be an opportunity for the congregation to bring brief expressions of spontaneous praise, both in words and in song. The keyboard player (or guitarist, or whoever is responsible for praise leading) might helpfully interject with an occasionally led song.

Variation on a theme How about an 'evening of appreciation' of, e.g., Isaac Watts, John Newton, Charles Wesley, Fanny Crosby, Graham Kendrick, Chris Bowater, in which something of the life and ministry of the particular hymn/song writer is shared, and the evening's praise consists of a selection of his/her songs.

Use of overhead projector The advent of overhead projectors and acetates brings the possibility of freeing the congregation from having heads buried in books while singing, and having the distraction from worship of looking up the next song. This is a particular problem in churches which have at least one supplement in addition to the regular hymnbook. A skilled operator of the OHP is a real asset in congregational praise, especially if all the hymns and songs are clearly typed on acetates. Such an arrangement also facilitates physical expressions of worship. Now we really can thank our God 'with hearts *and hands* and voices'.

Multi-media presentations The sensitive use of audio-visual accompaniment to music can be a most effective means of presenting the Christian message. One of my lasting memories is the beautifully crafted mime of the crucifixion by young people to a tape of Twila Paris singing 'O Lamb of God'. Each presentation brought several in the congregation to tears, and at least one person professed conversion as a direct result of the multi-media presentation. On another occasion a selection of slides of breathtaking scenes from around the world was presented on screen, while the musicians and singers led the congregation in the fine hymn 'How great Thou art'. In these and other ways musicians and singers can tap into the communication business in an imaginative and creative way, thus encouraging and enhancing the worship of the congregation. (See chapter 10 on 'Worship'.)

Further reading

H M Carson, *Hallelujah!* (Evangelical Press, 1980)

J D Douglas (ed), *The New Bible Dictionary* (IVP, 1962) art. 'Music and Musical Instruments'

G Kendrick, *Worship* (Kingsway, 1984)

D Montgomery, *Sing a New Song* (Rutherford House/Handsel Press, 2000)

J R Taylor, *The Hallelujah Factor* (Highland, 1983)

CHAPTER THIRTEEN

Small Groups

GRAHAM POLAND

Small is beautiful

In a world where big is often considered better, healthy churches have realised the indispensable value of small groups. These groups have always been around as a basic building block for church growth, but in recent years they have re-emerged around the world as a highly significant element in the expansion of the church, both as a means of preparing for and coping with either revival or persecution.

Historically, we can see their importance. Both John Wesley and George Whitfield made use of small groups in their day. Whitfield told his converts: 'You would do well, as others have done, to form yourselves into little companies of four or five each, and meet once a week to tell each other what is in your hearts; that you may then also pray for and comfort each other as need shall require.' Not only was it an efficient way of coping with unprecedented growth, for, as Wesley says, 'their primary purpose was discipline'. In more recent history we have witnessed phenomenal growth of the church in Latin America, China, South Korea and Africa where, in every case, small groups have been central to the process.

Pastorally, we can see their importance. In a growing church it is easy for pastoral needs to be overlooked and for people to lose their identity in the crowd. A small group structure ensures that people are more likely to be cared for and urgent needs met without delay. Bill Beckham observes the similarity with an efficient military structure: 'Armies are organised into manageable units appropriate for accomplishing the basic task. The most basic unit is the squad, which is made up of 9-12 enlisted men. This unit makes the difference in battle. All larger groupings of soldiers such as platoons and companies exist to support these basic fighting units. Five to 15 Christians are the basic fighting unit of the church.'

This consideration is particularly relevant for churches where the leadership structure is shared and predominantly reliant on volunteer help. People's time is limited, especially if they have to juggle paid work and family responsibilities with pastoral oversight in a church. The more the task is shared, the greater chance there is of people fulfilling their responsibility efficiently. A ratio of no more than 1:10 is usually recommended for shepherding, and a small group should not be allowed to exceed 15.

Our third consideration is that, *biblically*, we can see their importance. The 'Jethro leadership principle' (Exod 18:13-26) recognises that no one should take full responsibility for the needs of a large group. It also recognises that responsibility levels vary: not everybody has the capacity for pastoral oversight and leadership for the same number of people. To ensure efficient management Moses was advised to re-structure around smaller groups, delegating responsibility to others. Jesus is our prime example in his use of the small group. His ministry focused on the training and equipping of a dynamic small group of twelve disciples. They were a microcosm of the church that emerged in Acts and many lessons on small group dynamics can be learned from Jesus' dealings with them. (See chapter 4 on 'Discovering and training new leaders'.)

The cataclysmic explosion of numbers as the church grew through the book of Acts (see Acts 1:15; 2:41; 4:4) necessitated a structure that could manage such growth, so inevitably the early church had to be structured around small groups meeting in homes. According to Beckham, 'The small groups meeting in homes gave the first century church a way to absorb and nurture growth that was four or five times larger than their core congregation.' Michael Green traces the use of small groups in the book of Acts:

> As the story of the early church continues to unfold, private homes are depicted as becoming increasingly centres of worship and hospitality, of Christian teaching and missionary proclamation. Luke describes homes being used for 'prayer meetings' (Acts 12:12); for an evening of Christian fellowship (Acts 21:7); for Holy Communion services (Acts 2:46); for a whole night of prayer, worship and instruction (Acts 20:7); for impromptu evangelistic gatherings (Acts 16:32); for planned meetings in order to hear the Christian gospel (Acts 10:22); for following up enquiries (Acts 18:26); and for organised instruction (Acts 5:42). (*Evangelism in the Early Church*)

Much of Paul's ministry was accomplished in small group gatherings meeting in homes. The gaoler and Lydia opened their homes in Philippi; Priscilla and Aquila and Nympha had meetings in their homes (Rom 16:5; Col 4:15). In fact, it is hard to imagine the church in Paul's day functioning without such groups.

Some people today have resisted the move towards small groups because they fear becoming a house church and see little biblical warrant for such a move. However, it must be understood that most small group ministries exist within the context of a larger church, so that it is not a case of either house group or church, but the recognition of the church as people meeting both in various homes and all together. This would appear to be very much in keeping with what we observe to be happening in the early church.

Types of small groups

Many different types of small group exist in the church today, with a variety of functions:

The study group

If people have had any experience of small groups functioning within their church, it is usually at this level. Home Bible study groups have flourished in churches, college and university Christian Unions, and in the workplace. A multiplicity of study aids exists to resource such groups, enabling people who have had little theological training to lead small group discussions on a given passage or topic. Young Christians, in particular, have benefited greatly from such study groups because they have enabled them to get to grips with the Bible in a way that listening to sermons cannot achieve. Educationally it is a fact that people will learn more from what they discover for themselves in a context of interactive discussion, than by listening to a monologue. Some churches have created a healthy balance by linking small group discussion material to the topic or passage expounded publicly, either directly following the sermon, or subsequently in the following week's house groups.

For those adopting such a small group structure, care must be given to the style of leadership. A didactic approach, with the leader giving a lengthy lecture, can kill off participation and will have little lasting value. Basic training in the dynamics of small group discussion needs to be given for maximum benefit to be derived. (See chapter 5, Peter Cousins on 'Teaching'.)

The service group

The function of church leaders is to 'prepare God's people for works of service' (Eph 4:12). Some service can best be accomplished in a small group. For instance, evangelistic or hospital visitation benefits from a team approach, where training on the job and encouragement can be given. Practical ministry (e.g. decorating somebody's house or maintenance work in the church) can be done by a team who are called and gifted for such works of service. Drama teams, music teams or singing groups can not only serve together but grow together. Some churches have been able to structure their small groups in such a way that service groups can also be the place where you pray and study the Bible together, thereby avoiding the duplication of small group time and unnecessary pressure.

The support group

Many para-church or secular organisations exist to support people going through times of pressure or vulnerability. Alcoholics Anonymous, Cruse, Gingerbread and other organisations often look for premises and voluntary help from churches. Either as a back-up to existing groups, or as an evangelical alternative, Christians could make a considerable impact by participating in such groups. Some churches have set up small groups to support the deaf, the divorced, the bereaved or new parents.

The special-interest group

There are, again, a variety of options available to churches who wish to be relevant to their members and their communities. In many churches there are people with specialist skills who could offer evening classes in topics such as cookery, car mechanics, DIY, computer skills. Some people may object to the use of church premises for such activities, but, ironically, attend such classes themselves elsewhere. For those with sensitivity, such a service offered to the community could provide a fertile mission field and result in the person coming, say, to the cookery group becoming far less resistant to the invitation back into the same building to be fed with the word of life.

Special-interest groups exist within most churches and already function as small groups. People interested in overseas mission can pray for missionaries and organisations that reflect their own particular burden. On occasions we have divided our missionary prayer meeting into prayer corners, praying for different missionaries simultaneously and then inviting people to join another 'corner'.

People enquiring about Christianity often come to faith best in the context of a small group. The Alpha course combines introductory teaching with small group discussion. There are many other evangelistic courses available, designed to help people who are 'just looking' or wanting to discuss the implications of becoming Christians. Most of the conversion growth in our church has been the result of a small group meeting weekly in a home (entitled 'Discovery').

Committees are, in fact, special-interest groups and are often overlooked as an example of a small group ministry. Efficiently chaired, they can be the means of accomplishing much spiritual work, but without proper leadership they can be ineffective. As with any small group, the right leader is needed and the right training provided.

Although combining several of the elements already considered, a further category deserves specific consideration:

The cell group

In many parts of the world the cell church is the fastest growing model of the church. South Korea birthed the first mega church organised around cell groups and other thriving examples exist in places such as Singapore and Hong Kong. The impact of this way of organising church has been felt in many other parts of the world, but, curiously, has yet to have a major impact on churches in Britain. Jane and Andy Fitz-Gibbon describe cell church as 'a church composed of many cells. Each of the cells belongs to the same church under the same leadership. Programmes are jettisoned as the church holds two kinds of meeting: celebration, usually on Sunday and cell, usually during the week.'

A cell church is not a church with small groups, so much as a church of small groups. The goal of each cell is to multiply by seeing other people won to Christ and, within a targeted period, to reproduce itself again and again. It is a model primarily focused on numerical church growth with a strong emphasis on the training of new group leaders. It is a particularly relevant model for churches where it is impossible to purchase large buildings, but it is far more than a church with small groups attached to it, and anyone intent on pursuing this model should be aware of the underlying values and vision driving it.

Personal history

My own pilgrimage in recognising the value of small groups has taken me from considerable scepticism to the conviction that they are indispensable if your church is going to grow.

My initial reservations revolved around two things. Previous experience of small group Bible study had been of hoary-haired 'patriarchs' hijacking a captive audience to vent their frustrated

Bible-teaching ambitions or, alternatively, a lack of leadership resulting in a pooling of ignorance. Either way, I much preferred listening to a gifted preacher than participating in small group discussion. On reflection, however, I did recall teenage days when a forward-thinking youth leader facilitated our participation in discussion and I would come away having discovered for myself far more than I had ever learnt through listening to a monologue. I knew that, properly led, a small group could accomplish much, but I had experienced few good leaders and found it frustrating to have to lead a small group myself.

In recent years I have been involved in the leadership of a rapidly growing church and, as it has grown, I have recognised the danger of people becoming increasingly isolated. The loss of community in our postmodern society has left a longing for belonging in the heart of many people and the gap is not being filled simply by coming to church. I have also come to recognise that church is not a place where we go so much as a people that we are becoming. Peter says: 'You also, like living stones, are being built into a spiritual house to be a holy priesthood' (1 Pet 2:5). The inter-relating of people is far more important than the proliferation of programmes running a church. Church has to do with relationships, but I was in danger of perpetuating a religion of going to meetings. Yet, organisationally, it was difficult to know how to structure a church based on relationships when there were so many people; the bigger the church, the less intimate the relationships and the more isolated the individuals.

At this time I had the opportunity to visit Brazil and to observe, first-hand, the 'discipleship movement' which has permeated much of the church growth in Latin America in recent years. The relaxed way in which structures served relationships appealed to me as a more workable model than the somewhat regimented cell church approach. As a consequence we have, incrementally, introduced a network of discipleship groups within our church, linking all who wished to be in a discipleship relationship with somebody who would parent them as a discipler. However, we have insisted that nobody (including elders) is ever in a position of discipling others without themselves being discipled. In practice this means that most people belong to two groups (or pairs) of people. The purpose of these groups is for the sharing of life rather than information, supporting and praying for each other, and providing a place for belonging. Study takes place, but it is not the principal aim of the group.

We have found that the introduction of the above small group structure has enhanced fellowship at a level we had never known before. Leadership and pastoral responsibility is being shared rather than residing in a few, and people are coming to understand that they have a valid part to play in the daily running of the church. As a result, 'the whole body, joined and held together by every supporting ligament, grows and builds itself up in love, as each part does its work' (Eph 4:16).

Further reading

H Astin, *Body and Cell* (Monarch, 1998)
W Beckham, *The Second Reformation* (Touch Publications, Houston TX, 1995)
J Mallinson, *Growing Christians in Small Groups* (Scripture Union, 1989)

CHAPTER FOURTEEN

Evangelism in a Postmodern World

ALASTAIR SIMMONS

Facing the challenge

Once upon a time there was a mighty river. It flowed gracefully and elegantly across the landscape. Along its banks it gave life and sustenance to the tribes of aboriginal Australians who camped by it. For many generations this river was a central focus for life. Then, gradually, the river ceased to flow, becoming a stagnant pool. With the heat of summer it started to dry up. Around the banks of the disappearing symbol of their security, the people watched aghast. What could be happening to them? By the dried-up riverbed many sat, waiting for the river to flow once more. Yet others thought to look around and discovered the river was not gone. Still flowing, it had simply changed course upstream, creating a billabong on the curve at which they sat.

John Drane tells the above story by the Australian sociologists Peter and Sue Kaldor, in his perceptive and provocative book *Faith in a Changing Culture* (previously published as *Evangelism for a New Age*). It highlights with devastating impact the dilemma for many evangelicals in the postmodern world of today. Lest we mistake either the flow of his thought or the flow of the river, he continues:

Most Christians in the West can see that things have changed, and that the world has moved on. But too many are sitting by the dried-up riverbed, hoping the water will flow back the way it once did. It takes neither faith nor courage to do that. It is more demanding to step out and take risks, to experiment in order to find where God's life-giving Spirit is moving in today's world. To move away might mean the dismantling of our institutions or the sacrifice of some sacred cows, and that is always painful. But if the experience of the world Church is anything to go by, it might also mean a rediscovery of the gospel and some exciting surprises. Whatever the cost, this could be where God is calling the Church to go. For the size of the opportunity more than matches the dimensions of the challenge. (p.26)

The challenge of postmodernity for the church is that not only has the river changed course, but it will continue to change course with increasing frequency and rapidity. If the church is not to be left sitting by increasing numbers of smaller and smaller billabongs, then we have to ask some tough questions, accept that some ecclesiastical and theological noses will be somewhat dislocated, and seek to engage with society today.

A recent survey of church attendance in England and Wales identified an average attendance of less than 7.5% of the population. That is cause for concern enough. But even more so is the identified drop from 12% in the last ten years. This has caused some pundits from the Jeremiah school of prophecy to predict the potential demise of Christianity in this country in one generation. (Cf. the familiar dirge, 'Ah well, we're living in the last days.')

Yet at the very time when there is a marked decline in church attendance there is also an increasing openness to, and interest in, spirituality generally. People in today's postmodern society have a bigger problem with our church than with our God; a bigger problem with our jargon than with our Jesus; and a bigger problem with our medium than with our message.

These are the challenges we face. What is the message we are to preach? What is its content? Is there an irreducible minimum of faith? How are we to preach and evangelise? Indeed what do we mean by evangelism? What is the purpose of preaching and evangelism – to reassure ourselves or to reach others? What is the cultural context in which we seek to evangelise and what are the implications of that context for our approach?

Defining the terms

The *Independent* newspaper came up with a memorable explanation of postmodernism which went something like this: 'No one knows what it really means. Therefore if you want to impress people it is advisable to refer to post-modernism as often as possible.' This humorously highlights the difficulty of defining exactly what postmodernism is.

In a summarised Internet article ('The Post-modern Generation') Mark Titley hazards these simple pointers. (1) There is no such thing as an absolute, objective truth in matters of morality and religion. ('You have your truth and I have mine.') (2) Subjective experience supersedes logic and objective facts. ('Don't confuse me with the facts.') (3) The nature of truth and the nature of God are relative, not absolute concepts. ('You have your god and I have mine.') It is crucial to our attempts to evangelise in the 21st century that we seek to understand, and empathise with, the generation influenced by postmodern thinking and behaving.

In my opinion, the description, which best gives feeling and insight into the soul and psyche of postmodernity, is to be found in an article by Nick Mercer in *Encounter with God* (Scripture Union: April, May, June 1998).

> Post-modernity is one of the most exciting, painful, challenging, opportunity-filled, anxiety-ridden, faithbuilding, depressing, faith-destroying, enjoyable and contradictory of times to be alive. Post-modernity is the cultural climate that is increasingly pervading the world, spreading like a virus through TV, the arts, popular culture and new politics . . . Post-modernity is a transition, a staging post, a mood to help us on the journey to the unknown destination. So purpose is giving way to play; design to chance; founts of wisdom to pools of knowledge; the metanarrative, the Big Picture, to the micronarrative, the local story; reason to reasons. There is no lighthouse keeper. There is no lighthouse. There is no dry land. There are only people living on rafts made from their own imaginations. And there is sea.

I'm sure we share Nick Mercer's prayer, when we view this bleak philosophical landscape (or seascape), that 'we must be so in touch with our culture that we feel its pain and know how to apply the balm of the gospel'.

Postmodernism, by its very etymology, refers to something that comes after modernism. Therefore, to understand postmodernism and its influence, we must first examine modernism and its influence on civilisation in general and the church in particular.

Modernism, as a world view, grew out of the Enlightenment whose foundations were laid by Rene Descartes (1596-1650), famous for his Latin dictum *Cogito ergo sum* ('I think, therefore I am.' or, more correctly, 'I am thinking, therefore I am.') Descartes' understanding of human nature has had, in Drane's words, 'a profound and dominating effect on the whole of recent Western history. Personhood has been defined by what people think, and the process of rationality and argument, rather than how people feel.' This process of rationalism, logic and the pursuit of truth that could be proved, undoubtedly influenced evangelical Christianity in its thinking, and its preaching. Drane writes: 'The Church's indebtedness to Enlightenment thinking is beyond question. Writing of the development of the modern evangelical movement, David Bebbington observes that: "It is extremely hard to resist the conclusion that the early evangelicals were immersed in the Enlightenment. They were progressing fully in the progressive thought of their age.'"

The same modernist view which placed a premium on what could be seen and verified, also removed any need for supernatural intervention in the world. As if that were not bad enough it also laid the base for existential humanism and subsequently secular atheism epitomised by Friedrich Nietzsche's infamous pronouncement that 'God is dead'.

The challenge today is that people no longer ask, 'Is it *true*?' but more personally, 'Is it true for *me*?' Increasingly in a society engulfed by ennui and emptiness the question being asked is, 'Is it relevant?'

So what do we mean by evangelism? What do we mean by preaching? Is our preaching really Bible-based or is it something that developed more out of Calvin's *Institutes* (for example) than out of John the Apostle's insights? Are our evangelical minds, conditioned by centuries of Enlightenment-based, modernistic thought processes, able to accept the paradigm shift that will be required if we are to engage meaningfully with today's postmodern seeker who cares little for our skilfully honed abilities to cross every theological 't' and dot every exegetical 'i'?

Accepting the implications

I posed the question earlier, 'What is the purpose of preaching and evangelism – to reassure ourselves or to reach others?' Do we accept the implications of the scenario described? I suggest that, if we don't, we will miss the boat of opportunities for sharing the gospel in fresh relevant ways. Rob Warner, in one of the most influential and thought-provoking books I have read in recent years (*21st Century Church*), highlights the dilemma in a section entitled 'Stuck in Yesterday'. He writes:

> I rushed down the steps and onto the platform, only to see the train already leaving the station. The doors were closed, the train was moving and I was left behind. Anyone who travels by public transport will sooner or later have that kind of experience. You feel frustrated, but also powerless, as the train relentlessly draws away from the station. The same kind of experience now faces churches that refuse to adapt. The train of post-modernity is leaving the station, and forms of Christianity that are wedded to the dying culture of modernity will eventually die with it. Evangelicals are faced with a crucial question: Can evangelical

convictions be separated from the modernistic culture which has been their breeding ground for so long? (p.245)

I have deliberately included, at some length, illustrations of rivers, lighthouses and trains, to remind us of the challenge of change, the plight of today's society and the danger of churches failing to react and adapt to a society in transit. A picture is worth a thousand words. Don Carson addressed a Scottish conference of ministers and pastors in 1999 on the subject of preaching. He no doubt shocked many (Presbyterian and Brethren alike), when he stated that 50% of the time in sermon preparation should be devoted to mastering the text; and 50% to making it relevant. It is too easy for us to take refuge in Paul's statement to Timothy that 'the time will come when men will not put up with sound doctrine'. I don't propose that we give people what they want to hear. But it is a priority that we engage with, and communicate to today's society. The challenge for us is to communicate the gospel in ways that are both relevant and accessible to postmodern man.

Increasingly I find myself preaching what I consider to be thoroughly researched, well crafted, and, hopefully, well delivered sermons: yet the honest seekers in the pews are not engaged. (I am taking it as read that the whole process is immersed in prayer, and I acknowledge fully the sovereignty of God and the power and unction of the Holy Spirit.)

John Drane articulates this dilemma much more eloquently than I can when he writes:

There are four elements in effective communication: the message (and the medium through which the message is channelled); the audience and their responses; the process of feedback; and the communicator, with his or her aspirations and intentions. The relation between these four is cyclical, and there is no 'right' place to begin the process of communication, though Christians generally start with their message. They have something to say; therefore they search for the best words with which to say it. Inevitably, starting at this point they tend to choose words that suit themselves. Christians are typically orientated towards ideas – either complex theological concepts, or something that looks much simpler but which in terms of communication still has inadequacies (an 'ABC of salvation'). The trouble is, most other people are somewhere else. Their starting point is not our message. I once heard someone complain that sermons were simply 'answers to questions no one is asking'. While I would not have thought of putting it quite like that, I immediately recognised what was being talked about, for I must have heard thousands of sermons that fitted that description: the only people who appreciate them are the ministers who preach them. Much of what we imagine is evangelism is just the same. Effective communication involves a lot more than merely presenting a message. This is nothing to do with the truth or otherwise of what our message is, for it is perfectly possible for a thing to be 100% true, and yet totally irrelevant. (p.78)

Don Palmer in his chapter (15) in this handbook on 'Church-based evangelism' addresses some of the practicalities of this problem and earths them in the reality of church life. What I am seeking to do is to highlight the wider problem of evangelism in a postmodern world, and to examine whether our conditioning as a church has led us to the current state where our theology and spirituality suffer from a cognitive captivity that inhibits the development of a truly holistic gospel that will speak authentically to the needs of people in a postmodern world. Do we accept these implications? If so, this will be a huge challenge to the status quo for it will require us to put into reverse gear the way most of our churches operate. Reverse gear, of course, cannot be engaged while the vehicle is still moving forward in a given direction. My plea is that we 'stand still' and assess our message of salvation.

Identifying the cultural context

Crucial to how we present the message of salvation will be the cultural context in which it is communicated. Jesus knew how to be culturally relevant and yet call people to repentance. Supremely he demonstrated the need to bridge the gap. He incarnationally embraced the life of a Galilean peasant under Roman occupation and communicated in 'word and deed' in a way, and at a level, that was accessible to the common people. I recall Joseph d'Sousa, the director of OM India, saying 'India needs spiritually broken people: India needs culturally broken people'. So does Britain!

Too often, we seek to impose on genuine seekers our ecclesiastical and cultural baggage. I heard a story (it may be apocryphal) of a missionary who took the gospel to a remote tribe whose women were in the habit of 'going topless'. Some time later a visitor reported that some of the women who had been converted were still 'topless' but were now wearing hats! What a contrast to Hudson Taylor who rejected a monocultural approach to world mission, adopted a Chinese lifestyle and in so doing alienated his fellow missionaries, but furthered the gospel.

Paul's approach to 'Jews and Godfearers' at Pisidian Antioch

(Acts 13) is different from his approach to cynical sceptics on Mars Hill in Athens (Acts 17). The rules of engagement were totally different. The culture and context shaped his approach to the core of his message. Of course, some of today's ecclesiastically and theologically correct 'police' presume to criticise Paul for getting it wrong in Athens. Many times I have been 'shaken warmly by the throat', at the door, by some of that ilk when I have dared to preach on Paul's sermon on Mars Hill. 'The results weren't good, son! Paul then went to Corinth and "resolved to know nothing among them except Jesus Christ and him crucified". You go away and think about that.'

It is for each of us, in our own community, to adopt and adapt an evangelistic strategy tailored to local needs and idiosyncrasies. 'We need to remember that culture is not a national characteristic, but a local phenomenon. Even in the same town there will be several different cultures, each with their own questions and potential entry points for the gospel . . . This is why it makes more sense for us to share our attitudes to evangelism, rather than our blueprints.' (John Drane)

Revising our approach

Most experts on this subject (I am not one) stress the fundamental need to rediscover community as a central part of Christian faith and practice. 'God the Holy Trinity is community, and in that community of love we find our identity in the post-modern sea of shifting images and personal fragmentation. Jesus' command has never been more relevant: "As I have loved you, so you must love one another. By this (everyone) will know that you are my disciples." If we cannot demonstrably love one another, we might as well pack up.' (Nick Mercer)

Rather than offer specific personal revisions of approach, I feel I can do no better than offer Rob Warner's suggestions for a postmodern evangelicalism (I also urge you strongly to buy his book and John Drane's).

What then are some of the key ingredients for an evangelicalism reconfigured for the post-modern world?

- We need to recover a biblical *humility*. Our vision and theology are incomplete, for we see through a glass darkly. The apostle Paul is a great hero of evangelical exposition, and we need to recover his emphasis upon the mystery of the gospel. Anyone who thinks they have sewn up every last detail of Christian doctrine understands very much less than they suppose.

- We need to learn better how to be *generous* and *gracious*, both to one another and particularly to non-Evangelicals, recognising our common faith even where there is much disagreement among us on secondary issues. We also need to affirm that evangelicalism finds its place within orthodox Christianity, but is by no means the sum of orthodox expressions of faith.

- We need to create a climate of *openness*, learning once again to be creative, willing to experiment and eager to explore, both in theology and church life. The Word does not change, but we need to be open to new insights and applications derived from eternal truths of biblical revelation.

- We need to concentrate upon *guarding the essential gospel* rather than our particular package deal. While not dispensing with gospel essentials, we must be careful not to major on minors, over-emphasising our secondary concerns.

- We need to discover more about the *creative exploration and application of the gospel in a new cultural setting*. We should never change the heart of the gospel, but its expression always needs to be made new.

- We need to demonstrate a fresh willingness to *separate out the timeless gospel* from the cultural clothes of modernistic evangelicalism. The Bible is surely designed always to confront the subtle compromises of our ways of being church and pursuing the life of discipleship, and never should be so misread as merely to reinforce our instinctive theological and cultural prejudices.

- We need a style of preaching *that makes no claims to have all the answers*. We don't need preachers who impose upon us with overbearing authoritarianism, promoting specious standardisation for every Christian's prayer life, marriage, successful career and so on, often developing a compilation of mythical stereotypes of narrow saintly conformity. We are fellow sinners, understanding only partially the implications of the gospel and giving no more than a fragmentary expression to the gospel in our daily lives, so we need to beckon one another onward. The idea is not that others should meet us where we have already arrived, but that they should join us in a voyage of spiritual discovery, exploring and discovering a fuller, deeper conformity to the ways of Christ. We are fellow pilgrims, working out together what it means to live as 21st century disciples.

- We need to be more concerned with conforming to the

character and values of Jesus Christ than with the conventions of traditional evangelicalism. The disciples of Christ need to look a lot more like him if we are to make any significant headway and bridge our credibility gap to the generations of the 21st century. (pp. 256ff)

As Nick Mercer puts it: 'Post-modernity is a way of coping with life. It does not make sense of it. Christianity is also a way of coping *and also* a way of making sense of life. We need to let God grasp people's hearts and imaginations before we can restore their minds. Evangelism has never been easier; discipleship has never been harder.'

Further reading

J Drane, *Faith in a Changing Culture* (Marshall Pickering, revised & expanded, 1997). Quotations from this book are used by permission of HarperCollins Publishers Ltd.

R Warner, *21st Century Church* (Kingsway, revised & expanded, 1999). Quotations from this book are used by permission of Kingsway Publications, Lottbridge Drove, Eastbourne BN23 6NT.

CHAPTER FIFTEEN

Church-based Evangelism

DON PALMER

There seems to be a growing consensus that, in the words of Scottish evangelical theologian and historian, David Wright, 'A local congregation renewed for mission is God's primary evangelistic agency.' Similar sentiments are to be found in the writings of men like Bill Hybels, Robert Warren and Rick Warren who seem to be saying, in the words of David Watson's book title, 'I believe in the church'.

Whenever we hear of churches that are successful in their evangelism, we want to know their secret. People's attitudes range from an insistence on being faithful to the gospel and our particular heritage to a willingness to use whatever contemporary gimmick seems to work. I feel that *both* have lost the point. Those who want to remain faithful have forgotten much of Jesus' teaching and method of reaching people; and those who are attracted by the latest technique produce decisions without discipleship, and become discouraged. Even Paul's strategy – if he had one, apart from preaching in synagogues and discipling believers – was for his time and world. I believe that the NT does not give us a blueprint for evangelism any more than it does for church government.

In a highly significant book published recently on evangelism through the local church, *Natural Church Development Handbook*, Christian A Schwarz's basic premise is that church growth (and evangelism) is natural, or biotic. That is, instead of setting out the latest man-made technique for reaching others and building the church, we need rather to rediscover the in-built laws for growth, which God has already placed within the living organism, his church or body. He states: 'We should not attempt to manufacture church growth, but rather to release the biotic potential which God has put into every church. It is our task to minimise the obstacles to growth – both inside and outside the church.'

Similarly, in his typically Southern Californian way, Rick Warren states:

Surfing is the art of riding the waves that God builds. God makes the waves: surfers just ride them . . . A lot of books and conferences fall into the 'How to do it' category, trying to manufacture the wave of God's Spirit using gimmicks, programs or marketing techniques to create growth . . . but only God makes the church grow (cf 1 Cor 3: 6) . . . Our job as church leaders is to recognise a wave of God's Spirit and ride it . . . to recognise how God is working today in the world and join him in the endeavour . . .We shouldn't be asking "What will make our church grow?" . . . The question we need to be asking is: "What is keeping our church from growing?" What barriers, obstacles and hindrances are preventing growth from happening? All living things grow – you don't have to make them grow. It's the natural thing for living organisms to do if they are healthy.

So I want to share commonly accepted principles, which operate in a healthy church. I am convinced, through what I read, and through personal experience in York, that, where any church concentrates on removing the obstacles to growth and seeks to develop a healthy, friendly, biblically functioning community, such a church will grow and become evangelistically effective.

Signs of a healthy (i.e. biblically functioning community) church

'Are there distinctive quality characteristics which are more developed in growing churches than in those which are not growing?' asks Schwarz. There follow some observable principles, which seem to be emerging time and again wherever one reads and whatever type of growing church one observes. Though it would be a mistake to copy another church slavishly, especially one at a different stage of growth, there are proven principles which can be applied locally. The following are suggested as gauges to determine the health and potential for growth of your church.

Constant prayer
This must be at the heart of any church which wants to grow and be effective in its evangelism and pastoral care. It goes even deeper than having right beliefs or being orthodox. Prayer in the individual's life and built into the structure of the church's life is possibly the essential ingredient. It is a humble recognition of who God is and that we can achieve success only through him. It shows we want to hear from him and see clearly a vision of what our local church can be.

Respect for biblical authority

As well as committing themselves to prayer, the first Christian community devoted themselves to 'the teaching of the Apostles'. Here is the foundation for what we believe about God, the world and ourselves. How should we live? Why do we make disciples, baptise, and teach? Only the revealed word of God should be the foundation for shaping our world view and morals/values. To make anything else central in our life and worship is to destroy our very raison d'être.

Effective leadership

Schwarz describes this as 'empowering leadership'. Research indicates that churches which are growing – both in quantity and quality – are led by men and women with leadership gifts and servant hearts. As clearly instructed in Ephesians 4:12, such leaders concentrate on empowering other Christians for ministry. They don't merely use members to help gain their own goals of fulfilling their own ambitions. Rather they have a clear vision of what the local church should and could be. They keep people focused on it, incorporating others into the fulfilment of that vision and purpose.

Mobilised membership

We believe that it is God who assigns ministries and gifts in the local church. Leaders should ensure that this is recognised and practised. Schwarz puts it powerfully: 'The discovery and use of spiritual gifts is the only way to live out the Reformation watchword of the "priesthood of all believers" [men and women!] . . . yet in a survey of 1600 active Christians, 80% could not identify their gifts. This appears to be one of the primary reasons why the "priesthood of all believers" has, for the most part, never been achieved in the lands of the Reformation.'

Eventful worship

This means worship which is inspired by the Holy Spirit, so that it is living and dynamic. This is not about feeling good. True worship means encountering the living God and being moved and changed by the experience. There is also, as Rick Warren has said, 'incredible persuasive power in the witness of a crowd of believers worshipping together'. He gives twelve sound, practical reasons why worship should be used, even at an evangelistic seeker-service. There is ample evidence that that is what was taking place in Acts 2: 1-12 among the first disciples.

Continuous evangelism

Some churches wake up and realise they haven't had special evangelistic meetings for some time. So they have them, with elaborate publicity and an imported evangelist. Occasionally they see results and feel better for having engaged in evangelism. This is not the sign of a healthy, growing and effective church. It is ongoing and relevant evangelism that is a clear sign that a local church is living up to what Bill Hybels calls 'its redemptive potential'. Evidence points to the fact that most people come to faith gradually, usually as a result of the influence of a friend. Building relationships with unchurched friends and neighbours is the soil for effective evangelism. If our churches have little or no contact with 'the world', then structures and attitudes within them need to change. Peter Wagner estimates than less than 10% of Christians have a gift in evangelism. For most of us, it's a matter of building friendships, focusing on the needs and questions raised, and using our gifts and time in response. It may be years before our friends are ready to attend a Sunday service. We need to be prepared for that. Some excellent training resources are available to help equip your local congregation. *Becoming a Contagious Christian* (part of a pack of books, videos and tapes produced by a team from Willow Creek Community Church and published by Zondervan in 1995) is one of the best. I can also recommend John Allan's superb book *Rescue Shop* (Paternoster, 1988) and a very useful 26-page booklet by Janice Price called *Telling your Faith Story* (Church House Publishing, 1999).

Community life

One of the most difficult decisions we had to reach when starting our church in York at the end of 1993 was what to call ourselves. Eventually we decided on 'Community Church' because we are a *church* (and most people can relate to what that means, even if they do put more stress on the building than the people); and we are a *community* of people who exist for and in a local area as a visible Christian presence of the kingdom of God. 'Community' stresses what we become, so that when individuals come into contact with us they sense something of the presence of God. It has been well stated that 'people are looking to belong before they are looking to believe'. And it is still true, as we know from experience. I believe this is the secret of the success of both Alpha and 'seeker-services'. Individuals enter into relationship with a group of Christians living in community, and what they see, hear, and experience becomes all the more relevant to their own lives. This is what we see, too, in the early church (Acts 2 – 4). Schwarz refers to these life-changing small groups, as 'holistic small groups' in which individuals can do more than listen; they can discuss the relevance of what they have heard to their daily lives and bring up their immediate questions, needs, and concerns. (See chapter 13 on 'Small groups'.)

Compassionate service

The epistle of James stresses that one's faith needs to be seen as well as heard. The old fear of the danger of preaching a 'social gospel' is no longer relevant. It is imperative for each church to sit down, seek God, and read their local newspapers looking for practical ways of meeting needs in the local community in the name of Christ. (See Chapter 16 on 'Serving the Community'.) Otherwise, their message will be ignored and their witness remain invisible.

Openness to change

One church in central Scotland, which has been in existence for at least twelve years, is still called 'West Glasgow New Church', because they believe in an unchanging God who is constantly doing 'new' things! That's what change is all about. Paul says: 'And we, who with unveiled faces all reflect the Lord's glory, are being transformed into his likeness with ever-increasing glory, which comes from the Lord, who is the Spirit' (2 Cor 3:18). A Christian or a church which is not constantly being changed by the sovereign activity of the Holy Spirit is either dead or dying! Our churches constantly need to adapt to be relevant to the needs of the world around them. Our church mission statement includes the words 'culturally relevant and biblically pure'.

Released resources

Finally, it costs time, effort, possessions and money. We are only stewards of whatever we possess for the advancement of the kingdom of God. A healthy church will be a generous church – not a church which 'buries its talents' in the ground. Paul indicates that our giving will be in direct comparison with the measure of the grace of God among us: 'Each one should give what he has decided in his heart to give, not reluctantly or under compulsion, for God loves a cheerful giver. And God is able to make all grace abound to you, so that in all things at all times, having all that you need, you will abound in every good work' (2 Cor 9:7-8).

Conclusion

I apologise if the above is not what you expected. If you were hoping for a list of books, techniques, initiatives that you could try, then you will be disappointed. If you require such, it is relatively easy to find what you are looking for in your local Christian bookshop, or through a local fraternal of church leaders where you can learn from what others have done.

I would commend to you as a plan of action that you do not content yourself with having read the principles listed above, but that you analyse where you are now in each area, project where you want to be in a set period of time, and then decide how you intend to get there. And I strongly recommend that you discuss this with the congregation and carry them with you on each step of the process.

Further reading

B Hybels, *Rediscovering Church* (Zondervan, 1995)
C A Schwarz, *Natural Church Development Handbook* (BCGA, 3rd ed., 1998)
R Warren, *The Purpose Driven Church* (Zondervan, 1995)
R Warren, *Launching a Missionary Congregation* (CPAS, 1995)
D Wright, *Local Church Evangelism* (St Andrew Press, 1987)

CHAPTER SIXTEEN

Serving the Community

FRAN BECKETT

Overload could overwhelm us as we turn to yet another aspect of church life and how to manage it better; that is, if we see them as so many activities or projects that we must struggle to support in our own strength. Instead, we should realise that churches are groups of people who have the person and passion of the living God at the centre of their life together, as well as individually, and out of this flows the vision and capacity to embrace God's priorities, expressing his heart for the world around us in relevant accessible ways.

Reasons for action

So much of what we should be about as Christians concerns engagement with the world around us. We cannot read the Bible without encountering a God who is deeply, passionately committed to people, the most breathtaking expression of this being in the person of Jesus Christ.

Literally hundreds of verses reflect God's concern for those who are poor and marginalised, with God himself described as the defender of the poor (Psa 146:6-9). The white-hot intensity of his anger against injustice rings down through the centuries to us through the voices of men such as Amos and Nahum. And the implications for us are clearly spelt out in Jeremiah 22:13-16 where we are unequivocally told that we don't know God properly if we fail to seek justice for the poor. Intimacy of relationship with God is vividly described in Isaiah 58 with the consequences impacting all areas of life, in particular being expressed through an active commitment to social concern and justice. An integral part of Jesus' ministry was going around 'doing good' (Acts 10:38), and the lifestyle of disciples such as Dorcas (Acts 9:36-42) challenges us today.

At the heart of the Godhead, in the mystery of the Trinity, is community. The Bible exposes us repeatedly to God's commitment to people being in life-affirming relationships with each other. His investment into building communities which are to be characterised by integrity, generosity and compassion is plain to see. How can we then fail to embrace his concerns, and be indifferent to the fragmenting communities and broken lives around us?

Yet maybe it's not as simple as that for those of us who struggle with the social action and evangelism debate. The answers to some key questions posed by Ron Sider in *Evangelism and Social Action* will help us see where we stand, as well as challenge our thinking. How should we understand sin? Is it just personal, or do we encounter it also in unjust structures and oppressive systems such as those that perpetuate racism or oppress women? When we think about people, we need to consider whether there really is (as is so often suggested) some kind of separation between 'soul' and body; how we understand wholeness in all its implications for those with disabilities; and how important community is for people.

Then there is salvation and the means of sharing the gospel. Is salvation only individual in its implications, an escape from the wrath to come and out of the world's evil? Or is there something more, to do with salvation now, which involves escape from the world's evil but not the world itself? Is it possible to communicate the gospel with actions as well as words?

Our understanding of Jesus' return is of relevance here, as well. Whether we see the world as a sinking ocean liner from which we need to rescue as many souls as possible, or believe that God intends to conquer the evil that has invaded his good creation, transforming the world, will affect how we engage with society. And if we believe that Christians should seek to impact society there is the question about how society is changed. Is it only as individuals are converted, or can it be through working for change in the social systems? And what is the role of the alternative lifestyle, the model, of Jesus' new community, namely the church?

The imperative of relevance

The answers to these questions, and our consequent response as we are moved to act by the God who is described in the Bible, have a context. We live in a fast-changing world and the necessity of relevance in what we do is undeniable. Yet, tragically, too often Christians are spending time answering questions that people are no longer asking and investing in activities that fail to touch people's felt needs or aspirations.

Perceptions of the church have changed with many seeing it as largely irrelevant. No longer is it the place where people readily turn for help. This is against a backdrop of significant change in how society functions. A marked decline in a sense of neighbourhood and community based on meaningful contact has had quite profound effects on people's experience of belonging. Demographic changes mean that the early years of the 21st century will see in the UK a dramatic rise in the number of single-person households, and an increasingly ageing population with all the problems of isolation and need of care that this will bring.

Current Government social policy with its emphasis on tackling social exclusion, yet limited effective means of narrowing the gap between rich and poor, looks likely to continue in the years to come. Central to this is the decreasing role of the Welfare State, the emphasis on self-help, and the opportunity for other groups to play a key part in providing care for the more vulnerable members of society. This, coupled with Government policy geared to community regeneration and building community responses to local need, provides exciting opportunities for action by churches.

All that we have considered thus far amply demonstrates that there is both a need and a place for churches to get involved in serving their local communities. In order to ensure relevance in so doing, there are a number of issues to grapple with. We need to be clear what we mean when we talk about 'the community', and we also need to be good listeners before as well as throughout our service of the community.

The word 'community' is used in a variety of different ways, and how we understand it will shape our responses. It can mean a geographical area such as an estate or an electoral ward with landmarks and natural boundaries including main roads or railway lines. A community can also be a group of people who have a common sense of identity rooted in lifestyle or ethnic origin. There are also groups of people who form a community of common interest. To illustrate from where I live, people talk about the Nunhead community as a geographical area with a row of small shops and a green at its centre. Within Nunhead and beyond its geographical borders there is a strong Irish community with much of its social life revolving around the local Catholic church and a few Irish pubs and clubs. People from different backgrounds in the area are linked with a local school, having a common interest in the education of young children.

When considering how best to serve the community it is always worthwhile to do some homework. This involves listening to the facts and also to what people have to say, all within a context of actively listening to God. It can involve the use of public opinion surveys that genuinely seek the views of local people and are not just a covert way of proclaiming the gospel. The results can be published in the local press and be a positive foundation on which to build credible local action. To demonstrate a genuine commitment to listen to the aspirations of the public accords people dignity, and says that their views count, which is something we are not always good at in the church. At the very least, such an exercise begins to put a human face to the church. However, don't do this unless you intend to follow it through with some form of action.

Factual information includes census information that gives the age profile and other details of those who live in the area you are focusing upon. Local authorities each year update their Community Care Plan and from this you can identify not just areas of social need but also their priorities and means of tackling them. If subsequently looking for funding, such information can be invaluable. Other churches or community groups may have carried out a community audit, so avoid reinventing the wheel if possible. Information can often be gained from libraries and town halls about organisations working in the locality, and many areas have some sort of Council for Voluntary Service which, as umbrella bodies for voluntary groups, can supply information about who is doing what in relation to particular needs.

In addition, take the time to build relationships with key professionals and others who are informal 'gatekeepers' into the community. The long-term benefits can be great and in the short term it will help build your picture of what needs exist, as well as of those to whom you can turn for assistance at a later date.

Engaging the church

If your local church is to get involved in serving the community it is essential that the members are enabled to engage in some way with it as early as possible in the process. This includes consultation on their views on local needs, finding out where their networks are, and identifying with them their gifts, availability and vision. This should be set within a context of biblical teaching about God's concern for the community and our role within that. Those already involved with social need in a voluntary or employed capacity should be affirmed and supported. Regular prayer for community needs and occasional introduction of community figures, whether Christian or not, such as head teachers, police officers and local politicians, all serves to build the church's awareness and vision.

Your church resources may be limited and so you may decide to try to get a grant for someone to do the research on the church's behalf. Whilst this is certainly possible, ensure that ways of informing and involving the church throughout are identified so that there can be true ownership of the outcomes. And whatever activity or project is subsequently developed, ensure that it is kept at the centre of the life of the church rather than tacked on to the edge. To fail to do so, can create problems in the long term. In addition, if as a result of the church's community involvement unchurched people come into the church, how will the church be enabled to respond positively?

Into action

Let us assume that the church is now ready for action. Be realistic about what you do. Start small and, if possible, start from where you are if there are already some contacts or experience. Be clear about what you are seeking to achieve and make sure that the church and those more directly involved understand the expectations that surround the initiative. Is this about improving the quality of individuals' lives, building more of a sense of local community, or getting people into church on Sunday? Where will praying with people, and sharing the gospel, fit in what you do, if at all? How overtly Christian are you going to be? However small or large the church's initiative, have some idea what will constitute success, and also give some thought to how, humanly speaking, the initiative can be sustained.

It may be that the church's starting point has been some existing activity such as a playgroup or senior citizens' gathering. The exploratory preparation above is still important, and you will still need to decide what approach to adopt in the future. Is partnership with others an option? Ensure that there is clarity around expectations, responsibilities and review, and ensure that there is enough shared vision at the outset.

There is a wide range of possible approaches to involvement. These include setting up a specialist project that can act as a bridge between the church and the community, such as an advice centre, a support group for carers of partners, or children with special care needs, or training for long-term unemployed people. You may wish to see your church buildings more fully utilised and so turn them into a multi-purpose community centre open to a range of community groups, including those who run church activities. Alternatively, you may decide to focus upon one particular area of need and run a family centre with a nursery, after-school clubs or parenting classes on your premises. If you have particularly large premises there may be scope for redevelopment in partnership with another organisation in providing accommodation for people such as those with learning disabilities or those recovering from mental illness.

These ideas may be too big for you to start with, let alone sustain, so maybe an annual community weekend or week would be more appropriate. Here the church could concentrate on practical tasks in the community such as gardening, clearing waste from communal areas, decorating, and holding a community fun day with food, games and a bouncy castle. An annual Christmas community meal for those who are older or on their own could be offered. Using your premises as a night shelter for homeless people in the cold winter months is another possibility, albeit risky for those to whom the church buildings are more important than people!

A local 'Good Neighbours' scheme could be established, elderly people or young people with disabilities could be befriended and supported by accompanying them on shopping or recreational trips. The church can also serve the community not by setting up new projects but by actively supporting individuals as they get involved with other local groups such as the Citizens Advice Bureau, or in becoming school governors or involved in local politics. Youth mentoring schemes exist in some localities, as do opportunities for professionals to give their services voluntarily in areas such as legal or financial advice. Supporting people involved in this way should include the recognition that this will take up time and therefore potentially restrict their involvement in other church activities.

Conclusion

The possibilities are endless but what is essential is a clear sense of the call of God upon what you do, active dependence upon him within it, and a practical realism that ensures both being able to learn from experience and being relevant in all that you undertake. If as a result people experience at first hand the deep and passionate love of our God it will have been worth it.

Further reading

F Beckett, *Called to Action* (Collins, 1989 – only available from the Shaftesbury Society)

D Evans and M Fearon, *From Strangers to Neighbours* (Hodder & Stoughton, 1998)

T Gibson, *The Do-ers Guide to Planning for Real* (The Neighbourhood Initiatives Foundation, 1998)

A Hope and S Timmel, *Training for Transformation*, Books 1, 2 & 3. *A Handbook for Community Involvement* (Mambo Press, rev. ed. 1995)

Resources / Packs

A Stricklen and J Mckinnon – *The Purple Packs for Planning Projects* (Southwark Diocesan Board for Church in Society, 1996 – 1999)

Action for Change – A subscription-based scheme to enable and practically support church community involvement (The Shaftesbury Society, 023-8239-5555)

Planning for Real – A tool for community-led neighbourhood improvement (The Neighbourhood Initiatives Foundation, 01952-590777)

Working for a Whole World – Video resource available from World Vision UK (599 Avebury Boulevarde, Milton Keynes MK9 3PG)

The Toolkit – A practice-based guide to participation within the community (TEAR Fund UK Regional Team, 100 Church Rd., Teddington, Middlesex TW11 8QE)

Organisations

The Shaftesbury Society, Development Department, 16 Kingston Road, Wimbledon, London SW19 1JZ

Oasis Trust, 115 Southwark Bridge Road, London SE1 0AX

TEAR Fund, UK Regional Team, 100 Church Rd., Teddington, Middlesex TW11 8QE

CHAPTER SEVENTEEN

Stimulating Involvement in World Mission

BARBARA BAIGENT

What memories are conjured up by the words 'missionary' and 'missionary meeting'! They include the 'missionary sewing class' where devout ladies sat around sewing, knitting and making up parcels for people in remote parts; or a slide show, probably highly interesting to those who prayed regularly for the people concerned, but to the rest of the church, especially the young people, deadly boring. Maybe, too, a missionary prayer meeting where letters were read from people we had never met and who obviously had needs but couched them in veiled language, being afraid to actually make them known. Or it may have been the Sunday for the missionary offering which 'today will be divided between Messrs. Brown, Black and White, working in three of the four corners of the earth, £20 each.'

These four illustrations highlight what leaves people uninterested in mission today and should set us thinking about strategies to improve the way we motivate people.

Don't leave it to the women: try a mission co-ordinator

The leadership of the church must be the motivators both to support existing mission and to extend it. Only God by his Holy Spirit can bring about motivated leadership.

Fifteen years ago our church had sent no one abroad, although we supported a large number of 'Echoes' missionaries in a rather unthinking way. The new leadership began to pray and to set targets for growth and vision, asking the Lord for a member to be called abroad in mission. Five years later we had five members commended and now five children as well! Don't belittle the power of prayer and vision!

If the church leaders are unconcerned about mission they need to change, or put into position a deacon or co-ordinator for mission, who may be male or female. A mission co-ordinator could be responsible for areas like the following:

To promote mission within the church fellowship by:
- arranging special speakers;
- writing articles for the church magazine to educate and inform about mission;
- keeping the church informed of the prayer requests of 'home-grown' members abroad;
- making the church aware of short- and long-term opportunities;
- encouraging specific participation by church members.

To be responsible for the collection and distribution of funds for mission:
- to encourage and promote giving through covenant and for specific projects;
- to raise funds for short-term experience.

To build and maintain links between the church fellowship and its members abroad
- by prayer, letters, e-mails and telephone calls;
- by sending birthday cards and gifts;
- by encouraging church members to visit members abroad.

To provide support for furloughs and re-entry of members abroad into theUK.

Don't try to cover the whole world at once

Aim to concentrate on just a few countries or people at first. If you have members of your own fellowship abroad who need support, begin with them. Make sure that all the church members get to know them when they are at home; that their prayer letters are photocopied and distributed to all church members; that members are aware how much they receive financially and whether or not this keeps up with inflation, etc.

Try to encourage people to go out and visit them. Church leaders should go and take a younger person with them if possible. Encourage people to send e-mails (fewer people have the gift of letter writing today).

If your fellowship does not have any of its own members abroad, choose someone from a nearby church or an 'Echoes ' missionary who lives near to you; or someone from an agency such as Tearfund, OM, Interserve who can visit you regularly. Today people like to support individuals they know or projects such as 'The Good Shepherd' project, OM India, or the Logos and Doulos ship projects, or the SGM 'Street Kids' project.

Don't leave it to a video or slide show

If you choose a person or a family, you must ensure that you can meet them regularly and get to know them as a church fellowship. There will be more support for those you know than for those whom people have never met.

We have two families abroad who were commended from our London church and from Scotland. They spend five months of their six-month furlough in Scotland (where it is cheaper to live) and one month in London, when they live with a couple in the church fellowship. This gives them opportunity to speak on Sundays, visit all the house groups in the week and have meals with people.

Don't relegate mission to a back seat

Give mission a high profile. Replace your Sunday morning teaching ministry four times a year with a mission Sunday. The whole church will be present on Sunday morning – more than you would ever get out to a 'missionary meeting'. Have a lively presentation, or get to know a couple better, or support a network that you didn't know about before.

In one year in our church the four Sundays covered (1) our own members abroad in Istanbul, (2) the COCM – Chinese Overseas Christian Mission – whose headquarters are 100 yards from our church, (3) ROPE – Relief for Oppressed People Everywhere, which is a relief organisation covering the whole world, (4) a session on short-term mission in which the chairs were arranged in five circles of 10 or 12, and five people who had been abroad during the summer gave a five-minute presentation of their experience to each group in turn. Other initiatives could be a Tearfund Sunday or a Suffering Church Sunday.

Liven up your prayer meetings

Since a young woman of 30 became our prayer ministry leader, our prayer meetings have been revolutionised. Sometimes we have a week of prayer and fasting from the media – no newspapers, radio, TV or videos; another time it may be prayer and fasting from drinking tea, coffee or Coke; or we may do a prayer walk and pray for the neighbourhood. When the prayer meeting is in the building we may do something different every 10 minutes of the hour – dividing into four and praying in four corners of the room for different countries or people (with maps and photographs to help us); praying in pairs for specific needs; praying in fours or fives for some world situation; splitting into two halves, half watching a short video whilst the others are praying, then vice versa.

We often begin with 20 minutes of worship and organise a few young people to lead this on flute, guitar and keyboard. This usually means that their boy/girl friends come too, so there are the first six people for the prayer meeting!

Publicise the giving to mission

Don't be afraid to set targets for regular giving. If as a church you believe that 30% of the total giving should go to mission (which is a good minimum ideal!) publicise how much this is and let the. church know how it is to be distributed. People will get excited when targets are exceeded or when projects are successfully covered financially. When a lad went to Indonesia for a year between school and university, the young people collected £500 for his air ticket. When eight young men went to France with 'Christians in Football' the church gave £2,000 in one special collection.

We took the decision some years ago to stop sending £25 each to twelve people, who were not much more than names to us and, instead, to send £300 to a person or family we could be much more involved with. This strategy itself increased the giving.

We give our monthly mission offering to our own mission workers and then set aside the four annual offerings on the months with fifth Sundays for other people in mission. One of these offerings is always set aside for short-term mission to enable our own people to go abroad in the summer or to visit mission situations.

Set an example as church leaders

Our last full-time elder was a man of vision who listens for God's directions. He believes the best way to interest people in mission is to visit those working abroad and take someone with him. He has friends in Serbia and before the Kosovo crisis he took a young couple there for a week. It was life-changing for that couple. At the height of the Kosovo troubles he drove to the Hungarian border with Serbia to bring out the English wife of his friend who was in danger and unwell. This sort of adventure excites the church. A couple have been to both Istanbul and Pakistan recently to encourage our workers there. Such 'living on the edge' is stimulating and I personally found watching those who work with the poor extremely challenging.

Encourage holidays and trips abroad

Don't go to the usual tourist places but on expeditions like those arranged by Oak Hall – often they meet local Christians so that you can get the feel of the church abroad, with its needs and strategies, in places as different as Iceland and Zimbabwe, Mexico and Nepal, Peru and the Philippines. There are also many opportunities for short-term trips abroad where Christians can experience mission. Discover which is most relevant to your local church by consulting the 'Short Term Service Directory' from Christian Vocations, Holloway Street West, Dudley DY3 2DZ.

Our church faces a common with football pitches, so much of our evangelism is done through football. Each summer two couples visit France with 'Christians in Football'. Others have gone on Oasis, Youth for Christ and STEP teams. Remember, too, that for a Londoner to go to Yorkshire with the gospel is as much 'cross-cultural evangelism' as for a Nigerian to come to London; and having made the break, the following year much further afield to a different country might not seem too daunting.

Involve the whole church in the re-entry of members from abroad

Of course, this can only apply if your church *has* members abroad! Make sure everyone is aware who is coming home, what they look like, where they will be living and when they are expected. If your church is growing and changing, the returning members may not know half of the church and most of the worship songs you are singing!

The mission co-ordinator and team may have to find a house for those returning to live in – and if it is empty, furnish it. Very few missionary homes are available now and often a family cannot be accommodated with relatives. Today it is too expensive to rent a place in London for six months.

If they *are* located nearby, organise different church members to give invitations for meals; provide an initial welcome box of groceries; accompany them shopping in the supermarket, because there is a high level of 'reverse culture shock' when re-entering Britain with its vast choice of goods. Give them an idea of current prices; introduce them to the church on their first Sunday back but don't overburden them with new faces and engagements – they are home for a rest. Make sure they get around to visiting every house group.

It is also a good idea to have a 'de-briefing questionnaire'. This should be given to returning church members shortly after their arrival back on each furlough. It asks questions like: Did you achieve what you set out to do? Were there any disappointments?; Any areas of frustration or of conflict? How would you have done things differently? What hopes and aims do you have for the future? The questionnaire may be answered in private but it is a good thing for it to be worked through later with the church leaders and mission co-ordinator who can pray over it together with the returnees.

The church should also ensure that those returning have a medical check-up, such as that offered by Interhealth, and that they have a proper holiday. Maybe, too, they need a refresher course on a specific topic. When they are about to return abroad, arrange a farewell and give them a spot in the Sunday service to say goodbye. Our Sunday school children present the departing children with little gifts.

Get someone from the fellowship to send them tapes of the services or photographs of new members and encourage others to send viewcards from holiday, birthday cards and wedding anniversary cards.

Get round the problems

Yes, there are problems – lack of time, lack of interest, less than brilliant speakers to captivate the interest, minimal opportunity – but as leaders we must be positive, enthuse and aim at targets within our reach. There is no longer a 'Brethren missionary meeting' locally in this area and we only have one main service on Sundays so we cannot be forever having speakers from abroad or we would lose the flow of the Bible teaching. But we reserve four main Sunday services a year for mission and in this way have the whole church present instead of a handful.

We do not have a regular monthly mission prayer meeting but we have prayer in house groups every week and a mission prayer meeting about three times a year. We are not good at sending parcels abroad – all too often the cost of the postage is more than the cost of the contents. But we do try to visit once every two years and take goodies with us. Neither are we very good at sending tapes, videos and photographs, but we do send the church magazine every month and letters, e-mails and birthday cards.

Only when you yourself have visited do you realise what joy the local children have in receiving a comb, pencil, ruler, rubber or pencil sharpener sellotaped on to the back of an old Christmas card; or how new mothers love to receive a good quality second-hand sleep-suit or a little blanket for the baby. And only when you have been there do you know what it feels like to be the only one not to receive post in the mail-box; to be too far away from home to pick up the phone and talk for twenty minutes; to be unable to get cow's milk, tea-bags, cheddar cheese, Cadbury's chocolate, a paper with a crossword in it or the latest book from the library; to smell the scent of roses or trample through autumn leaves; to relax in a deep foaming bath or spend 24 hours in peace and private.

Why bother with mission?

When we look at the Psalms, the song book of the Jews, we find at least 12 references to all nations, the whole world, coming to give God glory and praise. Psalm 8:11 is a good example ('Proclaim among the nations what he has done'). Others include Psalms 18:49; 67:4; 86:9; 96:3; 97:1; 98:2; 105:1; 108:3; 113:3; 117:1; 145:12. God intended that Israel should be a God-fearing, holy people to show him and his covenant love to the watching world. They failed. They turned to worship the gods and idols of other nations. They forsook God, their husband, and committed adultery with other gods. Eventually they 'crucified the Lord of glory'.

So in the prophets God speaks of a future day when a new people of God will be given a similar chance to 'declare his glory' to the world. ('From the west they acclaim the Lord's majesty, therefore in the east give glory to the Lord; exalt the name of the Lord in the islands of the sea.' Isa 24:14, 15. Cf. also Isa 42:1; 45:22; 49:6; 56:7; 59:19; 66:19; Joel 2:28, 32; Amos 9:12; Mal 1:11.)

Between these prophecies and their fulfilment, Jesus came into the world to live, to suffer, to die, to rise again and to send his Holy Spirit upon the church, the new people of God, with the new commission fresh from the lips of the risen Christ (Matt 28:19; Mark 16:15; Luke 24:47).

Jesus had said: 'I, when I am lifted up from the earth, will draw all people to myself' (John 12:32). Are we going to fail the Lord as the people of Israel failed him? Are we going to turn to the gods of this world, to materialism, possessions, comfort, family ties, friendships or even to church activities? Or will we take our vision from the one that John saw as he penned his Revelation? 'After this I looked and there before me was a great multitude that no one could count, from every nation, tribe, people and language standing before the throne and in front of the Lamb. They were wearing white robes and were holding palm branches in their hands and they cried out in a loud voice "Salvation belongs to our God who sits on the throne and to the Lamb"' (Rev 7:9).

Some practical issues

Tent-making

We need to be aware of the opportunities to serve the Lord abroad while working in paid employment as one way of bringing the good news of God's love into countries where it no longer possible to have the word 'missionary' on one's passport. There are teachers, nurses, doctors, agriculturalists, engineers and many other professionals who can work in this way in countries such as Bangladesh, Afghanistan and those in North Africa.

Tent-dwelling

Although many people are called for life to a country, we need to guard against the 'house-building' mentality. Paul did not stay much longer than three years in any one place. He established a group of believers and left them (and the Holy Spirit!) to organise a church. It may be that we have made the mistake of staying too long as foreigners in one place in another country. Often the local church grows and matures when the missionaries leave. We should encourage long-term involvement in mission but church planting by expatriates should be short-term wherever possible. The local Christians are the best evangelists, but from the West we can send Bible teachers, for example, on short-term assignments.

Isaiah speaks of 'enlarging the place of your tent' (Isa 54:2). Patrick Johnstone comments on this passage : 'There is something dynamic about a tent. It is flexible...mobile...temporary; the very nature of a tent is impermanent. We have lost that concept of flexible, mobile and temporary structures as necessary for the church.' So we don't go to establish mini-Anglican, Methodist or Brethren churches which are copies of Western ones. We take the good news, God's word and allow the Holy Spirit to build the church.

Cross-cultural evangelism

What a joy it was when we visited Pakistan this summer to meet a Japanese lady who had been converted in Japan through an Irish missionary and was herself now working in Pakistan. Apart from English-speaking people, there were also young Christians working there from Sweden, Germany, Finland, Norway, Korea – all of whom had to learn English first in order to learn Urdu at the language school which was taught in English! We need to be reminded that the top ten sending countries of the *non-Western* world in 1988 were: India (8, 905); Congo (2, 731); Nigeria (2, 595); Myanmar (2, 560); Kenya (2, 242); Brazil (2, 040); Philippines (1, 814); Ghana (1, 545); Zimbabwe (1, 545); Korea (1, 184). (Source: Robin Thomson, *World Christian*, (Lynx/St John's Extension Studies, 1992, in P Johnstone, *The church is bigger than you think*).

The local church is the launch pad

How many people are working abroad from your church fellowship? *Operation World 1993* has compared the number of congregations of believers in a country with the numbers of members sent abroad on mission from that country. The surprising result is that only from Singapore has there been more than one missionary sent per congregation. On average the number is one for every eight churches. Norway, Finland and New Zealand have sent nearly one per church. How is your church doing? Will you be praying that in the next three years you will be able to send someone abroad? But watch out! It may be you!

Further reading

A Brown, *I Believe in Mission* (Hodder & Stoughton, 1997)
S Gaukroger, *Why Bother with Mission?* (IVP, 1996)
P Johnstone, *The Church is Bigger than You Think* (Christian Focus Publications/WEC, 1998)
P Johnstone, *Operation World* (21st Century Edition, Paternoster, 2001)
B Knell, *Encouraging World Mission* (Global Connections, 2001) (obtainable from Global Connections, 186 Kennington Park Road. London. SE11 4BT)

CHAPTER EIGHTEEN

Commendation for Service

PETER MAIDEN

At an important moment in the history of the church the Holy Spirit said to the worshipping church at Antioch: 'Set apart for me Barnabas and Saul to do the work to which I have called them' (Acts 13:2). Thus began a vast missionary enterprise of which the church around the world today is the magnificent result. This had been God's purpose from the beginning. In Genesis 12 we see God blessing Abraham's descendants, so that through him 'all peoples on earth will be blessed'. This theme is never lost, but we do not see the followers of Christ going to make disciples of all nations on a significant scale until Acts 13 when Paul and Barnabas, having been commended for service by the church in Antioch and rejected by Jews opposed to their message, declared: 'We now turn to the Gentiles.' (Acts 13:46)

The church today has a vital role to play in this eternal purpose of God. So central is this role to the church that I believe it is no exaggeration to say that a church is not a church in the NT sense of the word if the eternal purpose of God, to bring blessing to the nations, is not at the core of its existence. William Temple once declared that the church is the only society on earth that exists for the benefit of those who are not its members. We exist to worship God and to bring his blessings to the nations. In scripture and throughout the history of the church, God has been calling people to leave their normal employment and often their familiar surroundings to serve him on a full-time basis.

Who sends?

What is the role of a local church in this divine activity? I address this issue as a leader in a missionary society and as an elder in a local church. Often I hear dissatisfaction being expressed from both the sender and those sent. Those sent may feel that their sending churches are not truly interested in them. Sending churches often feel that, once the individual has received the financial support of the church, they are not interested in the sending churches.

The basic question is who calls and sends Christian workers. In Acts 13 the call was from God to Paul and Barnabas through the church leaders (v.2); 'the two of them were sent on their way by the Holy Spirit' (v.4). How does this happen? The NT indicates more than one way. In Acts 13 God spoke to the church leaders, and they spoke to the individuals involved. But when Barnabas and Saul faced such difficulties in their relationship that they parted company, they took the initiative in choosing their co-workers. 'Barnabas took Mark' (Acts 15:39); 'Paul chose Silas' (v.40). Paul obviously looked for the commendation of the church before moving off again (v.41) but he seems to have taken the initiative in choosing Silas and, later, Timothy (Acts 16:3). There is no evidence in the NT, however, of individuals doing their own thing. The church was not always the initiator but it was always consulted and involved in the sending of workers.

This is the heart of commendation. An individual senses the call of God to a particular ministry. The leadership of the church recognises the appropriate gifting and spiritual maturity of the person concerned, and calls the church to support them. The church then confirms the calling and sending of the Holy Spirit, and sends them out. So a church leader was able to write recently about his church: 'We minister today in India, Brazil, Japan, Uganda and the Philippines.' He was referring to the countries in which that church had serving missionaries and his language shows that the church which sent them viewed them as its representatives in those countries. In NT times there was a continuing relationship between the sending church and those it had sent. That was why at the end of their missionary journey, Paul and Barnabas reported back to the church which had sent them out (Acts 14:26-28).

These are the bare bones of the process. How is it working out in our churches today? One significant change from NT times is that in the vast majority of cases the initiative appears to be with the person who senses the call. I hear very few examples of what happened at Antioch – the Holy Spirit speaking to the church leadership about individuals in the congregation, and the leadership approaching them. Though, as I have already said, this is not the only way, I do believe that one of the responsibilities of elders is to be constantly listening to God and overseeing the congregation, seeking to discern those whom God may be calling into ministry.

Many churches today recognise that their role in commendation goes beyond a mere interview of the potential candidate and a valedictory service, and that they have a vital role to play in both the preparation of the candidate for ministry and the continuing care of the person sent. I commend this more serious approach to commendation, and would like to make some practical suggestions.

What is involved in commendation?

We need to recognise what we are saying when someone is commended. The church is saying: 'We know and have confidence in this person, concur with their sense of call, and believe that they are to some degree equipped and ready for the ministry towards which they are moving.'

The consequences of commending unsuitable or unprepared people are potentially very serious both for the individual concerned and for those with whom and among whom they are working. Therefore we should not be afraid to slow people down as they move towards involvement in Christian ministry, if this seems to be necessary. Often there is real enthusiasm at the thought of moving into full-time ministry, but we should encourage adequate preparation before the move is made. Evaluation should take place during the preparation process. It may become clear in some cases that it is right not only to slow them down but also to help them re-evaluate their sense of call, and suggest alternative vocations. It is better to ask the hard questions during the preparation process than when the move into ministry has taken place.

When it is clear that a person is being called into ministry a preparation or training process should be agreed. This process will depend on the person's spiritual maturity, ministry experience and the nature of the ministry to which they are called. Clearly, a person who is interested in a short term of service for a month or two will need different preparation from someone considering long-term service. The candidate for service could be assigned to an experienced Christian worker, within the congregation if possible, to assist them through the preparation programme. Retired Christian workers may be an excellent resource here.

Preparation for short-term work

Many Christians are now getting involved in a short period of training and mission involvement, normally between one and three months, often during the summer. I believe that these experiences are always valuable in the lives of those who participate. I remember talking to a missionary in Brest, France, who had recently arrived in the city with the intention of planting a church. He wanted to make it known in the city that he was there and was organising various events for the community. So we sent him a number of young people for a month. They distributed invitations to those events, played football with the young people, used sketch boards on the street corners. At the end of the month, hundreds of people knew of this missionary's existence and it provided a real 'kick start' for his church plant.

However, we should not underestimate the challenge of these experiences. The participants often meet new cultures and very different church situations from those at home, join teams with members from a variety of nations and church backgrounds, and face challenges they have not faced before. Those in church leadership should meet with those planning to get involved and suggest ways in which they might be prepared to handle them. Obviously any in the church who have had previous experience might be encouraged to meet with those going and share with them their experience. It is also good to help them think through the goals they hope to achieve through the experience and, soon after returning, meet for a time of debriefing. This could include asking whether anything has been experienced which they found to be difficult; whether they have learned things about themselves or their gifting which might lead to further training or to involvement in particular ministry in the church; whether they achieved their goals and if not why not.

Preparation for a 'gap year'

An increasing number are considering a year of Christian work as a 'gap year'. Again I believe this to be valuable, and many organisations are putting together some excellent programmes to accommodate such people. Clearly this is a much greater commitment and I believe that a brief preparation programme should be organised. It is crucial for those making such a commitment to be able to sustain themselves spiritually. Although many of the organisations put a high priority on pastoral care, participants will inevitably go through times of loneliness and will feel the pressure of living in what is often a very different situation from the one they are used to, as well as facing ministry pressures which, again, may be new to them. The ability to sustain a regular devotional life will be invaluable. The ability to adapt to new situations is also important. Covering subjects such as working with people from different theological, denominational and cultural backgrounds may save much agony for both individual and colleagues. However good the preparation, in most cases not everything will go smoothly, so some teaching on conflict resolution will be worthwhile. The need to communicate with those sending them, and how this might be done, should also be covered. It is also vitally important to discuss with all who are considering such involvement how they see it fitting into their long-term future. Don't be surprised if many are unsure about this, but encourage them to ask God to show them how the experience is likely to fit into their long-term future.

Preparation for long-term service

Those who are considering a longer term of service will need all the above and more. Depending on their planned ministry, special issues may need to be covered. Those going into a church planting ministry, for example, may benefit from a course on the principles of church planting . All who are planning long-term ministry will need to think about pension plans, retirement and, where children are involved, educational needs should also be fully discussed. In broad terms, the preparation programme could involve the following: time with an experienced worker; planned reading assignments; correspondence courses; involvement in the ministry of the sending church (this will not only be good training for future ministry but will provide a greater understanding of the sending church and will enable church members to get to know the person they are sending); special courses; Bible college training.

Where the person is to work with an organisation, it will avoid confusion and duplication if the preparation process is discussed together early in the process. A service of commendation in which the church expresses its commitment to the individual and vice versa will be meaningful for both. Again, where an organisation is involved there should be consultation and a joint commendation service.

Continuing communication along lines discussed before the person leaves is essential. This must be honest, not hiding problems and only highlighting successes. The information received must be carefully used by the church. If a number of workers have been sent it may be best to share the highlights with the whole church and to have a support group for each worker, with whom full information can be shared. If the church has house groups, each group might take an interest in one worker. With e-mail making regular and speedy communication possible, two-way relationship can be maintained. If there is to be intelligent prayer, then plans that the church is considering should be communicated in sufficient time for the person to be involved in the discussions. Tapes of church services may be another way in which the worker can be kept informed as well as receiving valuable spiritual input.

Travel is so easy nowadays that visits to workers can take place. They may include mutual evaluation and sharing in the ministry of the worker, but if the person is working with an organisation it will be wise to know their process of evaluation and the part that the church can play in it.

The time that the worker spends at home having a break should be well used. Make sure that it includes a real break. Are they able to afford a holiday? If not make it possible. Advise them about study courses which would be useful for them. Make sure you give them the right profile in the church. And don't forget that this is an ideal time for prayerful evaluation. (See chapter 17 on 'Stimulating involvement in world mission'.)

Conclusion

The damaging myth is getting around that the rest of the world no longer needs Christian workers from western nations. They are too expensive: let the western nations provide the funds and the two-thirds world the workers. I believe that the reality is that we need workers from throughout the world to go throughout the world, and that certainly includes our own nation. We still need churches which see the development, training, sending and caring for such workers as a privilege and a priority.

PART THREE

Church Management

CHAPTER NINETEEN

Church Membership

ALASTAIR PURSS

A church full of attenders is one thing: a church full of participating members and ministers is another. Many churches are full of sincere Christians, good people who regularly attend services, but do they really understand what the local church is all about and, more importantly, the part they should be playing in it? Rick Warren correctly points out in his book, *The Purpose Driven Church*, that we need church attenders before we can have participating members. Then he goes on to say: 'Once you've gathered your crowd of attenders you must begin the important task of forming them into a congregation of members. The crowd must become a Church.'

Is it enough simply to profess Christ? Is there really any need to identify oneself with a particular local church? Is it desirable to have a formal membership in a local church? What does it mean to be a member of a local church? These are some of the questions I have been facing in the church I serve and what follows is based on our attempts to find answers.

Is formal membership of the local church a human invention or a biblical concept?

While the term 'church member' never occurs in the NT, the concept is implicit. Believers clearly identified themselves with a local church, committed themselves to it and became participating members of it. (Rom 16 et al.) Barnabas and Saul committed themselves to a local church even though they were in the area for only a year (Acts 11:26).

How does the Bible define church membership?

There can be no doubt that in the NT we are presented with a church, not of attenders but of participating members. 'Just as each of us has one body with many members, and these members do not all have the same function, so in Christ we who are many form one body, and each member belongs to all the others... The body is a unit, though it is made up of many parts; and although all its parts are many, they form one body... From Him the whole body, joined and held together by every supporting ligament, grows and builds itself up in love, as each part does its work' (Rom 12:4, 5; 1 Cor 12:12; Eph 4:16).

In these verses and many others, Paul points out that being part of the church of Jesus Christ is both a positional (1 Cor 12:12, 13; Eph 2:13-22; 4:3-6; Col 1:13-22) and a participative experience (Rom 12:4-8; 1 Cor 12:25-31; 14:12, 26; Heb 10:24, 25; 1 Tim 3:14, 15). The moment we become Christians we become positional members of the worldwide Body of Christ. Once you are in Christ you are in the body. This new position never changes and is eternal. However, to grow as a follower of Jesus Christ one must identify oneself with and become a participating member of a specific local church. This, I believe, is the biblical definition of church membership.

Of course one may be a member of a number of different churches in one's lifetime. However, nowhere in the Bible is a Christian encouraged to drift around from one church to another, rejoicing in their positional membership of the worldwide church without the discipline of being a participating member in a specific local church.

The process of becoming a formal member in the local church

Formal membership gives people an opportunity to decide whether they want to be attenders or participators, consumers or contributors. It is meant not to create a 'them and us' attitude, but to heighten the need for responsibility to be taken, commitment to be made, accountability to be welcomed and partnership to be established. These four areas will be dealt with later. They tend not to be given much emphasis in our world. It is all the more necessary, therefore, for the church to teach them consistently and take them seriously.

At the church where I am pastor, we have found the following four-stage process helpful, though we daily struggle to make it more effective.

The discovering stage

Any prospective new member is given a church vision document to study prayerfully. It contains the following:

1. A statement of the church's mission, vision and plan

The mission is what we are doing, i.e. building a biblical community in a broken world. The vision is what we are becoming, i.e. a biblically functioning community through worshipping God, equipping God's people and reaching God's world. The plan is how we are doing it, i.e., building on strong foundations, ministering through suitable programming and reaching our goals through the strategic allocation of resources.

2. Building on strong foundations – what we believe

We have a clear statement of faith based on that of the Evangelical Alliance. It states what we passionately believe are the foundations of our Christian faith. If we build on and practise what God has revealed to us in his word and through his Son we shall fulfil our vision to become a biblically functioning community.

3. Ministering through suitable programming – the 42-47 model and purpose for church (based on Acts 2:42-47)

- Enabling spiritual growth through *discipleship*
- Exalting and honouring God through *worship*
- Developing and deepening relationships through *community*
- Providing encouragement and opportunity for Christian service through *ministry*
- Expanding and growing through *evangelism*

A participating member will recognise and seek to be involved in, contribute to and benefit from these areas of church as they are essential for every follower of Christ in becoming mature.

4. Accomplishing through the strategic allocation of our resources – people, buildings and finance

The primary resource God has given us is people! People are the members of the Body of Christ. 'The Church builds itself up in love as each part does its work' (Eph 4:16). As each part does its work! We make it clear to prospective church members that this is the only way the local church can and will be built up. The nature of church membership is a 'saving faith and living commitment to serve Christ, build one another up and reach out'. It carries with it the following privileges, purposes and disciplines:

It gives a person a sense of *identity* (Eph 2:19-22)

By becoming a formal member of a local church a person identifies with a particular group of people with similar beliefs, principles and values. This provides a Christian believer with a basis for functioning as a child of God and part of the Body of Christ.

It encourages and promotes *responsibility*

Membership is not about signing a contract or joining a club: it is a covenanting together in spiritual life and service which therefore involves activity and cannot be something passive. A member has the responsibility:

- to support and attend church gatherings regularly (Acts 2:46; Heb 10:25);
- to have the right attitude to other members and to work, service and spiritual authority (Col 3:12-24; 1 Thess 5:12-13; Heb 13:17);
- to discover, develop and use their spiritual gifts, to glorify Christ and build up the Body of Christ (Rom 12:6-13; 1 Cor 12); (Some excellent courses are available, which can help believers to discover, develop and deploy their spiritual gifts into the local church. See the list of books for further reading, at the end of this chapter.)
- to be a good steward of their possessions and money, and to use them wisely to support themselves, their family and God's work (1 Cor 16:2; 2 Cor 8:1-9; 9:7; Rom 13:6-10).

It leads to increased *commitment*

Having a clear identity as a child of God and a growing sense of responsibility to the church leads to increased commitment to God and to God's people. We believe that for a church to know the blessing of growth and expansion, it is important for the individual members to be devoted and committed followers of Jesus Christ.

The evidence of this devotion and commitment will include: an ongoing relationship with God; a desire to read, study and understand the teaching of the Bible; a desire to pray; a desire to serve others; a life consistent with a Christian profession of faith; a desire to share the gospel with others.

It leads to increased *accountability*

Accountability is essential to life! Just as it is essential within our marriage, family, educational and employment worlds, and is, in fact, an integral part of our citizenship of the state, so it is essential in local church life and relationships (Eph 5:22-6:9; Rom 13).

The local church provides the accountability we need to grow and mature as followers of Jesus Christ:

- the support, care and encouragement of the Body of Christ (Gal 6:1, 2; Heb 10:23-25);
- the spiritual protection, guidance and authority of godly leaders (Acts 20:28-31; Heb 13:17).

It leads to an understanding and appreciation of *partnership*

We use the word partnership to convey the interdependent nature of the local church and to encourage members to work and serve together. Partnership is therefore the goal of membership. Identity, responsibility, commitment and accountability are all essential to real and genuine partnership.

This discovering stage makes clear to any prospective member that we are serious in our desire to turn attenders into members and ministers within the local church. It is therefore something they must consider prayerfully before God.

The consultation stage

Once a prospective member has been able to give careful consideration to the church's mission, vision and plan, two members of the leadership team meet with the person. The consultation is not an intimidating experience for the prospective member, but is a time of mutual sharing and enjoying Christian fellowship together. The consultation is purpose driven. During it four main things are done.

1. The prospective member shares their Christian testimony, as do the two members of the leadership team.

2. The prospective member shares their experience of and involvement in their last church. This is designed to highlight encouragements and blessings. It is also geared to highlight any hurts, difficulties, troubles, or a broken relationship between the prospective member and their last church. If any difficulties or troubles are discovered then they are dealt with sensitively and appropriately. Where there is a broken relationship we encourage reconciliation and offer to help towards it.

3. Talk through and share ideas about the contents of the vision document. This gives an opportunity to ask or answer any questions and to clarify any points regarding the church's overall vision. A prospective member will then be asked three questions. With regard to the mission: can you commit yourself to what we are doing? With reference to the vision: do you want to be part of what we are becoming? And as to the plan: will you devote yourself to accomplishing it with us?

These questions are needed in order to make it clear that church is no place for people who do not have a sense of responsibility and commitment to its vision and purpose, and who do not want to be accountable to anyone for their Christian walk and service. We want members who intend to become participants and ministers in the church.

4. Pray. After the consultation the two members of the leadership team meet with the rest of the team and share the results of the consultation.

The commendation stage

Apart from very exceptional cases, upon the agreement of the leadership team and the prospective member a commitment is made and a time is set to welcome them publicly into the membership of the church.

The celebration stage

During a Sunday morning service, two members of the leadership team publicly welcome and affirm the new member(s) of the church. This involves a very simple public acknowledgement of Jesus Christ as their personal Saviour and Lord and of a commitment to service in the church. The church also makes a commitment to love, care and build one another up (Rom12:9-13). This is followed by a short prayer of blessing and commendation with the laying on of hands.

Maintaining passion and enthusiasm within the members of the local church

The vision gets lost unless it is reinforced time and time again. So we seek to remind members of the church's vision and their participation in and contribution towards fulfilling it, on a regular basis.

Teaching and corporate worship times

Very regularly through the teaching programme, in times of singing, prayer, Bible readings and drama, the church is reminded of our mission, vision and plan.

Vision Sundays

The first Sundays of January and September each year are vision days when we remind members of their commitment to the mission, vision and plan of the church. We do four things on this day:

- we reinforce the mission, vision and plan of the church;
- we celebrate what has been achieved through the ministry of the church;
- we evaluate what we are doing; why we are doing it; and how we might do it better;

- we set goals to show where we are going, and where we want to be in, say, six months, a year, two years in our areas of ministry.

Every key leader of a ministry area in the church contributes in some way to the above. Every member and attender leaves church on this day with a one-page resumé of the four points above.

Celebration meals

In recent times we have started to have celebration meals. Nehemiah was never slow to ask God for success (Neh 1:11; 2:20), or to celebrate it whenever it happened. What a party it must have been (Neh 12:43)! It cannot be a bad thing to celebrate people's hard work and commitment, rejoice in success, and dedicate it to the glory of God.

We have had only one of these meals so far. All who are involved in our Alpha courses were invited to attend and that was an encouragement in itself as we realised that over forty members of the church were contributing to this ministry. We had Alpha teachers, discussion group leaders, carers, administrators, meal providers and so on. The oldest person present was in their mid-seventies and the youngest was a teenager. We celebrated people's hard work and commitment, rejoiced in the fact that a number of people had become Christians and were being added to the church, and dedicated this success to the glory of God. People left that evening encouraged, blessed and full of passion to keep on serving in this area of ministry.

Our vision is to have celebration meals once a year for every key area of ministry in the church. The message we are giving through this activity is fourfold:

- commitment is of great value to the church;
- commitment is worthy of commendation and celebration;
- commitment without commendation and celebration leads to loss of vision and passion;
- commitment with commendation and celebration produces increased vision and passion.

Church forums

Three times a year we have a church forum. This is a time when we focus debate and discussion on no more than three key areas within the life and ministry of the church. It is geared not only to highlighting encouragements but also to introducing new ideas, developments and changes. Usually every church member will receive a short written presentation on each area of focus a week before the forum, and will be asked to come informed and ready to contribute. Church forums are held on a Saturday afternoon, with a creche for young children and a buffet tea afterwards.

Conclusion

Turning attenders into members and ministers within the local church is a very challenging and sometimes daunting task. As a local church leader you are a key person in making this dream become reality. I do not believe that a formal membership approach in the local church, accompanied by well presented vision documents and high sounding mission statements, will achieve this on its own. However, I do believe that it provides a platform upon which leaders can, with integrity and authority, help people to move from being mere attenders to becoming participating members and ministers in the local church.

Further reading

R Warren, *The Purpose Driven Church* (Zondervan, 1995)

D Prior, *Creating Community* (Navpress/Scripture Press, 1992)

Membership Course, Saddleback Community Church (obtainable from their web site:www.saddleback.com)

Ministry Matters Course, Saddleback Community Church (obtainable from their web site:www.saddleback.com)

Network Course. Willow Creek (Zondervan)

The Church Leaders Handbook. Willow Creek (Zondervan)

CHAPTER TWENTY

Church Discipline

DONALD BRIDGE

What is church discipline?

Church discipline is the backbone of church life. Without it, the Body of Christ is like an organism without bones or muscles. The *phrase* is not found in the NT but the *principle* permeates its pages. Gospels, Acts and letters all declare its importance. British readers easily miss this because the English word 'you' is identical in the singular and plural. So we tend to read instructions addressed to groups as if they were intended for the individual reader. In fact they are instructions to the believing *community*. (In Geordie, 'Youse lot' rather than 'you'!) Notice, for example, the corporate appeal of Galatians 3:9, 12, 13, 15, 16: 'as God's chosen people...members of one body'. Church discipline is part of the process by which Christians express this corporate life.

Seeking to identify evidence of a true church, Reformation leaders added 'Scriptures rightly preached' to the Catholic 'Sacraments rightly administered', and it was left to the Radical Evangelicals to add the third essential ingredient, 'Discipline rightly applied'. They were committed to the simple biblical idea that the Christian church is made up of believing and practising Christians. They promoted the concept of the 'gathered church', believing that those who gather 'in his name' have the Saviour's promised presence 'in the midst' and are therefore competent to function as a local church, mending broken internal relationships, making binding decisions, and harmonising in prayer (Matt 18:15-20). In contrast to either 'catholic' or 'state' systems, radical evangelical movements have sought ways to express this principle. Each has found that evangelism and church discipline go hand in hand. 'The church without discipline is like a body without sinews', said John Calvin. 'Where this is lacking, there is certainly no church', added a sixteenth-century Anabaptist leader. (See D Bridge, *Spare the Rod and Spoil the Church*, p.3.)

Discipline is more than the occasional visit of the leadership 'heavies' to recalcitrant church members! It is more about education than execution; more about restoration than rejection; more about preservation than punishment.

Discipline is related to *discipleship*, as the verbal similarity suggests. The gospels describe Jesus calling disciples, sharing his lifestyle with them, teaching, training, admonishing and correcting them (e.g. Matt 16:23; 18:15-17; 19:14; 20:24-28). On one of the few occasions when he used the word 'church', Jesus pictured a community of people who care enough for each other to 'keep short accounts', to settle disputes promptly, to harmonise in prayer and to share in making difficult decisions (Matt 18:15-17).

Church discipline, then, is the total activity that promotes discipleship and preserves order in the church's life. It is 'the serious attempt to preserve the truth, order and standards of New Testament Christianity in the local church ... It is designed for the preservation of spiritual life, the authentication of the church's witness, the discouragement of sin, and the restoration of the fallen' (Bridge, *Spare the Rod*, p.159). It has to do with our corporate Christian life and our convincing Christian witness. It involves much more than emergency action when things go badly wrong.

The New Testament picture of church discipline

The book of Acts shows the early church expanding and adjusting to new situations in fellowship. It offers no 'canon law', but relates stories designed for our instruction, emulation and warning. Those first Christians 'devoted themselves' to a shared life. This fellowship (*koinonia*) involved learning, eating, worshipping, praying and working together (Acts 2:42-47). They faced threats with united prayer (4:18); they confronted hypocrisy as a threat to spiritual fellowship (5:1-6); they met strains on their charitable work by appointing 'deacons' (6:1-7); they tackled serious disagreement by frank consultation (15:1-21).

The NT letters demonstrate the same process. Notice the form in which these divinely-inspired documents are cast. Very human disciples are learning together in relationship. The aim was godly order rather than ecclesiastical system. Sometimes stern discipline was necessary – even expulsion (1 Cor 4:14-21: 'Put out of your fellowship the man who did this' 1 Cor 5:2; cf. 2 Thess 3:14, 15). But the context is wider than that of mere emergency action. The apostles are guiding communities into life in the Spirit and maturity in Christ.

Using the means

Today's church discipline is an ongoing exercise that enlists teaching, nurture, leadership and fellowship life. Ideally, most potential problems will be dealt with quietly before they develop into emergencies.

Truth taught

Teachers and preachers do not simply impart truth; they aim to change lives. Scripture displays its divinely inspired quality by its effectiveness in 'teaching, rebuking, correcting and training in righteousness' – the very exercises with which discipline is concerned (2 Tim 3:16, 17). The Holy Spirit takes biblical truths 'for all' and applies them with heart-searching relevance to particular situations, sometimes quite unsuspected by the one who speaks. Both consecutive expository preaching and topical/biblical teaching exercise enormous healing power. 'Without my needing to make a personal approach, I have seen stealing stopped, immorality abandoned, family relationships healed, bitterness melted, quarrels ended, tight-fistedness turned to generosity, occult dabbling disowned. This is antidote at work ... It is church discipline launching a pre-emptive strike before the evil has become overt.' (Bridge, *Spare the Rod*, p.32)

Life nurtured

New converts need basic training in faith and lifestyle. This is best given in association with baptism and reception into membership. Encourage the acceptance of new standards of personal and corporate behaviour in which old ways are 'buried' and new ways embraced (Rom 6:1-7; Gal 3:26-29; Col 3: 1-14; 1 Pet 2, 3). Here small-group instruction comes into its own. Pastor-teachers must try to understand the specific challenges to Christian morality and lifestyle posed by today's postmodern 'anything-goes' culture. Specific teaching should be given on how the local church works (including its discipline and leadership) as the alternative society.

Communion received

As we 'eat the Lord's Supper' (1 Cor 10:14-22; 11:23-26) our community life is sustained, our unity preserved and our vertical and horizontal relationships strengthened. Here, especially, we should 'examine ourselves before we eat' (1 Cor 11:27, 28). Breaking bread together offers another antidote to those sins and hindrances that otherwise mar the fellowship. In the words of *The Alternative Service Book* (pp.128, 132): 'We are the Body of Christ. By one Spirit we were all baptised into one body. Let us then pursue all that makes for peace and builds up our common life... As we eat and drink these holy gifts in the presence of your divine majesty, renew us by your Spirit, inspire us with your love, and unite us in the body of your Son.'

Leadership exercised

Leadership is crucial. We must combine in creative tension the *servanthood of* 'deacon', the *rulership* of 'elder', the *authority* of 'teacher' and the *gentleness* of 'pastor'. These virtues and gifts are rarely to be found in one individual: another strong argument for shared leadership!

Fellowship encouraged

Christians seriously committed to a shared life bear each other's burdens, share each other's joys, give and receive both encouragement and rebuke (Gal 5:13-15; 1 Thess 5:12-15). All are involved in creating this community life that displays both care and discipline. Jesus' phrase, 'Tell it to the church ' (Matt 18:17) is surely used in this context. Some have built on it a concept of the 'church meeting' which has more to do with democracy, populism or constitutionalism, than biblical principles. Is the mind of Christ really discerned in the biggest vote, the most persistent argument or the most skilful manipulation of the rule book? (S Murray, *Explaining Church Discipline*, pp.27, 28). Nevertheless, the 'gathered church' passage does assume that the whole local body of believers will share in consultation, support, understanding and action in the preserving of biblical standards of belief and behaviour. The disorders just described represent misunderstandings of Jesus' words, and should not be taken as an excuse to ignore them.

Grasping the nettle

Stern action is sometimes sadly necessary. We may have to offer private warning. If this is ignored, the offender may be asked to accept a period of pastoral guidance. Temporary suspension from Communion may be necessary until the issue is resolved. Jesus said: 'If he refuses to listen even to the church, treat him as you would a pagan or a tax collector.' (Matt 18:17; see Murray's very helpful explanation, pp.37-41). Paul advocates exclusion in some circumstances (Rom 16:17; 1 Cor 5:1-3, 11; 2 Thess 3:6; 2 Tim 3:1-5). The sinister phrase, 'handing over to Satan' (1 Cor 5:5; 1 Tim 5:20) probably refers to excommunication, for someone who leaves the body of the church and all it represents is 'back in Satan's territory', so to speak. That may lead to physical, emotional or spiritual suffering (as apparently in 1 Cor 11:30). Needless to say, the church itself should never engage in physical threat, emotional abuse, spiritual bullying or mental manipulation. Leave all that to the cults!

The ultimate purpose is always the restoration of the offender (2 Cor 2:7-8). This may be a gradual, ongoing process. Its expression will vary with the nature of the offence and may include a private apology and reconciliation; a request to be pastored and 'helped back'; or a public retraction of a public misdemeanour. Sometimes, I suggest, the happiest solution may be an agreed 'transfer' to another fellowship where care and restoration can continue. 'Bringing it to the church' should be at a late stage of the process. If repentance is found before that, it should be sufficient for leaders to carry the trust of the fellowship – and preserve the confidentiality of the offender.

The scope of pre-emptive action by the church is a subject calling for careful and cautious treatment. The NT offers no exhaustive list of offences: it gives examples. This suggests an elastic and pragmatic approach. What is important is the effect a sin is having on the person's discipleship; the way they are dealing with it; and the effect it is having on the fellowship. NT examples include those who confuse the fellowship and cause division (Rom 16:17, 18); sexual misbehaviour, greed, idolatry, slander, drunkenness and financial dishonesty, which have this (and little else) in common, that they degrade and distress the corporate witness (1 Cor 5:11; 6:1-11). In Thessalonika, Paul rebuked 'mild' offences of idleness and disobedience (1 Thess 3:6) in the context of possible shame brought on the new Christian movement in a society that was cynical about the motives and methods of religious itinerants (1 Thess 2:1-12). Timothy was tough with false teachers who disrupted the church with their speculations (1 Tim 1:20; 2 Tim 2:17, 18).

In all of this, the common feature is threat to the corporate witness. To recognise this as a basis for possible action is more profitable (and practical) than trying to reconstruct what the apostles meant by false teaching, or what degrees of immorality were serious enough for dismissal. It is difficult to operate either a detailed process of canon law or a systematic theology when neither is offered in the NT! Rather, we may ask of a troubling situation, 'Is Christian love violated? Is Christian unity threatened? Is Christian living compromised? Is Christian truth denied?' The last question assumes, of course, some basic acceptance of biblical and evangelical truth, and one of the tasks of teachers is to provide and sustain that basis. (A published basis of faith, like that of the Evangelical Alliance, can be a useful guide here.)

Some practical hints

In doctrinal differences, attitude and direction are crucial. A recent convert may have genuine difficulties with a fundamental doctrine (like the deity of Christ) but simply needs personal pastoring and help. In contrast, an established member may be seeking power or causing disruption by promoting a 'lesser' doctrinal issue (e.g. a particular charismatic gift, a particular understanding of apocalyptic writings or a particular experience-fad). This may require firm discipline, for the good of the church's community life.

Moral-sexual issues will almost inevitably arise in a church that is truly engaged in evangelism, for in today's permissive society, converts may bring 'baggage' with them. Some problems will respond to gradual pastoring, but others may be irreversible or indissoluble this side of heaven. For example, how can a divorced-and-remarried couple with children from all three marriages 'put things right'? Since that is impossible, must they be permanently barred from membership? If that be the case, we are really saying that gospel message and church life are unavailable to an increasing proportion of the population! Or, to take another example, what of established Christians who fall? Clearly some disciplinary action is needed, but how can we make its purpose healing rather than punishment? And is there a difference between an established Christian who offends and a new convert who has offended already? (See chapter 44 on 'Divorce and remarriage'.)

Divorce and remarriage poses real problems. Today's society renders totally unworkable a widely-followed traditional practice, in which Jesus' words in Matthew 5:31, 32 are interpreted as 'Divorcees can never become church members'. In fact, that passage says nothing whatever about church membership. A similar application to the words immediately preceding and following the statement about divorce would lead to expulsion for erotic thoughts, bad temper, oath-taking and failure to turn the other cheek, and would be likely to close our churches in three months flat! What today's changing society does require in many situations is a constant exercise of 'casuistry' within an understanding of grace – a constant effort to treat every situation as unique, and not susceptible to regulations.

Love is the best way. God's love is holy love, but it is also gracious, welcoming and restoring. Even his 'rod' is administered in love. In the exercise of church discipline it can be difficult to square this circle. Leaders need to earn the trust of church members, to exercise moral courage and to safeguard confidentiality. The Bible is to be treated not as a book of rules but as a declaration of

God's love and a stimulus to expressing it.

Conclusion

'Church discipline is about the credibility of the Church ... We do well to wrestle with these issues together, so that once again we shall have the right to call ourselves God's holy people.' (Baptist Mainstream magazine, issue 15, January 1984)

Further reading

D Bridge, *Spare the Rod and spoil the Church* (MARC, 1985)
S Murray, *Explaining Church Discipline* (Sovereign World, 1995)

CHAPTER TWENTY-ONE

Vision and Goal Setting

MARK THOMAS

The word 'vision' occurs many times in scripture in different contexts. For example, Abraham was given a specific vision when the covenant was revealed to him (Gen 15:1), and Paul refers to his calling in terms of a vision (Acts 26:19). A 'vision' is distinct from the more passive 'dream', although the two words are often loosely used for each other. (Cf. the words of Martin Luther King, 'I have a dream', which clearly mean, 'I have a vision'.) There is the further complication that both words can be used literally or figuratively. Vision involves two-way interaction between the individual receiving the vision and God (or his messenger) who gives it. Those who receive a vision are aware of what is going on and experience something which is distinct from the more passive experience of a dream, though visionaries are often referred to as dreamers.

Visionaries are not always leaders, but leaders without a vision are unlikely to see where God is taking them, their church and individuals within the fellowship. As someone once said, 'if you aim at nothing you are sure to hit it'. In his book, *Planning, Paperwork and Priorities*, Peter Brierley reminds us of Lewis Carroll's Cheshire cat and the conversation with Alice. 'Would you tell me, please, which way I ought to go from here?' asked Alice. 'That depends a good deal on where you want to get to', said the cat. 'I don't much care where', said Alice. 'Then it does not matter which way you go', replied the cat. The scriptures make it clear that God waits to direct us, and, as leaders, we would all want to echo Paul's words in Acts 26:19 about not being 'disobedient to the vision from heaven.'

Visions are normally given to be passed on. Those who receive a vision have to find a way of translating it into practical reality by inspiring and then motivating others to understand and implement it. This calls for a great deal of patience and communication; skills and qualities which are often missing from the person who has received the vision. The individual's vision needs to be tested, and leaders would do well to reflect on the words of 1 John 4:1, 'Do not believe every spirit, but test the spirits to see whether they are from God' before any vision is shared or adopted. However, this is only the beginning and there is a long way to go before any vision becomes a reality. David Pytches (using the words of John Haggai) goes further when he says that 'Nothing important was ever achieved by someone without energy.' It is not enough to have a vision; it must be made to happen, or it will be nothing more than a dream.

The Lord's words to Jeremiah remind us that there is a divine plan for his people. '"For I know the plans that I have for you", declares the Lord, "plans to prosper you and not to harm you, plans to give you hope and a future"' (Jer 29:11). It is much easier for an individual to establish what God is trying to say, than for leaders to understand the collective vision and resulting plans that God has for the fellowship.

As the result of an encounter with God, both Moses and Joshua were given specific information about the need to leave Egypt and how to take the Promised Land. But someone had to sit down, work out the details, and then communicate the plan to the people. There is little doubt that the plan had to be amended to cope with diversions (such as an extra 40 years in the desert); nevertheless there must have been a plan.

Similarly, the early church had to come up with a plan to deal with the problem of food distribution. The vision the apostles had was not enough on its own. They had to reorganise what they were doing so that all the people would get their fair share of food. This resulted in the appointment of deacons to take on the administrative load, but I suspect that this did not happen as a result of a single conversation or complaint. The apostles would have checked to see that the proposed remedy was in line with what they had been commissioned to do. Then they would have agreed the action plan recorded in scripture.

In the Partnership publication, *Ten Changing Churches*, the majority of the churches followed a similar pattern. There was an initial vision that inspired the leadership. After being tested and agreed, it was communicated to the church. It then had to be implemented according to a plan of action that needed constant reviewing.

The realities of church life today often require decisions to be made quickly, as events unfold, so it is vital that there is, in the background, a real sense of direction. A plan of action is needed which can be communicated to those around us so that they can understand why things are being done in a certain way. And it is important to recognise the distinction between those who lead and those who implement or manage a process.

In my experience, great leaders apply the compass rather than the map to planning directions. In the West the majority of us seem to plan by map, needing to know exactly how and when things should be done. The majority of the world's population, however, do not have the same view of how to live their lives, and yet they manage to be successful in what they set out to do. (It will not have escaped your knowledge that the fastest growing Christian communities are not in the West, and that Christians are coming from the East to evangelise our Western communities.) Leaders who have the compass rather than the map strategy know exactly where they are going and you will not be able to deter them from this inner call. They have plans and strategies, but it is the final destination rather than each day's agenda that drives them. Care must be taken that we do not put more emphasis on the day's task than on our ultimate goal.

This does not mean that we do not have a plan – quite the opposite. As already suggested, there is no doubt that Moses and his fellow leaders sat down together and worked out how to get to the Promised Land. They would not have left the preparation and planning of moving a huge number of people until the final night. Yet, when God finally did move his people, I expect it was a bit chaotic. They certainly had a few unforeseen problems along the way, like getting across the Red Sea in hours rather than days, and an extra 40 years in the desert. Moses knew what God had told him, he knew which way to go, but he constantly had to go back to God for more specific directions. Paul's call to Macedonia also happened in this way (Acts 16: 6-10).

The need to receive a fresh anointing and confirmation of God's call is vital to leaders today. Many churches are led by those who have not personally received the initial vision given to the church. They have probably grown up and accepted what was given to their forefathers as relevant today, and it may well be. However, as Luis Palau said, 'God has no grandchildren' and, although he was referring to an individual's need to have a personal encounter with God, the same principle applies to leadership. A leader who tries to implement the vision of a previous generation will soon find that there is a need to establish a fresh vision within the current generation. Anyone who has grown up in a fellowship that has second-generation leadership will know the difference when they step into an environment where there is a fresh call from God.

We have already noted that not all visionaries are leaders but that leaders need to have a vision. Visionaries are often unable to translate and communicate their vision in a language that everyone in the church can understand. They often talk about 'the big picture' or 'the vision', and miss out a lot of the detail that is needed by so many within our fellowships. For example, understanding how implementing the vision will affect the work among the senior citizens may be more important to some than hearing about a two-year plan. Leaders often forget that they have probably spent months of discussion on the vision and yet they expect their fellow church members to understand it within a 30-minute presentation.

Outlined below, is a step-by-step process which translates the initial vision into day-to-day reality. Before starting this process, it might be useful to define the terms you are using so that there is no misunderstanding about what is being said. People often get confused about the word 'vision' and cannot understand why there needs to be anything additional to the Great Commission of Matthew 28:16-20. The words that you actually use to define the process are less significant than the collective understanding that the leadership team has of them. The process outlined below is certainly not the only way to do it. There are many different models, for example, the one used in Peter Brierley's excellent book, *Vision Building*. Walter Wright's book, *Relational Leadership*, also has some good advice in this area.

Step 1. Clarify the overall purpose of the church

We are all part of God's general purpose (Matt 28:16-20) along with his call to live our lives in a way which brings us into an understanding of his will and purpose (Rom 12:1, 2). This applies to all Christians. Without this foundation, the church will surely crumble. Leaders need to set this in place before attempting to clarify any specific call.

Step 2. Establish the vision

Leaders should seek God's guidance about their specific part in the general purpose of God. For example, knowing that God has specifically called a church community to evangelise a low-income community will often determine where they are located, the method of evangelism and the welfare programmes. What is important is not the size or complexity of the vision but the call of God on our lives. For some, it will be high profile (such as Willow Creek or Holy Trinity, Brompton) and for others, it will be a story that is never told in this life.

As already stated, as soon as a vision is received it should be recorded and tested by those who lead. When this has been done, it may be appropriate to share it more widely with men and women who possess real wisdom. This will further test the vision and may reveal things that have been missed. It may not be wise to share it with the whole church at this point, for some people need a lot of detail before they are ready to buy into anything.

Step 3. Define the mission

Most visions are not fulfilled quickly and so a mission plan needs to be put in place. This is the short-term vision (possibly 2-5 years) i.e. the current plan designed to bring about the vision during the foreseeable future or within a defined period. It will normally include a mission statement and some clear thinking about where we are going. It is when churches miss out this stage that they get the next bit wrong. Without clear direction, strategic objectives tend to change too quickly. Whilst this may be necessary at times, it will cause confusion within the ranks if an outline plan is not generally understood.

A written document will start to put the meat on the bones and allow specific objectives to be set. For example, if we are to reach the low-income community we will need to be accepted by them. This may involve a new building; the starting of children's and youth activities; the appointment of someone full-time to be available in the community. Most of these things will take years and only when they are in place will the church start to be more effective within the community. Hence the need for the mission plan.

The plan is now ready to be documented and communicated. This process may take many months. Be patient with those who find such things difficult and be prepared for all eventualities.

Step 4. Strategic objectives

This step has to have the full support of the church before it can be attempted. The whole church should be involved in agreeing the objectives in line with the mission. The objectives are those things that we agree on as necessary to bring about the mission within a defined period. They are normally measurable and reviewed on a regular basis. They will have their roots within the mission statement. What happens quite often is that individuals or churches take on new or revised strategic objectives without seeing if they fit with the mission, and find that they get sucked into doing something that is outside of God's will for them. Leaders need to find a way to implement the call of God within the life of the church and then ensure that others confirm their thoughts on this. When there is unity of mind and heart a clear plan of strategy and action is needed, which in turn needs to be communicated clearly again and again. When you think that you have communicated enough, start again! In his book, *A Noble Task*, Neil Summerton affirms that 'Elders must find appropriate ways by which they can come to a common vision from the Lord for the congregation that they are responsible for. They must communicate the vision.' The biggest problem in churches today is a lack of communication. Always assume that you have never done enough in this area. (See chapter 22, 'Handling differences and managing change'.)

Conclusion

Care should always be taken to keep the unity of the Spirit. It is so easy to offend and so hard to restore broken relationships. No system or strategy will work in a church without the influence of the Holy Spirit. Where the Spirit of the Lord is there is unity.

Further reading

P Brierley, *Priorities, Planning and Paperwork* (Marc Europe, 1992)
P Brierley, *Vision Building* (Hodder & Stoughton1989, Christian Research, 1994)
B Hughes, *Leadership Toolkit* (Monarch, 1998)
G Macdonald, *Ordering your Private World* (Highland Books, 1984)
D Pytches, *Leadership for New Life* (Hodder & Stoughton, 1998)
D Spriggs, *Christian Leadership* (Bible Society, 1993)
N Summerton, *A Noble Task* (Paternoster, rev. ed. 1994)
V Thomas, *Future Leader* (Paternoster, 1999)

CHAPTER TWENTY-TWO

Handling Differences and Managing Change

PETER GODFREY

However much we might long to have unity and stability in the local church, it is inevitable that we shall go through times when we are faced with differences and change. Indeed it would be true to say that if we did not do so we would not be living in the real world – the world God created! Creation is full of diversity, and is dynamic rather than static. Change is going on all the time.

That diversity and change are facts of life is clear from both OT and NT. They were for the nation of Israel and for the church in its early days, and they continue to be so down to this day. We are certainly not going to avoid differences and change, hence the very reasonable question: How do we handle the former and manage the latter? In addressing the question we shall be disappointed if we anticipate a neat, ready-made procedure. By their very nature, differences and change present themselves in a limitless variety of situations. It is not, therefore, possible to devise a simple methodology for dealing with them. How much easier church life would be if it were! What is presented here, therefore, is not a procedure to follow, nor a methodology to be adopted. It is more a way of approaching situations which will, under God's good hand, be helpful when they arise.

General observations

Before offering some comments on differences and change separately, I think it is appropriate to make some observations which apply to both. I believe that many of the difficulties which arise with respect to these issues occur through what I would describe as the 'gnats and camels syndrome' (see Matt 23:23, 24). It is clear from these verses, and from much of the context in which they occur, that the Lord's major dispute with the Pharisees arose from the fact that they had difficulty in seeing the 'big picture'. In the same way, the reason why differences and change so often cause problems is that, all too frequently, we become preoccupied with 'gnats' at the expense of taking a large view of the purposes of God.

I would dare to suggest that the responsibility for this lies, in some measure at least, with the way in which the Bible has been taught in many of our churches. There has been a tendency, now fortunately changing in many places, to teach from a series of disconnected texts, maybe fifty-two, or even one hundred and four, in the course of a year. Thus a congregation may be presumed to be well taught, and indeed does know a great deal of scripture, but has not gained a comprehensive grasp of how the Bible fits together. As a result, there may not be a real appreciation of the overall purposes of God, nor an understanding of how to interpret the different types, or genres, of scripture, i.e. history, prophecy, wisdom, gospel, epistle, etc. (An excellent book to help in this area is *How to read the Bible for all it's worth* by Fee and Stuart, published by Scripture Union. See also chapter 5 on 'Providing balanced teaching'.)

If we accept that the purposes of God may be summarised in words such as these: 'For he chose us in him before the creation of the world to be holy and blameless in his sight. In love he predestined us to be adopted as his sons through Jesus Christ, in accordance with his pleasure and his will' (Eph 1:4, 5), then it follows that a Christlike character and a childlike relationship are the main things that God desires for us. If these two things were held as priorities in our churches, and in our individual lives, then many of the issues which arise from differences and change would be seen in their proper perspective, and would not give rise to the problems which, sadly, they so often do. Therefore, to assist in handling differences and managing change it is suggested that we should do well to ensure that we seek to 'proclaim the whole will of God' in the church, as Paul sought to do in Ephesus (Acts 20:27). In this way, people will be helped to understand differences and accept change within the context of God seeking to restore the close relationship and holy character that he intended for his creation. If we are concentrating on the major concerns that God has, we shall not have the time, nor the inclination, to engage in minor matters. When a church has a clear vision for seeing lives transformed into the likeness of Christ, and so is promoting discipleship, handling differences and managing change will be very much easier.

As indicated above, establishing and maintaining these priorities in the church will do much to reduce the negative influences that differences and change can have. However, since it is unrealistic to think that this will solve all the problems, we must turn to consider a number of specific points related, first to differences, and second to change.

The nature of differences

Obviously, differences can occur in many areas of our lives. Within church life there appear to be two which cause the majority of the problems encountered. These relate to doctrine and style.

Doctrine

Differences in this area have been very helpfully discussed in two articles in the Partnership publication, *Handling Differences in the Local Church* (Christian Brethren Review Journal No. 38, June 1987). The first article considers the fact that, even within the NT, we are confronted with the presence of differences; and the second draws a distinction between essential and non-essential matters. Acceptance that differences occur, as they did in NT times, is not normally the major problem: coming to agreement over what is essential and what is not usually is. In practice, this often comes down to the basic question of our understanding of scripture and how we interpret it. Some hold the view that every word in the Bible is to be understood literally as the word of God, not open to interpretation but simply to be obeyed. Leaving aside the issue of translation and the fact that it is absolutely impossible to be consistent if taking a literalist approach, it becomes difficult to discuss differences with those who hold this view of the Bible. At the other extreme, are those who effectively deny the supreme authority of scripture taking, for example, the position that the Bible *contains* the word of God rather than *is* the word of God. In such situations it is very difficult to agree on what, if anything, is an essential doctrine.

If, however, one accepts the authority of scripture, but nevertheless recognises that the Bible was written by many different authors, in a great variety of situations, over a long period of time, then it becomes essential to interpet the Bible in a responsible manner. The understanding of the difference between essential and non-essential issues calls for careful Bible study together. This study must be undertaken with humility and openness to the Holy Spirit. There is a danger that we can approach the Bible with our minds made up, looking only for that which will confirm what we have already decided. In contrast with this, I recall the account given by friends who were missionaries in Nigeria regarding questions which arose in a church there. Without previous experience, tradition, or any preconceived ideas, the believers went to the scriptures to see what God had to say on the matter. It is hard for us, with our own background of thinking, and the many other voices around us, to come to the Bible with a mind simply open to what

God would say to us. However, if by God's grace we can do that, we shall be greatly helped in discerning between matters which are essential and those which are not.

Style

Apart from issues of doctrine, the differences which often cause difficulties relate to what I would term style; that is the way in which we do certain things. We all have our own preferences, particularly in worship. Our character (exuberant or meditatative) our upbringing, the traditions to which we have been exposed – all influence what we like and dislike. These differences have nothing to do with right or wrong: they are simply based on what we happen to prefer! However, as Tony Lane points out in the book referred to above, although differences of practice, or style, are less serious than differences of doctrine, they can be more of a bar to unity in a church. This is because they impinge on virtually every part of church life, including our choice of hymns/songs/musical instruments, order and timing of services, leadership style, even down to what we eat when we have a meal together.

The danger of differences

Whilst recognising that differences exist, we need also to be aware of the dangers which they present, namely distraction and division.

Distraction

Preoccupation with differences can be a very real distraction from the priorities of the church. Indeed it seems to be one of Satan's most successful activities in spoiling both the work and the witness of the people of God. One of the occasions when this activity can be very obvious is the church business meeting. It is vital that opportunity is given not only for the leadership to inform but for the church membership to respond and ask questions. However, it is important that leadership leads on these occasions. We experienced a dramatic change in the atmosphere of these meetings when a positive vision was shared with the church rather than just holding a 'talking shop'. On one occasion when we had taken a much more positive approach, a couple who had recently moved into the area decided to join the church as a result of coming to a business meeting! Here again, it is the fact of making clear statements regarding priorities that puts differences in the right context and keeps them from being unhelpful distractions. Unfortunately, there are occasions when the nature of the differences becomes so important in the eyes of individuals, or groups, that they take over the whole energy of the fellowship.

Division

If study of the scriptures becomes difficult to carry out in an open-minded way, or does not lead to an acceptance of different views then, regrettably, division may have to be considered. It is obvious that, if this occurs in a fellowship, it causes an immense amount of hurt within it, and has a negative effect on the witness of the gospel to those outside the church. Such a step cannot, therefore, be taken lightly. Indeed it is one of the hardest decisions that leadership may be called upon to take. Shepherds are responsible for the care of the flock and to preside over its division is hard to bear. However, they will have to decide which is least damaging to the kingdom: maintaining outward unity with inward division, or separation by agreement. If separation comes, then everything possible needs to be done to ensure that it takes place with the exercise of grace by all the parties concerned. It is so easy for the bitterness which may have arisen to be carried into the future, so continuing to hinder God's work. Taking a positive approach to dividing is a very hard thing to do, but every effort must be made to limit the harm which inevitably comes when such a course of action is followed.

Living with differences

Recognising that differences are going to occur means that we have to learn to live with them. We need to take steps to minimise the problems that will arise. Two of these relate to boundaries and acceptance.

Boundaries

Having realised that, within the fellowship, there will be differences between people over many things, it is important for everyone to know that there are, however, certain limits. It is not that anything goes! Problems arise from differences when an individual, or group, seeks to impose their particular approach on the others. It is the responsibility of the eldership to make known, and to maintain, the boundaries within which the fellowship operates. It is clear from many of Paul's letters that this was his major reason for writing as he did to the churches for which he had a concern. This certainly does not mean rigidity and lack of personal freedom, nor does it mean that there is no room for change: this is clear from the way Paul wrote. However, it gives security to the members to know what they can expect within that local church. It is important that those looking to join the church, especially if they are joining from another fellowship, understand and accept what they are joining. It is very unhelpful when people come in, find that things are not quite to their liking, and then seek to change them. Again it must be emphasised that this does not mean that the leadership is not ready to listen to the promptings of the Holy Spirit directly or through others who are sensitive to what the Spirit is saying. Also it is important that the definition of boundaries is done in a positive manner and is carried out by example, rather than by any suggestion of legalistic imposition by an authoritative leadership.

Acceptance

Acceptance of differences is greatly helped by teaching being given on the subject, designed to enable people to gain an understanding of how differences arise and how they are to be dealt with. The positive emphasis on priorities, referred to earlier, goes a long way towards creating an environment in which differences are accepted in the right manner.

Managing change

It is unfortunate that change is often viewed negatively, particularly within the church. We may be influenced by various biblical passages relating to the unchangeable nature of God and also by the apparent attitude of some hymn writers. One of the most popular hymns of an older generation includes the verse:

Swift to its close ebbs out life's little day;
Earth's joys grow dim, its glories pass away;
Change and decay in all around I see;
O Thou, who changest not, abide with me.

A verse in another much loved hymn also tends, unfortunately, to convey a negative approach to change:

In heavenly love abiding,
No change my heart shall fear;
And safe is such confiding,
For nothing changes here:
The storm may roar about me,
My heart may low be laid;
But God is round about me,
And can I be dismayed?

We may also recall familiar texts, such as 'Jesus Christ is the same yesterday and today and forever.' (Heb 13:8) and 'Because God wanted to make the unchanging nature of His purpose very clear to the heirs of what was promised, He confirmed it with an oath' (Heb

6:17). Whilst it is certainly true that God's character and purpose remain constant, the manner in which God acts can, and does, change. As mentioned earlier, creation is not only full of variety but has change built into it. Although God always acts consistently with his nature, the way in which he acts changes according to the requirements of each situation. For example, God is always righteous and merciful, but the way in which these qualities are expressed varies, depending on the specific situation in which they need to be exercised. So we need to hold fast to the unchanging message of the gospel, while adapting the manner in which it is presented to the continually changing environment in which we live. In managing change it is important to keep both the unchanging nature of God's purpose and the ever-changing nature of the world clearly before us. It also has to be recognised that, for many people, change is often uncomfortable and consequently something they would prefer to avoid; although there are others who thrive on it and are unhappy if everything stays the same for too long! This makes it essential that change is carried out with sensitivity and care. The following observations are intended to help achieve this.

Understanding the need for change

A Partnership booklet published in 1999 and entitled *Ten Changing Churches* described the experience of considerable change in a wide variety of church situations. It was interesting and, I believe, significant, to note that much of the change which had occurred had been brought about as a result of growing concern to reach out into the surrounding community. This raises the point that one of the major considerations in managing change is that people should understand why it is being done. Change purely for the sake of change itself is rarely a helpful activity. It is important, therefore, that before change is initiated there should be a clear understanding of why it is being considered and the purpose that it is expected to achieve. A period of preparation for change is essential if people are to be ready not only to accept the change but to be positively supportive and have a sense of ownership of what is proposed. For some, this may require an exercise of patience, as it is important that adequate time is given for questions, and possibly fears, to be discussed. It will be appropriate to consider the reason for the proposed changes in the light of biblical principles and the situation in which the church is operating. This is not to say that principles are dictated by the society in which we live, but rather to recognise that the way in which our principles are applied must take account of what is happening around us. Again, it is clear from Acts and from the epistles that this was the approach taken by the apostles and the early church

Communicating the process

Jonathan Lamb, in his booklet, *Making Progress in Church Life*, quotes Nick Mercer who suggests that sudden change 'is a bit like having a baby without being pregnant for nine months. The leaders have spent many hours and days in discussion, in the gestation of an idea. Then the "baby" is suddenly presented at a church meeting which has forty-five minutes to make up its mind! No wonder there are so many unhappy births. The congregation must share in the pregnancy if it is to be a healthy baby.'

A vital component of managing change is that people understand not only the expected result but also the process for getting there. In this way they will be able to prepare themselves for change and therefore be in a better position to accept changes as they come. It is implied in the quotation given above that the leadership has spent a good deal of time considering the proposed change and is therefore familiar with the whole situation. It is too easy to assume that everyone else is up to speed when they have not been given any opportunity to consider the matter.

Of course, the exercise of communicating the process of change does require the leadership to have thought the issue through for themselves; if they are unable to communicate the process of change effectively it probably means that their own preparation has not been done properly. But that reinforces rather than detracts from the need for the church to be given adequate time to give consideration to the proposed changes before being asked to accept them.

Monitoring the result

Getting caught up in the activity associated with the change itself can sometimes lead to a failure to keep everyone informed about how things are progressing. If this is not done, it can lead to discontent as people go through the inevitable discomfort that change brings with it and wonder whether it is worthwhile. It is important, therefore, that there is on-going communication about the progress that is being made towards the expected results. No doubt much time has been spent in asking God to bless what is being undertaken, but time also needs to be taken to thank God for what, by his grace, is being achieved. In this way not only is the glory given to God but his people are encouraged.

Conclusion

Differences and change will always be with us. Owing to the variety of ways in which they come about, there is no standard method for handling them. There are, however, certain principles we can follow which should assist in minimising the difficulties they so often bring with them.

In handling differences, it is important that the priorities we have as the people of God are constantly in the forefront of our teaching, our thinking, our living and our activities. If we establish and maintain these priorities it will help us to see differences in the right context, even to the extent of seeing them as a positive contribution to carrying out God's purposes.

In managing change, priorities are also important because people need to know why change is being carried out. The communication of these priorities as well as the process through which change is to be brought about, is an essential element in successfully introducing change and accomplishing the purposes for which it is intended.

Further reading

D Cormack, *Change Directions* (Monarch, 1995)

G Jones, *Coping with Controversy* (Solway, Paternoster, 2nd ed., 1996)

J Lamb, *Making Progress in Church Life. How to handle change positively* (Paternoster/Partnership, 1997)

H H Rowdon (ed.), *Handling Differences in the Local Church* (Paternoster, 1987)

Chapter Twenty-Three

Handling Growth

Graham Poland

Growth is generally a sign of health. A healthy child grows; a healthy plant grows; a sound financial investment grows; and a healthy church grows. Growth, of course, must be measured not only in terms of size, but in other dimensions such as strength and maturity. However, for the purposes of this article we shall consider numerical growth as the principal criterion.

Church growth has become a buzz term in recent years, developing into a science to be studied in its own right. Church growth experts seem to suggest certain cause and effect principles that are guaranteed to produce immediate results when applied to an ailing church, rather like hair-restorer applied to a bald patch. Some sincere people have become disillusioned as they have attempted to implement principles that have worked elsewhere, only to find that their church is unreceptive and unresponsive. The problem (as in the parable of the sower) is not in the seed but in the soil. In healthy soil, there is growth; in barren soil, the same seed yields little or no results. What produces healthy soil ? Ultimately it is produced by God. We may sow, we may water, but only he gives the increase.

That certainly has been our experience. Grosvenor Church in Barnstaple was founded in 1842 at the inception of the Brethren movement, and its subsequent history has seen periods of growth and decline. In recent years we are grateful to God for giving us a period of growth. We are sure that the prayers of past generations have watered the good soil of those early days and we are reaping the result.

Midway through the 1980s, attendance at our Sunday evening evangelistic service stood at around 40 – almost all of those already church members. When morning family services were started and, later, a full-time pastor appointed, attendance started to rise and conversions regularly took place. In 1989, when a second pastor was called, attendance was consistently over 200, many of these first-generation Christians. The larger number of families attending brought a corresponding number of children, putting an ever-increasing strain upon the building's resources. Eventually a new site was acquired and, after an intermediate period of hiring the town's cinema on a Sunday morning, the church transferred to a purpose-built church-centre with a seating capacity of 400. Before very long the increased capacity was also filled, so that the most recent development has been to create two morning congregations with services running back-to-back, both similar in content and providing children's activities, but with the same preacher.

Rapid, yet consistent, growth has brought with it tensions that have stretched us to the limit at times. Some of the growing pains have made us sharply aware of our weakness and need for dependence on God's grace more than ever. There has been little time to build in long-term strategies and even less time to reflect, but certain lessons stand out as important.

Strong leadership

Leadership is the backbone of a healthy church. Connecting joints and ligaments only operate efficiently when the backbone is strong, but when both interact the body grows. We have found that the majority of the church will follow if the leaders will lead. A church consultant who visited us recently commented on how the church had been through several major areas of change in a short period of time, any one of these areas capable of causing the church to disintegrate, yet, in spite of sailing through rough waters, the ship had kept on course and very few had been lost overboard. He attributed this to the respect the congregation had for the leadership team and their willingness to trust their judgments and to follow their decisions. At times, from the inside, it appeared to be otherwise, but although the elders were not always unanimous, we never made a decision that affected the direction of the church until all elders were agreed on the course of action. That principle enabled us to speak with one voice and to stand shoulder-to-shoulder whenever decisions were criticised or resisted.

Change creates vulnerability, so it is essential that a large congregation has the security of knowing that their leadership can be trusted and followed. Consultation is not needed so much as sensitivity, so that the leadership is conscious of the climate within the church and can assess accurately when it is the right time to move forward and introduce change. This sensitivity cannot be produced mechanically but is an instinctive trait of the spiritual gift of leadership, as well as the result of much prayer. (See chapter 22 on 'Handling differences and managing change'.)

But leadership needs to be courageous. Every time we moved forward and grew a little bit more we had to step out in faith. The challenge of meeting the increased need created by growth initiated a cycle of calling for a further increase of faith. When the first pastor was appointed, the elders took a step of faith in pledging to pay him a salary; when the second pastor came, not only was a second salary needed but a house, so a further step of faith saw £90,000 raised in a short period. Since then a youth pastor's salary has been needed and a full-time administrator is also being supported – this on top of a building programme that has cost in excess of £500,000 (and all in a part of the country where wages are among the lowest). Growth creates further need for growth and, because of that, we anticipate that even greater steps of faith will be needed.

Vision

Closely allied to faith is the need for clear vision. Within our leadership team are those who will always be anticipating the next need for change and the next step of faith. If vision rather than need drives a church, an energy can be harnessed that generates its own mechanisms for handling growth. When a church congregation is only presented with need there is a likelihood that a burden will be imposed that they will not be able to carry. This is a real danger within a growing church. That is why people must be encouraged to own the vision. Our most recent expansion into two morning congregations was presented to the church as an opportunity to further implement our vision to reach the lost, rather than a logistical headache to find more seats. It has brought with it the need for twice as many children's leaders, two welcome teams, two worship teams, etc. If presented without the underlying vision, this could be seen as a crippling burden. The needs have been presented to the church, and we wait for people with corresponding gifts to respond voluntarily. When people own the vision they will give themselves willingly to serve. So, again, the task of leadership in a growing church continues to be one of vision casting, just as much as in a small church. Where the vision dies, the growth stops. (See chapter 21 on 'Vision building and goal setting'.)

Focus

When a church grows, ministries will start to multiply. The more diverse the congregation becomes, the more fragmented the vision can become. So it is important not only to have ongoing vision, but for the vision to have a clear focus. We have learnt the value of having a mission statement so that every person's individual vision can be measured against the church's stated vision. If, for instance, a new church member has a passion to start up a particular ministry and recruit helpers from within the church, we assess whether such a ministry will help or hinder us in fulfilling our mission statement. If it does not help we would encourage the person to fulfil their vision elsewhere or give financially towards the fulfilment of that vision elsewhere, or we would channel them into a ministry within the church that does fulfil our mission statement. If ministries are not rigorously evaluated in the light of the church's focus then a growing church runs the risk of diversifying so much that an intolerable strain is placed on resources.

Prayer

If leadership is the backbone of a healthy, growing church, the heart will always be prayer. The more we teach on prayer, the more conscious we are of our inadequate prayer lives and impoverished prayer meetings. Yet we know that if we do not keep prayer as our priority then the growth will stop. Praying within the church has evolved away from the more traditional prayer meeting to a multi-faceted tapestry of prayer groups (i.e. for revival, for world mission, for youth work) and an emphasis on prayer within home groups. The eldership meets every Sunday morning at 7.30 for prayer in addition to praying in their elders' meetings. It is often at these times that we sense the mind of God for the way forward into our next stage of growth. (See chapter 7 on 'Stimulating corporate prayer'.)

Small groups

In addition to the heart, a growing church body has other vital organs. In our case we would say that small groups are those vital organs. With an attendance in excess of 400 it is inevitable that people get overlooked and pastoral needs remain unmet. Our decision, three years ago, to abolish the term membership and replace it with the biblical concept of discipleship, created a network of relationships that enabled life to flow through the body. Every person (who requests it) has somebody else who is responsible to disciple (support, encourage, teach, parent, discipline) them. In most cases they will be discipled as part of a group of people, and nobody will disciple without themselves being discipled. As with trees, some branches are stronger than the rest, with many other branches growing from them; others may only be supporting a few twigs. This networking of relationships and sharing of pastoral responsibilities enables the church to continue to absorb more people and the capacity for growing (like a tree) is enormous. Without such shared responsibility for individual care we should have been unable to handle the level of growth the church has experienced. (See chapter 13 on 'Small groups'.)

Further reading

G Barna, *The Habits of Highly Effective Churches* (Available from Christian Research, £11.50)

W A Beckham, *The Second Reformation* (Touch Publications, Houston TX, 1993)

R Warren, *The Purpose Driven Church* (Zondervan, 1995)

CHAPTER TWENTY-FOUR

Reversing Decline

ROGER ROWE

In *A Grief Observed*, C S Lewis recorded how he sometimes felt himself to be in a vicious circle following the death of his wife, Joy: 'One keeps on emerging from a phase, but it always recurs. Round and round. Everything repeats. Am I going in circles, or dare I hope I am on a spiral?' The discouraged, despairing remnant in a church in decline is grieving in a similar way, grieving for the church they knew, grieving for their lack of numbers, grieving for their inability to understand what has happened. In such circumstances they turn in on themselves, and their backs face the world they are called to serve. But is such a decline terminal?

As always in grief, acceptance of the situation, as it is, can change overall perceptions. In bereavement, people often gain immense strength and encouragement from the fact that what they are experiencing and expressing 'makes sense'. This takes the panic out of experience.

What are we?

The small church is normal. Among English churches, 36 per cent have an attendance of 50 or less. That means that in 39,000 congregations, some 14,000 have fewer than 50 members. Of these congregations, 61 per cent are in rural locations and 75 per cent have 25 or less. (MARC) We are therefore not alone. This trend has been exacerbated by the increase in mobility in the second half of the twentieth century. Many Christians have abandoned their local churches in favour of commuting to large town and city churches and, as a direct result, the location of small churches often represents the real front line of mission. The very area where Christian witness is at its weakest is where small churches are most numerous. My own experience in working in a small church in a north Hertfordshire village, equidistant from four large towns, has highlighted this trend.

On the positive side, the declining church is usually a caring church. There is very little expectation in such a situation that the care extended by its members is going to produce large scale growth. Rather, care is seen not in terms of potential evangelistic growth but simply as something that the smaller church does because of the emphasis it places on people and relations.

Where to start in reversing decline

The major problem in many declining churches is that what may or may not be done has been raised to the level of Holy Writ. Biblical *relatives* have become *absolutes*. When discussing this with my son (aged 18), he reminded me that all too often, in churches of our tradition, both leaders and people were taught to observe certain religious practices, but they were never given the basic principles of how to 'do' church. Without doubt this is the most destructive attitude in a declining church, an attitude which must be challenged and defeated before any meaningful change and growth can occur.

An illustration may help us understand this. Many declining churches have immense experience in sending out those of their number called to work in foreign lands. Missionaries we used to call them – those engaged in cross-cultural mission. In that phrase is our clue. To be truly effective, the new missionaries must understand and be able to communicate in another culture, and to be able to do this they need to become immersed in that culture. Yet, unfortunately, most declining churches actively despise the surrounding culture, and are entirely divorced from it.

Like the cross-cultural missionary, declining churches need to be immersed in the culture of those they desire to reach. Instead, they live in a 'time warp' characterised by traditions and practices which have little or no meaning to the world they are trying to reach for Christ. Most would affirm that the gospel message they endeavour to communicate is an absolute that can never change, but they find it impossible to change the means used to communicate it in accordance with the culture of the people whom they are called to serve. Such means are *relative*, needing to change from place to place and from time to time. (See chapter 14 on 'Evangelism in a postmodern world'.)

Change, or die?

Accordingly, if the decline in the local church is to be arrested and reversed, the first step is obvious. There must be agreement that some change is necessary: the alternative is stark – continued decline and ultimate death. We must continue to wrestle not only with God's charge to us in the Great Commission, but also with how to apply it in our generation. Perhaps we shall make a few false starts, failures which must be forgiven. Yet no matter how many times leaders may fail, we must continue to strive together to fulfil God's purpose for the church so clearly set out for us in the Bible – communicating the Good News to the world around us. We must surrender all we hold dear for the sake of a world pouring into a Christless eternity.

This process necessarily involves an openness and willingness to change. Existing structures (non-absolutes) must be changed if they do not positively aid God's primary purpose for the church as revealed in the Great Commission, namely that of 'making disciples of all nations' (evangelism), and 'teaching them to obey all that I have commanded' (discipleship). The issues which all churches, of whatever tradition, face at the start of a new millennium are huge, complex and crucial to their survival; we change or die. Many have avoided such issues in the past, or perhaps approached them with emotions overcharged and minds already fixed, with the dead hand of tradition on the tiller.

As we approach them afresh we need to read our radical past in such a way that it will help us understand our less-than-radical present; to read our Bibles in such a way that they cast a light into the instinctive defensiveness of our hearts and minds. And then we must plan for the future.

- We must understand the culture and society in which we live, so bringing our predicament and choices into sharper focus.
- We must understand the strength and weaknesses of the church of which we are part, forcing us to face the prospect of change with courage.
- We must make progress in applying the necessary changes to enable us to engage better with the society in which God has placed us.

In this painful process, we seek together to rediscover the power and direction to become a growing and caring church at the local street level, engaged totally with God and totally with the community in which we are placed.

Some suggestions

Discover the key people for the future of your declining church and install yourself at their heart. Make it clear that you need their personal friendship. Spend time with them outside church activities. Work on deepening relationships, show respect, give love and thereby earn trust.

Set the tone and style for this group. Help everyone to feel accepted and let friendliness and openness flow out. Share personal things with them in transparent honesty, and ask direct questions designed to lead others into doing the same. Talk with openness and candour about your walk with God, your joys and hopes. Pray together, laugh together, enjoy each other's company. Do not be judgmental which, in my son's words, is 'the biggest turn-off there is'. Instead, learn to love in spite of people's failings.

Lead the group away from exclusiveness and into openness. Continually encourage its members to look out and draw others in. Encourage 'fringe' church members and friends to want to become part of the warm core of the church. Instead of being exclusive, encourage people to belong – belief will follow as the Lord works by his Spirit in the hearts of those who regularly hear his word.

When it comes to turning a church into a family, declining churches have a huge advantage. The fact that there are few people, probably with many shared memories, is a very real strength. Build on this by setting up church family social events – parties, video evenings, Spring fairs, coach trips, rambles and the like. Sadly, many independent churches look down on social events, thereby displaying profound misunderstanding of human nature. Our Lord knew better. He did not live in a religious vacuum, but in the everyday world of laughing and crying, talking and listening, eating and drinking, with the occasional fishing party thrown in.

If we are to stimulate a discouraged, despairing remnant in a declining church, we need to rediscover ourselves as a noisy, hectic family with our social and spiritual lives converging. Focusing on acceptance of who we are, rather than grieving for what we were, makes it possible to turn grief into joy.

Further reading

M Breen, *Growing the smaller Church* (Marshall Pickering, 1992)
G Davie, *Religion in Britain since 1945* (Blackwell, 1994)
J Lamb, *Making Progress in Church Life* (Partnership, 1997)
M Robinson and D Yarnell, *Celebrating the small Church* (Monarch, 1996)
N Summerton, *Local Churches for a new Century* (Partnership, 1996)

CHAPTER TWENTY-FIVE

Knowing When to Close

STANLEY JAMIESON

Though scripture has much to say about the planting and nurture of churches, it gives no obvious guidance for their closure. A church facing the prospect of closure may feel a sense of failure, exacerbated by the disruption to the lives of Christians who may have enjoyed fellowship and service for many years in that church. In some circumstances, however, closure may be viewed positively and, following prayerful consideration and – literally – waiting upon the Lord, can be undertaken with the assurance that it is in accordance with the divine will.

The Lord's statement to Peter that he would build his church and that 'the gates of Hades will not overcome it' (Matt 16:18) has sometimes been understood as a promise of the preservation of individual groups of his people, as well as of the worldwide church which is the Body of Christ. But this is not necessarily so. Nearly three centuries ago, Matthew Henry commented on these words: 'While the world still stands, Christ will have a church in it...The church may be foiled in particular encounters but in the main battle it shall come off more than a conqueror.' A battle may be lost, but ultimate victory is assured; soldiers of the cross may be unaware of the Lord's overall strategy.

Reasons for closure

A number of indications may point towards closure, though it should always be a last resort. They include the following:

1. The increasing average age of the membership may make continuance of the church's activities impossible. Octogenarians do not make good Sunday school teachers; nor are they well suited to distribute tracts from door to door. Pastoral care of the church becomes an impossible burden for an elderly leadership with an even older congregation. Such a situation will surely have been foreseen, however, and only if honest efforts to enlist younger

believers to the fellowship have failed should closure be contemplated.

2. Severe decline in numbers may suggest closure if the adequate performance of the church's tasks of evangelism and Bible teaching becomes impossible. In anticipation of such circumstances, measures should surely have been taken to halt or reverse the decline. For example, if another, larger, church is within travelling distance, arrangements might be made for a cross-section of older and younger members from that church to come to the aid of the smaller one. (In this case, much grace will be needed on both sides to ensure harmonious relationships.) Or amalgamation with another church might be considered. This, too, will require careful management. The siting and nature of the accommodation and proximity to a mission field of housing, as well as the relative sizes of the congregations, will need to be taken into account. The division of responsibility between the respective leaderships will call for wise and gracious decision-making.

3. The loss of a 'mission field' of local housing. A city centre church might find that the local population is being decanted to peripheral housing estates, as the central district is redeveloped for commercial purposes. In such a case, relocation rather than closure might be appropriate.

Crucial questions

If, after careful consideration of all the possibilities, the leadership believes the Lord is leading them to close the church, then certain questions need to be asked:

1. Are the members unanimously in favour of closure? If general agreement is not reached, then those in favour of closure should delay action in the hope that further prayerful consideration will bring about the hoped-for unanimity. But how long should the leadership wait? One respected Christian writer recommends decision by the majority, but counsels that the parties should act in grace (F F Bruce, *Answers to Questions*, Paternoster, 1972, p.186). Another describes majority rule as bad, but minority rule as worse (C F Hogg, cited in loc. cit.).

2. Will individuals and families be able to find an alternative spiritual home with another congregation of Christians whose doctrines and practices are in general harmony with their own?

3. Will a gospel witness be provided in the neighbourhood by another group of believers?

4. Can the church's buildings and contents be put to appropriate alternative use? To many, it would be distressing if the premises

were to reopen as, say, a betting shop or some other establishment inimical to Christian witness.

If all of these questions can be satisfactorily answered, and the reasons for cessation of worship and witness in that place leave the church with an easy conscience, after careful thought and earnest prayer it is likely that the closure is within the permissive will of God. There can be no general prescription.

The experience of one church

The congregation had been functioning for more than a century in an industrial part of a large city. They occupied a solidly built stone 'mission hall' that had been recently renovated at considerable cost, and the membership looked forward to renewal within the church. However, the neighbourhood was decaying. Working-class housing in the surrounding streets was gradually being demolished. Small-scale industry had been steadily vacating nearby premises, and the only shop in the street had been shut. The local authority and a development trust started a programme of wholesale demolition and site clearance in the immediate surroundings of the hall.

Subsequently an industrial estate was built on the cleared site and, for cosmetic reasons, the developer rebuilt the outer wall of the church's meeting place, at no cost to the church. The Lord was preparing the accommodation for a new occupier but the congregation saw their mission field shrink as the residents moved away and attendance at Sunday school, family services and women's meetings steadily dwindled. Nearly all the few remaining members resided in other parts of the city but continued to worship in the place they had attended when younger.

The elders reluctantly considered closure and for a period of two years waited on the Lord for guidance. The membership was consulted and prayerfully considered the options. Several factors led the elders to the conviction that the Lord was guiding towards closure.

1. A Christian charitable trust intimated that they were keen to purchase and occupy the building.

2. A new church which had been established fifty miles away needed the furnishings and equipment that closure would release.

3. A Christian witness in the near vicinity was provided by other evangelical churches.

4. At meetings of the whole (though small) church, alternative spiritual homes were identified for all members.

Agreement on closure was reached, a date was fixed for dispersal, and arrangements were made for transfer of the building and its contents to grateful recipients.

Consequences

The elderly elders have been happy that the closure has been effected while they were still of sound mind and body, and before depletion of their numbers laid a disproportionate burden on the survivors. Other churches warmly welcomed the additional members they received. Funds were distributed to a variety of missionary and charitable agencies.

All involved have experienced the truth of William Cowper's verse:

> Ye fearful saints fresh courage take;
> The clouds ye so much dread
> Are big with mercy and shall break
> In blessings on your head.

CHAPTER TWENTY-SIX

Planting a New Church

PAUL SANDS

Some people have reservations about church planting, fearing that it will harm the parent church by breaking up an existing Christian fellowship, violating its love and unity, and demanding too high a cost. This is to forget the NT exhortations to generous giving (Luke 6:38; Acts 20:35) and the numerous examples of church planting which it contains.

There are many reasons why we should be actively engaged in planting churches.

- The nature of the church directs us towards church planting (Acts 2:38-47).
- It is the biblical pattern (Acts 14:23; Rom 15:20).
- New churches have more vitality than well established ones and are more effective in evangelism. 'It's easier to have babies than to raise the dead.' (Peter Wagner)
- Church planting is one of the best ways to encourage the development of new leadership and to utilise the gifts and talents of church members.
- The opportunities are unlimited, for many people are still unreached, and congregations that die need to be replaced.
- To reach the unchurched we need to offer them a variety of options. 'Each new generation must be evangelised on its own terms.' (Peter Wagner)

God must be sovereign in church planting

This is a fundamental biblical principle. All ministry starts with a vision of the Lord himself (Josh 5:13; Isa 6; Acts 9). Jesus is the Lord of the harvest (Luke 10:2). Churches are built by God (Matt 16:18). Churches exist by the will of God (Rev 2:5). We can expect evidence of God's sovereign, supernatural work in the establishment of churches (Mark 16:20; 1 Thess 1:4, 5).

Examples of God's sovereignty in NT church planting are numerous. They include the new churches in Samaria (Acts 8:4-8); Antioch (Acts 11:19-21); Iconium, Lystra and Derbe (Acts 14); Macedonia (Acts 16:6-10). Scripture makes clear the difference between a church built by the Lord and one built by man (Psa 127:1, 2).

In our own times, God's sovereignty has been evidenced in cases such as the Icthus group of churches in South London and overseas, led by Roger and Faith Forster; Paul Yonggi Cho's church in Seoul, South Korea; and the Park Christian Fellowship/Borehamwood Christian Fellowship Cell Church, part of the International Gospel Church (formerly Woodcroft Evangelical Church).

Practical consequences follow from this. Church planting must be soaked in prayer. Church planters must carefully maintain their own spiritual life. They must watch to see where God is at work, and run with that. They must enquire of the Lord before taking any action. They must put the church in God's hands – and keep it there.

Church planting and spiritual warfare

Evangelism, salvation and church planting go hand in hand. They are part of a process called spiritual warfare leading to the establishing of God's rule (the kingdom of God) through the setting up of central communities (parts of the church, the Body of Christ) in hostile territory (the world). Whenever a person comes to faith in Jesus Christ a stronghold of Satan is torn down; every time the sick are healed or the poor are helped we wield the sword of the word of truth against the spirit of evil. Not only is the enemy resisted but the glory of the Lord is revealed.

Church planting is a major part of the master strategy of fulfilling the call to spiritual warfare. Wherever we plant a church a fortress is set up. A place is established where people come to be healed, restored, saved and grow in relationship with God and one another. A new community is formed within the greater community, modelling biblical principles through lifestyle. God's family on earth is set up in a particular location, with Jesus as its head. It is not only a place of wholeness (salvation) but of equipping and sending out the gospel of Jesus Christ to the surrounding society. The Holy Spirit starts working upon a community.

Church planting needs a call from God

This follows from the above. Only God through Jesus in the power of the Holy Spirit can build his church. Planting churches is warfare and in war the commander-in-chief must be in control. So, in order to plant a church you (i.e. a group of likeminded people with a vision from God and, usually, a recognised leader even within a plurality of leaders) must have heard God's voice of command.

God speaks in five major ways: through his word (the Bible); through people full of his Spirit and wisdom (the counsel of the brethren, Acts 6:5 etc.); through visions and dreams (see *Divine Guidance* by G H Lang); through the gifts of the Spirit in a prophetic word or revelatory picture; and through the peace of Jesus Christ working in your heart (Col 3:15; Phil 4:7). God always directs through a cross-section of the above. He will not remain silent. He always speaks in relation to new areas, direction or decision. He loves us and cares about us.

Church planting requires a team of the right sort of people

Motivation is vitally important. Some people have wrong motives for joining a church planting team. They may want position or power; be looking for a change because they are bored or tired of what they are doing; or even see it as a way of escape from problems, people, positions or circumstances which they find difficult.

Personal motivations for church planting may be positive, negative or neutral. Positive motivations include compassion for people who are 'lost'; desire for more expressions of Christ's body in the form of local churches; desire to expand God's rule and influence in the world (his kingdom); a burden to reach a specific people group/need; a specific calling from God. Among the negative motivations are dislike of the present church's style or vision; inability to get along with other Christians; desire to be in control and do one's own thing; urge to discover one's significance and prove one's worth. Other motivations may be neutral. These include some specific personal or theological agenda; a desire to be involved in preaching or leading; lack of open doors in established churches.

The kind of person God uses in church planting

A study done in 1990-4 showed that the person who does best in church planting is someone who has vision; co-operation/support from the spouse (if any); ability to create ownership of ministry; flexibility and adaptability; faith; commitment to church growth; ability to build group cohesiveness; strong motivation; responsiveness to the community; ability to utilise the giftedness of others and effectively build relationships; resilience; and the ability to relate to the unchurched.

Research undertaken by Paul Sands shows the need for strong, visionary leadership; ability to identify, recruit, train, deploy, monitor, nurture and reproduce leaders; a proven track record under supervision; an indigenous support group or a solid lifeline to a regional church; a clear, written plan; willingness of leader (s)/planter(s) to take responsibility for the growth of the new church (under God); a strong supportive marriage; effective gathering techniques with highly motivated, well-led and organised meetings, and ruthless evaluation of them; ability to think through and solve problems; certainty of their call, optimism and faith about achieving results.

A personal experience illustrates the need for leaders to take responsibility for church growth. After 18 months on Grahame Park Estate, Colindale, North London, the 23 people sent out from Woodcroft Evangelical Church (though still remaining part of it) to plant a new church had been reduced to 21! Steve Brothwell, a church elder now planting a cell church in Dublin, and Paul Sands were very despondent. After a walk together one hot summer afternoon, they returned to pray, cry out to God and seek him anew. They were desperate! He answered: 'I have much people in this city' (Acts 18:10). Steve and Paul had a witness in their spirits that the Holy Spirit had spoken. They shared the message with their fellow leaders and within three months numbers had grown to 50, and within six months to more than 70. It had been their responsibility to seek God's face; it was his to bless – and he did!

A biblical/spiritual perspective

Church planters need to possess character and personality traits such as:

- absolute commitment to Jesus Christ (Phil 3:8-10);
- a track record of fruit of the Spirit (Gal 5:22, 23);
- genuine love for people and a desire to serve them (Rom 9:3);
- a high level of attainment of the qualifications for an elder (1 Tim 3:1-7; Tit 1:6- 9);
- freedom from major problems with ambition, owned or hidden agenda of empire-building etc (Phil 2:3; Jas 3:13-18);
- faithfulness in ministry already given (1 Tim 1:12; 2 Tim 2:2);
- willingness to work hard, endure loneliness, make sacrifices etc (Phil 3:14; 4:11-13).

They must also possess gifting in areas such as the ability to command the support of others, to teach, organise, plan strategically; empowerment and the ability to impart it to others (Eph 4:7-16); a God-given vision; and the ability to believe God and to work for the fulfilment of that vision.

It is essential that they be called. The call is first of all to Jesus himself, and then to ministry for him (Mark 3:13-15). A call to ministry should be quite specific, as in the case of Nehemiah (Neh 1: 4), to a particular place or people, for a definite purpose. It should be confirmed by scripture, prophecy, spouse, pastors/elders and others.

Since church planting is essentially team work, training is required through membership and involvement in a local church. There is no place for mavericks or loners who are unable to work with others. Church planting teams need to be sent out by and report back to the church from which they go out (Acts 13:1-3; 14:27, 28).

How to determine whether someone is suited for church planting

The brief answer is: look first at their strengths; then at their track record. Carefully consider their personality, character and leadership style. Then look at their experience and their certainty of a call from God. Have they a passion, first for him and then for his work? And have they a sober estimate of their skills and abilities?

Team leaders are essential

According to an article in an American management and marketing magazine, partners are four times as likely to succeed as individuals since they ensure the best use of time and giftedness.

A church planting team needs a strong, recognised, overall leader who will develop other leaders and not feel threatened by them. Four strong, clearly called couples will be required (including the overall leader and spouse). All leaders should fully share the vision and values of the team. They should be totally committed to the leader and spouse, both as leader and persons, and to all members of the leadership group. They must be capable, responsible people who are available, not afraid of hard work, and both teachable and responsive. They will need to possess strong hearts as well as heads, and a good deal of knowledge and experience.

Worship leaders are the first requirement, then evangelists, then small group/cell leaders or youth workers. As a general rule, avoid having too many.

Tips for team building

- Get to know each other intimately, and build strong relationships.
- Discover the motives, call and vision of team members, and make sure they are committed to the same vision and ethos.
- Set out vision, goals, objectives and strategy clearly. Let them buy into it voluntarily.
- Make sure they have counted the cost and know what commitment is all about.
- Warn that lots of work will be expected – but let them know that it will be fun!
- Make sure they are risk-takers – after all, faith is spelled 'risk'!
- Ensure they both love and like the leadership and accept the overall leader as the first among equals.
- Do not appoint to positions prematurely. Take your time about it. Look for reliability as well as potential.
- Weed out any who are disloyal and rebellious.
- Pray a lot, and listen to advice.
- Be an intercessor, for the enemy will be defeated on your knees. Ask the Lord to reveal to you the principalities and powers in your new area and also the institutions, social functions and key people in which they are active. Wrestle in prayer until they flee. Major victories will be associated with intercessory prayer (Jer 33:3; Luke 10:2).

Relationships with your sending church

Maintain intimate relationships with your sending church, before, during and after leaving to plant a new church. They will have had to pay a heavy price, emotionally, spiritually, and financially, to release you to go. So, communicate with those you love and respect. Share with them your hopes, fears and dreams. Be honest with them, admitting mistakes and failures, as well as sharing joys, gains and victories.

New Testament models of church planting

In general terms, NT church planting was characterised by informality, relationships, cultural relevance, urgency and vigour, concern for continuous multiplication. Eight models are discernible:

- the mass evangelism church plant (Acts 2; cf. Mark 6:39);
- the mega-church plant (Acts 6:7);
- the maybe church plant (Acts 10; 16; 19);
- the mushroom church plant (Acts 11);

- the mobile church plant (Acts 13:20);
- the mini-mission church plant (Acts 13:20);
- the mother church plant (Rev 2;3 – assuming that Ephesus spawned the other churches);
- the multi-cell church plant (Acts 20:20; 28:30).

Arguably, the idea of a core group is central to all eight models. It is reflected in the home group at Bethany and the cluster of house churches recorded in Romans 16.

The 'cell church' is probably the fastest growing model in the world. It commences with the formation of small *cell groups*. A cluster of such groups come together as a *congregation*. A cluster of such congregations come together for *celebration*. Having tried other methods before cell church, I believe this model to be the most holistic and biblical approach. It is also the most successful because discipleship, training, evangelising, worship, teaching and application happen in relationship with one another, and this automatically leads to growth and reproduction. (See the books by Astin, Beckham and Neighbour, listed below, for full discussions of the cell church model.)

Building a church : the first three years

What follows is an attempt to summarise the cell church method over a notional period of three years. It assumes that you are totally committed to the approach, and that you have already been led to the location and the people to whom you are to minister. It also presupposes that you have not made the mistake of committing yourself to a pre-planned, programmatic approach.

Phase 1. Laying the foundations

This starts with Phase 1a, which is one of gathering and forming. Keep things simple (cf. the niche retailer versus supermarket strategy). Build with an eye to the future; an ear turned to the Lord; your feet on the ground; and your heart pure in God's sight. Constantly tell your story; tell his story; explain the mysteries of life; disciple; explain the infrastructure; live in brokenness and dependency on God; re-evaluate and remain flexible in what you are doing.

It continues with Phase 1b which is the building process in which core groups are established. Objectives should be to develop personal relationships; to learn to minister to one another's needs; and to become accountable to and intimate with each other. The biblical basis should be studied in Acts 2:42; 4:32-35; Romans 15:1, 2; Galatians 5:13; 6:2.

Throughout Phase 1 the process involves, first, 'people finding' experiences. This means making personal contacts in the secular community, using the media (e.g. newspaper, radio) as much as possible. It includes establishing personal contacts with members of the Christian community (churches, para-church organisations, etc.).

'People developing' experiences are crucial. Who we are and what we are aiming to do need to be clarified. The purpose of the group meetings which are arranged must be clearly stated.

Above all, 'people relating' experiences are of fundamental importance. First, they should be designed to establish a climate of love, sharing, caring – and fun. This will enable relationships to be formed between members of the group. There should also be a climate of discussion, vision building and shared planning, leading to a sense of common ownership.

Progress needs to be evaluated with a view to knowing when the time has come to move on to Phase 2. Key factors are the degree of intimacy felt, shown and acknowledged in the group; the amount of voluntary interaction evident on a daily basis; and the level of sharing – physical and circumstantial, and also spiritual and emotional.

Phase 2. Establishing a caring community

The aim of this second phase is to establish a caring community along the lines of Romans 1:11, 12; 12:6; 15:7; Hebrews 13:1; James 5:16; 1 Peter 4:9, 10; 1 John 1:7.

The objectives include progress in receiving and using spiritual gifts; seeing spiritual, emotional, social and intellectual needs met; developing an increasing willingness to make friends; raising the levels of intimacy, caring and sharing – i.e. increasing love.

The process involves providing opportunities for the gifts of the Spirit to be taught, modelled, received and practised; learning to live together by means of daily and special events and retreats; developing new relationships through participation in social events; encouraging deeper levels of intimacy; and providing opportunities for discussions on direction, plans, vision, events, etc. in which people can talk freely about their feelings and ideas.

As always, progress needs to be evaluated. The group is ready to move on to Phase 3 when members are growing in their use of spiritual gifts; when they are expressing their needs at all levels (spiritual, emotional, personal, social, etc.) and these are being met by the group; when new members are getting involved in the group; and when members are manifestly being honest with God and with one another in a deepening intimacy.

Phase 3. Multiplying groups

This phase focuses on group multiplication. Its biblical basis is to be found in passages like Matthew 5:16; John 4:35; 2 Timothy 2:2; James 2:1; 1 Peter 2:9.

The objectives are to develop a sense of mission which will result in a desire to reach out to others; to create new groups through dividing, seeding and adopting; to discover who is best at befriending and nurturing new people; and to identify those who have gospel witnessing or special ministry ability and match them with those who need it.

The process can best be pursued by drawing attention to effective models (i.e. testimonies of past victories in this area) by providing space for new people to be integrated into the group through planting new ones; by providing modelling and training on 'how to be friends' in order to help people become absorbed into the group; and by encouraging group members to reach out to their families and any sphere in which they have influence (cf. NT households).

Evaluation is needed in order to determine when the group is ready to move on to the next phase. It is ready when new members are being regularly added to groups; the number of groups is expanding; members are extending their outreach into their individual spheres of influence; and relational skills are being developed and refined.

Phase 4. Establishing congregations

During this phase, the various groups which have been formed are brought together on a regular basis to function as congregations along the lines of biblical passages like Matthew 18:19, 20; Mark 16:15, 20; Acts 2:41, 42, 46, 47; Acts 20:20; Galatians 6:10.

The wide-ranging objectives of this phase are to bring together the various cell groups for fellowship; to develop ministries that meet the felt needs of the community (e.g. parent and toddler groups, advice centre); to foster ongoing penetration of the unchurched community through relationship and friendship/ bridge-building activities; and to receive those who are being reached through these activities.

Ways in which this process can be accomplished are numerous. The needs of the cluster of groups which now also meets as a congregation for fellowship, worship, teaching, facilities and mission should be assessed, and appropriate ways of meeting these needs developed. Congregational leaders need to be recognised and released for training. The community should be surveyed in order to discover felt needs which might be met by the congregation. Training should be provided in each area of function and ministry. Strategies should be put in place for reaching specific groups in the community. Encouragement and training are required for group/cell members, to enable them to absorb and integrate those reached through community initiatives.

Progress made needs to be evaluated with a view to discovering when the time has come to move on to Phase 5. That time will have come when the process outlined above is operating to the satisfaction of the congregation, as evidenced by full commitment of their time, energy and money; and there is a sense that the congregation is being propelled by the activities rather than the activities being propelled by the congregation.

Phase 5. Establishing celebration

This phase commences when a group of congregations comes together regularly for celebration, in accordance with scriptures such as Matthew 6:33; Romans 15:6; 1 Corinthians 14:23-26; 1 Timothy 3:10; 5:22).

In this phase, the objectives are to discover and develop an appropriate style of celebration; to recognise and/or affirm pastoral/worship/teaching leadership; to assess facility needs; and to deal with any legal/financial/tax requirements.

The process will involve exploring, experimenting with and evaluating format options for the celebration needs which have been identified; clarifying everyone's responsibilities, authority and relationships; following a planning process which includes choosing and exploring facilities and opportunities; and seizing opportunities to acquire assets, land, facilities, equipment, etc.

Progress needs to be evaluated as in phase 4. The phase will be complete when the process is operating to the satisfaction of the congregation, shown by full commitment of time, energy and money; and there is a sense that the congregation is being carried along by its celebration activity which is felt to be beneficial, fun, enjoyable and thoroughly worthwhile.

Tips for coping with times of struggle – which will come

• Overcome the 'smallness syndrome' with vision and faith.

- Maintain your vision at all costs.
- Train leaders to care for the flock.
- Insist on the miracles of God.
- Fight the enemy with vigour.
- Overcome criticism with love and determination.
- Remember that success awaits faithful church planters.

Conclusion

Much more could be said. It must suffice to outline the kind of church we should be planting. Antioch – where Christians were first known as such – provides the model (Acts 13:1-3). It was a multi-cultural local church with a global view. It enjoyed plurality of leadership drawn from diverse racial, ethnic and cultural backgrounds. Led by the Holy Spirit, it did everything with one accord in mind and purpose. A worshipping church, it excelled in corporate worship. As a caring church it demonstrated the love of God in a practical way. It was a missionary church which sent out Paul and Barnabas, and a praying and fasting church which continuously sought and did the will of God.

Further reading

H Astin, *Body and Cell* (Monarch, 1998)

W A Beckham, *The Second Reformation* (Touch Publications, Houston TX, 1993)

R W Neighbour, *Where do we do from Here? A guidebook for the cell group church* (Touch Publications, Houston TX, 1990)

S Murray, *Church Planting* (Paternoster, 1998)

CHAPTER TWENTY-SEVEN

Interchurch Activity

BETH DICKSON

In scripture

The NT demonstrates that, while the local church was the dynamo for the preaching and teaching of the gospel in a locality, each church had wider responsibilities, chiefly to recognise and support the work of similar churches in other places. Paul shows Epaphras (probably in Rome) agonizing in prayer for the churches at Colossae, Laodicea and Hierapolis (Col 4:13) and the letter Paul wrote to Colossae was to be read in each of these churches in that area (Col 4:16). NT churches received into communion itinerant preachers, teachers, and possibly travellers from whose ministry they were then able to benefit. This was a general principle of church life (3 John 8) and sometimes a result of apostolic instruction (Col 4:10). Timothy, who was from Lystra (Acts 16:1) was left by Paul at Ephesus to continue the work there (1 Tim 1:3); Tychicus also worked in Ephesus (2 Tim 4:12). Titus worked in Crete (Tit 1: 5) and Dalmatia (2 Tim 4:10). There is a great deal of evidence of the use of itinerant workers throughout a variety of churches.

Churches were also called on to support each other in times of need. The church at Antioch sent aid to the believers during the Judean famine (Acts 11:27-30). The church at Antioch also spearheaded new initiatives in mission by sending out Paul and Barnabas and probably supporting them materially to some extent. Churches met to sort out disagreements, as when the church at Antioch sent Paul and Barnabas to Jerusalem to explain that Jewish Christians were preaching the need for Gentiles to be circumcised if they were to be truly Christian (Acts 15). The NT shows a number of local churches striving together for the furtherance of the gospel and the establishment of God-glorifying Christian churches throughout the known world.

In our history

It was on such a biblical basis that Brethren churches and churches with Brethren roots, though self-governing, thrived by abundant co-operation in specific enterprises. Evangelism is the most obvious example and the present bodies, such as Counties in England and Scottish Counties Evangelistic Movement (SCEM) in Scotland, are the fruit of early evangelistic campaigns. For overseas evangelism – missionary work – it also seemed right to set up Echoes, not a missionary-sending organisation, but a conduit where information from the field could be relayed back home and vice versa. The Scottish sister organisation, the Home and Foreign Missionary Fund, is now known as Interlink. In this process a great deal of useful knowledge was built up by the staff at both offices and they were much respected and consulted for advice on a range of issues, though, of course, any local church was free to disregard such advice if it felt it had the mind of the Spirit. A number of financial organisations were also established to help churches to build accommodation or to support a variety of other church-based enterprises. The Laing Trust, Stewardship Services and the Aitchison Trust are all still in existence.

What is not always recognised is that there were many invisible forms of interchurch activity which were productive in all sorts of ways. Generally speaking, churches read either *The Witness or The Believer's Magazine* which, in addition to giving them Bible teaching, also kept them abreast of church affairs – the progress of evangelistic campaigns, the dates of larger conferences where the most able Bible expositors could be heard, as well as news of personalia. The free course of information and the sense of belonging to a group larger than that of the local church itself, gave the movement a sense of purpose and direction which accounts for much of the atmosphere of activity and effectiveness which it enjoyed in its heyday.

Today

The principles of those days are important for any local church wishing to be effective in contemporary society. It is vital that local churches have a sense of their identity as part of the Body of Christ. This encourages small churches not to stagnate because there is much good work going on and it means that large churches may not become complacent – no matter how successful they are in their own terms, there is still much to be done.

The first and most obvious area of interchurch activity is in evangelism. Counties and SCEM can bring expertise to a locality in order to facilitate outreach. If churches group together, then the work and resources involved in such a mission are shared – as are the benefits. People are likely to be converted and church members can see at first hand the activity of God among them. They can also see that they are gifted in evangelism.

Churches often use the services of a full-time worker. The Church Planting Initiative (CPI), supported by Gospel Literature Outreach (GLO), Counties and Stewardship Services (SS), provides resources for those looking to establish a church in a particular area. At Tilsley College in Motherwell, GLO provides full-time educational courses for people thinking about going to Bible college, or going on mission, or to some other area of full-time Christian service. The Partnership Link Up Service (PLUS) aims to link people who are looking for full-time positions in Christian service with local churches which are looking for full-time workers.

It is also useful for churches to come together to share good practice. As society changes, churches must find new ways of staying relevant, in order to make sense to their own members and to provide an experience of 'church' which is comprehensible and attractive to those examining the claims of Jesus Christ. Partnership aims to provide support services for local churches in such areas. It has a publishing programme through which members can become informed about how they might go about tackling difficult areas of change; it runs seminars where leaders can come together and discuss how they have implemented change and whether it has been successful; such a forum is indispensable in disseminating good practice, and provides leaders with news, encouragement, advice and the support of those who understand what a difficult activity implementing change in church can be. Despite the fact that many churches with Brethren roots now define themselves as independent evangelical churches, it still makes sound practical sense to be in touch with churches who share similar organisation and values simply because the areas of mutual value, mutual understanding, mutual difficulty and mutual support are greater than they would be across denominational groupings.

Most Brethren churches or churches with Brethren roots can see quite clearly what they have in common with other evangelicals. Within the Body of Christ, those Christians who hold that a relationship with Christ is of fundamental importance, that the Bible is the word of God, that people need to be converted and that the people of God should work hard to spread the gospel, are our nearest relations. Here too we can find help with evangelism. Many groups will provide teams trained in relevant evangelistic techniques; and may run training courses in evangelism. Saltmine is just one example and others can be found in the section on 'Evangelism' in the UK *Christian Handbook*. Other organisations are interested in training people in social action. Large evangelical holiday programmes such as Spring Harvest provide the opportunity to hear the best evangelical preachers, to study aspects of Christian life with a depth and rigour which local churches who do not have the necessary specialised knowledge cannot match, and to meet and be stimulated and encouraged by other Christians who share the same outlook on the faith.

Scripture Union (SU) is famous for its work among children and young people, and its promotion of Bible study for all ages. Again, it provides a natural home for the children of believers to grow in their faith, either at camps or in school groups, and it provides a framework in which young people and others can learn to share their faith, and be given responsibilities which will prepare them for future church life. The Universities and Colleges Christian Fellowship (UCCF) provides teaching and opportunities for students in tertiary education.

The Evangelical Alliance (EA) provides a meeting point for all UK evangelicals. With strong and developing work in the nations of the United Kingdom (there are offices in Glasgow, Cardiff and Belfast), the EA represents, through churches and individual members, around a million evangelicals. In recent years the EA has developed its relations with the media and is now often invited to present an evangelical perspective on contemporary issues. Internally, the EA's theological study group, ACUTE, has produced important reports on areas where evangelicals disagree. Homosexuality was discussed in the report 'Faith, Hope and Homosexuality' and ACUTE has also discussed the doctrine of Hell. Supporting EA is a very real way of supporting evangelicals in their call to be salt and light in their communities.

It is also possible for evangelical churches to be involved with groupings of local churches of a variety of denominations in the same area, often under the auspices of Churches Together. This presents another opportunity for evangelicals. Apart from the deep satisfaction that comes from getting to know other Christians in an area, it also forces evangelicals to realise that other Christians do things differently and that joining with them requires respect, humility and confidence (not arrogance) in the evangelical ability to contribute constructively to such a group. As the number of Christians in Britain continues to decline, the issue of mission is becoming unavoidable for many denominations and, for many individual members, involvement in mission in not something of which they have much experience. With tact and encouragement, evangelicals have much to offer in this respect. In the past it has not always been thought profitable to be involved in such bodies but the changing nature of the relationship between church and society makes united action and the pooling of resources that accompanies it an altogether different proposition.

It is quite likely that representatives of Roman Catholic churches may also sit on local branches of Churches Together. To meet Catholics on a religious footing such as this might be a new or unusual experience for some. However, such a meeting can be extremely constructive if those involved concentrate on what unites them. In morality and social justice, Catholics and evangelicals have much in common. In such areas united action is possible; in areas where there is difference over doctrine mutual respect should characterise relationships, especially as those involved see the common life of Christ in each other. It should, however, be noted that some evangelicals may be uncomfortable linking themselves to non-evangelicals. Elders thinking over this issue would need to communicate clearly and sensitively with their flock in order to familiarise themselves with the range of opinion in any local church before taking precipitate action.

John Donne said, 'No man is an island, entire of itself; every man is a piece of the continent, a part of the main.' This is as true of churches as of individuals. We are members of a body. We lose much of the richness of the life of God if we keep ourselves to ourselves. Our churchmanship while being principled, coherent, confident and worked out in a specific location, should potentially be as inclusive and as various as the 'many-splendoured wisdom of God' which the church truly is.

Some useful addresses

Counties
30 Haynes Rd
Westbury BA13 3HD

Echoes
1 Widcombe Cres
Bath BA2 6AQ

SCEM (Scottish Counties
Evangelistic Movement)
916 Tollcross Rd
Glasgow G32 8PE

Interlink
Challenge House
29 Canal St
Glasgow G4 0AD

GLO (Gospel Literature Outreach)
78 Muir St
Motherwell ML1 1BN

Stewardship Services
PO Box 99
Loughton IG10 3QJ

Tilsley College
78 Muir St
Motherwell ML1 1BN

Partnership
Abbey Court
Cove
Tiverton EX16 7RT

PLUS (Partnership Link Up Service)
Alan Batchelor
15 Barncroft
Berkhamsted
Herts. HP4 3NL

Saltmine Trust
PO Box 15
Dudley DY3 2AN

Evangelical Alliance
Whitefield House
186 Kennington Park Rd
London SE11 4BT

EA Scotland Challenge House
29 Canal St
Glasgow G4 0AD

EA Northern Ireland
3 Fitzwilliam St
Belfast BT9 6AW

EA Wales
20 High St
Cardiff CF1 2BZ

Scripture Union
207 Queensway
Bletchley
Milton Keynes MK2 2EB

Scripture Union Scotland
29 Canal St
Glasgow G4 0AD

Scripture Union Northern Ireland
157 Albertbridge Rd
Belfast BT5 4PS

UCCF (Universities and Colleges
Christian Fellowship)
38 De Montfort St
Leicester LE1 7GP

Spring Harvest
14 Horsted Sq
Uckfield TN22 1QL

Churches Together in Britain and
Ireland
Inter-Church House
35 Lower Marsh
London SE1 7RL

Action of Churches Together in
Scotland
Scottish Churches House
Kirk St
Dunblane FK15 0AJ

CYTUN Churches Together in Wales
11 St Helen's Rd
Swansea SA1 4AL

Irish Council of Churches
Inter-Church Centre
48 Elmwood Ave
Belfast
BT9 6AZ

PART FOUR

Pastoral Matters

CHAPTER TWENTY-EIGHT

Encouraging Godly Living

PETER COUSINS

In 2 Timothy 3:12 Paul sums up the Christian life style as 'to live godly in Christ Jesus'. Elsewhere he describes God's saving purpose as being expressed in 'lives that are self-controlled, upright, and godly, in this present world' (Tit 2:12). But in 'this present world' living 'in Christ Jesus' is not always straightforward. Although God loves the world, which he made 'very good', there is a sense in which Christians are not to love the world (1 John 2:15) and should remain unstained by it (Jas 1:27).

Two generations ago, evangelical Christians were frequently supplied with simple guidance about godly living. It entailed giving a due place to religious observance, avoiding the kinds of behaviour that would, in effect, interfere with earning one's livelihood and (partly linked to the former) abstaining from a specific range of 'worldly' activities.

NT priorities are rather different. In 1 Timothy 6:18 believers are to 'do good, to be rich in good works, generous, and ready to share'. Paul's attitude in the previous verse (17) ('[God] richly provides us with everything for our enjoyment') resembles that of Jesus, who was denounced as a glutton and a drunkard. Although he loved his Father's good world he warned his disciples against the systems of power and religion which dominated society and the hearts of men and women. Indeed, he rejected this so emphatically that he was accused of being demon-possessed. Jesus thought of his disciples as being in the world, although not of it, and told them not to hide their light but to shine in the world's darkness. They must be salt, seasoning or preserving society.

Preserving the world

A second-century document, the 'Apology to Diognetus' contains a remarkable description of how Christians then understood the question:

Christians are distinguished from other men neither by country,
nor language, nor the customs which they observe. For they
neither inhabit cities of their own, nor employ a peculiar form of
speech, nor lead a life which is marked out by any singularity.
The course of conduct which they follow has not been devised by
any speculation or deliberation of inquisitive men; nor do they,
like some, proclaim themselves the advocates of any merely
human doctrines. But, inhabiting Greek as well as barbarian
cities, according as the lot of each of them has determined, and
following the customs of the natives in respect to clothing, food,
and the rest of their ordinary conduct, they display to us their
wonderful and confessedly striking method of life. They dwell in
their own countries, but simply as sojourners. As citizens, they
share in all things with others, and yet endure all things as if
foreigners. Every foreign land is to them as their native country,
and every land of their birth as a land of strangers. They marry,
as do all [others]; they beget children; but they do not destroy
their offspring. They have a common table, but not a common
bed. They are in the flesh, but they do not live after the flesh.
They pass their days on earth, but they are citizens of heaven.
They obey the prescribed laws, and at the same time surpass the
laws by their lives. They love all men, and are persecuted by all.
They are unknown and condemned; they are put to death, and
restored to life. They are poor, yet make many rich; they are in
lack of all things, and yet abound in all; they are dishonoured,
and yet in their very dishonour are glorified. They are evil
spoken of, and yet are justified; they are reviled, and bless; they
are insulted, and repay the insult with honour; they do good, yet
are punished as evildoers. When punished, they rejoice as if
quickened into life; they are assailed by the Jews as foreigners,
and are persecuted by the Greeks; yet those who hate them are
unable to assign any reason for their hatred.

To sum up . . . what the soul is in the body, that are Christians
in the world. The soul is dispersed through all the members of the
body, and Christians are scattered through all the cities of the
world. The soul dwells in the body, yet is not of the body; and
Christians dwell in the world, yet are not of the world. The
invisible soul is guarded by the visible body, and Christians are
known indeed to be in the world, but their godliness remains
invisible. The flesh hates the soul, and wars against it, though
itself sustaining no injury, because it is prevented from enjoying
pleasures; the world also hates the Christians, though in no wise
injured, because they abjure pleasures. The soul loves the flesh
that hates it, and [loves also] the members; Christians likewise

love those that hate them. The soul is imprisoned in the body, yet preserves that very body; and Christians are confined in the world as in a prison, and yet they are the preservers of the world . . .

We need to be clear about one basic fact: God is not greatly interested in 'religion' or even in 'spirituality' as such. What concerns him is relationships – with him, with the world he has made, and with the persons whom he has made in his image and for whom Christ died. Isaiah dismisses religious observance as 'temple trampling' (Isa 1:12). It is because of their concern for others that the 'sheep' are invited to share the 'joy of their Lord' (Matt 25:33). Prayer and theology and spirituality are part of something larger and all-embracing. Living in harmony takes precedence over 'worship' (Matt 5:23, 24).

It is not particularly difficult to define the distinctives of a Christian way of life. We are still called to 'act justly, and to love mercy, and to walk humbly with [our] God' (Mic 6:8). Jesus himself summarised the requirements of the law as loving God and one's neighbour. He insisted on the importance of forgiving others. 'If you do not forgive others, neither will your Father forgive your trespasses' (Matt 6:15). Paul reckons the chief characteristic of the unbeliever is a refusal 'to honour ... God or give thanks to him' (Rom 1:21).

Although this is not hard to grasp there has been a good deal of misunderstanding about 'what the Lord requires' of Christians. People have imagined that they are called to be soul-winners, theologians, prayer warriors and so on. But, as we have seen, the biblical priorities are quite different. What they amount to is that God's saving and re-creating purpose is to develop the capacity of every son and daughter of Adam to be fully human: that is, to love, praise and serve God and to live in his world in fellowship with the rest of humankind.

Too often the hymns and songs we sing, whether pietistic or triumphalist, distort scripture by ignoring this. It is no accident that *Songs and Hymns of Fellowship*, to mention one popular collection, while it includes songs about 'signs and wonders', omits one of Charles Wesley's greatest hymns, presumably because it is 'merely' about a godly daily life.

Forth in thy name, O Lord, I go,
My daily labour to pursue,
Thee, only thee, resolved to know,
In all I think, or speak, or do.

The task thy wisdom hath assigned
O let me cheerfully fulfil,

In all my works thy presence find,
And prove thy good and perfect will!

Thee may I set at my right hand,
Whose eyes my inmost substance see;
And labour on at thy command,
And offer all my works to thee.

Give me to bear thy easy yoke,
And every moment watch and pray,
And still to things eternal look,
And hasten to thy glorious day.

For thee delightfully employ
Whate'er thy bounteous grace hath given;
And run my course with even joy,
And closely walk with thee to heaven.

If Christians are enjoined to live like this it follows that church leaders should help them do so. For those of us fortunate enough to be in work, Monday means neither a day of exorcisms nor an extended prayer meeting but a day of service to our fellows and thus to the Lord. How can we promote this kind of worldly spirituality which will glorify God while both challenging and blessing our fellows?

Example

The most important way is to model it (1Tim 4:16). We may wonder at Paul's temerity in telling people to imitate him but we can all remember men and women who have influenced others not by their words but by the way they lived. Church leaders have a fearsome responsibility in this respect. The way they behave to fellow believers and the way they are known to behave in their daily lives in the world are immensely significant.

But designated leaders are not the only important influences in a church. Many Christians glorify God in their daily lives as the Holy Spirit makes them more and more like Jesus. Sadly, a worship-orientated, triumphalist church can easily obscure the attractiveness and the challenge of such lives. But one of the ways in which home groups can enrich a church is by giving members greater insight into the way Christ works in the hearts and lives of others. As members share their experiences they are able – usually unconsciously – to show each other what it means to them to live and think and feel Christianly. Mature Christians are often challenged as they hear how the Holy Spirit has empowered relatively immature believers to make brave and costly choices in daily life.

This has implications for the kind of Bible study material used in home groups. However closely a passage is studied or some aspect of Christian faith examined there should always be an attempt to work out the practical use of the knowledge gained. What has this to do with the way I feel or behave in this situation or that? How does it challenge the way I live?

Teaching

Although the influence of example – from leaders and fellow-believers – is obviously important, formal teaching can also be helpful. But how often is it? There is a tendency, found not only in traditional Brethrenism but in FIEC evangelicalism and charismatic circuits, to offer congregations either perfumed pastilles or chunks of meat without seasoning or sauce. Charismatic churches tend to alternate watery gruel with spoonfuls of seasoning. All make the same mistake of failing to relate to the real world.

By and large, preachers don't find it easy to tell fellow-believers what it might mean to 'walk humbly' with God at half-past two on Monday afternoon. It is often easier to share a personal anecdote or even to explain a difficult passage of scripture than face the importance and the difficulty of showing forgiveness to those who have wronged us. But teaching through preaching or through group study fails unless it examines the implications for daily living. Sometimes this can be the most difficult aspect of preparation. A good commentary can help in dividing and explicating a passage – but after this has been done the preacher is left with the question of where the biblical truths or situation impact the experience of the hearers. We dare not overlook the obvious fact that every day brings new challenges to think and behave Christianly. There are problems with relationships at work and in family life, with the expectations of employers and managers, with current events in the community or the nation. If such problems are never mentioned from the pulpit it isn't surprising that the salt should lose its tang and lamps grow dim.

What about evangelism?

If the church is to fulfil its function of worship it must do so through the sacrifice of daily living (Rom 12:1). But how about the imperative to evangelise? Might there be a danger that emphasising the importance of living a godly life would detract from this? This is a valid question – answered by two scriptures in particular. Jesus said that people would be moved to glorify God when they saw the good works of his disciples (Matt 5:16). And Paul, after referring repeatedly to Christian teaching as 'sound/wholesome/healthy /reasonable', strikes another chord altogether when he describes what happens when Christians live the life. The result, he says, is to make the gospel attractive (Tit 2:10). Perhaps churches which work hard at evangelism yet see little reward for their labours should look again at the NT principles of godly living.

Further reading

R Foster, *Celebration of Discipline* (Hodder, 1989)
R Foster, *Money, Sex and Power* (Hodder, 1985)
Jean-Pierre de Caussade, *The Sacrament of the Present Moment* (1861; Harper & Row, 1989)
M Greene, *Thank God it's Monday* (SU, 1992)

CHAPTER TWENTY-NINE

General Principles of Pastoral Care

GWEN PURDIE

A woman with a blank expression starts attending your church on a Sunday morning. She seems lifeless and hassled with two young children. She listens attentively but isn't keen to converse with anyone. Some of the women try to draw alongside her but have an uphill climb. One of the children is causing difficulties in Sunday school. Eventually the story unfolds and the pastoral issues come to the fore. She is pregnant to the man she lives with. He is not her husband nor the father of her two children. He abuses the children. One child has Aspergers syndrome, recently diagnosed, and therefore struggles to mix with his peers and does not behave well. The lady pours out her story and includes that she is planning to have an abortion within two weeks. She wonders if the church could help her?

Increasing problems and a rewarding role

I write this contribution from my experience as a qualified social worker and then as a Christian counsellor. I have been practising biblical counselling for 16 years. As one church leader said to me: 'We are not used to dealing with such things – you are dealing with these complexities daily.' He was right but, increasingly, pastoral issues have to be addressed by church leaders. We need to learn how to deal with situations as they arise. There may be need for some training in pastoral care, in listening or in consulting. Reading this book in itself does not make us experts! However, God is waiting to use us as his channels of love as we make ourselves available to him and to others. It's an exciting and rewarding role.

Pastoral problems are increasing these days, or perhaps I should say more problems are being presented. People are coming to church with a lot of baggage. This is a fact of life. Some will and some will not have been raised in a Christian home. They will look perfectly normal most of the time. Yet the secrets they have are amazing. They will be looking to church to help them with their past hurts, their present difficulties and their future fears.

I believe it is realistic for people to expect substantial opportunities for healing in their places of worship. Of course we are 'new creatures in Jesus Christ' (2 Cor 5:17) but more often than not the problem is how far we appropriate – or fail to appropriate – this life. Some have been well taught, others haven't. Some have a clear view of sin, others are rebellious. In view of the kind of baggage people bring into their Christian lives, or even what they pick up as they go along, it is no surprise that Jesus is not automatically given his rightful place as Lord. Agreed, everything is dealt with at the cross of Jesus, but we need to give him access to our hearts and to the pain that we carry around. Yes, his divine power has given us everything we need for life and godliness (1 Pet 1: 3-9) but how often do we go through life unaware that we are actually short-sighted and blind? Life is not easy: we all experience trials, sorrows and difficulties. There may be besetting sins, snares and awkward circumstances.

Basic principles

This subject is so extensive that I have decided to list some important points. If we get these principles right, we won't go too far wrong in our attempt to pastor our people to a high standard.

Pastoral care involves shepherding the flock. This is a loving way of caring for people rather than controlling them. We always have to leave people with the element of choice. We can shepherd people only if we have a shepherd's heart. God promised to give his people 'shepherds after my own heart, who will lead you with knowledge and understanding' (Jer 3:15).

Shepherding involves protection, tending to needs, strengthening the weak, encouragement, feeding the flock, making provision, shielding, refreshing, restoring, leading by example to move people on in their pursuit of holiness, comforting, guiding (Pss 78: 52; 23). God has much to say about shepherds who don't do their job well (Jer 23:1, 2; Ezek 34:1-6). Our example is Jesus (John 10:1-21). To function well pastorally we must model ourselves on Jesus as the Good Shepherd.

All pastoral service must come out of our love for Jesus. He will give us love for his people, even the love that sometimes requires us to stand back and watch them making unhelpful choices. The person must be loved and be seen and dealt with as distinct from their behaviour or their sin. We need to accept people as they are, not as we would like them to be, or as we believe God would want them to be (Acts 10:34, 35). I take great comfort from remembering that Jesus chose Judas as one of his disciples, knowing that Judas would betray him. Our motive for pastoring has to be love. It is not enough to pastor people simply because it is part of our leadership role.

However, we have been blessed with 'every spiritual blessing in Christ' (Eph 1:3). There is an answer in God for every situation we may come across, including depression, divorce, being HIV positive or a perpetrator of child abuse. Would your church have a policy or procedures to integrate such people into the full life of the church without putting anyone at risk, and at the same time offering opportunities for full redemption (Psa 130:7)? What if the child abuser wanted to become a Sunday school teacher?

Pastoral care involves caring and loving. 'Dear friends, since God so loved us, we also ought to love one another. No one has ever seen God; but if we love one another, God lives in us and his love is made complete in us' (1 John 4: 11, 12). Again Jesus is our example: 'When he saw the crowds, he had compassion on them, because they were harassed and helpless, like sheep without a shepherd' (Matt 9 : 36). We need to care for the whole person – spirit, soul and body. It is not enough to think only of people's spiritual needs. Selwyn Hughes of Crusade for World Revival, suggests that every human being needs security, significance and self-worth. His book *A Friend in Need*, is well worth reading.

We are to love people as they are. In a helpful book on healing, Leanne Payne identifies three great barriers to healing in our lives: failure to forgive others; failure to receive forgiveness ourselves; lack of self acceptance. How true! (*The Healing Presence*, p.72)

Pastoral care includes accepting people with all their emotions. Don't be afraid of outbursts or tears (John 11: 35, Psa 126: 5, 6). People are emotional beings. It is never right to repress our emotions. People should be allowed to cry until they have finished. All the same, it is good to put boundaries on people for their own safety. One girl asked how angry she could be. I said that she could express her anger, she could talk about it, feel it and even experience it, but she could not act it out or go near the third storey window! She honoured those limits and helpfully expressed her anger before we took it all to the cross of Jesus where he spoke peace to her heart. She found a safe place to be angry (me) and then a safe place to dispose of her anger (Jesus). In another situation where violence was in the air I stated that if it continued I would call the police. This I did when the situation deteriorated. It is always important to follow through on issues, therefore just as important not to say something if you don't intend to do it or haven't the strength to follow it through. As church leaders we cannot be held responsible for making people happy or even taking away their pain. The Lord wants to change us first, rather than our circumstances. He would prefer that we move towards holiness, after which our emotions will come alongside.

Most people need help at one time or another in handling their emotions, or their circumstances, or their relationships. They may get help through the church service or the teaching, without communicating their specific need. But how good it is when church leaders are available, if required, to draw alongside even for a short while. Remember it is not the event that is the problem but the needy person's perception of that event and the consequent emotions. Jesus said, 'Take care of my sheep' (John 21:16).

Pastoral leaders should lead by example. Our attitudes are very important here. We should have an attitude of service (1 Pet 4: 10, 11, 1 Pet 5: 2, 3). We should be humble (1 Pet 5: 5, 6). We should have integrity (Titus 2: 7, 8). We should avoid criticising, being judgmental and prejudiced. We should understand but not condone. We should apply to God for abundant levels of wisdom (Matt 7:24; 2 Tim 3: 15-17; Prov 2: 6; James 1:5).

Pastoral care requires good team work, as Moses discovered when he learned the art of delegation (Exod 18:15-26). It is wrong to think that we can sort things out single-handedly. Some church leaders have devolved responsibility for pastoral care. It is worth considering setting up a pastoral team which includes women and other men with specific gifts. As a team, it is important to decide what are the individual and group limits and responsibilities.

We can help someone only if they are willing to work with us towards change. Usually we cannot take people's pain away, but we can stand with them in it. We can show them the options. We can teach them from God's word what he requires from them. We can instil hope (Luke 1:37; 1 John 4:18). We have unique resources for problem-solving in our churches today and we should be shouting it from the housetops. We have God himself – Father, Son and Holy Spirit (Heb 13: 5, 6; John 16: 13-15; John 14: 6, 16, 17). We have the word of God (Psa 119: 89, 105; Matt 24: 35; 1 Pet 1: 25; Heb 4: 12). The word of God must be used appropriately and sensitively when we are dealing with hurting people. Merely to throw in a Bible verse or to produce a text for everything does not reflect good care. We need to have a good understanding of biblical principles and of how to apply God's truth to troubled lives. We must be willing to learn how to do this. We also have prayer to offer people (John 17: 20; Rom 8:

26, 34; 1 Thess 5:17). Being prayed for and being prayed with are very powerful ways of expressing care. People really appreciate individual prayer. Praying with people is liberating and demonstrates love. It shows that we, too, rely on the Lord and his abilities. He is the One who solves problems.

We can be there, even if we cannot see the next step. We must be available and be there where people are. We are responsible to love, care and provide as far as is possible.

We need to learn to recognise our limits and to know when we are out of our depth. We need to know when to ask for help. Let's be humble, knowing our inadequacies, and learn what our strengths and weaknesses are. Our own responsibilities as well as the law of the land more or less dictate that we must refer to the authorities any case of child abuse. (See chapter 51 on 'Social care legislation'.) Other instances may well need help outside the church, for example when they involve crime or mental health. Prompt referral could prevent needless pain and could prove to be a vital ingredient for getting much needed help. Does your church have access to specialist help for pastoral issues? It is vital for everyone concerned to seek help if you or others are out of their depth. There is a danger of pastoral workers thinking of themselves as amateur counsellors. Counselling is distinct from pastoral care. A fifty-hour course in Christian counselling does not equip you to take on all counselling issues. Another danger is not taking into account the effect of continued involvement or over-involvement with a disturbed person. Your own emotional well-being can be seriously undermined by someone who may be more interested in rehearsing their difficulties than in getting help to change.

Our own experiences will likely not provide answers to other people's problems. There is no one way that God works. We have to be clear that we do not have and will not have all the answers, despite our status, or prayer life, or our access to the resources of heaven. We will make some glaring mistakes. The skill is to learn from them and not make the same mistake twice. We must be prepared for failures and disappointments; prepared also to say sorry if we are in the wrong. *Pastoral care is not so much about giving answers as it is about listening.* It certainly is not about giving advice. What is the goal of pastoral care? Surely it is to meet people's needs, to encourage a lifestyle of repentance, and to help people towards wholeness and holiness.

Careful listening shows how much you care, and could avoid a number of pitfalls. How a situation looks is not necessarily how it actually is. Many problems presented have deep roots. God deals with the root of the problem as well as the symptoms (Heb 4:12, 13). A thorough job is worth taking time over. Healing is a process which usually comes to its complete end only in heaven. God heals us, layer by layer, as we can cope with it. In John 11, Jesus raised Lazarus from the dead, but asked the people to remove Lazarus's grave clothes. Surely Jesus could have done this too? This is a lesson for us. It is the pastoral job of the church to help release people from their past lives, sin, and grave clothes so that they can be entirely free.

Listening involves empathy, which is trying to understand how it feels to be in the other person's shoes. It is having the desire to understand rather than to be ready with an answer. It is imperative that we do not jump to conclusions or assume things that we have not been told. Resist the temptation to pigeon-hole people. To listen carefully allows the person the dignity of having the right to feel any emotion and the free choice to choose any action, whether it be right or wrong in our eyes. Be genuinely caring and kind. People under stress are well able to identify our motives. It is always possible to say that you hear what is being said but that time is required before a response can be given. This can be done in a loving and supportive way. Make sure another time is set for meeting, otherwise the person will become anxious.

Some of what we listen to may shock us. If there is some crime involved or if someone is in moral danger we would have to take immediate action or seek help sooner rather than later. But do remember also that the person has probably lived for some time with what sounds so shocking to you and that it may not need an immediate response from you. The pastoral team should agree through discussion and much prayer what constitutes a genuine crisis so that appropriate action can be taken. Bear in mind that crisis management is not always the way we should respond. We need to hear from the Lord what we ought to do and take time for prayer and consultation with others, if need be. Of course the person will always want help immediately and will present their case from their own perspective. I personally have seen over the years that it is preferable to help people to get themselves out of their crisis rather than to go in with all the resources available in one particular moment. This does not mean inactivity on our part.

Listening to God regarding pastoral issues is of great importance. Listening to God as a routine changes our lives (1Sam 3:10). We will then be channels for God to speak through us. We also need to wait on the Lord for discernment. An active prayer life has often been the reason why people survive with pastoral responsibilities (Eph 6:18;

1Thess 5:16-18). Discernment flows out of a close walk with God.

Each individual regardless of class or area is of value, dignity or worth. This means, among other things, no casual sharing of information which should be regarded as confidential. It is because this happens too often that some people feel they cannot talk to their church leaders. They fear that what they have shared from their hearts about their personal lives may not be guarded within the conversation they are having. Pastoral workers must come to an agreed understanding about confidentiality so that preparation can be made in advance for situations which are unclear or intricate.

Pastoral care has to be practical. It may mean, for example, a pot of soup, a phone call once a week, accompanying someone to an important meeting, being there for someone who has been in trauma, reminding someone of an appointment, inviting a lonely person for a meal, sending a card or a letter, providing transport, etc.

Gender issues have to be thought out and handled sensitively. For example, it may not be appropriate for two men to visit a woman on her own.

Conclusion

Here are two major conclusions drawn from my own experience:

1. Human beings are fearfully and wonderfully made. They are complex, but have an amazing capacity to survive, to be repaired, to choose to get well despite very difficult circumstances.
2. God is able to do immeasurably more than we can ask, think, dream, or imagine (Eph 3:20). God meets people where their need is, every time. We can have much hope because of who our God is.

Pastoral care is an obligatory role for church leaders (see John 10:13; 1 Tim 3) and we can learn to do it well. (See chapter 2 on 'Leadership: roles, tasks, qualifications and style'.)

Further reading

F Bridger and D Atkinson, *Counselling in Context: developing a theological frame-work* (Darton, Longman & Todd, 1998)
P Hicks, *What could I say?: a handbook for helpers* (IVP, 2000)
S Hughes, *How to help a Friend* (Kingsway, 2000)
R Hurding, *The Bible and Counselling* (Hodder & Stoughton, 1992)

CHAPTER THIRTY

Pastoral Care of Men

MAX SINCLAIR

Living as a Christian man in today's world is more confusing than it was a couple of decades ago and, therefore, issues of pastoral care are more complex. It is not simply a question of knowing the Bible, though that is our guidebook. The challenge comes in applying timeless principles in the real life situations of the world in which men live.

Some of the confusion arises from the permanent changes to society's attitudes achieved by the feminist movement. A man who is attempting to be considerate will open a door for a woman or give up his seat on a train to her, but cannot be certain of the response. More than 70% of women in the UK now work. Where there is overlap, co-operation, or competition in the workplace, some women might find help patronising.

A man's role as a husband and father is not as clear as it was. I was brought up in a world where the man was the breadwinner. Today, many men's wives earn more than they do. Househusbands who assume responsibility for childcare, running the household and cooking are relatively common, whereas they were unheard of in my parents' generation. As a father, is it acceptable today to follow the traditional role where I leave primary responsibility for the children to their mother (though, of course, I will change the occasional nappy in an emergency)? Or is it a more Christian view to be a 'millennium man' sharing childcare equally with my wife, making sure I get up to the children at night as often as she does and taking my share of household chores?

All these complexities, and many more, demand understanding of our culture and godly wisdom, as well as a thorough knowledge of God's word. I want to look now at some of the key areas which can help us pastor men better.

Cultivate an atmosphere of acceptance

Effective pastoring can happen only in a fellowship where there is a pervading sense of loving acceptance of each other. While this is a cardinal principle for all pastoral care, it especially applies to men because of our cultural background. A man who has just been made redundant may be reluctant to attend church because of the way our society links a man's identity with his occupation. He may well be feeling that he has either failed or lost part of his identity. The man who has been bereaved or suffered some other grievous loss may stay away from church because he fears breaking down and shedding tears. The man who finds himself in constant tension with his teenage children, who feels that his marriage is slipping away, or is shamed because of constant struggles with sexual temptation may be persuaded that he is a failure and be caused to hold back from involvement in any kind of service within the fellowship itself. Our culture is intolerant of men who fail. So, even if he is simply suffering the normal buffetings of life, he may feel himself to be a failure. If he has failed and this is known, the problem is even more acute. A man who has an affair, loses his business, or falls into some other kind of trouble which everyone gets to hear about, knows he is in real trouble if his fellowship is not a loving one.

As always, our example is Jesus. As a leader of men he reversed many of society's norms, and he needs to do the same for us as leaders today. His loving acceptance of people was shocking in its total disregard for their present situation or past failures. Jesus mixed freely and comfortably with prostitutes and tax fraudsters. He forgave one of his closest associates who had blatantly lied, even denying that he knew Jesus, and promoted him to the highest position of leadership in the first church. We need to ask ourselves as leaders if our church accepts and affirms men, or criticises them. Of course this does not mean that we should condone sin or encourage failure, but it does mean that we are more concerned to restore, heal and lift men up than we are to stand over them in judgment.

So how do you cultivate an atmosphere of acceptance within a Christian fellowship? It will always start with the attitudes of the church leaders, and spread downwards. If leaders are open, warm and approachable, the example spreads. If they are open and honest about their own lives, including their disappointments and failures, that attitude of being real with each other will spread among other men in the church. This creates a context in which pastoral care for men is being real rather than pretending, being honest rather than putting up a front. Specifically it will probably lead to men seeking pastoral help at the onset of a problem, rather than waiting till the situation has overwhelmed them and it is virtually too late. It also makes it much easier for a church leader to approach one of the men and say, 'I would love to have a personal chat with you some time.' Correction and rebuke are received only when a man knows that he is being approached for his own good by those who are prepared to be real and honest about their own lives.

But it is not just the leaders. Things can be done in the life of the church fellowship to develop closer bonds between the men. My church organises five-a-side football matches twice a month, takes on local teams – and wins. Sport is great for building bridges. Of course not everyone is sporty, and other activities can be equally good for building relationships – anything from painting the church hall to restoring a sound system. Men like to do something together, whereas women are often happy to sit and chat as a means of getting to know one another, whether or not they are doing anything else.

Having said that, I belong to a small group of men who, over the past ten years, have been meeting to talk. It began as an outreach with five of us Christians inviting friends on the fringe to share a meal and then discuss the Faith for an hour over coffee. I have never belonged to such an intimate group of men. After an hour's Bible study, we share personal concerns and pray together for twenty minutes. Last week, one man told us his wife wanted a divorce; another asked us to pray for a change in his bank manager's attitude which could save his financial situation; a third asked for prayer for his new wife's ex-husband who had vowed to destroy her business – and so it goes on. These are men being real with each other, caring for each other because they know their secrets are in safe hands.

Pastoral care can never be effective if this atmosphere of loving acceptance is missing.

Understanding a man's roles

Every man's life involves balancing a number of roles. I can easily think of ten kinds of relationship which require different responsibilities. Much of our pastoral care will be to enable men to sort out conflicts of roles in different areas of their lives and we shall not be able to help them bring their lives into a biblical balance unless we understand the roles and recognise the conflicts. Here are some of the roles that men may have to assume.

Son

From youth to middle age, men will probably have one or both parents to relate to. Scripture tells us: 'Honour your father and mother' (Exod 20:12). We have to work out what that means at each stage of life. Many men's deepest pastoral problems arise from a bad relationship with their parents, or particular incidents which happened during their upbringing. A friend recently told me that his brother had gone to live in America as soon as he could leave home because he was desperate to get away from his father who had repeatedly told him he was no good and would never amount to anything. He is now a success and happily married, but he is still living with the hurt and bitterness. We have to find ways to help our men process the baggage of their upbringing, rather than let them try to bury it. Their problems range from the young man who says, 'My parents don't deserve any respect' to the middle-aged man who never had a good relationship with his parents but, instead of living at peace with himself in an attitude of forgiveness, still holds on to bitterness and hurt.

As parents become elderly, the son's role can soon become that of carer. This is a task which can be exceedingly difficult, but Christlike, selfless caring is something we need to urge men to embrace gladly rather than carry out reluctantly.

Husband

This vital role will be the privilege and responsibility of many men in our fellowship. Once again, scripture does not leave us without direct guidance regarding the job description: 'Husbands love your wives, just as Christ loved the church and give himself up for her' (Eph 5:25).

The whole idea of loving the most wonderful girl in the world sounds easy when you are falling in love or just married, but it becomes more difficult when tensions arise. There may be an immediate conflict with the role of being a son. We need to help our men understand that marriage alters our relationship with our parents. We will continue to honour them, but they must move out of the central place they once occupied. Genesis 2:24 tells us clearly that a man must 'leave' his father and mother and 'cleave' to his wife (AV). A number of Christian marriages fail because a man has not emotionally left his parents. Instead, because of a false sense of loyalty, he puts them before his wife.

Our fellowships must provide quality pre-marriage preparation with both teaching and time for open talking. Our church programme must include regular teaching on marriage and the roles of husbands and wives. (When did you last hear a sermon on this subject?) I have seen dramatic changes in marriages that were going downhill, as well as others that merely needed strengthening, as a result of seminars. These don't have to sound heavy or threatening. Titles like 'How to stay happy though married' help to dispel the notion that you must be in big trouble if you attend the seminar. And what about having a 'Renewal of Marriage Vows' service in church, say every five years, inviting everyone to attend, especially couples married in church over the last five years. An evening with a good meal, followed by renewal of vows, can make an appealing occasion. (See chapter 43 on 'Marriage enrichment'.)

Such simple, thoughtful action by church leaders has strengthened many a husband's commitment to his wife and even saved a marriage which would otherwise have been lost. In the background is the constant caring atmosphere which enables husbands to know that, if they have a problem, they can open their hearts in confidence. Make a rule that you will never pass on any secret a man shares with you, even for prayer with other leaders, without that man's permission. Don't expect a good pastoring relationship with the men of your church if you fail to keep that rule.

Husbands need not only to be challenged with their responsibilities (e.g. to be faithful, to be the leader of the home, to be a spiritual example); they also need considerable encouragement. The devil is out to wreck marriages, so don't be surprised if husbands are tempted to have affairs or, at least, become selfish and unloving. The battle against temptation need not be lost, especially if people are praying for you, and slips in our Christian character are always redeemable if we allow Christ to change us.

In these days when our fellowships are going to have increasing numbers of husbands in second marriages, and sometimes the complication of step-children and ex-wives, we shall need much wisdom and compassion as well as knowledge of scripture.

Father

The Bible gives fathers all kinds of helpful guidance. Ephesians 6:4 sums up much of it: 'Fathers, do not exasperate your children; instead bring them up in the training and instruction of the Lord.' A study on what the Bible says about being a father, and the principles of the fatherhood of God, could be of great value to those who are pastors, as well as to the church. As fathers are encouraged to train their children in God's ways by teaching and example, children will not be exasperated by unloving parental expectations.

Never forget when pastoring fathers that every one walks around with mixed feelings about their children – an extraordinary amalgam of pride in them, frustration at their behaviour, disappointment in certain areas, perhaps deep hurt at some points, for example when a teenager appears to reject the loving care of his father and adopts a lifestyle that rejects all that the family holds dear. Unjudging acceptance is essential for pastoral nurturing of fathers in need.

The Bible makes no promises that good Christian parents are guaranteed model Christian children who will grow into committed Christian adults. I know Christian fathers who have done everything right, but whose children have rebelled. Studying scripture and life have convinced me that our pastoral care needs to be supportive and non-judgmental if we are going to develop a fellowship where fathers feel free to share the toughness of their role. The teenage daughter who gets pregnant, the young child who seems totally undisciplined, the son who swears at his parents, or the youngster who is dabbling with drugs are already testing their fathers to the limit. This is hard enough to bear without being told that their upbringing was at fault. Of course there may be problems in the home which we need to look into. Assuming the best rather than the worst, though, will usually enable a man to share his heart as a father, while the opposite will cause him to keep his mouth shut.

Worker/boss

Scripture makes it clear that everyday work is important to God and a significant part of a person's life. A man's role at work is therefore a good starting point in discussions with men. Some of the issues involved are the problems of being a Christian in the workplace: how to witness; what to do when conflicts of conscience arise; motivation; ambition. As church leaders, we need to be careful, for in our anxiety to fill the gaps in the ranks of Sunday school teachers and youth leaders, and a host of other church activities, we need to make sure that we do not exalt the value of serving God through assuming a church responsibility above serving him through daily work.

We live in a day when many men have huge demands placed upon them in the workplace. Pressure of work causes most men to wonder how they will ever be able to cope with other parts of their life, including church. If our pastoring and preaching is laced with phrases which constantly challenge men to be 'more committed' by doing more at church, you will probably find that the church's 'Situations Vacant' column will increase. Prayerfully discerning how a man's overall balance of life can be secured is key to effective pastoring. Matching a man's gifts with his service in the church is a vital part of this process and a man who is serving in the right place will actually find this not one more stress but, rather, a joy. Bernard Langer, the celebrated professional golfer, once said that before he gave his life to Christ his priorities were 'golf, golf, golf' but then he came to see that he needed to rearrange things a little and the order is now 'God, family, golf'. While we need to encourage men to see work as a God-given calling, we also need to help them get their priorities straight. More than once I have counselled a man to look for a new job when he has told me that his work pressures are such that he finds his prayer life dwindling, his church attendance sporadic and his family and marriage relationships falling apart. Work is a God-given calling, but no man was ever called to be a workaholic, and pastoring will require the discernment to support men in their work but also to help them keep it in perspective.

Conclusion

There are many other roles a man may be called upon to play – such as those of lover, competitor (in business or sport), brother, mentor or discipler of other men and, of course, church member. Pastoring men in today's world is indeed complex, but it is not impossible. We need to read as widely as possible on the subject. Maturity and experience may help, but youth and inexperience are no bar to quality pastoral concern. We shall need the patience of Job, the wisdom of Solomon and certainly the power of the Holy Spirit.

Further reading

J Lawence, *Men: the Challenge of Change* (CPAS, 1997)
G Macdonald, *When Men think Private Thoughts* (Nelson, 1996)
R McLoughry, *Men and Masculinity* (Hodder & Stoughton, 1992)

CHAPTER THIRTY-ONE

Pastoral Care of Women

JOAN SHORT

Over half the average congregation is made up of women –
sometimes more. How are their pastoral needs to be met?

A disparate group with many different needs, it includes the
following: the elderly – often lonely, feeling they have outlived their
usefulness, and longing to 'go home'; the acute and chronic sick;
single parents struggling with the heavy task of bringing up the
children on their own, often with big financial burdens; young
marrieds who went into marriage with high expectations only to be
faced with the stress of young kids and a busy husband – and often
a job as well; the large group of unmarrieds – often, though not
always, longing for a husband with whom they can share their lives
and seeing the possibility of having children slipping away as they
approach their 40s (some of these find the emphasis on family-
dominated services quite hard to bear); the middle-aged women
who are trying to cope with a very busy husband and difficult
teenagers battling with a world in which everything goes and every
other young person is apparently allowed to do anything! Many
parents fear their youngsters will get involved in drink and drugs,
sex and pregnancy. What a catalogue of woes! But there are many
joys too, and a wonderful peace that only the Christian knows as
she walks along the rough places with her Lord. Most women I
know would never wish to change their feminine role for a male
one, and derive immense joy from being a woman.

What are the pastoral needs?

Everyone needs time to be really listened to – and for many women
that is the greatest need. They have no one who cares sufficiently to
make time to listen in strict confidence to their problems. So often
the husband doesn't realise how much a woman needs to be
listened to. Many women could fulfil the needs of other women in
this respect, but listening is a skill that needs to be learned and

ideally needs training. Christian Listeners do a very good course in this area which can be highly recommended. Much need will only surface as one gets to know the individual, and this takes time and practical love.

The sick, whether acute or chronic, young or old, often need practical help. Simple meals, especially soup; helping to take folk to hospital or to take relatives to visit their dear ones in hospital; manning the telephone so that the carer can have some rest; taking out the frail in a wheelchair or car for a short drive: the needs are endless. Sometimes it is appropriate to offer a brief prayer and leave a verse of scripture which can be savoured like a sweet. By the way, visiting usually needs to be short so that the patient is left 'longing rather than loathing'! Fewer women can do these things these days because so many are working full-time. What about considering a job share in order to be able to take part in this joyous work for the Lord? 'I was sick and you visited me', said Jesus.

Singles are often the backbone of the church, both in prayer and as faithful workers. They need to be recognised and consulted by the elders, and their views should be taken seriously. Singles need others, preferably in the same age group, to talk over their interests and problems. They need to have the opportunity of being accepted into families and not always being lumped together. Prayer triplets are a good way of incorporating single and married women in a supportive, productive relationship where all members are on an equal footing. Because modern society puts such emphasis on sexual activity as a route to human fulfilment, unmarried women are often made to feel keenly the fact that they do not have a sexual relationship – they may be regarded as 'odd' by their non-Christian peers. In the church, marriage and singleness must be regarded as equally valid states. Single people have needs associated with being single, and a caring church will be mindful to provide that support as it supports all its members. The frustrations which may accompany singleness should only be expressed to loyal and trusted Christians friends: they are not a matter for public consumption.

Many parents would appreciate help in good parenting, bearing in mind that some have poor role models and often come from homes where there was no Christian influence. They may not know much of the Bible for themselves, so the church should provide good relevant teaching. Care for the Family, Scripture Union, and other organisations produce good teaching material. Many marriages would benefit from marriage guidance and marriage enrichment classes, and there should always be pre-marital counselling. The elders should be prepared to identify and train someone, or better still a couple, in counselling and listening skills.

Widows with young families, and other single mothers, greatly need a father figure, especially if there is no suitable male relative. In the case of boys, this can often be best met by a male Sunday school teacher or Bible class leader who will take a practical interest in the boy, arranging outings and visits to his home for games. Parents with families of similar age could include the children in a family outing – picnics, hill walking, etc. The single mother herself, who is often very lonely, can benefit from some Christian social contact without people expecting her to return the hospitality. She often has much to contribute, and involving her in a committee consisting of both men and women can provide her with an interest and a role which can be of great mutual benefit.

Work outside the home can bring great benefits to both men and women. It helps to support the home financially, and can be a source of enjoyment and social support. However, there is a need to balance this with the responsibility, taught in the Bible, that a mother's most important role is as a wife and mother. Many women have no choice and they must work full-time. Others are in the position where they could work part-time and therefore have more time to be homemakers. The decision is a very personal one, and the church would be wrong to make a woman feel guilty. Church members should provide support in practical ways, such as baby-sitting, so that the woman is able to get out to a home Bible study, or so that the couple can have an evening out together without incurring the cost of a baby-sitter (money so often being tight). Young mums need praise and encouragement in the difficult task they are doing. So often, they are unable to attend meetings and are so tired that they have little spiritual input and are in need of understanding pastoral care.

A number of women in our congregations are high flyers and have very responsible jobs in the world. Indeed, even if they are not high flyers, many women work and are treated responsibly and respectfully in the workplace. When they come into the church what opportunities do they have to exercise their gifts? Too often, all they are invited to do is to make the tea, tidy the church, and cook the odd church meal. Is this right? Even if it is not considered appropriate for them to be elders, can their skills and talents not be harnessed as advisors? A woman looks at things in a different way from a man, and her input is a complementary and very necessary one. Yet how common it is for the men to make all the decisions. Women play a vital role in bringing up children. This should be recognised by the church and they should be given pastoral responsibilities in the church.

Many women are drawn to a relationship with Christ because he is so willing to listen to what is on their minds and able to empathise with the issues that are important to them. It is therefore all the more disappointing when the church becomes a barrier to this relationship. Churches can often make women feel guilty about themselves – particularly over the issue of working mothers. If work outside the home has benefits for men, it has similar benefits for women. It helps to support the family financially, and it can be a source of enjoyment and social support. If children can be looked after properly, then the church should affirm and support that family's decision; there may not be scope for choice.

The early years of child-rearing are so exhausting that mothers may not be able to attend all the services of the church or do the number of voluntary tasks they used to undertake. They should be made welcome at the services they can manage, but attendance at services should not become yet another task they have to perform to please people; they should not be made to feel guilty. When women are looking after pre-schoolers, real care should be taken to ascertain their spiritual needs. Are they not coming out to services because they are tired? Is there another reason? Would they like to come out to weekly Bible study groups if they had free and reliable babysitting? Just because someone has become a mother does not necessarily mean that they are enjoying all the bliss which is stereotypically associated with it. When a woman is constantly giving out of herself to look after her children, those with pastoral responsibility in the church should ensure, particularly if her attendance decreases, that someone is putting something back into her spiritual life by praying with her, praising her hard work, and ensuring that she understands how much God cares for all mothers – joyful, working, or reluctant.

Older women can play a great part in prayer. They need to be helped to see that this is one of their most important roles and they should be kept up to date with specific needs and information as to how God is answering their prayers. This could make all the difference to their own needs as they see that, in spite of their frailty and age, they can have the most vital role of all.

Is there a role for the men?

Finally, where do the men and particularly the elders come in all this? I feel that although the main responsibility is for women to deal with women's needs, there is a place for men to visit from time to time in hospital and home, and always to be ready to respond to requests from the women who are trying to meet the pastoral needs.

Over the years I have been greatly concerned when patients in hospital have said that most others in the ward have been visited by the minister and they have been asked, 'Where is your minister?' They have felt sad and let down. In our church, during the past year, we have commenced a regular meeting chaired by an elder who is a retired businessman with a real heart for pastoral needs. All those involved in visiting have been invited to attend, there has been prayer, and we have gone through the names of those who are ill, to see that their needs are being met as far as possible. This has been a great success, although only the needs of the chronic and acute sick have been considered and those whose needs are mainly spiritual have missed out.

CHAPTER THIRTY-TWO

Pastoral Care of Young People

CORINNA SUMMERTON AND DONALD BLACK

Young people are frequently excluded from pastoral care, often intentionally, as there is an underlying belief that young people do not need pastoring. They are a group seen as 'difficult to deal with' both in society and within the church. Usually there is a fear of young people because of their behaviour, culture, music, fashion and so forth. I think that many older people have forgotten that they were once young themselves. Perhaps, too, older people think that young people are different now from what they used to be, and therefore they don't think that they can help them. There is a need to recognise that times have changed and young people today are facing new pressures and have greater expectations than those we experienced. There is now a longer transition period between childhood and adulthood which cultivates an uncertainty of what the future may hold, and hence a tension regarding what is acceptable behaviour.

Young people are part of God's family and therefore church leaders have a duty to care for those individuals who are associated with the church. If our young people are accepted and cared for, then we shall keep them within the church.

Cultivating good relationships

The key to good pastoral care is relationships. Good, honest, mutual relationships come from 'working and playing together', rather than from a determined effort. Young people need to share the common aim of building the church. If they are involved and have a sense of ownership, they will feel that they belong and will participate at all levels rather than feeling they are being treated as 'customers' and therefore acting as such. If there is a strong bond between pastoral carer and the young person, much can be achieved. What is needed is a desire to see the individual becoming fulfilled, not an Elastoplast mentality of 'making it all better' whenever a crisis arises. Any relationship, whether between parent and child, teacher and pupil, or between friends, should seek the best outcome for the individual concerned rather than condemning them or looking down on them because their activities are considered to be sinful.

For a successful relationship to develop, a few basic principles should be considered.

Be yourself Young people are very suspicious of older persons who want to get to know them. If you start to behave like a young person and it is not really how you would act naturally, then you are unlikely to gain approval from the group concerned. You are more likely to be ridiculed.

Respect young persons for who they are When I was training staff to work with homeless young men, I would remind them that they would need to give respect if they were to gain it. Often there is a belief that, as an adult, 'I am a person of authority and, with my wealth of experience, I should be respected.' However, for many young people who have had bad experiences of a person in authority (an unfair teacher, an abusive adult) this does not necessarily follow. For them to give respect, they need to know that you can be trusted.

Trust young persons Help them to aim at achievable goals – let them lead a Bible study, for example. Allow them to make mistakes and support them when they do. Remember that all of us have fallen short of the glory of God. Encourage them, and build them up when they fall down. At times like this we need to hold our tongues rather than saying, 'I told you so!'

Pastoral care is about discipleship We need to be willing to challenge, to allow for individuals to fulfil their potential. This means that there is a need to guide and discipline young persons to ensure that they know the boundaries and consequences of their actions.

We should allow our young people to lead the church of today, not of tomorrow It is so important to let young people run their own affairs and activities because they are part of today's church and, as believers, are perfectly capable of doing so under the leadership of the Spirit and some wise oversight by people not much older than themselves. Giving young people responsibility within the church develops in them a sense of ownership and therefore makes them more willing to be committed to the church long term.

Pray for them The Spirit's intervention can be the best tonic for healing and support, especially when we are at a loss to know what to do or say.

Love them I think this is the most important ingredient in any relationship. Young people may be angry, resentful and/or deeply hurt. As the relationship develops you may sometimes feel that you are the target for all their negative feelings. Jesus taught us that we need to love our neighbour as ourselves. By having the heart of Christ we will be given the strength and compassion to care effectively.

Casual meetings can often be more fruitful than planned, formal meetings. I have often found that driving or washing up with someone can be the setting for more productive pastoral care than the formal, traditional one of sitting face to face. Having an open door policy encourages young persons to feel that they 'belong' as they can visit whenever, knowing that you will be happy to see them, talk to them and, more important, listen to them.

Protection of the carer and church There is a need to consider the protection of the church and the carer when dealing with people. By being proactive and having a bit of common sense and a sensible attitude, hopefully many of the mistakes we hear about that cause criticism of the church can be avoided. (See chapter 51 on 'Social care legislation'.) There follow a few practical measures that should be taken when any form of pastoral care is undertaken within the church.

Support for you as the carer When dealing with an individual who has demanding pastoral requirements, there is a need to ensure that there are clear reporting lines and support (see 'Confidentiality' below) so that you do not burn out by carrying other people's emotional baggage. Church leaders have a duty of care for those individuals who are doing the caring. If they are not cared for, the overall standard of care will decline. So, for example, provision should be made for those with pastoral responsibilities to share with specific individuals, in a confidential setting, the issues with which they are dealing and, more important, to pray through them together.

Confidentiality There needs to be an agreed and understood confidentiality policy within the church. Individuals engaged in pastoring need to be sensitive to the Spirit and recognise how confidentiality is interpreted in each set of circumstances they face.

Same gender caring is advisable, where appropriate. There have been many occasions when inappropriate relationships have developed when the carer has been of the opposite sex. Whether these relationships become sexual or just emotionally dependent they can cause long-term damage not only to the individuals concerned but also to family, friends and the church. These relationships may happen over a period of time, and may not have been intentional, but they can ruin the reputation of the carer and the young person's trust in the church responsible for their care. Same gender caring also reduces the risk of individuals with paedophile tendencies taking advantage of young people.

It may, therefore, be more sensible to have a couple carry out pastoral responsibilities since this will reduce the risk of dependency on one person. True, a single person advising a young person not to have sex before they are married will command more respect, provided they acknowledge the difficulties they face, than a married couple who already enjoy the intimacy marriage provides. However, this does not disqualify married people from counselling young people on sexual matters, provided they make it clear that they can remember what it was like to be single, and that they did not find these matters easy.

Seek professional help There will be times when it may be appropriate to seek professional advice from counselling services or other professional agencies. There is an onus on us as leaders to recognise when we are out of our depth. We need to be honest with ourselves, acknowledging when our skills no longer match the task.

Conclusion

I think that successful pastoral care of young people is down to strong honest relationships and allowing them to feel that they belong.

CORINNA SUMMERTON

SELF-EVALUATION SCHEDULE

These questions are intended to focus attention on the pastoral care of young people. It would be good for a church to answer them as honestly as possible and propose relevant action where this is called for.

- Does the church have a network of pastoral contacts for teenagers?
- Are there people in the church with the gift of relating easily to teenagers?
- Do they have opportunities to exercise this gift?
- How does the church ensure that at least some of its ministry is culturally acceptable to teenagers?
- Are young people consulted about their needs?

- Would the church involve teenagers in its decision-making?
- What does the church do about sex education?
- Does it help with the relationship problem?
- Are there social as well as spiritual activities encouraging friendships among teenagers?
- Is prayer for friends and partners for its teenagers a settled priority in the church?
- How does the church support families?
- How are the teenagers helped to cope with conflict with parents?
- Does the church help parents to understand their teenagers?
- Does the church regard parents (even non-Christian ones) as partners in its work?
- How does the church help its teenagers to resist the pressures to conform to the world's standards?
- Are there church activities which teenagers can enjoy without being regarded as freaks?
- How does the church avoid turning its teenagers into lonely isolated freaks?
- Does the church have a Child Protection Policy?
- Is there someone in the church to whom a teenager with a problem could speak and who would know what to do?
- Are youth workers alerted to the signs of abuse?
- Are parents of wayward teenagers embarrassed to come to church?
- Is church the last place a prodigal would be happy to return to?
- Can a church welcome 'publicans and sinners' at the same time as wagging its finger at them?

Further reading

P Brierley, *Reaching and Keeping Teenagers* (Marc Europe, 1993)

DONALD BLACK

CHAPTER THIRTY-THREE

Pastoral Care of Children

PETER KIMBER

Parents send children to school so that they grow up to be like their parents. Jesus encouraged parents to be more like their children (Matt 18:3).

It is tempting to find children something of a nuisance in church life. We like to have them around as long as they can be taken out of earshot while we adults get on with the serious business of worship or teaching. Yet working with children is not only more important but also far more productive than working with adults. Eighty per cent of church leaders come to Christ before they are eighteen years old, yet churches often put an undue emphasis on evangelism and pastoral care of adults. When one of my African colleagues returned from a week's preaching his wife asked how many people had been converted. 'Four and two halves', he said. 'You mean four adults and two children?' she asked. 'No, four children and two adults. The adults had wasted half their lives already.'

The English Church Attendance Survey (ECAS) has shown that over the past decade there are half a million fewer children and young people attending church – 1,000 per week have left. 'The church is bleeding to death', said George Carey, Archbishop of Canterbury. It has never been more important to care for children than today. A few brief comments on their pastoral care follow.

Don't patronise or marginalise children

Children are integral to a healthy church and have a contribution to make. I am reliably informed about a four-year old boy who came into the pastor's vestry shortly before the service began. The pastor was trying to pluck up courage to tackle a difficult issue and was therefore astonished when the small boy climbed on to his knee and said, 'God says, "Why are you prevaricating?"' In less dramatic ways the questions children ask are usually shrewd: they can see when the emperor has no clothes.

Children are an integral part of the church

It may be theologically difficult for some churches to accept children as an integral part of the church, where a firm dividing line is drawn between those 'in fellowship' and those who aren't, but we have a responsibility to care for them pastorally whatever our opinion of their spiritual state. Time and again the OT presses upon parents (and by inference, upon the church) the need to 'teach these things to your children and their children's children' (Deut 4:9). They are to be taught 'these things' in a way that is appropriate to their ability to understand. This brings us into an area of cultural and educational debate. In Muslim countries children are encouraged from an early age to commit the Koran to memory and it is not so long ago that children in this country were similarly encouraged to learn by heart. At the age of five my first encounter with Sunday school was being persuaded to learn 1 John 1:1 that way. I can still remember it; but it was a long time before I began to understand it, and that is the nub of the matter. Contemporary Western education takes the view that children need to understand something before they can effectively learn it. Oriental cultures see it the other way around: learn it first and in due course understanding will – or will not – come. However, the Western approach is more fun and it is important that children's experience of church builds on what happens in school.

If children are an integral part of the church, what form should their contribution take? The adult part of the church needs to know and appreciate the work that children undertake during the year. This morning, I was preaching in a church where a small group of women danced a call to worship, in place of the opening hymn, which all the children watched with absorbed interest. At the end of the service while we adults were drinking coffee and talking, each woman had drawn two children to her so that they could learn the dance the adults had performed – and very moving it was. Old and young together will probably perform a similar dance in the town square on Easter Sunday. Whatever gifts the children are developing need to be recognised, appreciated and used in the congregation.

We must build long-term relationships with them and their families

This is counter-cultural because our society shrinks from

commitment. Leaders who give a month on and a month off to children will not establish the sort of trust which is the basis of good pastoral care. This will require commitment of a high order from those responsible, but there is no substitute for it. We cannot build quality relationships simply from the time spent in collective activities on a Sunday. There needs to be time out of church for weekday activities of some sort, best of all a weekend away or a church camp.

Churches must have in place acceptable policies covering child protection legislation, (see chapter 51 on 'Social care legislation') and everyone involved with young people needs to know how the policies govern their conduct with children. There have been distressing incidents where well meaning, trusting churches have been infiltrated by practising paedophiles, and such incidents do great damage to a church's witness. Jesus' advice to be wise as serpents and harmless as doves applies.

More and more children these days will come from disturbed backgrounds and, inevitably, their leaders may be drawn into the stresses of family life. It is tempting for churches to be wary of involvement in family disputes, but it may be inevitable. If children honour us with their confidences we must treat them with utmost care. However, churches need to be in contact with professional agencies if they are drawn into supporting broken families in any way. Such support is a long-term commitment and cannot be dropped when the going gets rough – but it is enormously rewarding.

Children must be treated as individuals

This means that we should learn as much as we can about them and remember it as a friend. On many Scripture Union (SU) missions and holidays the teams make a point of noting the birthday of every child in their group so that they can send a birthday card and a letter at the appropriate time. Recently we had an astonishing testimony to the value of this personal contact when a woman wrote to us saying that a mission leader had written to her son every birthday for 25 years, and that this care had been a crucial support to him through a painful divorce. That is pastoral care of an exceptional kind.

Answer children's questions honestly

This includes saying so when you don't know the answer. Talking to children about God and discussing the Bible with them is a wonderful way of finding out whether you understand it or not. If you can't say something that is both true and simple you haven't understood it, and children will usually tell you so. This implies that we have to use simple language in place of theological words. In my view, John 14:20 is the most profound verse in scripture, yet it contains 21 monosyllables and only one word of two syllables. Language cannot be simpler or more profound than that. As they grow older we have to build up their spiritual language, bit by bit, so that they come to understand ideas like faith, sacrifice, resurrection, repentance, and sin. But remember that children don't think in abstract terms until around puberty. Stories which illustrate these ideas have to be developed and shared so that children build up concepts which they can hold on to and develop as they grow older.

Treat children with the integrity they deserve

We must never be tempted to apply emotional pressure on children to make decisions in relation to God. There is such a thing as spiritual abuse and its long-term effects are destructive. In later life children will resent and repudiate emotional manipulation. Jesus never applied pressure on anyone to follow him. He invited people to become disciples but he cajoled no one. The rich young ruler was allowed to go away sorrowful though Jesus loved him and saw how near he was to the kingdom. Similarly we may explain the nature of discipleship to children and invite them to find Jesus as their Saviour but it is the Holy Spirit who guides us into truth, just as it is he who convicts and convinces. It is our job to teach and explain but not to cajole, threaten or coerce.

Be a bridge between the secular and spiritual worlds for children

The comments made above about knowing how and what children are taught in school is a necessary background. Primary education relies heavily on practical activities. Educationalists suggest that children can concentrate on an activity for only roughly twice their age in minutes, so they need things to do. This may seem a gross overestimate to tired parents and teachers, but it is not a bad guide. Knowing what goes on in primary schools is essential background knowledge.

Leaders who know what television programmes children watch may sometimes be appalled, but used wisely this can be a great asset. I watched the leaders of an SU holiday base a week's teaching

about the Ten Commandments on excerpts from Neighbours and
Eastenders. Children make moral judgments about things from a
surprisingly early age. No one has to teach children the meaning of
'It's not fair'. It seems to be imbibed with their mothers' milk,
although their sense of fairness is mainly directed at their own
interests rather than those of dispassionate justice. They understand
ideas about bullying, stealing, lying, truthfulness, punishment and
forgiveness from the playground, and these are the raw materials of
spiritual understanding.

Conclusion

If Jesus gave a dire warning to those who would lead children
astray (Mark 9:42) by implication there are rich rewards for those
who lead them to him. No job is more important for the future of
church and society we are here to serve.

Further reading

F Bridger, *Children finding Faith: How can we help children know God?* (SU/CPAS,
    2000)
P Frank, *Bringing Children to Faith: Training adults in evangelism with children*
    (SU/CPAS, 2000)
D Gatward, *Mission Impossible: Ideas and resources of children's evangelism*
    (SU/CPAS, 2000)

CHAPTER THIRTY-FOUR

Pastoral Care of Leaders and Their Wives[1]

JOHN REDFERN

Leaders and their wives often find themselves in a very lonely position. Many church members tend to put them on a pedestal, imagining that 'unlike us mere mortals' they don't have problems and don't need pastoral support. Also, because of their desire to avoid giving the impression of showing favouritism by becoming too friendly with any in the church, their friendships are kept at a fairly superficial level. In consequence, real pastoral care of leaders and their wives becomes difficult.

Yet the pressures on church leaders and consequently their need for pastoral support can be very great. All leaders experience 'down' periods for a variety of reasons: personal, family- and church-connected (e.g. they can be made to feel scapegoats and, besides being focal points for criticism and gossip, they can be pressurised by criticism of their children). Their wives can feel particularly isolated, especially if their role within the church is restricted because there is a young family to look after. With her husband of necessity absent several nights of the week, the wife is left to cope alone with the children.

I want to cover the pastoral care of leaders and their wives from two angles – 'without' and 'within'. By 'without' I mean pastoral support from outside the immediate church fellowship; and by 'within' I mean pastoral support from within the church fellowship in which they are working. I shall be particularly concerned with those who serve the church as leaders full-time, but much of what I have to say relates also to church leaders who also have full-time jobs (or are retired). They, too, may feel lonely, come under pressure and experience 'down' periods. So they, too, need pastoral care.

Support from 'without'

Pastoral care can come from this direction through belonging to a fraternal of local church leaders. If the fraternal is operating well, it will provide an opportunity for the leader to share his worries and concerns with fellow leaders who understand the pressures of leading a church. For this to happen, a measure of mutual trust and caring is required. Sadly, some fraternals do not provide this, being somewhat formal and stiff.

Second – and this is to be regarded as an extremely high priority – there should be at least one, and preferably several, mature and sensitive Christians outside of the church to whom the leader relates well and with whom he can share problems at any level. He can pour out his troubles to them without fear of criticism or judgment; he can enjoy a game of golf with them; they can go for a long walk, enjoy a meal or pray together in depth. There needs to be a bond of trust between the leader and his supporter so that, when a 'down' period strikes, the leader can confidently ask for support, knowing that he will receive a sensitive, understanding and thoughtful hearing.

All this applies equally – even more – to the leader's wife. She needs a shoulder to cry on and someone to share her particular burdens. These may be physical, including the sheer tiredness caused by looking after home and children, or they may lie at a deeper, spiritual level where she is needing help. She may be missing the fellowship and shared Bible study and prayer of which she is deprived because her home commitments keep her away from a home group.

Support from 'within'

It is always important to start as you mean to go on. From the very beginning there needs to be clear understanding in a number of practical areas between a leader and the overall leadership of the church (be it an eldership, a diaconate or a leadership team). Agreed terms should be set down in writing so that they can be referred to should any questions be raised at a later time. This is a valuable preventative measure which will lessen the risk of future aggravation. Practical matters which need to be covered include a job description and a contract of employment. The latter should clearly specify the following: the remuneration package, including pension arrangements; terms and conditions; accommodation; position within the leadership; grievance procedure; outside pastoral support. (See chapter 1 on 'Leadership structures'.) Approaching such matters in a businesslike way and getting right the vital first steps helps to establish the partnership on a proper footing from the very beginning, and avoids the possibility of confusion at a later date. It also provides the foundation for good ongoing pastoral support of the leader and his wife.

The next key element is good communication between the leader and the overall church leadership of the church. This calls for constant and regular communication at this level and also between the leadership as a whole and the church. It is especially helpful if a good understanding develops between the chairman of the leadership team and the leader. Regular meetings between them for conversation and prayer enable them to raise any difficult matter which may arise without any undue feeling of anything 'special' or 'ominous'. Built into the contract, there should be an opportunity, once a year or at an agreed interval, carefully to review together the leader's work, and jointly to agree any adjustments that need to be made. It is important that all communication is two-way and at a real rather than a superficial level. This will enable the leader to share any pastoral matter concerning himself or his wife with a high degree of trust, and the matter will not stew beneath the surface.

All leaders, like the rest of us, experience crisis periods brought about by troubles within the family, sickness or bereavement. In addition, leaders are particularly vulnerable to feeling exhausted, stale, or dispirited about the work. Sometimes they bring this upon themselves, reaching the point of exhaustion because of their failure to delegate, or their feeling that the work will collapse if they don't work flat out. They do themselves, their family and the church no good by adopting such an attitude. Gently, but firmly, this needs to be taken up with them. At such times they need support, understanding and prayer. The leadership should be sensitive enough to spot the problem and act accordingly.

How should such problems be tackled? If the problem relates to the church, they should be prepared to release the leader for a suitable period, making arrangements for helping him, maybe sending him on a retreat. If the problem is family illness or bereavement, then probably the most helpful thing is to release him from engagements for a time to enable him to come to terms with the particular family pressure. In either case, it may be appropriate to provide the leader with the wherewithal, for the problem may be exacerbated by financial pressures.

What is certain is that problems don't just go away! If left alone, they will only fester, loom larger and larger, and will ultimately cause more disruption than if they had been tackled immediately they became apparent.

Conclusion

The above may sound like a counsel of perfection, but attention to these key elements will handsomely repay the leader, his wife and family, the leadership of the church and the church itself.

To sum up: good relationships; common sense; trust and understanding; good communication are needed. It is also important to remember that the position of a leader, his wife and family can be a very lonely one, and the leadership should therefore endeavour to show friendship and consideration in such ways as giving hospitality and introducing that little (or not so little) surprise from time to time.

Footnotes

1 As women play an increasing role in leadership please read 'husbands' for 'wives', 'she' for 'he' etc., as appropriate.

CHAPTER THIRTY-FIVE

Pastoral Care of Older People

BILLY GILMOUR

In biblical times and until comparatively recently, those who were older than most were generally looked up to with respect because of their wealth of experience, knowledge and wisdom. Not so today, when old age is commonly regarded as a disadvantage. The problems facing older people can be formidable. They may include the following:

- Bereavement, not only of a spouse, but of employment with its accompanying status, and the fear, often followed by the reality, of the loss of a much loved home and removal to an 'Old People's Home'.
- The decline of physical strength and the onset – or exacerbation – of disabilities.
- The onset of mental limitations and fear of Alzheimer's disease.
- Reduced financial income and fear of unexpected financial outlays.
- Difficulty in coping with change, including changes in church life.
- Reluctance to give up responsibilities in the church in favour of younger people, especially if they feel able to continue and fear for the future of the church.
- Fear of being marginalized.

Whether we like it or not, many of us will, sooner or later, join the ranks of the elderly, and a good proportion of members in many churches have already done so. Their pastoral needs are not inconsiderable. Church leaders should try to ensure that the elderly are well cared for. Such care should include at least three elements.

Help to prepare for old age

Just as, in an economic context, people need to start early to prepare for retirement, it is essential that Christians be encouraged to begin as soon as possible to build up 'spiritual capital' on which to sustain themselves in later life. This will include the following:

- Establishing personal, spiritual disciplines – notably, regular private prayer, Bible reading (with the help of good, published daily notes), meditation and communion with God (cf. Robert Burns' interesting phrase: 'a correspondence fixed wi' heaven').
- Developing truly Christian values, standards and perspectives – learning what it means, in Paul's language, to have 'died with Christ to the basic principles of this world' (Col 2:20) and to assess circumstances from heaven's standpoint.
- Cultivating a range of recreational interests and hobbies – at least some of which should be capable of extension into old age – and as that old age draws nearer, one more thing.
- Forming a positive mental attitude to retirement – seeing it as ushering in an era of fresh opportunity, rather than being a signal to lay down one's arms.

The teaching and pastoral programmes of the church should reflect constant awareness of these needs.

Encouragement to accommodate to change

Which of us has not at some time experienced the sense of threat or confusion which comes when our familiar and well-tested routines are replaced by what is new, untried or unknown? Even when, on an intellectual level, we recognise that change is an inevitable part of human progress, we are often left feeling vulnerable and defensive. There is a serious obligation on church leaders, therefore, to mediate the process of change with special understanding and patience towards the elderly, who are perhaps more sensitive to change than most.

For instance, leaders must try:

- To control the pace of change within the church – too often it is the elderly who feel specially disadvantaged by sudden, poorly-explained change; and neither the fact that the change is a good or reasonable one, nor that the elderly themselves seem to be stubborn and resentful, is justification for the aggressive or precipitate driving through of that change. (See chapter 22 on 'Handling differences and managing change'.)
- To create opportunities within the mainstream of church activities (even, and perhaps especially, when changes are taking place) for elderly members to function as usefully and for as long as possible. Leaders should take account of the very positive benefits which can derive from extended experience of life and of

the ways of God, as well as the devastation to morale when we feel ourselves no longer needed ('surplus to requirements').

- To maintain a strong corporate awareness that the church serves an unchanging Lord – one who remains constant and unvarying, utterly faithful within the ebb and flow of even the most confusing events and circumstances.

Provision of a balanced menu of support

Where the church fellowship is small, it will almost certainly be unnecessary to have any formal support structure. In a larger church, however, it could be particularly helpful for there to be a carefully thought-out framework within which pastoral care for elderly people is provided. Some churches may be large enough to consider the possibility of appointing a part- or full-time worker with responsibility for pastoring older people (cf. youth workers).

The framework proposed might incorporate the following aspects:

- Additional pastoral input, activated when members become less fit to attend church regularly, or less actively involved in front-line service. It might take the form of more frequent home visits, phone calls, correspondence, (e-mails?), etc. Church leaders should share this responsibility with suitable church members, including women.
- The development of self-help or mutual support groups. It scarcely needs arguing that the primary responsibility for supporting the elderly should fall to immediate family members, particularly when such members are both Christian and living locally (cf. 1 Tim 5:8, 16). Where this kind of support is not available, a valuable substitute could be provided by peer group prayer clusters or small, appropriate leisure activity clubs, within which the elderly might find companionship, stimulus, and various kinds of practical support and help. Relatives and leaders alike should avoid any approach which could contribute towards an unhealthy 'dependence culture', for although some older people are weakened by self-pity, many more are instinctively and sturdily independent, and this attitude should be fostered wherever sensible and possible.
- Organised support and counsel which is particularly needful in the case of those who are advanced in age or particularly frail, and where the physical, emotional or mental needs of elderly church members are beyond the capacities or resources of family, or where there are no relatives in the area. Many contemporary

churches have members with special expertise in medicine, nursing, social work, finance, legal affairs, etc., who could provide significant help for the needy elderly or their families. They might function separately or as a team. Church leaders should also keep in mind the need to provide ongoing spiritual and emotional support for family members who fulfil the very demanding role of carers – not least where they have felt compelled to allow their loved ones to go into permanent residential or nursing care.

Conclusion

Leaders who take seriously their responsibility for elderly members of their church fellowship should give consideration to the following:

*   sensitivity is needed in identifying those who qualify as 'elderly';
*   preparation for growing old starts now, and applies to everyone;
*   accommodation to change can be especially difficult for the elderly;
*   the elderly should be encouraged to function usefully within the mainstream of church life for as long as possible, since their gifting and experience are valuable;
*   a church culture is to be fostered in which older members feel valued and are encouraged to maintain their sense of independence;
*   carefully planned and balanced provision should be made for those who are of advanced age and increasing frailty;
*   full and wise use should be made of the spiritual and professional resources existing within the church;
*   constant awareness is to be maintained that we serve a faithful, compassionate and unchanging Lord.

Further reading

R M Gray and D O Moberg, *The Church and the Older Person* (Eerdmans, 1962, 77)

P Tournier, *Learn to Grow Old* (Harper & Row, 1972)

CHAPTER THIRTY-SIX

Home Visiting

DAVID AND JOAN SHORT

The duty of church leaders

It is the duty of church leaders to try to know each church member individually. This can usually be done best by visiting them in their own homes. Paul reminded the elders of the church in Ephesus that he had taught the believers not only publicly but also 'from house to house' (Acts 20:20). Many of the successful church leaders of the past have made a practice of visiting all their members, in their own homes, at least once a year. There is a special need for visitation at times of sickness or when a member is unable to attend church. James, in his epistle, encouraged Christians who are seriously ill to request a visit from the elders (Jas 5:14).

The need for visitation is too great to be met by pastors alone. In congregations where there is a considerable proportion of older members, the burden may be too great for the pastor and elders together. Church visitors need to be enrolled and trained to share the burden. It is a form of Christian service for which some are more naturally gifted than others; nevertheless it is a gift which develops with use. It is a sphere of Christian service for which women are especially fitted by reason of their innate empathy and practical skills in the home. Nevertheless, there is a real place for the men to back up the women and, particularly, to visit those in hospital.

In the church with which we are associated, one of the elders has been given the task of co-ordinating visiting. He has a designated deputy who stands in when he is not available. They are backed up by a caring group which meets regularly to share information. The whole fellowship has been circulated with instructions to look out for anyone needing help, and either deal with it themselves or notify the co-ordinator.

Advice for visitors

Visiting is an immense privilege. In his parable of the sheep and the goats, the Lord made this profound statement about visiting the needy: 'Anything you did for one of my brothers here, however humble, you did for me.' (Matt 25:40, NEB) Is it possible to imagine a greater privilege than that of visiting the Lord? We need to remember, too, that we shall all need help ourselves at some time in our lives.

Some needs are acute. They require immediate help for a relatively short time: e.g. an emergency in the home or admission to hospital. It is necessary to think about transport to and from hospital, washing, and care for the family at home. Children may need to be met from school or looked after while the parent visits, manning the phone would enable the relative to rest.

Other needs are chronic: not so urgent, but more lasting. Older folk who are frail and largely confined to their homes much appreciate a visit to bring news from the outside world. Such visits need not be long. Sometimes what they like best is to get out of the home and go for a ride in the car. Some can go out in wheel-chairs, if there is a strong person to push them. Others are able to go for a short walk if they have an arm for support. Some need a bit of shopping or small jobs done in the home or garden. Those who have poor sight might appreciate a book read to them. Many older people are hard of hearing, so it is necessary to speak up (without shouting) and speak slowly, letting them do most of the talking. Almost all old folk love to talk about the past, about families who are far away, and to bring out old photographs. They have so few people who can give them time. Sometimes they want to talk about fears they have bottled up. Everyone needs time to be really listened to. Christian Listeners do a very good course on this subject.

When you go for the first time, introduce yourself and make it a very short visit. At the start, it is good to greet the person warmly, but not too enthusiastically, with a friendly smile and a handshake – adapted to any disability the individual may have and proceeding gently in case their right hand is painful. If you do not know the individual well, it may be necessary to introduce yourself and indicate how you heard about them. The first words should be of sensitive enquiry. 'How are things today?' or 'What sort of a week have you had?' are useful opening gambits. If you simply ask: 'How are you?' the danger is that the person you are visiting may interpet your question as an invitation to enlarge on his or her physical ills. What is needed is a question which will open up their basic feelings and concerns.

At some point, not necessarily on the first visit, it might be appropriate to say: 'I don't know you well. Tell me a bit about your life.' It is sometimes valuable to ask what what they look back on as the most interesting, exciting and memorable phase of their life. It means much for one who is shut-in to talk about the past, and it can be fascinating for the listener. It is important to remember to keep visits brief, especially in hospital. Few invalids can stand long visits. Five to ten minutes is usually quite long enough for a first visit.

There is no need to take a gift; it is you they want. If you do take something, then often an old magazine or book you have enjoyed, or a bowl of soup, or a little home baking is a real treat. Try to call back again before too long so that they can remember your face. When you do start to visit a shut-in person, it is important to keep it up, so that you are really able to get to know each other. They need to be needed, just as we do. In between visits, a brief chat on the phone shows that they are not forgotten. Sometimes a telephone call may be more appropriate than a visit.

Simply visiting a lonely person is a Christ-like act, but if a visit is to have maximum value, it must be a means of bringing God into the situation in some way. This is surely what Jonathan did when he went to David at Horesh. We are told that he 'helped him to find strength in God' (1 Sam 23:16). Undoubtedly, Jonathan's friendship, in itself, would have been an encouragement. In addition, he might have encouraged David by some argument, e.g. by pointing to his skill in evading capture, or by promising to do all in his power to protect him from the king. But, instead, we are told that he helped him to find strength in God. How exactly he did this we are not told, but it was probably by reminding him of his anointing by Samuel as God's chosen king – in effect a promise.

God's promises are utterly reliable, and the most valuable service we can render to those we visit is to leave them with a relevant promise or statement from God's word – adding whatever explanation may be necessary to apply it in their specific situation. It is the actual words of scripture that bring blessing. For example, in the case of someone who dreads going into hospital, you could read (reading is better than merely quoting from memory) the promise in Hebrews 13:5: 'Never will I leave you: never will I forsake you.' You can point out the double negative – 'never, never' – and the way the promise covers every eventuality, including going into hospital. And you can add that God has never failed any of his children.

A visit by a pastor or elder should normally be concluded by prayer. When over 2, 000 patients in hospital were asked about the ministry that had been provided them by chaplains, prayer emerged as the element of the chaplain's visit that they considered by far the most helpful.

We all feel inadequate at times, but the Lord will help us in our weakness. What is required is a love for those who are lonely and in need, and a willingness to serve God without thinking of ourselves and our feelings of inadequacy and embarrassment. When on your way to see a stranger, you can repeat to yourself the words of the Apostle Paul: 'I can do all things through him who strengthens me' (Phil 4:13). It is important that we do not pretend to know all the answers to God's ways, and give trite replies. We must be honest, and when we don't understand, we should say so, and then remind each other that though we don't understand, we do know that God's love and care are as true now as ever.

If the person seems unlikely to recover, a valuable approach is to ask if there is any particular hymn or verse of scripture going through their mind, and go over it with them. Those suffering from Alzheimer's disease or other forms of brain failure need to hear very familiar scriptures. Some devoted Christians lose their sense of communion with God, and feel guilty that they do not find any comfort in the word of God. It may encourage them to hear that the saintly Harold St John, at the end of life, said: 'I am too weak to pray. I'm too tired to love him much. But I'm just lying here and letting him love me.'

Further reading

Richard Baxter, *The Reformed Pastor* (various editions)
R E O White, A Guide to Pastoral Care (Pickering paperbacks, 1976)

Pastoral Care of The Ill and Dying

PAULINE SUMMERTON

Though it may seem to devalue the gifts and expertise possessed by some, the fact is that caring for the sick calls mainly for sound commonsense. What matters is that you go to see the patient – and do it promptly. The thought, 'No one cared.' can haunt both patient and carer. For any but the most seriously ill, visiting is not usually very difficult. If time is limited, say at the start how long you can stay, and indicate, before leaving, if and when you will revisit. Don't raise hopes beyond what you can – and will – fulfil: be realistic. It is often helpful to give advance warning of the time you would like to call.

Visitors should bear in mind that the rarest commodity in life is listening, and having time for people. This is particularly true if the patient has a communication problem. Staff and even family (if there are any) rarely have much time to spend with the patient. Visitors often feel they have to entertain the patient, and are over-anxious about what to say. Be careful not to be the sort of visitor who uses the opportunity to say all the things you have wanted to say many times before. It is not fair to take advantage of the person when they cannot escape. They are vulnerable and, sadly, some pastoral carers act like the salesperson who comes to the door and, once they have their foot in the door, are loath to go. Don't stay too long. Twenty minutes is usually long enough, and it is better to come again than stay too long. If you are a bringer of information, you may be able to bring it in written form (e.g. the church notice sheet) which you can leave with the patient.

Confidentiality is very important. Be sure to obtain the patient's permission if you wish to share something confidential with others or mention it in public prayers.

Some visitors are unsure about praying or reading the scriptures. This may reflect their own embarrassment and inhibitions rather than those of the patient or carer. A simple remark like: 'It is usually my practice to pray when I visit people; may I pray for you?' will

clear the air. It has afforded me opportunities to pray and/or read
to a wide spectrum of people, including rigid Brethren, those of
Jewish faith, Jehovah's Witnesses, those of other faiths and those of
no faith. The response to the question often gives an indication of
where the patient stands spiritually which may not have been
known previously.

Those who are sick, even those who are not seriously ill, and even
those who are young, may be anxious, since it is at times like this
that they are brought into touch with their own mortality, what life
is all about, whether it is worth living, and how it will end. This is
specially true of those who have had a brush with death. Listening
to them express their thoughts and feelings and telling the story of
the event is usually therapeutic for them. But it also gives the
pastoral visitor an insight into where the person is, spiritually, and
provides an opportunity to support and help. If they are members
of your congregation, it may be that others are anxious too and
would benefit from some teaching on the subject.

Don't forget that, even though the patient may be unable to
respond to you, they can usually still hear. Therefore, never make
inappropriate comments to them or about them, in their hearing.
Use the fact that they can probably hear to talk, comfort, encourage,
read the scriptures and pray with them.

Though the patient may be very sick they may resent it if you or
indeed anyone else talks to the staff or others out of their hearing –
i.e. behind their back. This may be because they have real fears
about what may be arranged for them – e.g. placement in a home,
or an operation. The attitude of doctors towards telling patients
things as they are has changed in recent years. Why should pastoral
carers be any different?

The point of death can be a long time coming, and sitting with a
patent can be hard and time-consuming. I think I should like quiet,
supportive company at such a time, but some patients have no one
to be with them, for while some have supportive family members,
others may belong to families whose members are estranged from
each other, or even at war. The pastoral carer needs to be sensitive
to this and to act with the utmost tact. One may not know the full
truth of the matter and, almost certainly, may not know how the
patient is feeling about the situation at the time. Mum/Dad may be
feeling that it would be the answer to their prayers for family unity
to have the whole family round their bed, even at this late stage.

Sometimes, dying patients will seem to delay the final moment.
Clinically, they should have gone: what are they waiting for? Maybe
a relative is flying back, or an anniversary date is imminent. If this
is likely, it is possible to comfort the family by expressing these

things. Sometimes dying people appear to want to slip away quietly, without being watched. It may be necessary to explain to the family that they need to take it in turns to be with the patient, in order to ease the departure.

Relatives and friends are sometimes reluctant to ask for prayers at this stage, since they fear it might indicate to the patient that they are dying. Yet on occasions when the patient has recovered they often say how grateful they were for the prayers. It seems that it was the relatives who were having difficulty facing up to the death! Bear in mind that, if we believe that God answers prayer, the patient may well improve. Sometimes pastoral carers and, indeed, relatives, are a bit surprised when this happens – and quite often it does.

Funeral arrangements

If the patient has planned their own funeral it is a tremendous help, both for the relatives and for the officiator – to say nothing of the therapeutic effect it will have had on the deceased. Helping someone make such plans is a very worthwhile experience. In modern times, when families are scattered, there is rarely a family grave or plot. And there may be conflicting views as to where, when and how to proceed. Undertakers are used to these things, and are usually exceedingly helpful. Since it is usual for the undertaker to charge an inclusive fee for the whole procedure, the minister's fee will be included. If, as a charitable soul, you do not wish to accept the fee, the best thing to do is to take the cash (which is usually the form in which it is given) and return it to the family personally – or give it to an agreed cause. (See chapter 38 on 'The funeral service'.)

Pre-natal death, stillbirth, cot deaths, etc.

Sometimes babies miscarry or spontaneously abort. In the case of multiple births, only one may live – a bittersweet situation for the parents. These are very sad and painful experiences.

Before birth, the baby will have had no contact with anyone but the mother. Hence, in the case of a miscarriage, the mother may have difficulty in believing that any baby existed, putting it all down to her imagination. It is therefore important to talk to the mother about the baby, asking whether she gave it a name, how much it weighed, whether a photo (or ultrascan picture) was taken (if you were not able to see it yourself). If you are present with the baby, do stroke it, or gently pull aside the shawl to at least see its hair. Don't entertain in your mind thoughts such as: 'She's only such and such an age; she can try for more.' or 'She already has two lovely children.' No two babies are the same, and each is special to the mother. Usually, even decades later, she will not have forgotten her child, and will remember anniversaries. 'Can a woman forget her child?', asks scripture.

Things have changed in the health service, and staff realise the importance of a formal ending. Many hospital chaplains are able to arrange, for the bare cost of the crematorium or cemetery basic fee, a simple, short funeral service, in which, at the parent's request, the pastoral visitor can take part. In the case of a burial, this can take place at the graveside. The baby has had little, if any, outside contact, so a short service for those who have had contact with the baby, or maybe just the parents, is more appropriate than a service in a largish church with a tiny white coffin alone at the front. It is better not to use it as an opportunity to witness. That can come later.

The father will often find all this most difficult. He has not carried the baby during the pregnancy, and therefore has had even less contact than the mother. He may well have been taught that men should not show emotion, and he may not have grasped the idea of being a father. For these reasons, it is often difficult for him to show his grief, and it may take a long time before he does. If there are other siblings, try to include them in the ending event, by bringing a flower, or a letter to the baby they had hoped for. Encourage the parents to allow them to come. They often survive these events better than the adults – and better than the adults had imagined they would.

CHAPTER THIRTY-EIGHT

The Funeral Service

BOB TRIPNEY

'In conducting a funeral service the Christian pastor simultaneously performs a social service, with legal overtones, offers a ministry and bears a Christian witness in one of the crucial experiences of life.' (R E O White) It is right that society should respectfully and reverently dispose of the dead, thus safeguarding the dignity of the individual and, especially for the Christian, affirming underlying belief in the destiny of man. Any society that does otherwise usually has scant regard for the living as well. The funeral service is unique in that it is man- rather than worship-orientated. It is intended to help the living: family, friends, the church, the community. Do good service here and you will greatly assist the grieving process and ease the pain of saying 'Goodbye'. Therefore, pastoral concerns must be uppermost. Pastoral care treasures the memory of the deceased's life and affirms hope, while at the same time facing the mystery of death. The emphasis must rest on 'service' which is not just a matter of conducting a church service, but also of consulting the bereaved beforehand and being concerned about their aftercare too.

The pre-funeral visit

Any view of life which does not include death, is not worth having. As the Prayer Book says, 'in the midst of life we are in death'. It brings us all to the edge of our existence in this world. In Jesus' ministry we see him confronting disease and death. For him it is an alien (evil) intrusion into the goodness of God's world. He is indignant at the grave of Lazarus and weeps (John 11:33). The Christian view of death is ambiguous, for paradoxically Jesus dies and in death suffers the judgment of God, that we through faith in him, might never experience that same judgment (Rom 6:33; 8:1, 2). He has drawn the sting of death. The last enemy has been overcome, but the pain remains.

The death might have occurred suddenly, giving no time for

preparation and leaving the family in shock. If it has been long expected and even prayed for, possibly by both the deceased and their family, there will be relief mingled with sadness. If the death is that of a child or has occurred by suicide, violence or accident, there may be feelings of total disbelief, anger, guilt and even resentment against God. The bereaved would be less than human if they did not look around for help and comfort at this time, but Bible promises may sound hollow. Great wisdom is called for and a total absence of superficial comment and synthetic sadness. Therefore, it ill becomes any to make this visit in triumphalist fashion. You must go in the quiet assurance of hope. Be prepared to get it wrong, but not before you have consulted and prayed with fellow elders. There are helpful comments in *Patterns and Prayers for Church Worship*. Do not go it alone.

Your role at the pre-funeral visit is:

- To bring comfort by sharing the great affirmations of the Faith in a quiet, sincere (not artificial) manner.
- To find out details of the person's life, spiritual history (faith or otherwise) -see *Tribute* below.
- To discuss details of the service, where it is to be held, whether at church and cemetery/crematorium, or wholly at the crematorium, and in what order, e.g., the usual order or burial/cremation first, followed by a memorial service. There are endless variations in the order of service, but scripture sentences, a 'welcome', prayers, hymns, scripture readings, an address/tribute and blessing should be included. The tribute might be given by a family friend, and prayers and readings done by family or fellow elders. Someone might have composed a poem. Adopt a flexible approach adapting to personal requests. You must ask what tone is to be set. Often in our circles it is that of thanksgiving.
- Give practical assistance. Local conventions and procedures vary. Do not despise these, but rather extract the maximum significance from them. In some areas the coffin will be kept at home till the funeral though, increasingly, chapels of rest at undertakers' are used. The relatives have to attend to a whole variety of practical matters and good undertakers provide written guidance for this. Be advised – undertakers are excellent and do undertake. Sound advice from the pastor is that the bereaved should not make any hasty decisions. Matters about the immediate future need to be settled, but major decisions should be left till the days of shock and bereavement have passed and things can be seen from that new perspective. Don't hesitate to

consult fellow elders and/or undertakers on anything you are uncertain about.

The funeral service

You arrive at the day and time well prepared as above, recognising that it is an honour to be asked to conduct the service. The three essential elements to the service are: a recollection of the great truths of the gospel leading to worship and thanksgiving; a tribute to the one who has died; prayers of thanksgiving and remembrance for the life of the deceased and for assurance and strength for those left to mourn.

Initial procedures

When the coffin arrives, meet the undertakers at the door and greet the family. It can be very reassuring for them to have you do this. Walk ahead of the funeral party into the church reciting some of the following scriptures: John 11: 25, 26; Deut. 33:27; John 3:16; John 5:25; Rom 14:7-9; 1 Cor 2:9. Alternatively, stand on the platform and read the verses. Speak in a clear, firm voice without histrionics, leaving the time-honoured scriptures to yield their own depth and power. From the platform, courteously dismiss the pallbearers when they have positioned the coffin.

The welcome

E.g. 'We have come to say farewell to – to thank God for his/her life and to commit – and ourselves to God's care'.

Depending on the family's wishes, you may say that the service is to be a celebration of a fulfilled Christian life or a service of thanksgiving for a wonderful mother/father etc.

Prayer, asking for strength and assurance.

Scripture

Readings may be selected from the following list. It can be helpful to group them under headings, but please note that there is considerable overlap:

The sovereignty of God, who gives life and takes it away (Job 1:21; Pss 8; 90; 121; 138; 139:1-14; 1Tim 6:7).

The God of comfort (Deut 33:27a; Psa 23; Isa 66:13; Matt 5:4; 2 Cor 1:3-7, Rev 7:7).

The God of compassion: (Pss 103:1-4; 116; Lam 3:22-23; 2 Cor 1:3-7).

Assurance: (Psa16; John 5:19-27; 6:35-40; 14:1-6; Rom 8:18, 35, 38, 39; 14:7-9; 1 Cor 15; 2 Cor 5:1; Heb13:5; Rev1:17, 18).

The Christian hope of immortality and reunion confirmed by the resurrection of Jesus Christ: (Pss 30; 130; John 3:16; 11:25; 1 Cor 15:1-4, 20–26, 35–38, 42-44a, 53-58; 1 Thess 4:14-18; 1Pet 1:3-9; Rev 21:1-7).

Victory: (Pss 27; 118:14-21; Rom 8:18; 1 Cor 15: 54, 57; Phil 3:10, 11, 20, 21; 1 Pet 3:3-9; 1 John 5:4; Rev 21:7).

Eternal reward: (1 Cor 2:9; 2 Cor 4:7-18; 1Thess 4:18; 2 Tim 4:8; Rev 7:9-17; 21:1-7) .

The sensitive pastor should select prayerfully, depending on freshness and relevance. The selection may then be used as part of the tribute, or if someone else is doing that, form the basis of a short address emphasising the great theme of the Christian funeral service – eternal life. Against the transitory nature, fragility and vulnerability of human life, should be set the permanent nature, solidity and invulnerability of God-given and guaranteed eternal life (1 Cor 15:22).

Tribute

The Christian
Here the fullest opportunity is given to say farewell and to bring before the congregation the sense of completion, of victory and of a life fulfilled in the grace of Christ. The main events of the person's life should be highlighted, their human and spiritual history. Include special recollections from the loved one's life; memories sacred to the bereaved of love, home and friendships. Mention their role in the local and wider church and in the community. It helps relatives to know the respect in which others held their loved one. Congregations are genuinely interested in the details of the deceased's life and even in apparently ordinary lives you will find events of real significance. We need to remember their importance to God, in whose presence the first shall be last and the last first.
N.B. Never forget to pay tribute to those who have cared for the deceased.

The Christian adherent
This is not an occasion for speculating about the person's true position or probable destiny. Exercise discretion and kindness. Give thanks for them, express regret at losing them and pay tribute to their known character – these alone are in order. 'Only God knows any heart's true story.' Therefore, make the great Christian affirmations without any suggestions as to whether they were or were not fulfilled.

The Non-Christian

It is not uncommon to be asked to bury a non-Christian who is known to be such. This is where the introductory remarks about the service being for the bereaved are especially relevant. The service we conduct is a Christian rite and gives opportunity to discuss the great truths of the gospel with relatives prior to the funeral, and to affirm on the day a Christian theology of death. This may be the only time the public hears what Christians think. In the context of human bereavement, the story of Christ's death and resurrection gains tremendously in relevance and power. You must not proselytise a captive audience. Rather take for granted the great truths of the gospel and conduct the service in a quietly triumphant manner.

Special cases – The child

Great care is needed here. Avoid sentimentality and trite explanations; admit that there are questions and mystery. Allow for expressions of grief. Affirm God's love and assume the child is in the circle of divine compassion (Matt 19:14).

Special cases – Death by accident, violence or suicide

There may be considerable delays before the body is released for burial/cremation.

Let the writer suggest that you concentrate on the bereaved, relying heavily on prayer and consultation with other pastors and leaders to give you guidance and support.

Hymn

Prayers

Either set or extempore prayers should be made, giving thanks for all that God has done in Christ and for the life of the deceased. The comfort of God for the bereaved should be requested and the victory won through Christ should be stressed.

Blessing

At some point you may have to mention arrangements for the burial/cremation and where and when refreshments are to be provided.

Committal

Note that if the service is wholly at the crematorium, then this part will be included there.

The body is reverently lowered into the grave and committed to the ground or, at a prearranged signal, a curtain closes around the coffin, which then goes off to be cremated. Give clear instructions to the congregation about watching these events, so that they are not left wondering what to do or where to look. Maintain the emphasis on the hope of resurrection to eternal life through our Lord Jesus Christ. He will change our earthly bodies to be like his glorious body (Phil 3:21). Appropriate scripture verses could be: Romans 8:31-39; Philippians 4:7; Jude 24, 25.

Careful planning reserves verses and prayers for this time and allows opportunity for relatives to let go. Advise them gently that: 'Here you have left the earthly remains of your loved one, but you have committed them to the safekeeping of a loving God.' Remember that this can be the most harrowing moment for the genuinely grieving and they will need much support.

This part of the service should be brief.

After care

Good pastors will keep a watchful eye on and remain in regular contact with the bereaved until they know they have either come 'through' or have not, in which case they will need specialist help. The deepest, most genuine feelings are often those most carefully controlled and concealed. (See chapter 39 on 'Bereavement counselling'.)

Further reading

Alternative Service Book (SPCK, 1980)
D Atkinson et al, New Dictionary of Christian Ethics and Pastoral Theology (IVP, 1995)
Common Worship: Funeral (Church Publishing House, 2000)
Patterns and Prayers for Church Worship (Baptist Union, 1991)
M Quoist, Pathways of Prayer, pp 42-45, (Gill & Macmillan, 1989)
M Quoist, Prayers of Life, pp 30-31, (Gill & Macmillan, 1963)
E Smalley, Christian Burial (Baptist Union, 1981).
R E O White, A Guide to Pastoral Care (Pickering & Inglis, 1981)

CHAPTER THIRTY-NINE

Bereavement Counselling

MADGE FORD

Loss is an experience we all share. For some it may be the ultimate loss of a loved one through death – a bereavement. However, loss of any kind produces grief in varying intensity, depending on the significance of what has been lost. Grief is a normal emotional response to the experience of being bereaved. It is part of the cost of loving and then losing. 'Bereavement is the experience of losing a loved person or object. Typically "bereavement" describes a person's reaction to the death of someone they love, although the term may also be used to describe other losses.' (D J Atkinson, *New Dictionary of Christian Ethics and Pastoral Theology*, p. 190) Jesus said, 'Blessed are those who mourn for they will be comforted' (Matt 5:4). It is only as we mourn and grieve that we can truly and fully experience the comfort God would offer us.

However, being a Christian with access to the comfort and truth of God's word does not render us immune to the hurt and bewilderment that bereavement can inflict. Bereavement often produces feelings and reactions which may seem strange and frightening. Given time and support, most people are able to cope with them and work through the process of grieving.

Sometimes Christians have unwittingly discouraged others from expressing their very normal feelings of grief and loss. Perhaps we accept too readily the view that, 'She is a Christian so she will soon get over her grief.' In an attempt to be positive and helpful we quote scripture verses like, 'Blessed are the dead who die in the Lord' (Rev 14:13), or 'With Christ which is far better' (Phil 1:23). These can be of immense comfort at the right time. But that is the key issue. When is the right time? To be able to judge that, it is important to be aware of at least two things.

First, what is the family situation of the person who has been bereaved? Do we know what are the circumstances of their loss? Have we sufficient understanding and awareness of their need and culture which will inform the way we express our care and support? If they are believers they can accept that their loved one is blessed, but they are hurting so much at the severance of the relationship that they may be unable to hear words of comfort even from scripture.

Second, bereavement inevitably introduces a period of transition in the life of the bereaved person. This time of change offers them the opportunity to reflect on the relationship which has ended, and an opportunity to review and consider the past and the future. It is a time to *mourn* the one who has died. With a supportive person alongside they can be enabled to explore their feelings, thoughts and memories. It is intended to be a healing and recovery period and can last, even in normal grief, for as much as two to four years.

While the most natural bereavement support system may be that of family and friends, there are times when additional help and support is needed. Sometimes family members are just too close to the situation. Also friends, desperately wanting to help, may try to make things 'better' too soon. There is now a greater awareness of the value of bereavement counselling and the need for it in today's fractured and hurting world. Many statutory and voluntary agencies offer bereavement counselling training and also offer a counselling service. In many churches people have undergone this training and have then put it to good use in their own church and community. Bereavement counselling training gives the skills which enable one to deal with many aspects of grief. It provides a very helpful preparation for those who care pastorally for others both in and outside of the church. Also in our multicultural society today it is essential that we have some understanding of how those in other cultures deal with their grief.

Understanding the grief process

This process entails a series of responses or 'stages of grief'. It involves a sense of *shock*, followed by a painful awareness of the *reality* of our loss which, if unhindered, leads to *acceptance* and emotional healing. The desired outcome at the end of this process is a *readjustment to life* without the loved one, a looking forward, acknowledging that although much has changed there is still a life to be lived.

These 'stages of grief ' do not necessarily follow one another in a specific order. They often overlap and are not always clearly defined. To work through them requires time and effort, which for the bereaved person can prove unexpectedly demanding and exhausting.

Shock

This is perhaps the most obvious initial response and is often seen before and during the funeral. It is the mind's way of coping with the horror and pain of the loss, a closing down of our ability to face what is happening. This sense of numbness and shock protects the bereaved person from feeling the impact and significance of the loss. They are thus enabled to carry on and get through the formalities of and preparations for the funeral. It may last beyond these early weeks and can persist even for months, particularly following a sudden or unexpected traumatic death.

Reality

As shock gives way to the reality that the loved one has died, the acute pain and finality of the loss begin to be felt. 'The loss of a loved person is one of the most intensely painful experiences any human being can suffer', writes J Bowlby (*Attachment and Loss*, vol. 3, p. 7).

People cope with this pain in varied ways, perhaps by unconscious denial, e.g. by continuing to set a place at the dining table for the one who has died, or by delaying decisions about the dispersal of their personal effects. For the Christian there is also the risk of retreating into a superspirituality which refuses to face the pain of the loss. Often there are feelings of guilt, anger and resentment towards the deceased which are felt to be unworthy and must somehow be denied. These feelings can then lead to depression, a not uncommon response in grief. Some have a need to idealise the dead person and refuse to allow a negative thought or comment to be made. Others speak of restlessness and lack of concentration. This, together with feelings of deep sadness and loss, coupled with a fear of breaking down in tears, may make it impossible for the bereaved person even to sit through a church service.

Acceptance

As time passes and the reality of the loss is faced, a new phase of grieving begins. Memories of the loved one become more realistic. The negative as well as the positive elements of the relationship and of the person begin to be acknowledged. There is a gradual 'letting go' of the person, perhaps by saying goodbye to any clothes or personal effects which may still be around. For many the recognition of acceptance begins when they experience satisfaction and a sense of achievement in learning new skills.

A widow struggled through her first year of grief with feelings of dismay and frustration at being so suddenly left unprepared for widowhood. In his wish to protect her, her husband had always handled financial matters and also actively dissuaded her from learning to drive. With the help of her counsellor she worked through these and many other issues. As the first anniversary drew near she decided, at the age of 61, to take driving lessons. She passed her test first time, bought her first car and realised that she had turned a corner. She had taken a huge step towards independence and begun to accept her new status.

Acceptance leads into the fourth and last stage of the grief process.

Readjustment

Recovery and readjustment are indications that mourning is moving towards a conclusion. Life begins to beckon again, and there is a new sense of hope and expectation. It is a significant moment when the bereaved person is able to look beyond their grief and begin to invest emotional energy into other aspects of life and relationships. The loved one is not forgotten, but the pain recedes, the intense feelings diminish. It does not mean that grief is forever ended but rather that the loss is no longer the primary focus of life. However, on special occasions, or significant anniversaries, painful memories may be reawakened which elicit those pangs of longing for all that has been lost. These feelings are usually temporary and, once acknowledged, do not inhibit the move towards a new independence and freedom.

Helping the bereaved person

Be there

Sometimes we feel inadequate or fearful of upsetting the one who is mourning. We may feel quite helpless in the face of their loss. It is often painful to share another person's grief, but our loving, caring presence is a priceless gift they will deeply appreciate and value. As friends and relatives become absorbed in their own lives again, the bereaved can feel isolated and abandoned within a few weeks of the funeral. So keep in regular touch with them. Don't assume they prefer to be alone. They may, but give them the choice. In her contribution in *Facing Bereavement* (p.50) Elizabeth Boot speaks of her wish for visits from Christian friends and her sense of shock when one of them said, 'We felt you needed to be left alone.' She comments, 'How did he know what we felt or needed?' Job expressed it well when he said that his brothers, friends, guests and servants had all forgotten and alienated him (Job 19: 13-15).

Listen

While talking helps the person come to grips with the fact and reality of their loss, good listening facilitates the expression of their grief. They will want to talk about the one who has died, reviewing memories and events over and over again. This is not the time to share our experience of loss and how we have coped in a similar situation. It is their time. While we are with them we put our own concerns and worries to one side. By our attentive attitude and body language we allow them to see that we are not in a hurry. If we know we can only be with them for a brief moment, it is kinder to say so and arrange for a longer visit another time.

We don't interrupt their outpourings of grief, nor do we offer solutions or advice. If there is a silence it can be more helpful to allow it, rather than rush to fill it by asking questions. Allow the tears to flow without endeavouring to stem them. Listen for the feelings behind the words – feelings of guilt, anger, disappointment, depression. Throughout, listen to God. Pray for the prompting of his Spirit to know when to intervene with the comfort of his word and when to hold back. It may not be the moment to quote a verse from the scriptures.

Should our approach be different when we are listening to someone who does not share our faith, or whose loved one has lived a life without God? Not necessarily so. We express our shared humanity and respect for them as individuals as we acknowledge the commonality of grief. However, we may have to adjust our approach and take more care before offering overtly Christian answers, Bible texts or suggesting a prayer. In our eagerness to help, beware of manipulating the experience of grief in order to bring them to faith. C S Lewis wisely wrote after being bereaved: 'Don't come talking to me about the consolations of religion or I shall suspect you don't understand.' (*A Grief observed*, p.23)

In such a situation it is even more important that we follow closely the bereaved person in their thinking and in reflecting together on their feelings. We will sense when it may be right to ask if they would like us to pray or read a scripture, but often this will be only after some of the doubts about where the deceased has gone have been discussed. This is the moment to stay with their questions and doubts and to ensure that we are answering only what is being asked.

We know that death is the end of the earthly body, but not the end of the person who has died. But it is not for us to say where their loved one is, unless of course we know that they became a Christian before they died. In our compassion and concern to share Jesus and the 'certain hope' that we have, it may be tempting to divert the discussion to issues of faith. The appropriate time may come when the bereaved will want us to talk abut faith, but it has to be in their time and on their terms. It is essential to be honest and admit when we do not have the answers, balancing this with our experience of faith in a God of love who, knowing all things, always does what is right (Gen 18:25). He is merciful and forgiving, and can be trusted not to judge harshly.

Support

There is no short-cut through this pain. For the bereaved Christian it can be a particularly tough time. They know the scriptures but their deep feelings of loss, perhaps anger and fear, may seem to deny those scriptures. A Christian widow exclaimed: 'How can I be angry? He was an active Christian with a strong faith. He is much better off.' She was finding it hard to acknowledge that she felt let down and abandoned. She had been left with many worries and concerns and in reality was fearful and deeply angry.

It takes courage to grieve, and not be afraid to ask questions of God. It also requires courage to become vulnerable by admitting and sharing questions and feelings that are often inexplicable and disconcerting. For some it may feel that God has abandoned them and they are losing their faith. They may feel angry with God and yet horrified to admit it. In these moments it can be immensely reassuring to have the non-judgmental, empathic support of another Christian.

Unresolved grief

During the months following the death of a loved one there may be signs that resolution is not taking place. The depression may persist and deepen. The bereaved person may repeatedly break down in tears, but be unable to say why. They may never talk about the deceased or share memories or anecdotes. In some cases the room of the deceased is left as it was prior to their death, becoming almost a shrine to their memory. In others they remove photographs or anything personal that would be a reminder.

Unresolved grief may lie dormant for years, often until another significant death takes place. A lorry driver, whose elderly mother had died some months earlier, was referred to a counsellor by his doctor. The patient complained of a phobia related to driving his lorry over bridges. Approaching the bridge caused him physical symptoms, intense stress and anxiety. In counselling it emerged that his father had died suddenly from a heart attack while driving over a bridge. The patient was now the same age as his father had been when he died. During the sessions he was enabled to grieve for his father, acknowledging that, as a teenager, in the shock and pain of this sudden and unacceptable loss, he had pushed the feelings away and never grieved.

Grief may be unresolved, delayed or become complicated for many reasons. The following are some examples:

- when the cause of death is unknown;
- if there is no body to which to say goodbye;
- if the person has committed suicide;
- if the death has resulted in litigation;
- when the loss is due to an abortion, miscarriage or stillbirth.

In all of these losses grief can be a particularly difficult and prolonged journey.

Infant death

This is also true in the case of Sudden Infant Death Syndrome (SIDS or Cot death). The loss of a baby, however it happens, is traumatic and often emotionally disabling. More so when it is not clear why the infant has died. The parents may blame themselves, feeling they have failed in caring for their baby. They may have to face questioning by the police, which adds to their sense of unreality and shock. It is unlikely that the couple will travel the road of grief at the same pace, which can place a strain on their relationship and add to their confusion. With a wish to protect each other from the pain of their own grief, one or other may withdraw into themselves, believing they will upset their spouse by sharing how they feel.

Supporting parents whose baby or child has died calls upon all the skill and sensitivity we possess. The parents may be ambivalent about the level of support they would like, sometimes wanting to be left alone and at other times wondering why no one has been in touch. It is better to err towards a regular pattern of visits or telephone calls, checking with the couple what they would prefer. As in all grief we need to give thought to the words we use to offer comfort. It is not helpful to suggest: 'Baby is now in a better place.' or 'Jesus doesn't only want older people in heaven'. Some parents have been told: 'It's good you have other children. They need you.', or 'You will soon have another one who will take his place'. We tend to use these phrases because we are unsure what to say, not realising how hurtful and unacceptable they are. Often a sympathetic touch of the hand and a whispered, 'I'm so sorry' is sufficient at that moment to ease some of their pain. (See chapter 37 on 'Pastoral care of the ill and dying'.)

In caring for the parents the other children in the family will be also enabled to grieve. It is natural to want to protect them, but in doing so we may deprive them of the opportunity to experience grief appropriately and at the right time. 'A child can live through anything, so long as he or she is told the truth and is allowed to share with loved ones the natural feelings people have.' (Eda LeShan, *The Courage To Grieve*, p.8).

Referral

If we are aware that we do not have within the church fellowship anyone with sufficient skills and resources to accompany someone on their journey through grief, it is wise to seek an alternative. The ability to recognise and acknowledge this is an important step in helping the bereaved person. It may mean suggesting a visit to their doctor, or exploring with them what resources are available locally. Bereavement support groups organised by local voluntary agencies can provide the opportunity for those in grief to share together and support each other.

Conclusion

Bereavement and loss are an integral part of being human, but for the Christian it has a dimension that offers hope and reality beyond this life. The goodbye is not for ever. Therefore the pastoral care of those who grieve includes nurturing their faith in a God who comforts. To move forward creatively into a future where the comfort they have received may be used to comfort others (2 Cor 1: 3, 4) adds purpose and meaning to their pain and loss. For all who grieve we look for that moment when they experience the reality of God's promise: 'I will turn their mourning into joy, I will comfort them, and give them gladness for sorrow' (Jer 31:13).

Further reading

D J Atkinson and D Field (eds.), *New Dictionary of Christian Ethics and Pastoral Theology* (IVP, 1995)

E Collick, *Through Grief – the Bereavement Journey* (Darton, Longman & Todd, 1986)

J Goodall, *Children and Grieving* (Scripture Union, 1995)

M Heegaard, *When Someone Very Special Dies* (Children's Workbook) (Woodland Press, Minneapolis, USA, 1988)

C S Lewis, *A Grief Observed* (Faber & Faber, 1966)
C M Parkes, *Bereavement* (Harmondsworth, 1985)
J Tatelbaum, *The Courage to Grieve* (Cedar, 1980)
J W Worden, *Grief Counselling and Grief Therapy* (Tavistock Publications, 1983)
A Warren (ed.), *Facing Bereavement* (Highland Books, 1988)

Where to find help

National Association of Bereavement Service (NABS), 20 Norton Foldgate, London E1 6DB (020 7247 0617) for nationwide information on all types of bereavement.

CRUSE Bereavement Service, 126 Sheen Road, Richmond, Surrey TW9 1UR (020 8940 4818) for counselling, advice, social contact for the bereaved and training.

The Stillbirth & Neo-natal Death Society (SANDS) 28 Portland Place, London W1N 4DE (0207-436-5881) for research, advice and support.

The Compassionate Friends, 53 North Street, Bristol BS3 1EN (0117 966 5202) a nationwide self-help organisation for parents whose children of any age have died.

The Child Bereavement Centre, Brindley House, 4 Burkes Road, Beaconsfield HP9 1PB for support for families, training and research.

Winston's Wish, Gloucestershire Royal Hospital, Great Western Road, Gloucester GL1 3NN (01452 394377) for residential weekends and midweek support for bereaved children who live in the county; also training nationwide.

Association of Christian Counsellors (ACC) 173a Wokingham Road, Reading, Berks RG6 1LT (0118 966 2207; acc.office@zetnet.co.uk) for nationwide accreditation, information and directory of Christian counsellors, including bereavement counsellors.

Depression

RUSSELL BLACKER

Depression is a very common experience, and most people will have felt miserable and sad at some time in their lives. However, in some people, through no fault of their own, depression can get out of hand and become severe – so severe that it stops them from being able to manage at all.

There are many causes for becoming severely depressed like this, but relationship problems are probably the most common. Physical illnesses and bereavements often lead to depression, but less dramatic things like stress, overwork or unemployment, and money worries can also be important. A few people become severely depressed without ever being able to pinpoint the reason, a problem well recognised by doctors.

A true case

Terry has been having difficulties with a younger colleague at work who has now complained about him to his supervisor. Terry is in his fifties and worries that he might be made redundant. His wife doesn't work and has recently been ill. He worries that if he loses his job he won't be able to manage financially or look after her. He hasn't told his wife because he doesn't want to upset her, but neither can he discuss it with anyone at work. For several months now he has become increasingly anxious and dreads going to work. He is sleeping badly and finds that he cannot concentrate at work, or do the work as well as he used to. His mind is full of fears for the future, and the less well he copes the more he fears he will lose his job. His wife notices that he has become very withdrawn and irritable at home, and it is clear that he is off his food and losing weight. At night he can't sit still, or watch television, and he spends his time walking about the house smoking cigarettes. His wife suggests that he go and see the doctor for a check-up, but he refuses. Privately, he thinks that his doctor will think him weak or might even tell his boss that he can't cope.

Seeking help

It is when this depression gets out of hand, when it goes on for weeks on end and nothing seems to make it better, that we need help. Family and friends can give a lot of support and reassurance, and talking things through with them can be enough to help us out of it. But if this doesn't work, if family and friends start to become concerned, or if you start to have thoughts that people would be better off without you, then a visit to the family doctor is the most sensible decision.

Of course we may be unaware of just how depressed we have become because it has all happened so gradually. Some people are determined to struggle on, and may need to be persuaded by others that it is not a sign of weakness to get help. Occasionally, depression doesn't show itself as normal misery and comes out in other ways such as troublesome aches and pains, or worries about our health. If you think this is happening to you then it will help your family doctor considerably if you tell him about any recent upset or how you have been feeling lately.

Symptoms

The symptoms of severe depression are well recognised and may give you or your family a clue that you need professional help. One such symptom is a loss of interest in things that used to give pleasure. Another is a loss of drive and motivation that makes even simple things difficult to do. Depressed people often find it difficult to sleep or find themselves waking up very early in the morning. Going off one's food, losing weight, and feeling weak and tired are important symptoms. Some depressed people become quite irritable, snappy, tense, and restless and may also worry about things unnecessarily, or find it difficult to concentrate. Wanting to stay away from friends and social contacts generally, or finding it difficult to show affection even to those they are close to, are common experiences of depressed people.They may also lose their self-esteem and confidence in situations that they normally handle well. They may even feel worthless, or bad, or feel that the future is bleak and hopeless. Suicidal thoughts are also common signs of depression and they should not feel ashamed to tell their doctor or family about them as they will want to do something to help.

Of course, severely depressed people are unlikely to have all these symptoms, but the number and intensity of them does tend to increase as the depression worsens. Severe depression also tends to go on for quite a long time and, without professional help, you could be feeling like this for six months or longer. Anybody – men and women, young or old – can be affected, although men often find it difficult to tell others and may start to use alcohol to lift their feelings and boost their confidence.

Case example

It is another month on, and Terry has felt so bad some mornings that he has had to skip off work. His boss has phoned up to find out where he is, and has been given the excuse that Terry has 'flu. He still refuses to go and see the doctor, but his wife has now told him and he has offered to see Terry at home. His wife is also concerned that he is drinking so much at home, especially at night when he can't sleep. She notices that he looks dishevelled and thin, and she can't get through to him any more. If she tries he becomes angry and she is frightened that something dreadful will happen.

What you can do to help yourself

There is a lot you can do to help yourself, such as not bottling things up. It helps to have a good cry, and to tell people close to you how you feel inside. If you've recently had some bad news or major upset in your life, then it is good to go over this with others, even if you have done this several times before. Re-living painful experiences is part of the mind's natural healing mechanism, and you should find that the painful feelings get less as you talk things through.

It is important to get out of doors and take some regular exercise, even if it is only a long walk. This will help your sleeping and encourage your body in its natural healing mechanisms. In the same way you may not feel able to work, but it is always good to try and keep up with some work or housework, or some aspect of your normal routine. This will help take your mind off the painful thoughts and feelings which only make you more depressed if you dwell on them.

Make yourself eat a good balanced diet – maybe a diet better than you're normally used to – even if you don't feel like eating. People with depression often lose weight and run low on vitamins, which only makes the situation worse. Fresh fruit and vegetables are a good idea even if you don't normally eat these things.

Above all, avoid using alcohol to lift your mood or help you sleep. Alcohol is a dangerous drug to use when depressed. Despite the temporary relief it may bring, it actually makes depression worse. The other dangers to one's physical health by drinking too much are well known, and these are increased in depression.

Many people find sleeplessness one of the most difficult symptoms of depression to cope with. If you find you cannot sleep, don't get into a state about it. Listening to the radio or television while you are resting your body will still help, even though you are not actually asleep, and you may find that you go off to sleep better when you stop worrying about not sleeping.

It is often helpful to remind yourself that you are suffering from depression – something many other people both now and in the past have gone through – and that you will come out of the other side as they did, even though it doesn't feel like it at the time. Depression can sometimes be a positive experience in that people emerge stronger and better able to cope than before. Situations and relationships may seem clearer and you may now have the wisdom and strength to make important decisions and changes in your life that you were holding off before.

Relatives and friends

Family and friends often want to know what they can do to help someone who is depressed. Being a good listener (and a patient listener if you've heard it all before) is very important. Practical support and making an effort to spend time with a relative or friend is worthwhile. Encourage them to talk and to keep up with some activities. Reassurance that they will come out the other side will be appreciated, although this will need to be repeated since severely depressed people often lack confidence and are full of worry and doubt. Ensure that they get some exercise and eat well, and help them stay away from alcohol.

If it looks as if your relative or friend is getting worse and is starting to talk in terms of not wanting to live, or even to make suggestions that they might hurt themselves, then it is important to take these statements seriously and to insist that their doctor knows about it. The Samaritans can also be very helpful and are experienced at dealing with depression, but the doctor should know about things as well.

Case example

It is now two months further on, and Terry's doctor has seen him at home. Terry is now officially 'off sick' and has not been into work for weeks. His doctor thinks he ought to have treatment, but Terry refuses either to talk to him or to take tablets. His drinking is now quite a problem, and this is made worse by the fact that he sleeps only a couple of hours each night. He feels wretched inside but can't find words to communicate this to others.

He wears his wife out with his worries about money and his incessant demands, and she too is beginning to feel she can't cope.

Treatment from the doctor

It may be that you've tried all these things and nothing has had any effect. This may not be your fault as, generally speaking, severe depressions don't respond to the kinds of simpler, self-help techniques that I have described here. If you've tried and haven't got any better, then the sensible step would be to go and discuss other forms of treatment with your doctor. Nowadays, there is a range of safe and effective treatments for depression, and your doctor will know which is the best for you, and which are available.

Severe depression is a dreadful experience which is far worse, many think, than physical suffering. The important thing is to recognise what is wrong with you in the first place and then make sure that someone, preferably your doctor, knows about it as well.

Case example

Terry eventually reached a point where he could no longer cope, even at home. His doctor asked a psychiatrist to see him, and he persuaded Terry to accept counselling from a community nurse to help control his drinking. Terry refused any medication but the psychiatrist did arrange for him to speak to his boss who, contrary to his fears, was very understanding. The troublemaker at work had been sacked, and Terry has been assured that he won't be made redundant. Nevertheless, it is several months more before Terry is sufficiently recovered to return to work. Many people think he is a changed man. His wife and doctor wish he had accepted help in the first place.

Further reading

J Lockley, *A Practical Workbook for the Depressed Christian* (Word, 1991)

P R Moore, *When Spring Comes Late. Finding your way through depression* (Baker Book House, 2000)

J White, *The Masks of Melancholy. A Christian psychiatrist looks at depression and suicide* (IVP, 1982)

R Winter, *The Roots of Sorrow. Reflections on depression and hope* (Marshalls, 1985)

Marriage Preparation

BOB TRIPNEY

This chapter, which cannot be exhaustive, is intended to provide basic information for route finding in the maze of relationships between men and women and between both and their God. The material has been arranged into four sessions which, of course, can be varied. Busy pastors find it difficult to give more than one or two sessions of preparation, so why not use the services of a mature couple within the fellowship?

Marriage is God-given

The scriptures teach us that marriage is a gift from God in creation and a holy mystery in which man and woman become so closely united with each other as to be called one flesh. We are called to marriage on God's terms. It is a way of life all should honour (Heb 13 : 4). But it is not easy. To take two disparate people and place them together for life, for better for worse, for richer for poorer, in sickness and in health, to love and to cherish, with death the only escape, is not easy. Therefore it must not be undertaken carelessly, lightly or selfishly but reverently, responsibly and after serious thought. A newly married Canadian couple came to stay with us on their rather unusual cycling honeymoon. In the course of conversation they mentioned their grandparents, long thought of as an ideal couple, and said: 'They have not found marriage easy. We expect to have to work at it as they have, but we have our faith to help us.'

SESSION 1. GETTING TO KNOW YOU

However well you may think you know the couple, you will be endlessly surprised at the information that emerges at such a session.

General

This session should be approached sensitively, flexibly and prayerfully with a mental check-list in place. Bring each partner from childhood to where they are now, en route gently teasing out achievements and failures, hopes and fears, attitudes and aspirations. A question might be slipped in here about health, and whether a premarital consultation with the GP might be advisable, if not already done.

Relationships

Family

Relationships within individual families should be explored to discover particularly whether parents have been good role models for marriage. One partner might be a first-generation Christian from a broken home. If so what hopes do they bring with them? Is there parental support for the marriage and if not, why not? How does each feel about the prospect of leaving home and setting up on their own? If there are other brothers and sisters, do they get on well together and how supportive are they? Treading carefully and phrasing questions with the utmost diplomacy, enquire whether there are any (deep) hurts stemming from childhood that need healing.

Example: 'Mother tells me that she is giving the speech at daughter's wedding this Saturday, because father does not get on well with her.'

School, work, friends

Enquire gently about school results and how the transition from school to work was managed. Was school enjoyed and were there good relationships with teachers? Have friendships made at school lasted and have new friends been made at work? Is work looked forward to or is it sheer drudgery?

Note: The problem of non-Christian friends was a real one for an earlier generation and still needs to be explored today.

Careers

Each partner in the late 20th century is likely to have ambitions about a career – discuss whose will be sacrificed, at least temporarily, when children come along, or do they intend to further each other's career in turn? Bear in mind Marjory Foyle's wise words: 'Previous expectations used to be security through a hierarchy – God, husband, wife, children and servants in that order of submission. Today the major expectation is for a high level of personal achievement and growth to be experienced by both partners.'

This is a useful point at which to discuss their attitude to having children especially if there is a variation of opinion.

Notes

1. Use gentleness and humour throughout this session.
2. You are unlikely to cover all this ground.
3. With permission, make notes, which will be useful for the wedding address and will ensure accuracy of facts.
4. No one is trying to turn you into a counsellor if you are not already one, but you are the pastor and need not abrogate responsibility, unless you feel specialist help is needed.
5. Any problems uncovered can be noted and addressed in later sessions.
6. *Marriage Preparation* (Mother's Union) has a useful section on 'How well do you know your partner?'

SESSION 2. EXPLORING THE BIBLE BASE

'Conscientious disciples of Jesus know that Christian action is impossible without Christian thought – we have to hold our people to the divine intention, not what might or might not happen to disrupt a relationship as a result of human weakness.' (John Stott)

What is marriage?

It is God's idea not ours, 'instituted by God in the time of man's innocency' (1662 Marriage Service). Because it is a creation ordinance preceding the fall, it should be regarded as God's gracious gift to all humankind, not just to Christians. In all societies it is a recognised and regulated institution. It is rightly approached by young people with high ideals, for God has chosen the marriage relationship to communicate some of the most profound spiritual truths (Eph 5:25-33). Many couples believe their marriage should be an integral part of their ministry, demonstrating the truth of what the Bible teaches. They expect it to be a good experience.

The creation account

Genesis 2: 19, 20 details Adam's naming of all the animals, but says that nowhere could a suitable helper be found for him. God states, 'It is not good for man to be alone. I will make a helper suitable for him.' Eve was taken from his side, not his head or foot, stressing the complementarity of the couple. Adam joyfully recognises Eve's distinctness as a new creature (woman), but also her suitability to be his helper. The given reason (2: 24, 25) for a man's leaving his father and mother, being united with his wife and becoming one with her, is that she was taken from him. This is a view strongly endorsed by Christ (Matt 19: 4-6, Mark 10: 6-9) who added, 'What God has joined together, let no man separate'.

Leaving, cleaving, becoming one flesh

Leaving

This has to do with mature choice, being voluntary in nature. It is done for a relationship of love and will, not of power or family control. Each partner should have ceased struggling with the issues of growing-up. He or she should not still be attached to mother's apron strings or be father's pet respectively. When problems arise, they should be resolved, whenever possible, within the relationship. They should be encouraged that in so doing, strength and joy will be brought to their relationship. What is private and intimate should not become the public property of the families that have been left.

Leaving close family ties does not mean abandoning them. However, couples might be advised that, while they are lost in each other for a while, loving parents will experience a sense of loss and go through a grieving period.

Note: There should be a healthy separation, both emotionally and physically, if true marriage is to result.

Cleaving (being united with)

This opens up a rich vein of thought that includes 'becoming one flesh'. It goes right to the heart of the relationship between husband and wife. It is about being very close – glued together – closer than anyone or anything else.

Beautiful prose has been written on this subject (see the article on 'Marriage', in *New Dictionary of Christian Ethics*), which might be addressed under the following three headings:

1. Mutual support which includes:

* *Stickability* Husbands and wives should stick together through thick and thin. They should be able to count on each other and

not have the rug pulled from under their feet when in a tight corner.

- *Acceptance* Each should be accepted and affirmed by the other as a unique individual.
- *Deep sharing* They should be able to share deeply from their inmost beings without fear of criticism or censure, and feel safe in so doing.
- *Recognition of vulnerability* As human beings with all their weaknesses and failures they should be open and vulnerable together, i.e. 'naked' physically, psychologically and spiritually. Doors should not be closed and defended. A continual search must be made to find the key that opens all the doors in the relationship.
- *No superiority of one over the other* Ephesians 5 raises the potential of the marriage union to sublime heights by comparing it to the union of Christ with his church. And if the wife is asked to submit to the man, it is in the context of his submission to Christ and in a loving, caring, cleansing and self-giving atmosphere.
- *Openness to God* The marriage should be open to God, so that it is conducted on the spiritual plane. Shared insights deepen faith as well as their relationship.

They will need encouragement to read the Bible and pray together.

2. Healing

We all bring baggage with us from the past, as much from hurts given as hurts received. Deep scars may have been left by childhood experiences of dysfunctional relationships. Everyday life itself can impose severe trials, hurts and disappointments on either party. The marital home should be a place of security and sharing where troubled hearts and minds are settled.

Note: Marriage with its mutual support and right relationship is the best place to heal childhood (and other) hurts, by love.

3. Growth or Self realization

The best marriages thrive on the uniqueness of the two individuals. Each should stimulate the other to achieve their full potential and so become mature persons. This involves not only sharing, but allowing space to the other. Many interests may be held in common, but there must be enough confidence to allow each other to do their own thing, but then come back and share. Ephesians 5:27 allows for spiritual growth and maturation. There is no better vehicle for growth to maturity, i.e. being the best you can be under God, than marriage conducted on the spiritual plane.

Notes

1. Alan Storkey's book, *Marriage and its Modern Crisis*, has an excellent table (3:1, pp. 51, 52) under the headings: 'Life...to be shared...failure'. During the recent preparation of a couple, it proved valuable to go down this list sharing their ideas and comparing them with his.
2. *Marriage Preparation*, (Mother's Union) has a good practical section on decision making.

Becoming one flesh

'God's intention is that "becoming one flesh" should be a reciprocal commitment of self-giving love which finds its natural expression in sexual union.' (John Stott)

This means:

- Sexual union as created by God is pure and legitimate, expressing the far deeper union that already exists between the inner lives of husbands and wives.
- It is part of their desire to give themselves to each other totally, not just physically.
- It is a matter for full and joyful acceptance.
- Its proper setting is within marriage, in an atmosphere of tenderness, affection and faithfulness.

The couple need to learn:

- to give and to get;
- to know how good it is to hug and cuddle without the necessity of genital contact each time;
- what pleases (gives pleasure to) the other.

Paul is much misrepresented for his supposed anti-marriage views. Yet one only has to look at 1 Corinthians 7 to see what sound, sensible advice he gives concerning mutual sexual duty on the basis that their bodies belong to each other and they should 'not deprive each other', except by mutual consent and even then only 'for a time' (vv. 4, 5). All this is in the context of 1 Corinthians 6: 19 – 'your body is a temple of the Holy Spirit'. The Bible takes a high view of the human body and we should not let modern reductionist thinking persuade us otherwise. We are not 'naked apes' at the mercy of our instincts, and prey to every whim of desire.

Furthermore the Bible has set sexual intercourse within a framework of morality – a proper way of behaving under God, whereas the reductionist reduces morality to the level of biology.

'For some couples physical pleasure is alien, and silly inhibitions which have nothing to do with the Christian faith make them try to drive with the handbrake on.' (Gaius Davies)

Note: 'Becoming one flesh' must not be divorced in thought from 'leaving and being united with'.

SESSION 3. CHILDREN, FINANCE, WHEN THINGS GO WRONG

Children

Marriage and family are intertwined, but we have tried to show that marriage must stand on its own. It is seen by some as a unique covenant of troth (fidelity, truth, love and commitment) between husband and wife. A childless marriage is not incomplete. A couple need to be advised clearly, that being a wife and husband is different from being a mother and father and that the arrival of a new baby, wonderful as that is, must not take over their roles as wife and husband. It is easy at such times for the wife to be so totally absorbed in caring for the little bundle of life, that the husband feels neglected. Fortunately, nowadays, the sharing of care relieves this difficulty, but it is a time when men have been known to wander, contradictory as that seems.

These days, with the lack of the infrastructure of extended family support that used to exist, together with the removal of constraints of kinship ties, inheritance and economic dependency, it is even more important that the marriage relationship should be solid and sustainable in itself.

On a practical level, most women have access to a series of antenatal classes conducted by a midwife at the GP's practice or at hospital. Included in these are sessions on parenting. Husbands are welcome and the demand is high.

Finance

'The trouble is there is too much month left at the end of the money.' It is beyond the scope of this chapter and the competence of the present writer to discourse on financial matters, but it is a legitimate subject to raise with the couple because, as in the rest of their marriage, Christian principles and openness must prevail. There should be emphasis on mutuality and equality of resources. Unless one partner is a proven profligate the current account should be joint and each should have a 'flexible friend'. After all, do they not trust each other and are they not accountable to each other for the way they use their resources? Similarily, the house should be jointly owned, and efforts should be made to have equality in pensions and insurance, though tax advantages may favour one over the other.

And how much should be given to the Lord (2 Cor 9:7)? Surely the emphasis of this text is on the Lord having 'first slice of the cake', first call on whatever he has given us. It is fashionable to say we are 'not under law but under grace' with the implication that we need not give 10% of our income. But surely, however you compute it, the Lord must have at least that much and generations of Christians have proved the truth that, 'He is no man's debtor'.

Note: It is often helpful to seek the advice of an independent financial adviser. (See chapter 46 on 'Wealth, poverty and debt'.)

When things go wrong

The opening quotation of session 2 stresses that 'the divine intention' should be held before our people and an attempt has been made to do this. The burden of this chapter has been to enable partners to function well under God, but the attentive pastor should make provision for some sort of follow-up after several months of marriage. If problems and stresses are detected which the couple cannot resolve themselves, then they would be well advised to seek help rather than suffer unnecessary pain.

Notes

1. Many excellent Christian counselling resources are available. (See chapter 43 on 'Marriage enrichment'.)
2. During recent preparation classes the couple were given the Care video, 'Marriage Matters', featuring Rob Parsons, and were also invited to go along to a Care seminar, with much benefit.

SESSION 4. THE MARRIAGE CEREMONY

'There is no magic in the ceremony, just vows before God and an unqualified commitment to marriage which the couple then keeps. Clearly the wedding service allows an overt recognition of the God-given nature of marriage...it is the right and best way to get married, but perhaps there needs to be a massive transfer of Christian attention from weddings to lived marriages.' (Alan Storkey)

This session easily absorbs a whole evening.There are certain procedural and legal matters that need to be covered, but usually the couple are 'well ahead of the game' by the time they come to this session. However, make sure they have booked the registrar to witness and register the marriage.

The service

Enquire whether they have chosen hymns and what order of service they would like and also whether they wish any relatives or family friends to participate, e.g. to give one of the prayers?

The writer uses either *Altenative Service Book* (1980) or, for preference, *Patterns of Prayer for Christian Worship* (Baptist Union, 1991), for the conduct of the wedding service. Set formulae must be adhered to for the actual marriage, but there is considerable flexibility in the choice of Bible readings and prayers which introduce and accompany the service. There are set prayers in both books which beautifully encapsulate the God-given truths of this great ordinance – better than many extempore prayers often heard.

You might consider the following:

1. The couple normally choose to repeat their responses phrase by phrase after the pastor in traditional manner, but the alternative is to give printed cards from which they can read the responses.
2. When it comes to 'giving away' the bride, most parents would now opt for 'My wife and I do', or better still, 'We do' – and how right this is. Why not do the same for the man?
3. Families and congregation might then be asked if they will give their love and help to uphold and care for the couple in their life together.
4. The responses at giving of the rings may be said separately or simultaneously.

Note: The four points raised in this paragraph must be gone through with the couple. It is their wedding and their choice must prevail.

After the union is sealed by God, prayers of blessing follow and this is always a most moving and spiritual time in Christian marriage.

The Address

How many marriages one has been to where the address was either a few blessed thoughts by a pastor who clearly did not know the couple, or was a heavy gospel sermon preached to the unbelievers present, so as not to miss an opportunity, and delivered as if the newly weds were not there. The address, in this writer's view, is primarily to the couple with the congregation privileged to listen in. Here is an excellent opportunity to use your hard-won knowledge of the couple to highlight the main points of their lives' journeys, especially the spiritual ones. A specific biblical message should be sought from the Lord, that they will always look back on as blessing them on their way. Fifteen minutes is long enough.

Then the register is signed and witnessed and it's off to confetti, photographs and reception.

Note: See chapter 42 on 'The Marriage Service'.

Further reading

Alternative Service Book (SPCK, 1980)

D J Atkinson et al. (eds.), *New Dictionary of Christian Ethics and Pastoral Theology* (IVP, 1995)

P Beasley-Murray, *Happy ever after? A guide to the marriage adventure* (Baptist Union, no date)

Marriage Preparation (Mothers Union, Guildford Diocese, 1998)

Patterns and Prayers for Church Worship (Baptist Union, 1991)

A Storkey, *Marriage and its Modern Crisis* (Hodder & Stoughton, 1996)

J Stott, *Issues Facing Christians Today* (Marshall Pickering, 1990)

Chapter Forty-Two

The Marriage Service

Gerald and Eileen West

It is obvious that a marriage is not simply a private matter for the couple themselves. Nor is it only a family matter. Furthermore, whilst for believers it is important that the ceremony should take place 'in the sight of God' even this is not sufficient! An important component in the service is the recognition that what is taking place involves the wider community. It is a public matter and is regulated by social norms enshrined in the law. For this reason the preliminary paragraphs of this chapter concentrate on the legal requirements that must be fulfilled if the service is to result in a legally valid marriage. The legal requirements are designed to ensure that the couple are free to marry, that they do not do so under duress, that there is a proper record with competent witnesses, and that the couple make appropriate verbal commitments to each other. It is these commitments that are at the heart of a wedding service and make the marriage. The 'piece of paper' is a necessary record, but only that.

This chapter deals primarily with services intended to meet the legal requirements when a marriage takes place in a church officially registered for marriages by the Registrar General for England and Wales. It does not cover marriages conducted in Scotland or in Northern Ireland. Nor does it cover marriages in England in an Anglican Church by a clergyman of the Church of England, or in Wales by a clergyman of the Church of Wales in a church of that denomination. The legal position of both those churches is special and the formal procedures for notice and the forms of service used by them are not valid if used in a place of worship which is not within their communion. Nor is a marriage conducted by the clergy of those denominations in a church not of their own denomination valid unless the requirements described below are adopted. As a result an Anglican clergyman who is invited to conduct a marriage in a nonconformist church must use a form of words different from the Church of England form, and the marriage is valid only if an appointed person or registrar is present.

Detailed information about the legal requirements for a marriage in England and Wales or in Scotland or in Northern Ireland can be obtained from the relevant registrar general. Contact details are appended to this chapter. There are a number of complexities which cannot be covered in this chapter which deals only with marriages where both parties are resident in England and Wales. If the service takes place after a marriage abroad or if one of the parties is not domiciled in either England or Wales there will be special considerations and the local superintending registrar should be consulted. Depending on the country, it may be necessary to have a legal marriage in England, and it may be permissible to have two legally recognised marriages!

Anyone asked to conduct a marriage needs to satisfy themselves about various matters before agreeing to conduct the service. Some further information will be required before the form of the service can be considered in detail. In many cases most of this information will already be known or it will be quite straightforward to obtain.

Questions about the couple

Usually the couple and the circumstances surrounding their decision to marry will be well known to anyone asked to conduct the service. (See chapter 41 on 'Marriage preparation'.) If this is not so, it will be necessary to enquire whether the couple are both believers and whether there has been a previous marriage. The matter of remarriage after divorce is not dealt with in this chapter. (See chapter 44 on 'Marriage and divorce'.) Current social conditions increasingly require leaders in the church to consider a wide variety of complex pastoral issues. This chapter assumes that, where necessary, these have been addressed and that the person conducting the marriage is in agreement with the policy adopted.

Questions about the church and its leaders

It is important to ensure that the leaders of the church in which the marriage is to take place know of the arrangements and approve of them. In mainstream denominations the minister is likely to expect to take the service and may wish either to restrict or exclude the involvement of others. This chapter assumes that this is not the case but, nevertheless, the leaders/elders of the church must be consulted and approve the arrangements. This includes the use of the church, the time and date of the wedding, and the person(s) who will be involved in the service. None of this is usually a problem but apart from all other considerations this is a matter of simple courtesy. Such courtesies can be forgotten but are necessary if one is to avoid subsequent ill feeling or embarrassment.

In some cases the answers received from the couple themselves may make it necessary to enquire further from the leaders of their churches. The person conducting the service will also wish to establish that the elders of the couple's church or churches approve of the marriage and will seek assurances that they are arranging appropriate marriage preparation. It may be that the person conducting the service will be expected to undertake this counselling. If this is not so and someone else is undertaking that responsibility, it will be necessary for the two people involved to consult one another so that the matters they discuss with the couple cover all the necessary issues, but do not overlap. Any such conversation must respect the confidential nature of the counselling process in which the couple are involved.

Questions about the law

The comments above will have made clear that it is important to establish as soon as possible whether the couple intend the service to be a legal marriage. There are circumstances in which a civil marriage may already have taken place either at a register office or abroad. There can be good reasons for a prior marriage. If this is the case it is likely to affect the character of the service, and whoever is conducting it must be aware of these circumstances and the reasons for them. This chapter cannot cover all the possible circumstances but if there is any uncertainty about the legal position advice should be sought from the local superintending registrar.

Registration of premises for marriages

If a legal marriage is intended it must take place either in a register office, or in approved premises, or in a place of religious worship that has been officially registered for marriages by the Registrar General for England and Wales. It is not possible to conduct a legal marriage in an unregistered building. All register offices have lists of buildings where marriages can legally take place. For a marriage to take place in a 'place of worship' it must first be registered as such. Registration for marriages is a separate process which can only follow thereafter. Both these processes can take some months. It would not be sensible, therefore, to plan a legal marriage in an unregistered church unless there is plenty of time. If this is not the case and the couple are particularly anxious to have a service in the church, it may be better to arrange a prior legal marriage in a church already registered for marriages or at the register office. The local superintending registrar should be consulted about the detailed process and requirements for registering as a place of worship and for registering for marriages.

Authorised persons

Some registered churches also have one or more 'authorised persons'. These are men or women nominated by the leaders of the church and approved by the registrar general. If there are authorised persons the church will hold a marriage register and will arrange for an authorised person to be present at the marriage. The couple should consult the authorised person as soon as they know when and where they will get married. The authorised person or the registrar must be able to hear the legally required words during the service. If that is not possible the couple will be asked by the authorised person to repeat them! After the necessary words have been spoken, the appointed person or registrar will prepare the register so that it can be signed during the service, and will issue a copy of the marriage certificate at the conclusion of the service.

Registrar

It is essential for either an authorised person or the registrar to be present if the marriage is to be legal. If the church is registered for marriages, but there is no authorised person, the registrar must be in attendance. It is in any case important for the couple to consult the registrar at an early date. There are civil preliminaries to be completed for which the local superintendent registrar is responsible. In all cases notice must be given by both parties to a registrar who is responsible for issuing the necessary certificates. Since 1 January 2001, two superintendent registrar's certificates have been required, one for each party (unless notice was given before that date). The authorised person requires these certificates before the marriage can take place. All the legal requirements must be complied with and the authorised person and the superintendent registrar will work together to guide the couple and to ensure this happens.

Questions about the service

The first discussion

It is important to establish as soon as possible what the person conducting the service is expected to do. Sometimes it is to take the whole service but it is not unusual for the couple to wish someone else to give the address, and for other members of the family to take part by reading a passage of scripture, by praying, or by making a musical contribution. The leaders of the church in which the service is to be held may also wish to take part. All this can be clarified only by an early conversation with the couple. It is wise at this stage to listen to the wishes of the couple but not to feel obliged to adopt all their suggestions. An important matter is the degree of formality or informality that the couple feel to be appropriate. However, the fact that they have selected a particular individual to conduct their marriage suggests that they have confidence in that person, and that they expect them to be able to interpret their wishes in a sympathetic way. This should enable the preliminary discussions to be dealt with easily and quickly.

Legal components

It will also be necessary to explain to the couple what is required if the service is to constitute a legally valid marriage. The law requires that at some stage in the service (and in the presence of the witnesses and the authorised person) each party makes declarations in one of the approved forms. There are two components to these declarations. The first is a declaration by each of them which identifies who they are, and which declares that they are legally free to marry. In the second component each of them says words (or makes vows) which establish a binding commitment to one another. There are alternative forms of words for each component.

The words most commonly used for the first component are either:

(a) *'I do solemnly declare that I know not of any lawful impediment why I* [name] *may not be joined in matrimony to* [name].' or,

(b) *'I declare that I know of no legal reason why I* [name] *may not be joined in marriage to* [name].'

The words for the second component can be either:

(a) *'I call upon these persons here present to witness that I* [name] *do take thee* [name] *to be my lawful wedded wife[or husband]'.* or,

(b) *'I* [name] *take you [or thee]* [name] *to be my wedded wife [or husband].'*

Wherever in these sentences a name is to be used, it must be the relevant full name including all Christian names and the surname. (Note that this is not the case in an Anglican marriage, but one of the above forms must be followed whenever the ceremony is held in a place of worship registered for marriages.) It is not required that the two components follow each other without interruption, but the order must be observed and the couple must both say the necessary words separately in the presence of the witnesses and the authorised person.

Except for these two declarations everything else in the service is at the discretion of the person conducting it. This leaves considerable scope to adapt the service to the needs of the occasion and the wishes of the couple.

Christian components

A marriage in church will be a Christian marriage and, even if the couple are not believers, they should have committed themselves to a Christian marriage. The service will therefore include much more than the bare legal requirements. The first discussion with the couple will have established what the person conducting the service is expected to do and what other elements they wish to see in the service. The next step is to prepare a draft order of service.

Typically, a marriage service will include a number of elements. Every one who conducts marriage services will develop their own preferences for the sequence and character of these. Some of the possibilities can be indicated. The headings below are not intended to suggest the sequence in which these elements should occur during the service but are in an order which roughly reflects importance and sequence. The headings are not exhaustive and the comments are intended only to give an indication of possibilities. No attempt is made to suggest a sample service. It is essential to consult the various denominational orders of service, some of which are noted at the end of this chapter. Care must be taken to use up-to-date editions and to make sure that the publication takes account of the relevant law. This is particularly important for material published in the USA. By judicious selection an 'eclectic' pattern can be developed to suit the needs of the particular occasion whilst retaining the legal requirements.

The marriage

This should not be delayed but take place towards the beginning of the service. Both the couple and the person conducting the service are likely to be somewhat tense, and this will only increase if the formalities are delayed. The couple have finally arrived at the moment they have longed and waited for, and there will be an atmosphere of expectation in the congregation who have come primarily to see the couple married. Everyone will relax and enjoy the service once the formalities are over. It is important to remember when conducting a marriage that a flawless performance is not required! Any mistake or slip can be corrected without embarrassment or fuss. This applies both to the person conducting the service and to the couple. It is important that all those taking part should be at ease from the beginning of the service.

Although the legal exchanges of words are all that is required for a civil marriage, these have, traditionally, been supplemented quite considerably. Most of the denominational forms of service derive from *The Book of Common Prayer*. They uniformly consist, first, of an introductory statement (or preface) which sets out the intent of the service and refers to the purposes indicated in scripture for which marriage was ordained of God. This is a salutary reminder, particularly to the congregation, and should be included in some form. (Note that in these comments the sectional analysis indicated by the headings introduced in *Common Worship* is not followed.)

The second section will incorporate the legal declarations and the vows, and these must be followed exactly. Note that at this point there are important differences between the Anglican service and the legal requirements for a service in a church registered for marriages. The Anglican service includes a specific invitation to the congregation to declare any reason why the couple may not lawfully marry. On the other hand, it does not require the couple to make positive declarations that they are free to marry; they are simply asked to declare any impediment, and silence is taken to imply that there is none. However, the Anglican service does include a question to each party which requires the traditional answer, 'I will.' The couple will most probably wish this to be included in the service, and this should be encouraged. For these reasons, although the statutory words must be followed to the letter, they are usually extensively supplemented.

These additions may include a preliminary reminder of the seriousness of the step the couple are about to take, and an introductory question to each of them regarding their willingness to take each other as husband and wife. The traditional words expand this to include a promise to be faithful to one another 'as long as you both shall live'. This is an appropriate reminder of the significance of Christian marriage. The declarations may be followed by a prayer.

The vows will follow and these will incorporate the second component of the legally required words. Again, these have been traditionally supplemented, for good reason, to include promises to love, honour, comfort, cherish (obey?), etc., and words to remind them that these promises are intended to last whatever the circumstances ('for better, for worse' etc.) and 'till death us do part'.

The fact that the ground covered by the additions to the legally required words will have been covered in the pre-marriage preparation is not a reason for omitting these statements. They are made, not simply for the instruction of the couple, but to remind the congregation of the nature of the act they are witnessing.

The traditional role of the father in the service has changed over the last generation. *The Book of Common Prayer* asked the question: 'Who giveth this woman to be married to this man?' This was reduced in the *Alternative Service* to a silent role but, in the *Common Worship* service, he does not even have a walk-on part! If the traditional question is to be included it is now increasingly common for both parents to give the reply: 'We do.' Some services also include a requirement that the bride and groom hold hands during the vows. The inclusion of this symbolic act is partly a matter of taste and partly a practical matter. It should be discussed with the couple.

Following the declarations and vows there will usually be an exchange of rings by the bride and groom, and this is accompanied by appropriate words. This is the modern practice. Traditionally there was only one ring for the bride. Finally, this part of the service may conclude with the proclamation of the couple's newly married status and a prayer for God's blessing on them. In less formal marriages the groom may be invited to 'kiss the bride' and there may be a photo opportunity.

Prayer

There are a number of points in the service at which prayer is appropriate. Usually there will be a prayer, either immediately the bride and groom have come to the front of the church or immediately after the first hymn. This is likely to be a general prayer for God's presence and blessing on the occasion. At the end of the formal marriage exchanges there is an opportunity to pray for God's blessing on the couple who have now been declared to be husband and wife. This may be expanded into a more extended time of prayer, giving the opportunity for other members of the congregation, and especially family and friends, to pray for God's blessing on the couple. This may be by prior arrangement and/or it can take the form of a time of open prayer. The person conducting the service may be prepared to contribute further. The set denominational services provide a wide range of examples of the kind of prayers that are appropriate. These are often expressed in more formal language and can be both thoughtful and helpful. There will also be a final benediction. This should be quite short. It may be one of the scriptural prayers of benediction and may include 'The grace'.

Worship

The character of the service will be shaped to a large extent by the way in which this element is handled. Much will depend on the wishes of the couple and the balance they wish to strike between the inevitable formality of 'The Marriage' and the possibility of informality in other parts of the service. It is important to remember that the congregation should not be faced with too many hymns and songs with which they are unfamiliar. It is sometimes not easy to strike a good balance, but some well-known traditional hymns are likely to play a part in the service. These may be printed on an order of service sheet. If this is the case it is necessary to ensure that both the words and verses printed are in the required version. There are a number of versions of many traditional hymns. The version used on the overhead projector should be the same as on the printed sheet!

Worship songs should be selected with care and the nature of any linking prayer or comment should be carefully considered beforehand. However, it is not always necessary to decide in advance precisely what form this should take. If there is to be freedom to respond to the spirit of the occasion, it will be necessary to have clear pre-arranged signals between the worship leader and the musicians so that they know what is required of them.

Music

Music forms an important part of a marriage service and can help significantly to create the right atmosphere. Everything depends on the skill and talent of the musicians available. This may involve organ, piano, and band. It is difficult to make particular comment but it is important not to overstretch their ability. Discuss the arrangements with the musicians and provide them with the information they need about hymns, songs, etc., at an early date. If necessary the music at the beginning and end may be played on a tape. This makes a wider selection available. An important issue is what to arrange during the signing of the register. This time is often used for a solo or other musical contribution. The couple may wish to involve friends in this.

Bible reading/s

Readings from one or more passages should be included in the order of service. The speaker should be consulted about possible passages and the couple may wish certain scriptures to be read. Consider which version should be used, taking account of the version available at the church. The couple may wish to nominate someone to read. Whoever is chosen should be able to read in public accurately and clearly. Some churches have a practice of presenting a Bible to each couple married in their church. Apart from emphasising the value of scripture in the life of a married couple, this provides an opportunity for the church to be involved in every marriage service.

Sermon

Interestingly, *The Alternative Service Book* suggests the sermon should be before the marriage. *Common Worship* suggests that the preferred place is between the declarations and the vows. In most nonconformist services the sermon comes after the marriage. It is important not to prolong the sermon. Experience suggests that the couple themselves are unlikely to remember much of it! Ten to fifteen minutes will usually be appropriate. However, it is important not to undervalue it and the opportunity it provides to underscore the significance of Christian marriage. In such a time span it will not be possible to cover all the possible themes. Married believers can be challenged to renew their promises to each other and to recognise their need to experience the grace of God in their lives if they are to live up to the ideal for marriage that the Lord sets before us. The unmarried and younger people can be reminded of those ideals. Unbelievers who are sceptical and consider Christian standards of sexual conduct are unrealistic can be challenged by testimony to the grace of God in individual lives. Above all, the sermon should reverberate with joy and thankfulness to God for his gift of love and send the couple out into their married life with enhanced confidence in a faithful and loving God.

Signing the register

At some point, usually towards the end of the service, the bridal party will sign the register. This may take place in full view of the congregation or in a side room. Somewhere out of sight of the congregation has the advantage of allowing the couple and their attendants time to relax and to prepare to re-enter the church prior to the end of the service. There must be sufficient time after the legal declarations have been made for the authorised person to complete preparation of the register. The register will be signed by the couple, by at least two witnesses and by the authorised person.

Welcome and announcements

It is usual to include some words of welcome, particularly to the members of the congregation who are not members of the church. In addition, there are likely to be some necessary announcements. It may be necessary to explain the arrangements for making a video of the ceremony and for photographs during the service. This should have been discussed with the couple and the church, before the service. Such activities should be limited and controlled during the service to avoid distraction. It may also be appropriate publicly to thank the church for allowing the service to take place in their building.

Some announcements may be required so that the congregation knows what is to take place immediately after the couple have left the church. There may be special arrangements for photographs with consequent advice as to how to leave the building, and information for those either going on to or remaining for the reception. The details will be different in each case and the timing of such announcements in relation to the service will take this into account. Such matters should be handled so that they avoid disruption to the service itself. For this reason it may be wise to make the necessary announcements before the bride arrives and the service proper begins.

The order of service and final preparations

Once a draft order of service has been prepared it should be discussed in detail with the couple so that the final arrangements can be agreed and everyone who will be involved can be given the necessary information. It is usual to arrange a final rehearsal at the church on the evening before the wedding. This is a valuable opportunity to bring everyone together to ensure they are all clear about their role and to iron out any last minute or unforeseen difficulties.

Further information

About the Marriage Service

These publications offer a wide range of ideas and suggestions. Not all are legally relevant or up-to-date. The reader must judge what is appropriate.

The Alternative Service Book, 1980

The Book of Common Prayer

Common Worship: Marriage. Services and prayers for the Church of England. (Church House Publishing. 2000) [This is an extract covering the marriage service]

S Lake, *Using Common Worship: Marriage. A practical guide to the new services* (Church House Publishing. 2000) [This includes an interesting introduction which explains the historical and theological background to the changes now introduced. The book itself makes many useful suggestions and there is a resource list for further reading.]

Evangelical Minister's Manual (FIEC, 3 Church Road, Croydon CR0 1SG)

Marriage Blessing (taken from *The Methodist Worship Book*) (Methodist Publishing House, 20 Ivatt Way, Peterborough PE3 7PG, 1999)

An Order of Marriage for Christians from Different Churches. The Joint Liturgical Group of Great Britain (Canterbury Press, Norwich, 1999)

The Wedding Service (taken from The United Reformed Church Service Book (OUP, 1989)

About legal issues

Advice and copies of the forms published by the General Register Office about the procedures to be followed in England and Wales can be obtained from any local register office (the address and telephone number will be in the telephone book) or from The Registrar General (Marriages Section), Office for National Statistics, Smedley Hydro, Trafalgar Road, Birkdale, Southport PR8 2HH.

Forms published by the General Register Office include:

Form 357C *Getting Married in England and Wales. The basis for a valid Marriage*

Form 357 *Getting Married. Notes on the Legal Requirements*

Information about marriages in Scotland can be obtained from The General Register Office for Scotland, New Register House, Edinburgh EH1 3YT.

Information about marriages in Northern Ireland can be obtained from The Registrar General for Northern Ireland, Oxford House, 49-55 Chichester Street, Belfast, BT1 4HF.

CHAPTER FORTY-THREE

Marriage Enrichment

TONY HOBBS AND EDWARD PRATT

For most people involved in pastoral care, the ideal pastoral problem is one that is self-contained, can be addressed with confidence and solved quickly. Pastoral problems related to marriage rarely fall into this category. Time and expertise may need to be invested in helping the couple in question, and may not always be available within the church. Pastoral carers need wisdom in recognising their limitations, while at the same time being aware of their special opportunities. A first-aider may save the life of an accident victim, but it is a foolish and arrogant first-aider who attempts open-heart surgery. However, we need to avoid the trap of thinking that the church is the amateur organisation and the true professionals are somewhere 'out there'. The NT sees the church as the locus for life-changing events. The external conference and expert has a place, but alongside the church, supporting it, not as a substitute for it. We need to know the power of God in our everyday pastoral care, and not assume that the Holy Spirit is more effective at an external conference centre.

Many problems that appear to be serious marriage issues are the symptom of deep individual issues. What may appear to be a joint counselling need may turn out to be an individual one, and much time and effort can be taken up addressing the symptoms rather than the actual problem. Of course, such a couple may benefit from a marriage enrichment event, but it may be only a step along the way to individual counselling or healing. Marriage enrichment can be of most value in helping couples to take a pace back from busy lives and to focus on each other and rediscover the joys of marriage that have become submerged by the everyday pressures.

Most of the Christian marriage enrichment providers work co-operatively with one another. Although all have broadly similar aims, we each have our different distinctives and focuses:

• some work with biblical material explicitly, others implicitly;

- some work to set scripts, others more flexibly;
- some use limited psychological pressure, others avoid it altogether;
- some target Christians, others the wider community;
- some work locally, others nationally;
- some are run by people with formal qualifications, others by lay helpers.

If a pastoral carer is looking for a marriage enrichment event for a particular couple, it's good to find out which is most appropriate for the couple in question.

The biggest obstacle for people attending an enrichment weekend is usually the reaction of their friends. Tell people you're going on a Bible weekend and people assume you're serious about scripture; tell them you're going on a prayer retreat and they'll assume you're really committed to prayer; tell them you're going on a marriage enrichment weekend and they'll ask what's wrong with your marriage.

Leaders and pastoral carers will inevitably be faced with dealing with some sort of marriage problems in their church. Whether or not they involve outside help and support at any stage, they will inevitably have to spend time alongside those in need of help. We shall usually want to give help and support based – explicitly or implicitly – on what the Bible says about marriage.

It is generally recognised that what the Bible says about marriage is not easy. But this may mean, not that it is complex or obscure, but that it is uncompromising in what it demands of us. What follows is intended to offer a framework to help those involved in pastoral care to think though some of the issues afresh, with integrity and biblical consistency.

Using scripture with integrity

A challenge facing those of us committed to the inspiration and authority of scripture is using the Bible with integrity. C S Lewis wrote: 'We must not use the Bible (as our fathers often did) as some sort of encyclopedia out of which texts (isolated from their contexts and not read with attention to the whole nature and purport of the books in which they occur) can be taken for use as weapons.' (*Letters of C S Lewis*, ed. W H Lewis, London, 1966, p. 47) If we want to have a biblical view of marriage, it is not adequate to work through all the references in a concordance and take as our conclusions a sort of mathematical average of the combined passages. Neither, if we're serious about the authority of all scripture, can we neglect the OT material. Rather, what we need to do is to identify the principles concerning marriage (which we would expect to remain non-negotiables) and how those principles were applied, which – theoretically at least – may be subject to change.

In our marriage ministry we have found it convenient to use what we call a four-stage model. We are careful to emphasise it is intended only to be a framework for approaching scripture with integrity (as opposed to a definitive interpretative tool) and also that we're not trying to sneak some form of dispensation theology past our readers! The model's stages reflect the status of the relationship between God and his people.

Stage 1. Man and woman before the fall

This is based primarily on the first three chapters of Genesis. The principles we can note are:

- It is not good for man to be alone. (And that this is not exclusively about sex.)
- Eve is not Adam 'Mark 2'. She is created differently from Adam. (Which raises, but doesn't necessarily answer, questions about gender and role differences.)
- The relationship between the two is singled out as special. The two become one flesh.

Stage 2. Man and woman post-fall: under the old covenant

Because we're apt to think of marriage as a so-called creation ordinance, we fail to be surprised how little change there is between pre-fall and post-fall. The fall is the catalyst for radical change in other crucial areas; but not marriage. Throughout the old covenant period marriage remains a special relationship among the people of God. (A review of marriage in the neighbouring societies of the Ancient Near East can underline just how special.) For example, marriage is given a special status in the Torah (e.g. Lev 18). A single verse emphasises the point: 'When a man takes a new wife, he shall not go out with the army, nor be charged with any duty; he shall be free at home one year and shall give happiness to his wife whom he has taken' (Deut 24: 5). Israel was, for most of its OT existence, under military threat of some kind. Yet newly-marrieds were exempted from military duty. By contrast, think of the Second World War. A claim that a man was newly married did not prevent his call-up.

Many of our theoretical difficulties relate to godly men having more than one wife during the old covenant period (e.g. Jacob, Elkanah, David). Although this raises important questions about their understanding of marriage, it is little more than a theological red herring for our pastoral issues. In the West it is a rare pastoral issue that has to deal with the problem of a man having more than one wife at the same time, though it can be a live issue to converts from cultures where polygamy is permitted. What we can note in this area is that men were expected to treat their wives well, and not as chattels, either physically or emotionally. David was not condemned for having more than one wife; he was condemned for destroying the marriage of Uriah and Bathsheba (2 Sam 12:1-15). Abraham incurred grief because, although it was apparently reasonable for him to do otherwise, he did not remain totally faithful to Sarah (Gen 16).

Stage 3. Man and woman post-fall: under the new covenant

Compared to the standards of the Ancient Near East (and, we might add, compared with much of today's secular society) the Israelites of the OT period had a very high view of marriage; metaphorically, an Alpine view. In Matthew 19, which is presented in the gospel as an independent block of Jesus' teaching, we find Jesus challenging the contemporaneous understanding of many of the roles in Jewish society. Popular understanding of singleness, childhood, wealth and poverty are all turned upside down. But with regard to marriage, Jesus emphasises God's original intentions for marriage and acknowledges the validity of the old covenant approach to actual marriage problems. What Jesus does challenge is this Alpine view of marriage. By the standards of the kingdom it's not high enough. He presents his hearers with a Himalayan standard.

In the NT, teaching on marriage has much closer similarities with the pre-fall period than the old covenant period. And that is what we should expect: lifestyle issues under the new covenant reflect those of the time before the fall, restoring things the way God intended them to be. Of course this is something of a theological over-simplification, and we cannot regard the new covenant era as an exact echo of pre-fall times. The new Adam can restore, and in many cases make things even better than under the pre-fall old Adam (Rom 5:12-21). But God does not make things exactly as they were. We are redeemed but mankind has lost its theological virginity. The NT teaching on marriage gives us no prompt to aim for marriages based on gardening, permanent nakedness and vegetarianism!

Many of the NT passages related to marriage have caused heated debate. Jesus' words in Matthew 19:9 require us never to treat divorce with the casualness that had crept into Israelite society, but we must note that some divorce is permitted. (See chapter 44 on 'Divorce and remarriage'.) Passages in the letters interface with questions about the role of women and thus have generated strong and differing views. One helpful way of approaching some of the Pauline passages is to recognise that Paul often uses a common rabbinic model for his arguments: outlining a theological principle and then supporting it with points of application. We can witness this in Colossians 3:1- 4:1.

Colossians 3:1-17 is all about theological truths (the 'why') and lifestyle principles (the 'what'). But there is scant help from Paul in these first 17 verses on specific application (the 'how'). But 3:18-4:1 is about how to implement the why and what of verses 1-17. Three twined relationships are cited: husbands and wives; children and fathers; slaves and masters. Paul does not present us with detailed lifestyle blueprints for each role. Instead, he gives warnings about particular pitfalls into which people in these roles can commonly fall and neither party is given additional scope because of the other's Christian obedience. Children have a tendency to be disobedient; even the best fathers can occasionally abuse their authority. Slaves (might we extend this to people in badly paid jobs?) have a tendency to work harder when the boss is watching; masters can slip into treating their slaves with less than perfect justice and consideration. But we are unlikely to mistake these brief comments for a complete summary of the relationships. And we can understand verses 18 and 19 in the same way. On a common-sense level most of us easily recognise that wives find that being subject doesn't always comes naturally. (Precisely because women are strong, not because they are weak!) And husbands can find it all too easy to be unloving and bitter when problems arise. (Is 'sulk' a male verb?)

Such an approach allows us to view the theological principles of 3:1-17 as non-negotiables but 3:18-4:1 as application, almost – without under-estimating the importance of the verses – seeing them as inspired 'helpful hints'. Application may not be non-negotiable; it may require understanding and perhaps even re-interpreting with regard to culture. Which, of course, is what most of us do with 4:3.

Ephesians 5:22-33 is perhaps the best-known of the relevant passages related to marriage. But reading it against the principle of verse 21 prevents inappropriate chauvinism. Husbands are to show love; wives respect. Here is not the place for an exposition of this passage but it's important to note that what Paul says is not lop-sided. It makes excellent sense in psychological terms. As a thumb-rule test: how many wives could be content with just respect from their husbands; and how many husbands would cope with love but no respect from their wives? Verse 32 complicates the interpretation of the passage, for it is not totally clear if Paul is referring just to the quotation from Genesis or some or all of his own argument as well. Incidentally, as the better translations recognise, the Greek text of verse 22 lacks a verb and is literally: 'Wives to your own husbands as to the Lord'. While '... be subject...' is a perfectly legitimate (and probably correct) understanding of the verse, it is, strictly speaking, an interpretation. A reminder that we should be sure about what the Bible actually says rather than what we think it says!

1 Peter 3:1-7 is another important passage. Whether or not we insist on a literal application of verse 3, it should not should detract from the emphasis on lifestyle and quality of relationship. Again, theological truth has an important psychological dimension. The truth here can banish deep-seated fears common in marriage. Genuinely lived out, this passage reassures the wife that her husband's love is not based on the beauty of her youth. And the husband that his wife's respect is not conditional on his achievements.

Stage 4. Man and woman post-fall: the resurrection

For the sake of completeness we must recognise Jesus' words in Mark 12:25 (and parallel passages): 'For when they rise from the dead, they neither marry, nor are given in marriage, but are like angels in heaven.' While we can recognise that Jesus' words here have echoes with certain contemporaneous Jewish ideas, what a resurrection relationship between a man and a woman will look like in practice we can hardly begin to guess. But of course this goes for much about resurrection life. Surely the principle is that, whatever it may be, we can conclude that it will be even better than stage 3.

Using scripture with consistency

1 Corinthians 7 is an important chapter concerning marriage, and a crucial starting point for many actual pastoral issues. In it Paul makes a distinction that would never occur to us if he hadn't emphasised it: a clear distinction between what is directly from the Lord and what is his own teaching (vv. 6, 10, 12, 25). Now, admit-tedly, this presents us with a hermeneutic complexity since we regard all of the passage as inspired scripture. Nevertheless, a clear

principle is laid down here by Paul: the distinction between non-negotiables and teaching that is more akin to wise guidance. It certainly appears that Paul's wise guidance is given with awareness of specific cultural issues. That we face different cultural issues should at least prompt us to approach Paul's wise guidance with discernment and sensitivity, even if we conclude that his guidance remains fully adequate. What we must not do is permit cultural issues and secular norms to undermine the divine non-negotiables.

If our pastoral care is genuinely motivated by love, we will inevitably encounter tensions between showing love and compassion and trying to remain true to biblical standards. While passages such as Ezra 10 should not be simplistically applied in our churches, they should put a break on compassion that stems more from our wanting to be nice people than to show true biblical love. Jesus' compassion to the woman at the well (John 4:1-42) and the woman taken in adultery (John 8:1-11) brings them back to God's standards ; he doesn't compromise. These examples don't make us uncomfortable; we can imagine using them as a model for our pastoral care. But are we equally comfortable with Jesus' response to the Syro-Phoenician woman (Mark 7:2-30) or the so-called rich young ruler (Luke 18:1-24)?

A complication for most of us is that, for whatever reason, we are apt to treat sexual sins and problems according to different standards from those we use for other sins and problems. Consider this example. The church leaders find out that a respected member of the church is having an affair, which, among other things, is damaging his family. The leaders are likely to treat the matter as a very serious pastoral issue, and may well remove the person from any positions of responsibility in the church. This would appear to be an appropriate biblical response (cf. 1 Cor 5).

Now suppose there is another respected member of the church. He is a successful business man, working long hours. The family have all the trappings of a wealthy lifestyle. He is not shy of admitting to considerable savings and investments. And he is generous with his donations. But one consequence is that his family see little of him, and quality time together is virtually non-existent. Will the leaders treat this as a serious pastoral situation, approached with equal vigour? Will he be removed from positions of responsibility within the church? Jesus has much to say about materialism. We are inclined to explain away verses such as Luke 14: 33 as applying to our attitude rather than understanding them as an actual lifestyle requirement. Yet we would not allow the first of our example men to use a similar argument with regard to adultery.

This is not to argue against treating adultery with pastoral rigor; nor is it a diatribe against materialism. The point is that we are more inclined to allow our pastoral strategy to be influenced by our 'unofficial league table' of which sins are more serious than others. We generally find it easier to be tolerant of materialism than adultery. Our strategy should be based on biblical standards, and applied with a consistency that is biblical.

Conclusion

In the NT it is the Christian's lifestyle and approach to family that are key indicators of maturity and holiness. The quality of their role within the family is one of the most important tests of their suitability for leadership (e.g. 1 Tim 3). But the stresses of twenty-first century living are putting pressure on family life. In a society struggling with relationships, non-Christians ought to be attracted to our churches because of the beacon of Christian marriages burning a message of what marriage can be under the lordship of Christ. Our churches ought to be full of people who treat their marriages with high priority; where, for example, husbands and wives turn down promotions at work so as to be able to devote more time to each other. Sadly, some of our real pastoral needs have become so much a part of our church lifestyle that we no longer recognise the problem until it becomes a crisis.

Further reading

R. Alter, *Genesis. Translation and Commentary* (WW Norton & Co., 1996)
D and J Ames, *Looking Up the Aisle?* (Mission to Marriage, 1994)
J Goldingay, *After Eating the Apricot* (Paternoster, 1996)
K Kuhne, *A Healing Season* (Marshall, Morgan & Scott, 1986)
T Sine, *Why Settle for More and Miss the Best?* (Word, 1989)
G Smalley, *Love is a Decision* (Word, 1989)
J White, *Eros Defiled. The Christian and sexual guilt* (IVP, 1978)

TONY HOBBS

RESOURCES

The Lord calls some to remain single but most to marriage. It has been said that the health of a local church is directly related to the health of its marriages. Good marriages lead to happy and stable families, vital for any church yet, sadly, the malaise that is affecting marriage in Britain has reached churches too.

So despite all the competing pressures of church life, every church with young or middle-aged members needs to have a marriage ministry. It is at least as important as young people's work. Not only marriage preparation but marriage enhancement and help for marriage difficulties need to be on offer, with warm encouragement to Christians to make use of them and to invite their non-Christian friends to do so

Introduction to marriage enhancement

The essentials of marriage enhancement activities are usually three-fold. First, the couple read a chapter of a book, or hear a talk, or watch a video on some aspect of marriage. Second, they each separately answer questions on that aspect, on a sheet or in a workbook. Third, they share their answers with each other and discuss them. It is good to have an optional extra: someone available later with whom they can discuss anything they wish, preferably someone from another church, with whom they may feel more able to share confidences. Couples will need assuring that marriage enhancement does not involve discussing their marriage with other couples attending an event.

A key part of preparation for any event is persuading couples that marriage enhancement is for all, however good their marriage. It is most important to follow up general announcements about events with personal spoken invitations. Why not help them by using the illustration of giving a marriage 'a service' after six months, a year, five years, just as one does for a car? Once you have had one event, couples who have been on it can then encourage others to come to the next.

Courses on church premises

A church can run its own enhancement course by using a video and workbook series, such as Marriage Resource's five-session 'Time for Each Other', presented by Eric Bird with Sally Magnusson. It is available from the Christian Publicity Organisation, (ref ZX52) Garcia Estate, Canterbury Road, Worthing, W Sussex BN13 1BW, Direct Order Line: 01903 263354, for £25.00 plus £2 per pair for extra workbooks (ref CPO 1716). There are extra sheets for Christian couples and for retired couples.

Another course is 'Marriage in Mind' by CPAS, Athena Drive, Tachbrook Park, Warwick CV34 6NG, Tel: 01926 334242. However, the video is only suitable for use early in marriage. The course costs

£50 (or £20 for the sheets alone). It includes additional sheets which can be used with young people or in marriage preparation.

Either course can be made more attractive by having meals together. 'Time for Each Other' can also be used by a couple in their home.

Holy Trinity, Brompton, have produced their seven-week 'Marriage Course' on Alpha lines, i.e. a meal together, a talk on audio cassette or by a leader (videos are in preparation), coffee, couples answer workbook questions and discussing their answers with each other (not in a group). The audio cassettes cost £20. The Leaders' Guide is £1.50 and the Participants' Manual £2.50. The Marriage Book (£5.99) covers the course material and much more. They are available to order from the Alpha Hotline on 08457 581278 and from Christian bookshops.

Another marriage enhancement course is 'Keeping Marriages Healthy' provided by Intimate Life Ministries over eight weeks. This is presented by those trained for the purpose. There may be some such person near you, or you could be trained yourself. Contact Alister and Christine Mort, 2 St Mark's Road, Leamington Spa, Warwicks CV32 6DL, Tel: 01926 421004.

CWR of Waverley Abbey House, Waverley Lane, Farnham, Surrey GU9 8EP have produced a video and workbook seminar for Christians, by Selwyn Hughes. This consists of two videos containing four sessions, a pair of handbooks and an audio tape for £40.

A simple course for a couple to use in their own home is provided in a series of five workbooks beginning with 'Communication in our Marriage', price £2.60, including post and packing, for two sets of five, from Light House, 1a Argyll Street, Coventry CV2 4PJ.

Several marriage enhancement organisations can supply couples to take enhancement days or weekends for churches. Some of these are:

Christian Guidelines (Northern Ireland only): Ruth McBurney, 7 Queen Street, Belfast BTI 6EA, Tel: 02890 230005.

Marriage Agenda: David and Maureen Brown, 10 Duke's Close, Cranleigh, Surrey GU6 7JU, Tel: 01483 272016.

Marriage Review: Derek Saunders, 9 Grosvenor Gardens, Upminster, Essex RM14 1DL, Tel: 01708 225344.

Mission to Marriage (including Northern Ireland): Dr Tony and Mrs Anne Hobbs, Forge Cottage, Fishery Road, Boxmoor, Hemel Hempstead, Herts HP1 1NA, Tel: 01442 215414.

Radiant Life Ministries (within roughly 100 miles of Manchester): Rev Walter and Mrs Lyn Crick, Radiant Life Ministries, 47 Gloucester Road, Alkington, Manchester M24 1HT, Tel: 0161 653

3040.

Saltmine: Brian and Chris Clark, P O Box 15, Dudley, West Midlands DY1 1YQ,   Tel: 01384 454809.

The following Marriage Resource Branches also offer marriage enhancement in their areas or nearby:

Bournemouth and Poole, Kidderminster and Wyre Forest, London South-West, Manchester and District, Norfolk, Sussex. Contact names are in the Marriage Resource Directory, or can be obtained from 24 West Street, Wimborne, Dorset BH21 1JS.

Courses off church premises

Christian Guidelines (Northern Ireland), Marriage Agenda, Marriage Review and Mission to Marriage also run marriage enhancement weekends for members of different churches, at pleasant locations around the country, as do several other organisations:

CWR: Contact Sean Gubb, Waverley Abbey House, Waverley Lane, Farnham, Surrey GU9 8EP, Tel: 01252 784700.

United Marriage Encounter: Contact Michael and Susan Watts, 79 Clarence Road, Horsham, West Sussex RH13 SS1, Tel: 01403 252553.

Marriage Encounter (Anglican): Contact David and Liz Percival, Trebakken, 11 Lambourne Close, Sandhurst, Berks GU47 8JL, Tel: 01344 779658.

Marriage Encounter (Baptist): Contact Bill and Brenda Reynolds, 26 Bellingdon Road, Chesham, Bucks HP5 2HA, Tel: 01494 782466.

Despite the organisations' names, participants in Marriage Encounter Anglican and Baptist weekends need not be Christians.

If a couple can get away from distractions at home, they will reap the benefits. Some couples arrange to look after friends' children to free those friends to go away for such a weekend; then later the second couple do the same for the first.

Enrich

Another helpful method of marriage enhancement is to do an 'Enrich Inventory' (questionnaire) with a 'Prepare/Enrich' practitioner. Each spouse does their own and these are then analysed to find the couple's strengths and the areas in which they need to grow. These are discussed with the practitioner in one or more further sessions. The cost is £20. Peter Brown of 41 Main Street, Cosby, Leics, Tel: 0116 286 6184 will put couples in touch with a practitioner near them.

National Marriage Week

The week was begun by Marriage Resource in 1997 and is now run by Richard Kane, 137 Middlehill Road, Colehill, Wimborne, Dorset BH21 2HL, Tel: 01202 887883, as part of a separate but related charity. The week always includes 14 February. An increasing number of churches are doing something in the week. One popular event is a Marriage Thanksgiving and Rededication Service. Marriage Resource provides ideas of how to do this, for £2 to cover costs. Ideas include a Valentine's Day Dinner with a speaker, a marriage stall in a local shopping area with leaflets, books, videos, etc., or a Marriage First Aid evening.

Marriage First Aid

This arose from the discovery that most people with marriage difficulties confide first in a friend, relation or colleague at work, rather than a counsellor, minister, doctor or other professional. Marriage First Aid is a training session to give anyone, married or single, Christian, or of other faith or none, some first ideas about how to help a friend who confides about marriage difficulties. The training session centres around a booklet written by Eric Bird of Family College (£1.50 each), given to each participant. Details of how to run the session on an evening are also in a pack from Marriage Resource for £4.00. You will need a speaker or a couple who have some experience of helping with marriage problems to lead the evening. Participants are encouraged to refer their friends on for help if First Aid is not enough.

Counselling

Another important part of a church's marriage ministry is to have a scheme for helping marriages in difficulties, beyond First Aid. Just as a church needs to proclaim the message that every marriage needs enhancement, it also needs to say from time to time that every couple experiencing difficulties needs to seek help, early. The majority of couples seek counselling as a last resort, and many leave it too late.

Many local counselling organisations which offer marriage counselling with Christian values are affiliated to Marriage Resource and their addresses and telephone numbers are in Marriage Resource's Directory, their newsletter, 'Briefing', and their website: www.marriageresource. org. uk

Marriage Resource is a national Christian organisation dedicated to helping marriage in any way. Churches which agree with its Objects and Basis of Faith can join it free and receive the directory regularly, together with other news and ideas to help them in various forms of marriage ministry. (Its Basis of Faith is virtually that of The Evangelical Alliance.)

Another source of names of Christian counselling organisations and private Christian counsellors is the Christian Counsellors' Directory (£15.00) obtainable from Grace Ministries, 2 Fifth Avenue, Lancing, West Sussex BN15 9QA, Tel: 01903 521462, or on their website: www. GraceMinistries.org.uk

Marriage Resource recognises two Marriage Counsellor Training Courses, through which couples who have done a foundation counselling course can be trained to do marriage counselling, e.g. over a series of Saturdays. Such a course would be best put on by a large church, or a Christian counselling organisation, with invitations to all other interested churches and Christian counselling organisations within reach, inviting them to send couples. Each course is designed to train married couples to counsel other couples together. Marriage Resource can supply details.

Marriage Support

Because of the great need for more mature couples to be equipped to help others with difficulties without long training, Marriage Resource has launched Marriage Support, which can be used by a small group of churches, a large church, a Marriage Resource branch or a counselling organisation. It involves two Saturdays of training for Supporter couples, together with use of the five-part 'Time for Each Other' video and workbook course in their own home to enhance their own marriage before they help others.

The training days include instruction in helping couples with difficulties to use 'Time for Each Other' to resolve them and to enhance their marriage, including having discussions with the Supporter couple. If a couple need more help, Supporters would refer them on to counsellors, a minister or somebody else appropriate.

Then a Marriage Supporters Group can be formed and its services advertised to the public in the locality, too. 'Support' is a much more friendly word than 'counselling', and couples are likely to seek 'support' in their difficulties earlier than counselling.

Details of how to run a Supporters' Training Day and to set up a Supporters Group can be obtained in a pack available from The Christian Publicity Organisation, Garcia Estate, Canterbury Road, Worthing, W Sussex BN13 1BW for £7.00 including p & p.

Healing and restoration ministries

There are two organisations which help those whose marriage has broken down to pray and work for its restoration. They rightly stress that marriage is a covenant made before God, which one party should not break when the other walks out. Both organisations have occasional Encouragement Days for those 'standing' for their own marriage to meet together to hear encouraging talks and have fellowship, and they also send encouraging literature. They are: Beulah (Mrs Nora Sanders), 21 Lanfrey Place, London W14 9PY, Tel: 0171 385 7682, and Covenant Keepers (Mrs Vivenne Osunde), P O Box 10728, Blackheath, London SE3 7ZL, Tel: 0208 297 0158.

For the most part marriage ministry is much appreciated and is encouraging, especially if supported by prayer backing, as it should be. Rarely do any couple fail to gain from a marriage enhancement event. Sadly, not all marriages in difficulties will be restored, but some that are will be a glowing testimony to the Lord's grace and will bring glory to his name.

Further reading

J Dobson, *Man To Man About Woman* (Kingsway, 2000)
J Dobson, *Love Must Be Tough* (Kingsway, 1998)
J Gray, *Men Are From Mars, Women Are From Venus* (Thorsons)
T and B LaHaye, *The Act of Marriage* [on sex] (Zondervan)
N and S Lee, *The Marriage Book* (Holy Trinity, Brompton, Publications, 2000)
M and K Morris, *Praying Together. How to pray as husband and wife* (Kingsway, 1994)
R Parsons, *Sixty Minute Marriage* (Hodder & Stoughton, 1997)
M Sheldon and D Ames, *To Bind up The Broken-Hearted* [on counselling] (£8 for churches or full-time Christian workers, if ordered from Mission to Marriage)

EDWARD PRATT

CHAPTER FORTY-FOUR

Divorce and Remarriage

DAVID SHORT

Divorce is, sadly, becoming increasingly common in Western society, and Christians are not immune. There is enough sorrow and heartbreak involved in any divorce without the addition of what are often perceived as harsh and unsympathetic religious rules. So what does our loving Creator teach us in his word about divorce and remarriage?

It is important to begin with a Christian understanding of the nature of marriage. The marriage service reminds us that marriage was a loving provision of God right from the start of the human race. 'It is not good for man to be alone. I will make a helper suitable for him' (Gen 2:18). God ordained marriage for the comfort and joy of husband and wife, and also for the nurture of children: 'Be fruitful and increase in number' was his command (Gen 1:28). Marriage was designed to be permanent: 'They will become one flesh' (Gen 2:24). This has obvious advantages for the children, who need both parents.

The four essential elements in marriage

Before going further, we should attempt to define marriage. Clearly a religious service is not essential. From the dawn of history, countless couples have lived together in faithful marriage without the benefit of a religious ceremony. From the Bible and elsewhere there would appear to be four essential elements: consent, permanence, public witness, and sexual union (A Cornes, *Divorce and Remarriage*, pp.39-44). A woman who is forced against her will to marry has not really married. Hence the first question asked in the marriage service is: 'Will you have (or take) this woman/man to be your … wife/husband?' There must be consent. With regard to permanence, Lord Penzance, the famous nineteenth-century English judge, defined marriage as 'the voluntary union for life of one man and one woman to the exclusion of all others'. So far as public witness is concerned, in Scotland, from before the Reformation until 1940, a couple could be married by simply expressing mutual consent in the presence of two witnesses, without any other form of ceremony. And then there must be sexual union. If a couple fulfil these four conditions, they are, according to scripture, 'joined together by God' (Matt 19:6).

The teaching of the Lord Jesus

Christians are committed to following the teaching and example of Christ, irrespective of what the law of the land may allow. So we need to ask what Jesus taught on the subject. The answer is found in three key passages in the gospels; Matthew 5:31, 32, Matthew 19:1-12, and Mark 10:1-12. (There is also important teaching in the OT which needs to be studied as a background to our Lord's teaching.) It would be fair to summarise our Lord's teaching as follows. First there is the basic principle that in marriage the two become one for life: 'A man will leave his father and mother and be united to his wife and the two shall become one flesh. So they are no longer two but one. Therefore, what God has joined, let man not separate' (Matt 19:6). The teaching is unambiguous. As John Stott puts it: 'The marriage bond is more than a human contract: it is a divine yoke.' (*New Issues*, p.330) Jesus called remarriage after divorce, adultery. If a wife 'divorces her husband and marries another man, she commits adultery' (Mark 10:12).

Jesus did *permit* divorce on one ground: sexual infidelity (*porneia*) 'Anyone who divorces his wife, except for marital unfaithfulness, causes her to become an adulteress, and anyone who marries the divorced woman commits adultery' (Matt 5:32). Much interest has naturally focused on the exception, the one ground for divorce, which is widely assumed to carry with it freedom to remarry. But nothing must be allowed to detract from the fundamental inviolateness of marriage in the teaching of Jesus.

The absolute prohibition of divorce – with the single exception of marital unfaithfulness – shocked the disciples who first heard it, and it is recorded that they exclaimed: 'If this is the situation between a husband and wife, it is better not to marry' (Matt 19:10). It has been suggested that the Lord might have been using hyperbole here (as he undoubtedly did on other occasions) but the reaction of the disciples is a sufficient rebuttal of that idea. He meant what he said to be taken literally.

In seeking to understand our Lord's teaching with regard to divorce, it is vital that we do not overlook his attitude towards those who had fallen into marital unfaithfulness. We recall the loving consideration he showed to the woman caught in adultery (John 8:1-11). Although he reminded her that her action was sinful, he treated her with profound compassion. We recall, too, the friendship and respect he showed to the woman he met at Sychar's well, who was living a profoundly immoral life (John 4:7-26).

In addition to our Lord's teaching recorded in the gospels, there is the teaching in the epistles. Jesus promised that when the Holy Spirit came he would guide the apostles into all truth (John 16:13). It is as one fulfilment of this promise that we should view the apostle Paul's teaching on marriage in 1 Corinthians 7:10-16. Paul fully endorses our Lord's fundamental teaching, saying: 'To the married I give this command (not I, but the Lord): a wife must not separate from her husband. But if she does, she must remain unmarried or else be reconciled to her husband. And a husband must not divorce his wife' (vv.10, 11).

Paul then goes on to deal specifically with the situation where one partner in the marriage is an unbeliever and the other a believer (i.e. converted after marriage). Writing under the guidance of the Holy Spirit, he says that, if the unbelieving spouse is willing to remain, the Christian must not initiate a divorce. If, on the other hand, the unbelieving spouse insists on a divorce, 'a believing man or woman is not bound in such circumstances' (v.15). Paul does not mention remarriage, but many think that he envisages this.

John Stott sums up the NT teaching by saying: 'Divorce and remarriage are permissible (not mandatory) on two grounds. First, an innocent person may divorce his or her partner if the latter has been guilty of serious sexual immorality. Secondly, a believer may acquiesce in the desertion of his or her unbelieving partner, if the latter refuses to go on living with him or her' (*New Issues*, p.336).

How has the church down the ages understood our Lord's teaching?

Historically, the early church was virtually unanimously against the marriage of divorcees while the partner was still living. Although we are not bound by the practice of the early church, it could be argued that, coming from the same culture as Christ and speaking the same languages, they would be better placed than we are to interpret his teaching aright. (Though it must be said that post-apostolic writers did not get everything right!) This early church tradition was continued in the Roman Catholic and Anglican churches up to the present time. The Reformers allowed remarriage in cases of adultery and abandonment by an unbelieving spouse. More recently, it has been suggested that physical or sexual abuse of spouse or child might be regarded as a stronger ground for divorce than an isolated instance of adultery.

Application of biblical teaching in principle

How should we apply the biblical teaching to the situations we meet in church life today? Clearly, we must be true to the teaching of Christ. It is to this that we as Christians are committed, rather than the more lax law of the land. It is often thought that, provided a couple has obtained a legal divorce, the man and woman are free to remarry. They may be legally free to do so, but unless their divorce was on the specific ground of the adultery of their spouse or the desertion of an unbelieving partner, it could be argued that they are not free to remarry in church.

It is sometimes argued that our Lord's standard is so high that he cannot have intended it as more than an ideal to be aimed at. The danger is that, if we follow this line, the vows taken at the marriage service would lose the force of promises, and decline into pious hopes. Scripture makes it abundantly clear that God views divorce very seriously. The prophet Malachi quotes God as saying: 'I hate divorce' (Mal 2:16). Clearly, Christians should not condone anything that God hates. Marriage should be viewed as a lifelong commitment: 'for better, for worse; for richer, for poorer, in sickness and in health ... Till death us do part.' So, the Christian should do everything possible to sustain a marriage, and Christian leaders should do all in their power to bring about a reconciliation. Where there are children to consider, the weight of evidence currently available seems to show that even a stormy marriage is less harmful than divorce. Cornes argues that there are occasions when a Christian may be justified in initiating a separation – hopefully temporary – for such situations as repeated physical or mental cruelty (*Divorce and Remarriage*, p.300).

Today, the conservative Christian position is divided between those like Cornes who believe that the one-flesh state persists in spite of any adultery and in spite of legal divorce, so that marriage is never legitimate in the lifetime of the divorced partner, and those like Murray who consider that both parties to a divorce on the ground of adultery are free to remarry without being guilty of another act of adultery (J Murray, *Divorce*, p.101). Even Cornes regards a second marriage as valid, though illegitimate; so it should not be undone. He believes that we can even praise God for all the good that has come out of the second marriage (*Divorce and Remarriage*, p.399).

If we claim to be Christians, we are committed to our Lord's teaching on the permanence of marriage. But, along with this, we must reflect the compassion of Christ. We must never forget the pain, guilt and fear associated with marriage break-up. This is often greatest for Christians. So we need to communicate unconditional love and acceptance. God hates divorce, but he loves divorcees. He hates adultery, but he loves adulterers, and is willing to forgive them if the sin is confessed and repented of, as in the case of David after his adultery with Bathsheba. Adultery, serious though it is, is not the unforgivable sin.

The difficulty lies in keeping the right balance. In showing compassion, we must not give the wrong signal regarding the standard expected of Christian couples. If sexual misconduct is seen to be tolerated in the church, in the way society now tolerates it, standards of morality will inevitably fall, and we shall lay up greater problems for the future. We must show compassion, but we must make it clear that immorality is sinful and unacceptable. We must be open and honest about sin – our own as well as that of others – recognising that our God is a God of forgiveness and new beginnings.

Application of biblical teaching in practice

Every marriage breakdown is different, so it is necessary to be very cautious about generalising. There are, however, certain broad categories. One is the situation where the marriage has broken down because of the persistent adultery of one partner. The question arises: Can the innocent partner remarry? Of course there are always two sides to any situation, and no one is totally innocent. The partner who has not committed adultery may have behaved in such a way as to make the adulterous conduct of the other at least understandable. Our Lord clearly stated that, as a general rule, remarriage after divorce is adultery; but if the breakdown of the marriage came about as a result of the sexual infidelity of the spouse, then it seems that he did permit divorce and remarriage. In OT times, divorce was allowed by God because of the hardness of the human heart; and there is no evidence that hardness of heart is a thing of the past. It has been urged, however, that a Christian should be forgiving over a single lapse, if the partner is sincerely repentant.

When a couple have married before either was a Christian, and one has subsequently been converted, it does seem clear, on the basis of Paul's teaching in 1 Corinthians 7 that, if the unbeliever leaves, the believer may be free to remarry once the original marriage has been annulled. The believer should not initiate the break-up of the original marriage, and should indeed seek the conversion of the unbelieving partner and endeavour to bring up the children in the ways of God. In some Christian circles, it is argued that a marriage contracted in pre-conversion days is not necessarily still binding, on the ground that he or she is a 'new creature', and in its place a new beginning may be made. But John Stott considers this to be dangerous reasoning. 'Does this mean that all pre-conversion contracts are cancelled by conversion, including all one's debts?', he asks (*New Issues*, pp. 335, 336).

If remarriage seems right, how soon after the breakdown of the first marriage should it be permitted? And what degree of celebration is permitted? Can it be a 'white' wedding? The service should undoubtedly include a clear statement of penitence. The hymn: 'The king of love my shepherd is' with its verse: 'Perverse and foolish oft I strayed. But yet in love he sought me' catches the right note.

May an adulterer remarry? It is difficult to find warrant for this in scripture. On the other hand, it is hard to contemplate condemning a deeply repentant young man or woman to a lifetime of loneliness. Nevertheless, it may be the price that has to be paid if standards are to be upheld; and it must not be forgotten that a single life, dedicated to God, is not a second best but a high calling. Hard though it may appear, Jesus' teaching must be good for individuals and good for society.

There is, of course, nothing to stop an adulterer getting remarried in a register office. But if the person is truly repentant, he or she will long for God's blessing on their union. One way which has been suggested is for the register office marriage to be followed by a simple service in which God's forgiveness and blessing are sought on the new union (R Warren, *Divorce and Remarriage*, pp.23, 24). The problem is that this will be seen as giving a seal of approval. On the other hand, I see nothing against seeking God's blessing on those who have taken an irrevocable step without scriptural sanction – provided there is open confession of sin. The whole subject bristles with problems. The pastor or church leader faced with a request for remarriage may have insufficient evidence to judge who is 'innocent' and who is 'guilty', particularly if, as is usually the case, he hears only one side of the matter. This raises the question whether separation rather than divorce might be the best solution in some cases, particularly where violence is involved. It has been claimed that the obligation to preserve one's life and the lives and well-being of one's children, and also to maintain our own dignity and self-respect, overrides our marriage vows (F Retief, *Divorce*, p.138).

In the face of such difficulties, it is tempting to refuse to consider marrying anyone who has been divorced on any ground other than the adultery of the partner, if the partner is still living. Such a stance would be justified on the belief that the divorcee is still married in God's sight. If that is the view that is taken, it cannot be right to encourage a Christian to remarry even in a register office. But if we adopt this attitude, we lose opportunities of helping those in need, and instead drive them away from the Christian fold. It has been suggested that we should simply set out the scriptural guidelines and leave it to the contracting parties to decide whether they can take their vows in good conscience. The danger here is that the testimony of the church would be compromised if the Lord's teaching was not followed. If a church adopts the rule that it marries divorcees only 'in exceptional circumstances', it does not avoid criticism, because people feel aggrieved if they apply and are turned down. Moreover, there would be an almost irresistible pressure progressively to relax standards.

I believe we should be very reluctant to reject a couple asking for a church marriage without careful consideration. They may have mixed motives in applying to a Christian rather than going to a register office, but it does give us an opportunity of telling them what a Christian marriage involves. If we refuse them out of hand, they will be unlikely to turn to the church again, and may well settle into a life of cohabitation. I know of a pastor who was approached by a girl who was young in the Christian faith and who wanted to marry a boy who was not a believer. The pastor said he would need to have several talks with them before he gave them a definite answer. After two or three talks, the boy came to a genuine faith in Christ, as a result of which he was happy to accede to their request. Several years later, they are jointly walking the Christian path.

Conclusion

The church needs to be much more thorough in its teaching regarding marriage – and singleness – than it has been in the recent past. We are up against a pervasive worldly attitude which actually commends people for getting out of an unsatisfactory marriage. We must insist on the scriptural teaching that marriage is lifelong; one flesh for life. We must also be more realistic about the problems of married life and the need for sacrificial love. We must do more to support marriages, perhaps by having an officially designated lay pastor or pastors to the family. And we must be prepared to work at reconciliation before matters have gone too far.

Discipline may be necessary in the case of those who have

disobeyed the law of God, especially if they knew full well that this was what they were doing. Such discipline should be applied lovingly, along the lines laid down by our Lord in Matthew 18:15-17. This may include exclusion from the Lord's Table for a time.

I close with some words from a godly mentor of my youth.

There is shown in the Word of God a principle of divine toleration of evils that cannot be completely cured because of existing conditions. The ideal ought indeed to be striven after. God aims at it, men ought to do so. But until this can be attained God tolerates much that is as yet irremovable. Walking on the lower level does indeed involve its due recompense of reward, but the full penal consequences are not always enforced. (G H Lang, 'Divorce and Remarriage according to the Scriptures' [unpublished manuscript])

Further reading

A Cornes, *Divorce and Remarriage* (Hodder & Stoughton, 1993)
J Stott, *New Issues facing Christians Today* (Marshall Pickering, 1999)
J Murray, *Divorce* (Presbyterian & Reformed Publishing Co., 1961)
R Warren, *Divorce and Remarriage* (Grove Books, 1992)
F Retief, *Divorce – Hope for the Hurting* (Word Publishing, 1995)

CHAPTER FORTY-FIVE

Homosexuality

DAVID SHORT

Every church leader needs to know something about this subject, because every fellowship of any size is likely to have one or two individuals in this category, with special pastoral needs. There is also a possibility – at present remote – of a legal challenge by a practising homosexual who is refused membership. This has already happened in university Christian Union circles. In spite of all that has been written about homosexuality, there is still a considerable degree of ignorance about it.

A homosexual may be defined as a man or woman who depends on someone of the same sex for his or her happiness and to fulfil his or her need of love – and engages in sexual acts with them. Female homosexuals are referred to as lesbians. Homosexuality is not a rare condition in the population at large, neither is it as common as is sometimes claimed. A survey in the USA reported an incidence of 2.8% among males and 1.4% among females (J Satinover, *Homosexuality*, p.53). A recent survey in Britain found that only 0.4% of men and only 0.1% of women considered themselves exclusively homosexual (K Wellings et al., *Sexual Behaviour in Britain*, p.183). Considerably more report having had a homosexual experience at some time during their lives. The impression that the figures are much higher is probably because the incidence is greater in celebrities such as entertainers and artists.

It is very important to distinguish between homosexual orientation and homosexual practice. There are many who have difficulty in relating to the opposite sex and cannot contemplate marriage but who, nevertheless, do not engage in sexual acts with those of the same sex. Such individuals deserve our fullest respect and support, because they carry a heavy burden throughout life, with sexual needs that cannot rightly be met.

What does the Bible teach regarding homosexuality?

There are six key Bible passages to consider. The first is the well-known story of Sodom, recorded in Genesis 19. Alongside that, we can place the story of Gibeah, recounted in Judges 19. Then there is the teaching in the book of Leviticus 18:22 and 20:13, which explicitly prohibit 'lying with a man as one lies with a woman'. In the NT we have the apostle Paul's portrayal, in Romans 1: 18-32, of decadent pagan society in his day. The inclusion of homosexuals in a list of sinners in Paul's first letter to the Corinthians (6:9, 10) is important because it describes homosexuals under two different terms: *malakoi* translated 'male prostitutes' and *arsenokoitai* translated 'homosexual offenders'. John Stott explains that the former refers to the one who plays the passive role and the latter to the one who plays the active role (*New Issues,* pp.390, 391). The final reference is in 1 Timothy 1: 8-11, where Paul gives a list of law-breakers and rebels'.

The obvious inference of all these passages, taken in their straightforward sense, is a strong condemnation of homosexual practice. It is important to note that there is no condemnation anywhere in scripture of homosexual orientation, only of homosexual practice. It is tempting to leave the review of scripture teaching at this point. But it has to be acknowledged that some modern biblical scholars have argued strongly that the traditional view is mistaken. For example, they consider that, in the cases of Sodom and Gibeah, what is condemned is a serious breach of oriental hospitality. Those involved in loving, committed homosexual relationships cannot believe that God would be displeased with them. This is the view of the Lesbian and Gay Christian Movement.

John Stott considers these and other objections in detail and answers them convincingly. He also makes the basic point that homosexuality represents a total rejection of God's institution of marriage, described in Genesis 1 and 2 and summed up in the words: 'For this reason a man will leave his father and mother, and be united to his wife, and they will become one flesh' (Gen 2: 24). This fundamental relationship was underlined by our Lord, as recorded in Matthew 19: 4-6, where he quoted verbatim the words of Genesis 2: 24. Thus he affirmed that (1) heterosexual gender is a divine creation; (2) heterosexual marriage is a divine institution; and (3) heterosexual fidelity is the divine intention. A homosexual liaison is a breach of all three of these divine purposes (*New Issues,* pp.391-406).

Contemporary understanding of homosexuality

If homosexual activity is to be regarded as sinful, but homosexual orientation as a handicap to be borne, how are we to respond to the present demand for a better deal for homosexuals. We need to understand how homosexuals feel in contemporary society. They feel themselves to be rejected and alienated, and they see no justification for this adverse discrimination. They do not regard themselves as being any more abnormal than if they were left-handed. They consider the attitude of society at large as being one of 'homophobia' – using the term 'phobia' not so much in the classical sense of an irrational fear – though it must be admitted that in some heterosexuals there are elements of fear and disgust – but in the sense of persecution. They demand that homosexual activity should be approved, that the age of consent for homosexual activity should be the same as that for heterosexual activity, and that they should be allowed to contract same-sex marriages with all the privileges which go with traditional marriage.

There are several problems with this point of view. In the first place, as we have seen, homosexual activity is contrary to the will of God. This immediately suggests that God may have a reason for prohibiting it. Sure enough, when we look into the matter, we find that homosexual practice is bad for the individual and bad for society. Although homosexuals like to compare their condition to left-handedness, it is in reality much more serious than that. Francis Bacon, one of the greatest British painters of the second half of the twentieth century, confessed: 'Being a homosexual is a defect. It is like having a limp.' A leading Scottish churchman recently described it, sympathetically, as 'a disorder, a handicap like a wooden leg'. Homosexuals strongly reject such sympathy.

Satinover, an American psychiatrist, has made an intensive study of homosexuality, and has written one of the most valuable books on the subject. One of the points which emerges is that homosexual activity is associated with a great degree of ill-health (*Homosexuality*, pp.67-69). According to his researches, the average life-span of men engaging in homosexual activity is reduced by as much as 30 years. This is partly, but by no means wholly, due to the high incidence of AIDS. Although promiscuous vaginal intercourse carries a risk of AIDS, the risk with anal intercourse is far higher. In addition, those indulging in homosexual activity are, on the whole, far more promiscuous than heterosexuals. There are, no doubt, examples of faithful homosexual relationship, but this is not typical. Satinover gives the average number of life partners of a homosexual as 50, with 43% having over 500 partners (*Homosexuality*, pp.54, 55). Not all male homosexuals indulge in anal intercourse, but many do, and they are prone to develop lower bowel disease. Promiscuity is also responsible for great emotional damage.

Likening homosexuality to left-handedness implies that it is something innate, a disposition with which the individual is born. This idea has been strengthened by the claimed discovery of a 'gay' gene. The existence of such a gene is far from being confirmed, and even if it is, it would not imply that homosexual practice was the inevitable result. A few years ago, genetic testing of the inmates of prisons showed that a certain genetic pattern was commoner in them than in the population at large, and it was thought that there might be a 'criminal' gene. But it was soon discovered that a proportion of normal individuals carried the same genetic pattern.Thus criminal conduct was not inevitable; there was an element of personal choice involved. The same would apply if the existence of a 'gay' gene is confirmed. The Wolfenden report of 1957, on which the Sexual Offences Act of 1967 was based, stated explicitly: 'There are no *prima facie* grounds for supposing that because a particular person's sexual propensity happens to be in the direction of persons of his or her own sex it is any less controllable that that of persons whose propensity is for persons of the opposite sex' (para 22).

Satinover does not accept that a 'gay' gene is the explanation of homosexuality. He believes, as do many who have studied the problem, that a major factor is a difficulty in parent-child relationship, especially in the earlier years of life. Dr Elizabeth Moberly has put it in the following way: 'The underlying principle is that the homosexual – whether man or woman – has suffered from some deficit in the relationship with the parent of the same sex; and that there is a corresponding drive to make good this deficit through the medium of same-sex or 'homosexual' relationships' (*Homosexuality*, p.2).

Satinover believes that the boy who becomes a homosexual is born with certain characteristics such as a sensitive disposition, a strong creative drive and a keen aesthetic sense which, combined with a poor relationship with his father, leads him to develop unsatisfactory relationships with the average boy. Longing for the father he never had, he feels a need for same-sex closeness. His first homosexual experience gives him a profound feeling of comfort, leading him to seek repeat experiences. Life becomes harder for him than for most males because of the guilt and shame he feels, and later the medical consequences he suffers.

Homosexual conduct is difficult to modify because, like other forms of compulsive behaviour, it becomes a habit 'embedded in the brain', 'engraved on the heart', as Satinover puts it (*Homosexuality*, pp. 221-225).

Can homosexuality be cured?

The Bible-believing Christian is encouraged by the knowledge that 'with God all things are possible' (Matt 19:26). In confirmation of this is Paul's statement, referring to sinners of many types, including homosexuals, and adding: 'That is what some of you were. But you were washed, you were sanctified, you were justified in the name of the Lord Jesus Christ and by the Spirit of our God' (1 Cor 6:11). It seems clear that Paul means that homosexuals had been converted and that they no longer indulged in sinful practices, including homosexual activity. We cannot, I think, conclude that their orientation had changed. They may still have had a battle with their sexual drive. But they were no longer practising homosexuals.

Homosexuals, for the most part, dismiss talk of cure, because they do not consider their condition to be a disease. The only problem in their eyes is the attitude of society. It is this that they consider needs to be 'cured'. In recent years, there does seem to have been some success in the healing of homosexuals, particularly following psychotherapy and perhaps rather more with Christian therapy, as practised by Leanne Payne and the True Freedom Trust (Satinover, *Homsexuality*, pp.197-207). There are some parallels between homosexuality and alcoholism, and some of the best results have come from an organisation called Homosexuals Anonymous, which works in a similar way to Alcoholics Anonymous, starting with the recognition of the need of help from a 'Higher Power'. Almost every homosexual feels a sense of anger and resentment, and healing requires the forgiveness of the one who is perceived as causing the damage.

What should the Christian attitude be?

Toward those with homosexual orientation, who are battling against temptation, and for whom marriage is not an option, we should have nothing but admiration, and we should seek to help them in every way possible. At the heart of the homosexual condition is a deep loneliness. What is needed, says John Stott, is deep, loving, lasting, same-sex but non-sexual relationships, especially in the church. He does not think there is any need to encourage homosexual people to disclose their sexual inclinations to everybody; this, he believes, is neither necessary nor helpful. But they do need at least one confidante to whom they can unburden themselves, who will not despise or reject them, but will support them with friendship and prayer (*New Issues*, p.417).

So far as practising homosexuals are concerned, we need to

remember that, sinful though their activities are in God's sight, homosexual practice is not the greatest sin, nor is it the unforgivable sin. Our Lord said that it would be more tolerable in the Day of Judgment for Sodom than for those who came face to face with him and yet rejected him (Matt 11:23, 24). Wilful unbelief – and pride – are more displeasing to God than homosexual practice.

John Stott goes into the question whether AIDS should be regarded as a divine judgment on practising homosexual men. His conclusion is 'yes and no' (*New Issues*, p.408). 'No' because Jesus warned us not to interpret calamities as God's specific judgments upon evil people (Luke 13:1-5). 'No' also because AIDS victims include many faithful married women who have been infected by their unfaithful husbands, with a substantial minority of innocent haemophiliacs and children. But 'yes' in the sense that Paul meant what he said when he wrote: 'A person will reap exactly what he sows' (Gal 6:7). The fact that evil actions bring evil consequences seems to have been written by God into the ordering of his moral world. But the fact that many people have contracted AIDS as a result of their own sexual promiscuity provides us with no possible justification for shunning or neglecting them, any more that we would those who damage themselves through drunken driving or other forms of recklessness.

We should not allow ourselves to be invariably suspicious of same-sex friendships. There have been many valuable same-sex relationships both between men, as in the case of David and Jonathan in OT times, and between women as in the case of the twentieth-century missionaries, Mildred Cable and Francesca French. Where caution is necessary is in the leadership of work among children because a high proportion of those with homosexual orientation are abnormally attached to children, with consequent risk of abuse.

Further reading

E R Moberly, *Homosexuality: a New Christian Ethic* (James Clarke, 1983)
J Satinover, *Homosexuality and the Politics of Truth* (Baker, 1996)
J Stott, *New Issues facing Christians Today* (Marshall Pickering, 1999)
K Wellings et al., *Sexual Behaviour in Britain: the national survey of sexual attitudes and life-styles* (Penguin, 1994)

FORTY SIX

Wealth, Poverty and Debt

KEITH TONDEUR

This is a vital issue about which Jesus talked more than almost any other subject. In the Bible there are about 2350 verses on the subject, compared to 500 each on prayer and faith. The handling of money could well be the most difficult area that people in churches and communities are currently facing. Jesus came to earth to teach us to love God and those made in his image and we should use money and possessions to help us do so. Sadly we live in a world that loves money and often exploits people to get it. Jesus tells us that we have a choice. We cannot serve God and money (Matt 6:24). The way we handle our money is in fact an acid test of our priorities, as we spend money on what is most important to us. Unfortunately, our lifestyle often reflects our culture more than our faith.

Acknowledging God's role

When it comes to money we need to acknowledge that it all belongs to him, for everything is his (Psa 24:1). As soon as we recognise this, every spending decision becomes a spiritual decision – 'Lord, how do you want me to spend your money?' This surrender cannot be overemphasised: 'Any one of you who does not give up everything he has cannot be my disciple' (Luke 14:33).

A need should not be confused with what we want or desire. We need food, clothing and housing: we may want a desirable property in the Bahamas! Remember, too, that the Lord loves us all equally but may well give us the responsibility of different sums to look after (Matt 25:14-30).

Fulfilling our role

God has given us the role of steward. 'You made him ruler over the works of your hands, you put everything under his feet' (Psa 8:6). This means we are to live recognising that we are God's hands and wallets on earth, and this carries both obligations and opportunities. We need to keep asking ourselves which is more important – money or others made in the image of God. We are called to hold on to things lightly and to be faithful with whatever we have, be it small or large. At this point it is also worth noting that we always define a rich person as someone who has more money than we have even though, in world terms, nearly all in Britain would be classed as rich! So, under stewardship:

• our possessions are a responsibility;
• we work to serve Jesus;
• we give because we love God;
• and we spend prayerfully and responsibly.

Living in a materialistic world

It is not possessing riches that God condemns, but rather clinging to them, coveting them, or centring our lives around them. Many of us when asked: 'How much is enough?' will reply: 'Just a little more.' Society has brainwashed us into believing that anything of value can be bought. It believes, and is encouraged to do so through things like the lottery, that money and possessions will bring love, happiness and peace of mind. But it is an empty illusion. The centre of materialism is always self – the worst four-letter word in the English language. Our society always seems to want more and be envious of others who have more than we have. As Christians are we different? Are we storing up treasures on earth or in heaven? Some of Jesus' most powerful teaching is directed at those who are self-centred on earth (Luke 12:15-21 - the rich man and his barns – and Luke 16:19-31 - the rich man and Lazarus).

The world seems to ask: 'What does somebody own?' whereas Christ asks: 'How is it being used?' The way we live needs to have an impact on the people we meet, demonstrating that they matter to us more than things. Possessions don't just cost money, they take up a great deal of time as well, which probably explains why we are becoming an increasingly lonely society. In the light of eternity many things fade into insignificance. We shall not be thinking about houses, cars or fashions in heaven. Today we are living in unprecedented affluence. We are constantly bombarded with manipulative advertising, pressuring us to buy more. Many of us buy things we don't need, with money we don't have, to impress people we don't even like! But we are told: 'Do not conform any longer to the pattern of this world' (Rom12:2).

Money – the root of all evil?

Money in itself is a neutral commodity. It can be used creatively to spread God's word or help the poor and needy. It can be wasted on frivolous activities such as lavish living or gambling, or it can be used corruptly for bribes or illegal trading. Wealth can be so seductive, and can easily erode our faith as we become arrogant, bask in *our* success and forget God. We need to remember that most individual tension, family friction and despair are caused directly or indirectly by the wrong use of money.

We are called not to imitate Christ's poverty, but to follow him in his example of love and self-giving, not caring how much money we have as long as we are obediently following him. On the surface, riches appear to do what in fact only Jesus can do – provide for our needs, bring contentment and give us peace of mind.

Contentment

It is vital for us to remember that all that we long for is to be found in Christ alone. Our society teaches that more is always better and that happiness is based on the acquisition of things. But this is wrong. Rich and poor alike long for real love, acceptance and intimacy, and it is only our Lord who can provide this. The word 'contentment' appears only seven times in the Bible and it always relates to money. Having much money does not bring contentment or make people what God wants them to be. We are told to 'keep [our] lives free from the love of money and be content with what we have because God has said, "Never will I leave you, never will I forsake you"' (Heb 13:5). Money can never hold and comfort, forgive and love unconditionally, which is what people long for. Only Jesus can do this and the way in which we use money and possessions can point others towards him.

The problems of debt in our society

Debt is endemic in our society today. It is largely hidden because most people are very reluctant to admit that they are struggling with it. But we are under constant pressure to borrow more, to feed instant gratification. At the same time, with very few jobs for life left, it is not surprising that there are now several million court summonses for personal debt each year, millions of Britons now having some form of credit restriction imposed upon them. The more one owes the more the creditors dictate where the money goes. 'The borrower is truly the slave of the lender' (Prov 22:7).

Things have got so bad that 'Mr. Average Great Britain' has been described as someone driving on a government bond financed road, in a bank financed car, fuelled by credit card financed petrol, going to buy store card financed furniture to put in his building society financed house!

The dangers of excess credit

By its very nature, credit encourages us to spend more than we otherwise would. Only about half of us clear our credit cards every month which means that interest will accumulate rapidly and each month that passes will increase the amount owed. In addition, whenever you take out credit you are making an assumption that you will be able to repay out of future income. Yet the Bible clearly warns us not to make such assumptions. 'Now listen, you who say, "Today or tomorrow we will go to this or that city, spend a year there, carry on business and make money." Why, you do not even know what will happen tomorrow. What is your life? You are a mist that appears for a little while and then vanishes. Instead you ought to say, "If it is the Lord's will we will live and do this or that."' (Jas 4:13-15).

The consequences of debt

It is almost impossible to overstate the pressures that debt brings. Many will have real fear – even of answering the phone or the doorbell. They may feel insecure, guilty and ashamed. They will certainly feel lonely. And the consequences of this are enormous, money problems being named as the major cause of relationship breakdown. Rational people can do irrational things under this sort of stress and on Credit Action's freephone counselling help line (0800 591084) we have heard of some of the desperate things that people have done in attempts to rectify the position. We know of cases where women have even toyed with prostitution and men have had breakdowns under the tremendous pressure it brings. Sadly we are even aware of some cases of suicide. But even when it does not reach such extremes it causes loss of self-esteem, health problems and increased loneliness. And these problems are rife within the church as well as in the community. The first guide we wrote on debt was specifically Christian and sold out in six weeks.

Trying to sort out debt

When looking at the problem of debt it is important to discover how people got into it in the first place. For some it will be unemployment, for others it will be benefit problems, relationship breakdown, overspending, addiction of some sort, or one of many other reasons. It is only by identifying the reason behind the debts that one can hope to provide a long-term solution. Once this has been identified, a plan needs to be put into place along the following lines:

Pray God wants us to clear our debts. 'Let no debts remain outstanding' (Rom 13:8).

Transfer ownership to God If we forget that God owns our resources we shall inevitably assume too much responsibility.

Establish a budget Everyone should be budgeting. If Christians are not doing so it is bad stewardship as, inevitably, money will be wasted. Those in debt need to know where their money is going in order to cut back wherever possible.

Look at assets Are there things that can be sold to reduce debts?

Establish a debt repayment schedule Confidence will soar as soon as the debt total begins to fall.

Seek advice This is a specialist area and good Christian professional advice will be needed.

Where to go for help

God People in debt feel deep despair and a feeling of hopelessness. But God says: '"I know the plans I have for you", declares the Lord, "plans to prosper you and not to harm you, plans to give you hope and a future"' (Jer 29:11). There is much in the Bible that will bring hope.

Husbands/Wives/Parents Many people, probably most, who are in debt do not share this with their partners. Inevitably the truth will finally emerge and often, with it, a total lack of trust. We must seek advice from those closest to us at the earliest possible moment. Working together on a problem avoids much recrimination.

Others who can help This will involve contact with creditors, the benefits' agency, doctors or anyone else who can help ease the pain.

Christian advisers Almost certainly much help will be needed before a debt problem is fully resolved. Credit Action not only has a freephone help line but a range of material, both Christian and secular, that covers all aspects of personal financial teaching including both escaping from and avoiding debt.

What the church can do to help

The first thing to do is probably to acknowledge that the extensive range of money issues in the Bible have not been taught as much as they should have been! Then there needs to be a recognition that every community, and probably every church, will have people with debt problems. And this may apply especially in affluent areas as all government figures indicate that the more people earn the more they borrow.

Once the awareness of the problem has been raised it is essential to ensure that resources are available to meet the need. Not all churches will be able to provide quality debt counselling, but books and phone numbers can easily be made available. A small hardship fund or food larder would also be handy.

Remember, the church is likely to see only the tip of the iceberg. Being able to reach out into the community offering help in an acceptable way is a tremendous opportunity for outreach and for demonstrating that you are a caring church. We are aware of our books being used in the community through personal outreach as well as through places such as libraries and doctors' surgeries.

And, whenever possible, we need to give practical help in a non-judgmental way, making ourselves available, giving time, and restoring dignity to those who are hurting.

And what about giving?

Space permits only a few thoughts here. Giving is all about sacrifice, so God counts not so much what we give but what we keep. It is all to do with priorities. Giving is not God's way of raising money because God can do that any way he likes. Rather, it is to make us more like Jesus who gave 100% for each one of us. It is all about attitude. What comes first in our lives? This is why biblical teaching on money should be in the forefront of our discipleship as we learn to accept that everything belongs to God, not just at most 10%.

So does this preclude saving?

There needs to be a balance here between saving for every extreme possibility and assuming that the Lord will simply provide for our needs. There is a difference between faith and presumption. In fact the Bible tells we should save to ensure we are not a burden to society, or our children, in our old age. 'Children should not have to save up for their parents, but parents for their children' (2 Cor 12:14). So we can save for our retirement and hopefully leave a small inheritance for our children (see Prov 13:22) but we really do need to know when enough is enough.

Conclusion

Jesus tells us very clearly that we have to make a choice. We cannot serve two masters. Given that we are going to be in heaven for ever, and that therefore our time on earth is as a blink of an eyelid, it should seem easy to decide our priorities. But the day-to-day pressures of the here and now so often blind us to reality. Perhaps we need to remember that money can buy all the cosmetics in the world but not beauty, all the books but not common sense, all the drugs but not health, the most comfortable bed but not sleep. In fact money can buy everything in the world except peace of mind and eternal life, both of which are free gifts from God.

Surely, as Christians, we need to show that we live by God's values, and use money and possessions to make known his love, grace and forgiveness to a lost, lonely and hurting world.

For further information please contact: Credit Action, 6 Regent Terrace, Cambridge CB2 1AA (01223 324034). Freephone helpline: 0800 591084.

Further reading

B Partington and M Jackson, *To will and to do* (Credit Action)
K Tondeur, *Your Money and your Life* (Credit Action)
--------------, *Escaping from Debt* (Credit Action)
--------------, *What Jesus said about Money and Possessions* (Credit Action)
K Tondeur and L Burkett, *Debt-free Living* (Credit Action)

FORTY SEVEN

Addiction

GWEN PURDIE

So let us put aside the deeds of darkness, and put on the armour of light. Let us behave decently, as in the day time, not in orgies and drunkenness, not in sexual immorality and debauchery, not in dissension and jealousy. Rather, clothe yourselves with the Lord Jesus Christ and do not think about how to gratify the desires of the sinful nature. (Rom 13 :12b-14)

Most people, when we see they see the word 'addiction' think of alcohol and drugs. Whilst these are chronic addictions in our society so are the following – listed in no particular order: coffee, coke, sport, gambling, paracetamol, spending, shop-lifting, computer games, sex, food, internet pornography, prescribed drugs and ...

What is addiction?

An addict is someone who is devoted or given habitually or compulsively to the use of a substance or exercise. In the case of alcoholism, for example, there are three main criteria: excessive drinking; growing dependence; and inflicting or sustaining social or physical harm. What characterises an alcoholic is being consistently unable to choose whether to drink or not, and whether to stop or not.

Quite apart from questions of law-breaking, addiction is a serious matter. The effects of addictive behaviour include: time off work; secrecy; accidents; crime; violence and aggression; impaired ability; blackouts; mood swings; theft; breakdown of relationships; divorce, loss of health; loss of self-esteem; loneliness and isolation; uncharacteristic behaviour; deceit and manipulation; guilt; depression; damage to the body and ill health; shortening of life; suicidal thoughts; financial problems. This is a horrific list. Not all of these effects will be experienced by everyone but even a few could cause major disruption.

After many years of counselling in all the above situations I have formed the opinion that addiction is a symptom rather than a root in itself. It is, in a sense, a self-inflicted curse. To become addicted you need to have made a whole series of wrong choices. There are always reasons why people become addicted.

Is addiction a sickness or a sin? Obviously sin can be involved in the sense that wrong choices may have been made. It is, however, simplistic and judgmental to assume that all addicts are primarily indulging in sin. It is important to look further at the roots of a person's addiction. Perhaps the addict was sinned against and this has caused a reaction in them. Their background may supply clues as to why they have chosen this route. Factors involved could include their environment, hereditary or social, circumstances, upbringing, lack of self-confidence, stress, and possibly ignorance of the addictive qualities of the substance or activity.

A person does not choose to become addicted. The process takes some time. At some stage in the process, besides being fully responsible for their wrong choices, the addict has become 'sick'. This is when the body craves for more of the same, having become physiologically dependent. To become an alcoholic takes a little longer, usually a minimum of approximately two years. But in terms of recovery, it is unhelpful to suggest that an addict is merely sick, because they will then imagine that a doctor can cure them. The basic philosophy of Alcoholics Anonymous or Gamblers Anonymous is the expectation that addicts will take full responsibility for their own behaviour and choices.

Some people have addictive personalities, like the lady known to me who is a Christian alcoholic, bulimic and also addicted to cigarettes. In view of her two divorces and her new 'friend', I am tempted to say that she is also addicted to unhelpful relationships. Often the addictive personality is very attractive – but also manipulative, driven to extremes and so capable of deceit and rationalisations in order to keep the habit going.

Among characteristics typical of persons who are addicted are:
- being easily offended if you don't believe them;
- self-rejection or self-alienation, leading to self-hatred;
- a tendency to complain a lot;
- seeing themselves as the centre of their world;
- thinking everyone else is selfish and not 'there for them';
- being immobilised by frustration, fear or depression;
- loneliness;
- anxiety to seek approval so great that they lose their own identity in the attempt.

Helping addicts

How we can help addicts within the church setting? It goes without saying that good teaching about addictions and how to prevent them would be a good investment for a church. But however far you may bend over backwards trying to help, both you and your help may be rejected. Some will need more help than we can give; for example residential care, therapy, help from psychiatric or specialist organisations, etc. They will also need support until they get help. Do not give up. Keep trying.

When attempting to help an addict it is good to assess the problem properly before embarking on a treatment plan. Help him or her to think through the following questions:

• What do you feel is your problem?
• What are your problem-solving goals?
• What are the forces working for change?
• What are the forces working against change?
• What help or support would you like from the church?

The addict has to want to be helped. There is nothing sadder than having to live with someone who has an addiction but will not admit it. But although we cannot force people to be helped we can pray for them.

An addict has to realise that they can have a new life in Christ Jesus. They must have the desire to put the past behind them and to begin again. The healing process usually involves help and support; also accountability. The past cannot be erased, but the Lord, who is full of grace, can remove the sting from the past (Acts 4:16). The implications of past behaviour may still have to be faced but the Lord promises to be there (Deut 31:6).

In all this, hope is basic. As church leaders we need to have hope ourselves and communicate it to others. God can and does change addicts. There is life after addiction. It is not only the person with the addiction who needs to have goals. So do we. For instance, to see the person's addiction broken; to communicate the power of God and the ability to help; to indicate that healing will happen but that it is a process; to establish a trusting relationship with the person; to help them sort out their own problem; to be caring and empathetic; to pray with and for the person; to offer ongoing support as needed.

There are conditions to being made well and to being able to leave an addiction behind. The addict must know that:

• God is good (Matt 19:17), desires to heal and is able to heal (Exod 15:26; Psa 103:3, 4).
• They are responsible for their behaviour (Psa 51:1-4).

- Freedom is a real possibility (Isa 61:1; John 8:36).
- They are powerless to control or conquer their habit themselves (1 Cor 10:13; 2 Cor 12:9, 10; Phil 4:13).
- They are capable of deceiving themselves (Jer 18:12; Mark 10:18; Rom 3:12).
- Self-control is a possibility that can be realised (1 Thess 5:4-11).
- God in all his graciousness has a plan for exchanging the heartache and the old ways for the new (Gal 5:19-25).

The acts of the sinful nature are obvious: sexual immorality, impurity and debauchery; idolatry and witchcraft; hatred, discord, jealousy, fits of rage, selfish ambition, dissensions, factions and envy, drunkenness, orgies and the like. I warn you, as I did before, that those who live like this will not inherit the kingdom of God. But the fruit of the Spirit is love, joy, peace, patience, kindness, goodness, faithfulness, gentleness and self-control. Against such things there is no law. Those who belong to Christ Jesus have crucified the sinful nature with its passions and desires. Since we live by the Spirit, let us keep in step with the Spirit (Gal 5:19-25).

For a Christian alternative to Alcoholics Anonymous, contact Arthur Williams, The Stauros Foundation, Ballyards Castle, 123 Keady Road, Armagh BT60 3AD (01861 527124;arthur.g.williams@ btinternet.com)

Further reading

O Batchelor, *Use and Misuse – a Christian Perspective on Drugs* (IVP, 1999)
G G May, *Addiction and Grace. Love and spirituality in the healing of addictions* (Harper, 1988)

PART FIVE

Legal, Financial and Practical Matters

Forty Eight

Trusts and Trusteeship

Gerald West

This topic covers a specialised and complex area of the law and many of the questions that arise cannot be adequately covered in a short chapter which relates only to the situation in England and Wales. The law is different in Scotland and Northern Ireland. When problems and questions arise it is important that trustees should understand their duties and responsibilities and should be able to obtain reliable advice. As a general rule trustees should take advice if they are in doubt. For churches which do not have help available through a denominational framework, there are three main sources of such advice: the Charity Commission, organisations such as Stewardship Services, and specialist solicitors.

Sources of further advice

One of the responsibilities of the Charity Commission is to provide advice to trustees. To this end they issue a wide range of leaflets and booklets and these should be consulted whenever necessary. A list of their publications can be obtained from them free of charge. Stewardship Services publish a *Church Trustees and Treasurers Handbook* and the latest edition of this should be consulted for further information (referred to below as *The Handbook*). Help, including legal advice, can also be obtained from Stewardship Services which is itself a registered charity with an evangelical trust deed. It is not easy to find solicitors whose practice regularly deals with these issues. The larger partnerships may include specialists. Such firms will service the larger secular and Christian charities and their fees will reflect this. The Association of Christian Lawyers can provide details of Christian lawyers but it is important to make sure that the lawyer concerned has appropriate experience.

Trust deeds

Most churches will operate under the terms of a written trust deed and the trustees can usually be easily identified. All Christian churches are charities (whether they have a trust deed or not) because they have as their purpose the advancement of the Christian faith. Many churches are connected with a trust which holds only the premises (a property trust). In these circumstances the trustees are not responsible for the affairs of the church. The trust and the church will have separate bank accounts. The trustees of the property trust would be likely to intervene only if the church began to use the premises for purposes not allowed by the trust deed and/or if the church departed from any doctrines and practices set out in the deed. Where there is a property trust and the affairs of the church are not managed by the trustees, the church is probably technically a separate trust, even though formal trust documents may not have been prepared. Where this is the case, the leaders of the church are probably operating without realising that they are in fact trustees of an undeclared trust. There are cases in which the exact relationship between church and trust is not clear. If necessary, advice should be taken.

Increasingly, under the impact of the provisions of the Charities Acts passed in the early 1990s, this position is being regularised. Sometimes it is possible to bring the church within the terms of the existing property trust, but this may require a change of trustees to include at least some of the present leadership of the church and to allow those trustees who cannot in practice exercise effective oversight of the church to retire. If the terms of the property trust do not allow this, the alternative is to create a separate trust relating to the church and its activities (a congregational trust). These are complex issues and their resolution will require legal advice. Any new trust should be drawn up by a lawyer with appropriate experience and will need to be submitted to the Charity Commission if the charity is to be registered.

Every trustee should have a copy of the trust deed and be familiar with its provisions. These will include statements setting out the purposes of the trust and the powers of the trustees. There will be clauses governing the appointment of trustees and the conduct of meetings and how decisions are to be made. The deed will include provisions dealing with the winding up of the trust if it is not possible to continue. In a modern trust deed there will be some provision allowing amendment to the terms of the deed. But great care should be taken when considering such provisions. They will usually be limited to procedural matters and will not allow changes to the purposes of the trust or the powers of the trustees.

Registration

There is a basic duty to register a charity. There are a number of exceptions which include the more established denominations. The application of the exceptions is complex and the Charity Commission do not themselves seem clear about some of the details. However, there seems to be little disadvantage in registration and significant advantages in relation to public perception of the status of the church. It will normally be sensible to seek registration. The Charity Commission will supply on request a registration pack consisting of a number of explanatory booklets and the main application form.

Purposes and powers

Any charitable trust deed will set out the purposes of the trust. These purposes are circumscribed by the requirement for them to be charitable. Over the years there has been a wide variety of ways of describing these purposes in legal language. In many cases the definition will include at least by implication a set of doctrines and sometimes a number of practices to which the church or any church using the premises must conform. Each trust deed must be carefully read to determine the purposes for which the charity exists and the trustees are bound by those purposes. They cannot do or allow anything which falls outside the purposes described in the trust deed.

In addition the trust deed will set out the powers of the trustees. In general trustees may act only in accordance with the powers given to them in the trust deed. There are exceptions to this and if in doubt legal advice should be taken. It is the duty of a trustee to act within the constraints of the trust deed. The power of trustees to sell or mortgage land is subject to special rules. In general an order of the Charity Commission is required, but there are important exceptions to this. The rules cover both freehold and leasehold land. The Charity Commission issue comprehensive booklets covering this matter and these should be consulted in all cases. Any solicitor involved also has special responsibilities when dealing with charity land and this is another reason for using a solicitor who has experience in this field.

Trustees

The trust deed is likely to place restrictions on the persons who can be trustees. In particular there may be a requirement that each trustee should affirm the beliefs and fulfil the practices and/or be a member of the church. In some deeds there is provision for automatic retirement if a trustee ceases to fulfil this condition. The deed is also likely to stipulate a minimum number of trustees. Care must be taken not to allow the number to fall below that figure. Further advice should be sought if it proves impossible to maintain the number.

The method of appointment of new trustees will depend on the provisions of the trust deed. A resolution of the trustees may be sufficient. Otherwise a formal deed of appointment is required. If the trust owns land/property it is necessary to ensure that the property is conveyed to the new trustees. If there is any doubt about the matter, advice should be taken to make sure that changes in the trustees are dealt with properly. Failure to do this is a frequent source of later difficulty.

Qualities of trustees

In order to carry out their responsibilities trustees need to have a sense of responsibility and be able to put to one side any personal preferences which might inhibit them from working strictly within the terms of the trust deed. Trustees should be scrupulous in complying with all the requirements of the deed and must understand the need to keep proper records. The trustees of a congregational trust should be actively involved in the life and ethos of the church and able to devote the necessary time to the task. It is important that the spiritual leadership of the church should be represented on the body of trustees.

There are a number of disqualifications under the legislation. These rarely apply but, if there is any doubt, take further advice. One disqualification which arises from time to time is that, unless there is specific provision to the contrary in the trust deed, trustees cannot be remunerated by the trust. For this reason it will not usually be possible for a paid worker in the church to be a trustee. In rare cases the trust deed may specifically allow otherwise. The Charity Commission can be reluctant to allow such a provision in a new trust deed and is highly unlikely to approve changes to an existing one to allow payment.

The need to distinguish between congregational trustees, the spiritual leadership of the church, and any members of that leadership who are financially supported by the church raises complicated questions. This is not the place to try to address them but it is important to be aware of them.

Liabilities of trustees

Trustees are responsible for administering the trust in accordance with the trust deed and for actively doing this. They will therefore meet at appropriate intervals. This should be at least once each year for a property trust and much more frequently for a congregational trust. Formal minutes of trustees meetings should be kept, approved and signed. Trustees are required to exercise proper care and are jointly and severally responsible. They are personally liable for any loss arising if they act outside their powers and they are liable to third parties under contract or tort.

Trustees indemnity insurance can be purchased but this will not cover dishonesty or folly! Trustees have an obligation to ensure that there is adequate insurance cover. (See the Insurance Section of *The Handbook* for further information.) Trustees should understand that if they enter into a contract for which the trust does not have the financial resources they will be personally liable for any debt.

Publicity, fund raising and trading

Registered charities with a gross income greater than £10,000 per annum are required to state on certain documents that they are a registered charity. These documents include: notices and advertisements soliciting gifts; cheques; invoices; bills and receipts. There are various approved forms of words. Failure to comply is a criminal offence! Banks seem slow to advise their customers of this requirement.

There are rules in the legislation regarding public charitable collections which require the permission of the local authority. Offerings and collections taken at church meetings are outside these rules. Sponsorship when advertised only at a public church meeting would also seem to fall outside these rules. Care, however, must be taken if canvassing generally for 'sponsorship' or when making house to house collections for unwanted clothing.

Charities should not engage in trade. The only exception is if the trade is fulfilling a primary object of the charity (e.g. selling Christian books, tapes and videos). Otherwise the *de minimus* principle can be invoked if the volume is very small in comparison to any primary purpose trading. Further information about these matters can be found in *The Handbook*.

Addresses

The Charity Commission has offices in London, Liverpool and Taunton. The

London address is: Harmsworth House, 13-15 Bouverie Street, London EC4Y 8DP (0870 333 0123).

Stewardship Services, PO Box 99, Loughton, Essex IG10 3QJ (020 8502 5600)

Association of Christian Law Firms, David Wells, Messrs. Ellis-Fermor and Negus, 2, Devonshire Avenue, Beeston, Nottingham

Forty Nine

Church Accounts[1]

Gerald West

Accounting records

It is the responsibility of trustees to keep proper accounts. This means that the records need to be accurate and comprehensive. They may be prepared by the church treasurer or by someone else under his direction. It is not necessary to be an accountant to keep such records. It does however require a somewhat pedantic temperament and a determination to do everything correctly. Not everyone has such a temperament and if the records are prepared on a slipshod basis or not kept up-to-date it becomes time-consuming and difficult to put them straight. There are a number of related tax and legal issues which can only be briefly referred to in this chapter. Further information is available in *Bookkeeping for Church Treasurers* and *The Church Trustees and Treasurers Handbook*, (*The Handbook*) both published by Stewardship Services. The April 2000 tax changes are covered in depth in *GivePlus – Churches Charity Tax Pack*.

If records of transactions are accurate and comprehensive, it is relatively easy for the average church treasurer to prepare the accounts. If necessary this can be done by someone else of appropriate skills. The skill required to prepare the accounts depends on the annual income. So long as the basic records are available it will also be a simple matter to have the accounts examined. The writer has learned the hard way that the records are fundamental, and these notes therefore emphasise this aspect of the matter. More detailed information about the preparation of accounts and the requirements of the Charity Accounting Regulations can be found in *The Handbook* and in the other publications listed at the end of this chapter.

Year end accounts

The requirements regarding accounts apply to all charities, whether they are registered or not. In practice, this means complying with the relevant parts of the Charities Statement of Recommended Practice (SORP). There are separate requirements for charitable companies. The complexity of the requirements depends on 'gross income' (GI) and 'total expenditure' (TE). Where GI or TE in any of the current or preceding two financial years exceeds £250,000, the accounts must be audited by a professional auditor. If GI or TE is between £10,000 and £250,000 per year the accounts are required to be examined by an Independent Examiner. The Charity Commission have produced *Guidance Notes* on the selection of independent examiners.

There is no requirement for an examination where GI and TE is below £10,000 per year. At this level, and indeed for GI up to £100,000 per year, the accounts can be prepared on a simplified 'receipts and payments' basis. However, as the income rises it becomes increasingly important to work on an 'accruals' basis. Accounts prepared in this way give a 'true and fair view'. For example, they would give a better understanding of outstanding debts. It is surprisingly easy to build up a significant debt without realising it, if the accounts are prepared on a receipts and payments basis.

Above £100,000 the accounts must be prepared on a full accruals basis. This means that the accounts must take account of amounts owed to creditors and by debtors at the end of each year. A church with this income level is, however, more likely to have paid assistance with the accounts and should have the advice of an accountant. The church treasurer should make sure that appropriate advice is available as required.

For accounting years beginning on or after January 2001, and where GI or TE does not exceed £250,000, expenditure classifications can be simplified, even where accruals accounts are prepared. Note: the simplification limit was £100,000 up to 31 December 2000 and only applied where accounts were prepared on the receipts and payments basis.

Annual report and annual returns

Every registered charity must file an annual report. Other charities may be under an obligation to prepare such a report. Registered charities must also complete an annual return for the Charity Commission. This must be submitted, together with the accounts, within 10 months of the year end. Copies of the accounts must be kept for six years. They must be made available to any member of the public who asks for them but a reasonable charge can be made.

Deeds of Covenant and Gift Aid

The legal provisions in connection with Deeds of Covenant and Gift Aid were changed in the Budget in 2000. The church treasurer will have received a pack from the Inland Revenue if the church is registered with them. The *GivePlus* pack from Stewardship Services gives comprehensive information, tailored to churches. There are two important general points to make. Treasurers should encourage members to take advantage of these arrangements. They should also seriously consider encouraging the congregation to give through one of the trusts which handles tax recovery for the donor and distributes the giving to whoever is stipulated. These arrangements are efficient, simple and flexible. They do cost something, but very often in smaller churches the treasurer does not have the time or inclination to undertake the necessary detailed work to recover the tax. If the volume of payments increases as a result of the tax changes, the task can become more onerous. If the tax is not claimed it was pointless to make the arrangement in the first place.

Other tax related issues

These notes do not deal with the tax position, generally, of churches. This may become an issue if the church carries on a trading activity. There are complex rules relating to VAT. Churches are not generally exempt but there are some detailed reliefs. Places of worship are generally exempt from rates and there are exemptions available in relation to stamp duty, inheritance tax and capital gains tax. All this requires specialist advice.

Churches who employ someone are subject to the same legislation as any other employer. This is a complex area and many churches are not equipped to handle the paperwork. Help is available from Stewardship Services who offer a payroll service. If it is not clear whether someone working with the church is employed or self-employed it is wise to take appropriate advice. This distinction is a complex one and the answer is not always obvious.

Resources (free unless otherwise stated)

Available from Stewardship Services, P.O.Box 99, Loughton, Essex IG10 3QJ (020 8502 5600):
Bookkeeping for Treasurers
Church Trustees and Treasurers Handbook (£5.00)
GivePlus Church Charity Tax Pack

Independent Examination Service Information Sheet

Make your Giving joyfully simple, wonderfully effective (Gift Aid services for individuals)

Partnership Account for Churches and Christian Organisations (Gift Aid administration for churches)

Seminars Brochure

Available from The Charity Commission, Harmsworth House, 13-15 Bouverie Street. London EC4Y 8DP (0870 333 0123):

Charity Accounts 2001: The Framework

Charity Accounts – under £10,000 GI/TE

SORP 2000 Accruals Pack (GI or TE less than £100,000)

SORP 2000 Receipts and Payments Pack (GI less than £100,000)

SORP 2000 Statement of Recommended Practice 'Accounting & Reporting by Charities' (Free, but additional copies £5.00)

The Carrying out of an Independent Examination (revised 2000). *Directions and Guidance Notes*

Association of Church Accountants and Treasurers, Alan Wilson (01623 795510; awilson30@83sheep.freeserve.co.uk)

Footnotes

1 I am indebted to Kevin J Russell, Manager, Accountancy Services, Stewardship Services for his help in preparing this chapter.

FIFTY

Premises

GERALD WEST

Church buildings reflect the commitment, priorities and values of those who built them. Their variety demonstrates the way these priorities and values change from generation to generation and from situation to situation. We can learn important lessons from this variety and from the fact that the life expectancy of church buildings (in common with that of all other buildings) is decreasing.

- Spiritual life is more important than physical structures. It is the life that generates the structures and not the other way round.

- Physical structures reflect our vision and values. The way these are expressed inevitably changes over the years.

- The need to change physical structures arises from changing spiritual needs and priorities and from the way that these are expressed in a changing spiritual environment. The pace of change is increasing and, just as our homes require regular updating, so do our church buildings.

It is not surprising, therefore, that at every stage in the life of a church there is a question about premises. These questions come in many forms and it is not possible to cover them all in a short chapter.

Renting or owning?

At some stages in the life of a church, and particularly at the beginning, it may be best to rent. The advantages of this arrangement are:

- short-term financial commitment at a time when longer-term needs are hard to define;

- ability to find larger or different accommodation as needs change;

- freedom to create an independent image related to the character and quality of the life of the church and not the images conjured up by traditional church buildings (of all kinds!).

The advantages of owning are:

* it gives a permanent expression to the commitment of the church to a particular community;
* it gives the church a clear public image (this is an advantage only if the physical image truly reflects the reality of the church);
* it can be cheaper in the long run.

Before entering into any obligation to rent or buy, check that your trust deed gives you the necessary powers. Not all trusts have the power to own a building.

Location/Site

Where should the building be? It must be visible and accessible to the congregation it is intended to serve. This includes the members of the church and those among whom the church has been called to work. These two groups of people may have different perceptions of themselves geographically. There can be a tension between these requirements to which there are no easy answers. In an increasingly mobile society a site closely related to good communication routes and to other community facilities such as the health clinic, local schools, shopping, etc. is to be preferred to one embedded within a limited residential area.

Before purchase make sure the site is of an appropriate shape and size, that access is available and that it can be easily provided with essential services: drainage, gas, water, electricity. It would be wise to undertake a proper feasibility study, which should include town planning enquiries, to make sure that the site is suitable for the purposes you have in mind. This should be done prior to commitment to purchase.

The church will need an appropriate legal structure to purchase a property. If you are contemplating any substantial project it is essential to check the legal framework under which the church operates. Does the church operate under a formal trust? (Many do not.) Do the trustees have power to own property? (Some do not.) Who owns the property the church occupies? If the church does not, what are the terms of the tenancy? These may be only informal or implied but at the least, the 'landlord's' permission will be required, and it may be sensible to consider changes to the arrangements, if that is possible.

Organising a project

Any serious building project, whether for a completely new building, or for alterations and addition to an existing building, requires proper organisation. It will be necessary to obtain professional advice (see 'Useful addresses', at the end of this chapter) and to set up within the church a group of members responsible for seeing the project through to completion. The leadership of the church will initially be responsible for making the necessary arrangements and the church will be consulted and involved throughout the process. Nevertheless it is important that there should be a small group (not more than three) who have the confidence of the leadership and of the church and who can take day-to-day decisions quickly.

The essential stages are:

• the development of a statement of detailed requirements;
• agreement of a design which meets those requirements;
• agreement of a timetable and of financial targets.

These three stages impact on one another and it is usually necessary to adjust requirements to meet cost or to improve the design. At the end of the third stage there should be a comprehensive statement, in words and drawings, of the user requirements, the design, the budget and timetable. Each element must be compatible with all the others. When this has been achieved one can move to the fourth stage:

• implementation and monitoring progress (both physical and financial).

If there is a group of professional advisors dealing with the design and procurement of the building work, it is important that one of them accepts responsibility for the leadership and co-ordination of the group so that together they can deliver a successful project.

Fund raising

The prime responsibility for raising funds for a project legally rests with the trustees but, in practice, it is likely to fall on the congregation. This is another reason why it is important that a young church should not burden itself with a major building project at an early stage in its life.

Some churches are able to undertake parts of the building work themselves. This can be an effective way of reducing cost if the necessary skills are available in the congregation. It is important, however, not to attempt more than the congregation can handle in a reasonable time. If care is not taken, the demands of the project can divert priorities away from the spiritual work of the church and leave the members physically exhausted and spiritually depressed. It is, however, tremendously exciting to see what God can do when a church moves forward in faith and unity.

Wherever possible, advantage should be taken of giving by Deed of Covenant or by Gift Aid. This may be administered directly by the church treasurer. However, the treasurer will have many heavy responsibilities in connection with the project and it is possible to reduce this load by making arrangements for the administration of tax recovery to be handled by a third party trust.

Timing of giving in relation to payments for the work must be considered in order to avoid having to borrow to cover a cash flow deficit. It may be necessary to borrow if the committed giving does not cover the costs or if there is a failure of cost control. Decisions on how to raise the funds necessary, including whether to include planned borrowing, must be carefully considered. Most churches (and trustees) will wish to keep loans to a minimum. Where appropriate, the church may consider short-term loans from members or from outside the church. Loans for building projects are available from Stewardship Services at rates of interest below commercial rates. Details of the terms and conditions are available from them.

Sources of advice (see 'Useful addresses' at the end)

No substantial project can be undertaken without appropriate professional advice. This will usually include advice from an architect, a quantity surveyor and a structural engineer. For most churches the problem is how to find and choose the right professionals. It may be that such advice is already available from within the church. If not, the best source of information is other churches who have been through the process and who can recommend professionals. Failing this, an approach to the various professional bodies can be helpful. The advice of an architect is usually required first.

When choosing professional advisors, do not feel inhibited from considering two or three possible candidates and asking them for the names of other clients for whom they have undertaken similar work. Take up those references, talk to other clients about their performance and, if appropriate, go to see the work they have done. Make sure that you understand the basis on which their fees and expenses will be calculated. Try to avoid time charges. Do not be unduly influenced by small differences in percentage fees. It is more important that you should feel comfortable with your professionals than that you should take the lowest fee.

It is not essential that they share your particular theological views, but you would be wise to appoint Christians who share your general values and who will understand your requirements. It is also an advantage if the professionals have worked together on other projects and respect one another. Take their advice about the other professional appointments. At the contract stage take their advice about possible contractors and sub-contractors.

Assessing space needs

A crucial first step when considering any building project is to assess space needs.

This will need professional help, but much can be done simply by listing the various uses to be accommodated and the spaces required. This will probably raise fundamental questions about the kind of church envisaged and how the work is to be done. Your architect may well be able to help you consider these issues. It is important to address these questions at an early stage and not to push them to one side. Only if they have been properly thought through and resolved will it be possible to give a coherent brief to the professionals. Visits to other similar projects will often be helpful at this stage. Do not leave these visits too late in the process, or you will be tempted to make changes to accommodate the 'good idea' you have just seen! This is also the stage in any project at which an architect can provide the most help, so long as he has freedom to think about the problem and is not unduly constrained by preconceived ideas as to how the various space needs can be met.

The space required for meetings of the congregation will require careful assessment. The form and type of service may require alternative seating arrangements, and space must be provided for worship leaders, speakers, musicians (together with their equipment: public address, overhead projector, etc.) and furniture (communion table, lectern, pulpit, etc.). Try to keep this simple but also practical. Because of the importance of this space in the life of the church it must be given the most detailed consideration. Contemporary informality can be constrained by spaces which do not allow a variety of ways of arranging things. It is particularly important, if spaces are to be used for more than one purpose, not to underestimate the need for storage space. It may be necessary to store chairs and other furniture.The storage of children's facilities can also make considerable demands on space.

Flexibility/adaptability

The uncertainty of future accommodation requirements and the desire to economise by doubling up the possible uses of space often suggest that a structure should be designed to be both flexible (capable of different uses) and adaptable (easily changed over time). In practice this is easier to suggest than to achieve. Any particular proposal will require careful discussion with the appropriate professional advisors. If a space is to be used for more than one purpose (e.g. for sport and for worship) it will be necessary to consider the detailed needs of each activity and to make sure all the needs can be met. Some compromise may be necessary and there may be some additional cost.

The changes that will be necessary each time the use of the space changes, and the workload these changes will involve, should be carefully assessed. There is no reason in principle why such arrangements should not be successful so long as they have been carefully thought through in the first place and the compromises and costs are clearly understood. It is particularly important to give careful consideration to proposals to use 'sound proof' movable partitions. Soundproofing is much more difficult to achieve than is sometimes thought.

It may be necessary to undertake a project in stages. A medium-term programme of development is often advantageous, but longer-term adaptability is a different matter. It is virtually impossible to predict accurately future long-term needs. These are usually best left to be considered when they arise.

Selection of materials and equipment

Select the materials to be used with care, taking advice. Bear in mind that finishes and equipment will require regular maintenance and that savings on initial cost may be outweighed by long-term heavy maintenance costs. Consider also the practical implications and cost of renewing electrical and mechanical equipment. Heating in church buildings is often intermittent, which raises particularly difficult design problems. Systems offering a reduced initial cost may not provide the most effective and practical long-term solution.

Control of costs

From the earliest stage there should be a proper estimate of cost. This will need regular review. The estimate will become more accurate as consideration of the details progresses. It is important to avoid cost overruns once the contract work has begun. These are most likely to arise from changes of mind or inadequate consideration before the work is begun. It is important not to put off decisions and not to put pressure on the design team and the contractors to start work on the site before the work has been thoroughly designed and costed.

When considering estimates of costs make sure they include all the likely expenses. It is not only the building costs that must be paid for. There will be various fees to pay, including professional fees and expenses – and V.A.T. There will also be the cost of furniture, fittings and equipment (musical instruments, public address, etc.). These can be expensive items. It is essential that there should be a regular review and report of cost estimates which includes all these items.

The control of cost throughout a project is imperative. No estimate is exact and there should always be provision for unexpected expenditure. If the cost of a project appears beyond the resources available, it is usually better to undertake the project in stages than to try to proceed with everything cut to the bone. The adage 'Penny wise – pound foolish' applies to building projects as much as to other aspects of life. Work not done properly will become a source of considerable additional cost later.

Disposal/redevelopment

Redundant churches are a familiar sight in both town and country. They are too often a sad reminder of expired spiritual life. But they are also a reminder that God does not stand still. He is moving on! The disposal of premises which are no longer required is usually the task of the trustees who must be guided by the terms of the trust deed. If the disposal arises from a decision to move to another site or because the accommodation can no longer meet the needs of the church, the trustees will normally seek to achieve the highest price.

It is particularly difficult to value church premises. There may be little demand for them as churches and it may be necessary to consider selling for an alternative use. Do not sell to the first person who offers a price, and be particularly wary of developers. (The issues raised by proposals to redevelop a site with a mixture of uses including a new church are complex and cannot be considered in this chapter.) It will probably be wise to obtain advice as to what alternative use the planning authority would allow on the site. This may be some form of community use or it may be residential use. If the site is within a town centre there may be a high value for commercial use. The most important step in these circumstances is to obtain genuinely independent advice. This is never easy unless there is someone personally known to the church who has genuine expertise and integrity. Time taken to find the right advice will not be wasted.

If the disposal arises from the demise of the church, the trust deed will determine how to proceed. Some trusts clearly set out what is to be done in these circumstances and these provisions must be followed. However, many trust deeds allow the trustees to exercise some discretion and in these circumstances there are many possibilities. If disposal to another church is an option, it may be possible to make a gift to the church and in this way enable them effectively to purchase the property at less than market value. In any case the value of church premises will depend on the restrictions placed on the trustees by the trust deed. If there is discretion, trustees should consider whether they should give some of the proceeds of sale to help those who are engaged in planting new churches of a similar type elsewhere. In this way the giving of one generation contributes to new spiritual life in the next.

Disposal of property by trustees is regulated by the Charity Commission. This is a complex area and trustees will need to seek advice.

Useful addresses

Professional bodies

Royal Institute of British Architects, 66 Portland Place, London, W1
   Contact the Client Advisory Service.
Royal Institution of Chartered Surveyors, 12 Great George Street, London SW1
The Institution of Structural Engineers, 11Upper Belgrave Street, London SW1
(The above are national addresses. Regional or local addresses may be in the
   Yellow Pages.)

Other bodies

The Charity Commission for England and Wales, Harmsworth House, 13-15
   Bouverie Street, London EC4Y 8DP
The Charity Commission issues leaflets dealing with a wide range of aspects of
   charity law. They also have statutory duties to regulate the charity sector. In
   general, they do not give legal advice.
Stewardship Services: P O Box 99, Loughton, Essex IG10 3QJ
Stewardship Services (formerly U.K.E.T.) is a registered charity which developed from a group of Open Brethren assemblies in the first decade of the
   20th century. They now provide a range of legal and financial services to
   evangelical churches, including legal advice on all aspects of charity law,

trust formation and Charity Commission requirements. They provide loans for building projects at favourable rates of interest. They undertake the administration of Deeds of Covenant and Gift Aid for a modest charge.

Charities Aid Foundation: Kings Hill Avenue, West Malling, Kent ME19 4TA

A registered charity which provides a wide range of services, including financial, to donors and both secular and religious charities.

Brass Tacks: l7 Osborne Avenue, Wallasey, Merseyside L45 1JD

An organisation providing building skills and expertise primarily overseas but also to churches in the UK.

The Church Planting Initiative: c/o P O Box 35, Fareham, Hants PO14 4TX

C.P.I. is a co-operative venture of Counties, G.L.O., and Stewardship Services which encourages the growth of new churches in the UK. It supports those called by God to undertake church planting and introduces them to opportunities to develop new and re-born churches.

FIFTY ONE

The Church and Social Care Legislation

HELEN WALKER

Partnership was the word for the 90s in social care. Following the implementation of the NHS and Community Care Act (1990) and legislation dealing with children, social work departments have undergone a quiet revolution in the way services are delivered and in their attitudes to working with other agencies. There is an increasing recognition that the caring task with older people and people with disabilities is often better carried out by those who are known to, or chosen by, those needing the care. Additionally, local authority social work departments now realise that there are some areas of the caring task that they do not have the resources to provide. This in turn has resulted in improved recognition for relative carers as well as an upsurge in 'Private Caring Agency' provision.

In the field of the care of older people some residential units run by the churches are offering to train staff to work in domiciliary settings. This has now been extended to work with those with learning difficulties, especially with the closure of long stay hospital provision, and with those needing respite from caring for a relative.

In the area of child care, too, many changes have been implemented in the last decade with the introduction of the Children Act 1989 (England and Wales) and the Children (Scotland) Act 1995. The protection of children continues to be uppermost in the mind of the public and local authority staff, with a few high profile media cases grabbing people's imagination. The churches and other charitable and voluntary organisations have played their part in this. As a result of some well-publicised child murders such as the Dunblane shootings, and abuse in residential care homes for children and young people, it is now time to consider the safety of some volunteers and employees in children's work.

Being seen as 'good upstanding' members of a Christian community does not automatically protect children if adults do not behave properly towards them and seek to protect them appropriately. This has made social and health workers suspicious of the apparent selfless motives of those perceived as 'do-gooders' in society. Those acting on behalf of a local church are either viewed with an unquestioning acceptance or with suspicion, and it is only since the middle of the 1990s that the churches and uniformed organisations in Scotland have begun to look more closely at those volunteering to work with children and young people on their behalf. This is welcomed by the statutory agencies. Many churches now have an established code of good practice to direct their work with children and young people.

Codes of good practice

These have been established as a result of the following reports and subsequent government legislation:

- The Children Act 1989 (England and Wales) which recognized the responsibilities as well as the rights of parents, and introduced a number of requirements for the monitoring of child care provision, particularly for childminders and day care establishments.
- The Children (Scotland) Act 1995 which introduced the concept of the child's welfare being the paramount consideration in decisions affecting them.
- The 1993 Home Office report, 'Safe from Harm: A Code of Practice for Safeguarding the Welfare of Children in Voluntary Organisations in England and Wales'.
- The 1996 report on Lord Cullen's 'Inquiry into the shooting at Dunblane Primary School'. Lord Cullen recommended that a system be set up to highlight any previous problems of a person who applies to work with children.
- The 1997 Police Act and Sex Offenders Acts. These aim to increase the level of access to criminal conviction information that will facilitate wider access to appropriate information about people's criminal records.

As a response to these, it has been recognised that the churches need:

- To set in place methods of checking the credentials of those volunteering to work with children by interviewing all potential volunteers; by ensuring the provision of an appropriate written reference; by keeping a register with basic details of all volunteers; by undertaking criminal records checks once this legislation is implemented in 2001; and by nominating someone to administer the above and ensure confidentiality for the volunteer and the information obtained.

- To be observant of the children in church organisations and be aware of unusual injuries, changes in their behaviour or their family background by setting in place a procedure for volunteers to pass on any concerns to the person nominated to make a decision about the appropriate passing on of information to the relevant authorities.

- To provide training for all volunteers; to observe safe practices when in contact with children; and to recognise signs of child abuse in children.

- To support church leaders, and provide forums for discussion and private sharing of concerns.

- To know what the procedure will be if situations are encountered which are beyond their resources to deal with.

Churches need to demonstrate that they are capable of managing this task. They need to show that they can anticipate the dangers for children and realise that people in their own ranks might abuse their own or other children.

Referral

The crux of every situation is going to be an ongoing assessment of the situation and the people in need, and an understanding about when it might be appropriate to refer on to the local social work department. These are located in every area, and a referral can usually be made by phone or personally. It is possible to make anonymous referrals, though the value of these referrals is reduced if the referrer does not identify him/herself to give credibility to the information being passed on. It is usually beneficial to obtain the permission of the person who is being referred, as this makes any contact from the social worker easier.

Social workers have a wide-ranging responsibility which, although encompassed in legislation, also gives them great flexibility and discretion. Here is an example of how it can work out.

When a young church family of four, aged between 7 and 17 years, was left in need of care after the death of their mother and long-term hospitalisation of their father, the church wanted to do something practical for the family. However, the long-term needs of the children were going to be great and there were legal and financial implications for the children. When the minister involved the local social work department, discussions took place about the needs of each of the children, their relationship with their father, and the support available from the local church and community. A friend who was a church member was identified to care for the youngest child, and another was enabled to leave home to study. Two others were maintained in the family home for a period until one requested to be placed with local authority foster carers. All the children were enabled to maintain contact with each other and their father. The church supported the family throughout, both in practical ways and emotionally, and their care was monitored and complemented by that offered by the local authority.

Hazards

Church leaders are often in a position to visit church members in their own homes and it is possible for their concern for an individual to be misinterpreted. Having a responsible position within a church community gives access to the lives and homes of people at vulnerable times in their lives. This can lead to a blurring of roles and emotions, leaving the church leaders open to being troubled by persistent telephone calls, e-mails or letters. It becomes very important to be aware of the potential for this to happen, and for advice and help to be sought at an early stage. The most helpful thing for anyone at the receiving end of these excessive contacts is not to be working in isolation but to have an advisor or group to offer support and assistance in reflecting how to handle the situation.

Equally, the youth leader who works with adolescent church groups may inadvertently be subject to unwarranted attention from a young person. It is helpful if youth leaders of both genders can work with any group. In extreme cases those in authority in the church may need to refer an individual on for counselling.

Conclusion

All of this amounts to a changing and changed role for the churches today. The social care offered by our congregations must be more responsive and forward-looking than it has been in the past, but it must also conform to the legal and statutory requirements of our time. In order to have credibility, we must be seen to be fulfilling a task not being tackled so well by other agencies, and yet we must be aware of the dangers and limitations incurred. By making a careful assessment of what it is we are trying to do and then referring on appropriately and working with others, we will achieve this credibility.

Further reading

Adults

B Hughes, *Older People and Community Care* (Open University Press, 1995)
Homes for Living in – Department of Health (HMSO, 1989)
The NHS and Community Care Act (1990)

Children

P Parkinson, *Child Sexual Abuse and the Churches* (Hodder & Stoughton, 1997)
S Wheatley, *Handbook for Child Protection in the Church of Scotland* (Parish
  Education Publications, 2000)
The Children Act 1989 (HMSO)
Convention on the Rights of the Child (HMSO, 1996)
Guidance to Churches: Protecting Children and Appointing Children's Workers
  (Churches Child Protection Advisory Service, 1998)
*The Protection of Children and Young People in the Church: A Code of Good Practice
  for Kirk Sessions and Congregations in the Church of Scotland* (Parish Education
  Publications, 1997)
Scotland's Children: The Children (Scotland) Act, 1995, Regulations and Guidance,
  Volume 1 *Support and Protection for Children and their Families* (HMSO, 1997)
The Police Act 1997 (HMSO)

Index

C